HENRY RICE
(1717–1818)

THE PIONEER
TENNESSEE
GRISTMILLER

AND HIS TWELVE CHILDREN

by

Melvin Weaver Little

HERITAGE BOOKS
2007

HERITAGE BOOKS

AN IMPRINT OF HERITAGE BOOKS, INC.

Books, CDs, and more—Worldwide

For our listing of thousands of titles see our website
at
www.HeritageBooks.com

Published 2007 by
HERITAGE BOOKS, INC.
Publishing Division
65 East Main Street
Westminster, Maryland 21157-5026

International Standard Book Number: 978-0-7884-3654-3

PREFACE

Henry Rice (1717?-1818), the East Tennessee Pioneer Grist-miller, was my great-great-great-great grandfather through James, George, Henry, and Marcellus (Sillus) Moss Rice and my mother Ruby Rema Rice Little. His long life spanned a century through the troubled colonial, revolutionary, and early Tennessee times. The story presented here has been compiled from numerous sources during the past eleven years.

Why This New Book? I wish to share what I have learned with numerous other descendants, distant and close relatives, and with all who are interested in the lives of the common people among the pioneers. As a child I became interested in family history while listening to the experiences of my grandfather, Marcellus Moss Rice (1873-1964). His life is the subject of the work by John Rice Irwin mentioned below (23). Later my mother and I traced our ancestry through the Rice line to the Revolutionary War to qualify for membership in the Daughters and Sons of the American Revolution. My curiosity to piece together additional details led to this book. It has been expanded somewhat from an earlier draft of limited circulation: HENRY RICE, The Pioneer Gristmiller, compiled by Melvin Weaver Little. 34 pages, illus. May 1979.

References. Henry Rice's life has been reported in several previous works as the ancestor to several lines of descendants. He is mentioned also in other books, pamphlets, periodicals, etc. Some of the most detailed are listed below. Numbers at left and numbers in parentheses in the text refer to Sources and Bibliography, page 251.

1. Rice Trails 1717-1977, by Nan (Frances) Rice Shute. This 1977 edition of a most extensive work is still in manuscript form and is being updated periodically. Mrs. Shute is a descendant of Henry Rice through his grandson Martin Rice. She has been most generous in sharing her information and encouraging me to continue my own researches. She placed a belated but prominent tombstone at Henry's grave site in Lost Creek cemetery.

2. Charles Rice, His Ancestors and Descendants, by Alva Silas Turnbow and Maude Ina Turnbow, privately printed, Eugene, Oregon, 1957. Charles Rice was a grandson of Henry Rice through James, and the ancestor of Mrs. Turnbow. Her maiden name is Finley.

3. Nicholas Gibbs and His Descendants, 1733-1977, by the Nicholas Gibbs Historical Society, 1977, Southeastern Composition Service, Knoxville, Tenn.; Davis Printing Co., Maryville, Tenn. Nicholas Gibbs was my great-great-great-great grandfather; two of his daughters, Elizabeth and Sarah Gibbs, married John Snodderly and Conrad "Coonrod" Sharp, and both were my great-great-great grandmothers.

23. The Story of Marcellus Moss Rice and His Big Valley Kinsmen, by John Rice Irwin, The Times Printing Co., Montevallo, Ala., 1963. The author is my first cousin and a direct descendant of Henry Rice through James, George, Henry, and Marcellus Rice and Ruth Annette Rice Irwin. He has worked diligently on local history and genealogy for many years.

27. Know Your Relatives (The Sharps, Gibbs, Graves, Efland, Albright, Loy, Miller, Snoderly, Tillman, and Other Related Families), by Genevieve E. Peters, 1957 and 1972. Mrs. Peters and I are related through Sharps, Gibbs, Graves, Efland, and other families.

30. Cantrell-Rice-Mackie, by Lucylle Rice Davis, ca 1960, Waynesville, Mo. Lucylle and her husband are both descended from Henry's son Levi Rice.

37. The Epistle, A Bi-Monthly Magazine for the Batchelder, Carpenter, and Rice Families, edited and published by Rosemary Batchelder, Post Office Box 398, Machias, Maine 04654. This publication contains historical and genealogical information on the above surnames for the entire country, largely submitted by interested readers.

Sources. Living in the Washington, D.C., area, I have access to many valuable collections of records. These include:

1. The National Archives. Military and pension records and census reports from the first census in 1790 through 1900. (The 1910 census became accessible recently after this search ended.) Also colonial records of many kinds.

2. Library of Congress. The Local History and Genealogy Room, for histories and family trees.

3. Library of Congress Map Division. Early maps.

4. Daughters of the American Revolution Library. Family histories and especially the "Patriots List" of persons known to have rendered service or to have been sympathetic with the Revolutionary War. Here are found many manuscripts and unpublished histories, as well as published family histories.

5. Potomac Genealogical Library of the Church of Jesus Christ of Latter Day Saints. This branch of the Genealogical Library at Salt Lake City, Utah, has or can borrow family trees of hundreds of United States families. The research facilities are not limited to church members.

6. U.S. Geological Survey, Map Division. The most recent and most detailed topographic maps.

7. Virginiana Collection, Arlington (Va.) Central Library.

State and County Sources. Records were examined also at these four state capitals and state libraries: Richmond, Va., Raleigh, N.C., Columbia, S.C., and Nashville, Tenn. Records of land grants, deeds, marriages, wills, deaths, etc., were seen at various county seats. Examples by states are: North Carolina, Yanceyville, Caswell Co.; Hillsboro, Orange Co. South Carolina, Spartanburg, Spartanburg Co. Tennessee, Clinton, Anderson Co.; Tazewell, Claiborne Co.; Jacksboro, Campbell Co.; Rutledge, Grainger Co.; Rogersville, Hawkins Co.; Knoxville, Knox Co.; Maynardville, Union Co. Some county records had been destroyed by fire. Information from all the above sources was fitted into that already published by the previous authors.

Plan of This Book. As detailed under Contents (page ix), this book begins with the Introduction (page 1), discussing possible colonial origins of Henry Rice. Of the 13 chapters, Chapter I (page 6) is devoted to Henry Rice himself. Each of the following, Chapters II through XIII, covers one of Henry's children. Some chapters contain additional information on later generations. The sources consulted are cited under Sources and Bibliography (page 251). The Appendix (page 292) contains 14 maps, plats, deeds, and other documents, such as pages from family Bibles and military records, listed on page 258.

Names of Persons and Places. For ready recognition, names of persons mostly are in boldface or heavy type. Index to Names of Persons (page 258) is detailed. A special effort has been made to index every person mentioned on each page. Thus, the reference value for tracing names is increased. Likewise, Index to Names of Places (page 286) is detailed and aims to make the information more accessible.

Errors. Among the published works one encounters contradictions and sometimes errors. For example, several persons may have had the same name, such as father and son or grandson, uncle and nephew, or even persons apparently not related at all. Sometimes several persons with the same name resided in the same county at the same time. Also, there are many examples of persons of the same name living in different parts of the country, such as in New England and the South, with no evidence of any kinship. Some persons with the surname Rice are of German or other non-British descent rather than the commonly assumed English, Welsh, etc.

Another cause for error, one that happened in my own line, could be the accidental omission of a page at some point in the preparation of a manuscript--leading to the actual listing of a completely erroneous set of children under my grandfather's name. And, of course, early records are subject to being misread and misfiled. For example, Longmire records were found filed under "S" as if the name were Songmire!

The possibilities for error and confusion are numerous. It is my hope that some errors are hereby corrected and some of the confusion resolved--and that no new errors or confusions are added; and please remember that "... to forgive is divine."

Acknowledgments. I am very grateful to all who have inspired and encouraged me, also supplied ideas, information, and records, especially Nan Rice Shute and John Rice Irwin. I am indebted to many persons, mainly close and distant relatives, who have shared their memories and knowledge of birth, marriage, death, and other records. Finally, I thank my mother Ruby Rice Little for assistance throughout and for typing the final manuscript, mostly on word processors.

Henry Rice's Mill. This mill at Church Hill near Kingsport (Hawkins Co.), is among the historic landmarks officially recognized by the State of Tennessee. I feel that it deserves greater publicity than it has received heretofore. The giant waterwheel is crumbling and the millrace has vanished, but the great stone foundation is intact and probably unique in East Tennessee history. It was built at a time when Indians were still a menace, although they had sold the territory in 1769 (no doubt for a pitifully low price). The great stone foundation rises two stories. At the southwest corner of the ground floor there is a giant fireplace (one could stand erect in it). It could have been used not only for heating and cooking but also for smithing and making guns and bullets. Area citizens who took refuge here during Indian uprisings would find its warmth most welcome. In addition, higher in the stone wall there are two rows of widely spaced small square openings that, while they originally held scaffolding supports, undoubtedly also become portholes during hostilities. Patterson Mill a few miles away was built about the same time and may have been similar and used also as a fort.

Readers may wish to visit the Henry Rice Mill. The Tennessee Historic Marker is on the right side of Highway US 11W (southbound) about 3 miles south of Church Hill. The present owner is a descendant of the Mr. Hord who bought it from Henry's son Daniel Rice and calls it the Hord Mill. I believe this mill should be preserved and restored.

Summary by Chapters. Following this Preface a brief summary of each chapter has been inserted (page v). These paragraphs combined may serve as an abstract of the book.

Future Studies. Finally, I hope that readers will continue the genealogical studies of these and other ancestors. Any corrections and additional information will be welcome.

Melvin Weaver Little

924 20th St. S.
Arlington, Virginia 22202
July 1983

SUMMARY BY CHAPTERS

CHAPTER I. HENRY RICE (Page 6)

Henry Rice was born in 1717(?) in Hanover County, Va.,
lived in Virginia, South Carolina, and East Tennessee; he died
in 1818 at Lost Creek, Tenn. (Campbell County, now Union).
Name(s) of wife or wives unknown. He had at least six sons
and six daughters, some born in Virginia and some in South Carolina. Near the middle of the century the family moved to the
"96 District" of South Carolina and settled on land known as
Indian territory. After several years at Rices Creek of Twelve
Mile River in South Carolina, Henry traveled with some of his
older children to Watauga Settlement, East Tennessee, where
he built and fortified a large grist mill. He spent the rest
of his 101 years here and at Lost Creek.

CHAPTER II. HENRY'S SON WILLIAM RICE (Page 22)

Born in 1743 in Virginia, William Rice probably was Henry's
oldest son. He probably was with his father in the Watauga
area (whether he was ever in South Carolina has not been determined) and helped build the mill as well as engaged in battles
with the Cherokee; he also served at the battle of King's
Mountain. He sold his Hawkins County land in 1805 and went
to Wilson County, Tenn., where he died in 1831.

CHAPTER III. CHARLES RICE (Page 29)

Henry Rice's son Charles was between 26 and 45 years old
in the 1800 census of Pendleton County, S.C. (present Pickens
County)--thus was born between 1755 and 1774. Since he already
had children between 10 and 16 years of age, he must have been
born around 1755-1760 (in Virginia?). He lived for a time in
the Pendleton District of South Carolina, was sold land in
Grainger County, Tenn., from his father Henry Rice. He sold
land for his father in South Carolina but apparently moved finally
to another State such as Georgia. Nothing was uncovered regarding his marriage, his children, or the date and place of his
death.

CHAPTER IV. JAMES RICE (Page 32)

JAMES Rice, third son of Henry Rice, born 1763 in South
Carolina, married Rebecca Miller in 1787. He moved to Lost
Creek, Tenn., about 1795, where he built a grist mill, prac-
ticed gunsmithing, and died there in 1829. He had ten children, four sons and six daughters. The James Rice grist mill

was operated by the **Rice** generations, **George, Henry,** and my great-uncle **James Rufus Rice.** It was kept in continuous service on Lost Creek until 1935, when the Tennessee Valley Authority moved it to its present location on Clinch River at Norris Dam. **James Rice's** wife **Rebecca Miller** is said to have been the daughter of a **John Miller** who died in 1771 at the Battle of the Alamance. **Rebecca Miller Rice** was born in 1767 and died after 1830.

CHAPTER V.   DANIEL RICE THE GUNSMITH (Page 56)

Daniel Rice, fourth (?) son of **Henry Rice,** was born presumably in South Carolina about 1765-1770. The name and date of his first marriage unknown. His sons **Henry, Lewis, Thomas** and his daughters **Temperance** and **Patience** were all adults by 1830. The second son **Lewis** was born between 1790 and 1800. **Daniel** sold land as late as 1836 but the exact date and place of his death were not learned.

CHAPTER VI.   JOHN RICE, THE OLD PREACHER (Page 61)

Very little is known of this **John Rice** except that he was a preacher. Also his daughter **Sally** was married to the famous outlaw **Willie Harpe** (whose life was quite short). **John** was possibly born in South Carolina before 1775; he was in Tennessee by 1797. Later he migrated with **Sally** (a "reformed" young lady) to Illinois (?) and was recognized at **Ford's** Ferry on the Ohio River as late as 1820. **Sally** had an unnamed daughter of, maybe, an unknown second husband, when they were seen on the ferry.

CHAPTER VII.   LEVI RICE (Page 65)

Levi Rice, a preacher, was perhaps **Henry's** sixth son, born presumably in South Carolina around 1770 (he had married **Mary Catherine Mitchell** before 1789). **Levi Rice** married **Jane Simmons** in 1801, Grainger County, Tenn.; they settled in middle Missouri. The sons **John, James,** and **Joel,** and two daughters, may all have been born to this marriage, according to 1810 census records. There may have been other children born after the 1810 census, since in 1830 there were two females under five years of age. **Levi** died after 1835. **Lucylle Rice Davis,** or Waynesville, Pulaski County, Mo., and her husband are descended from **Levi,** and she wrote a book (30).

CHAPTER VIII. MARTHA (PATSY) RICE - DAVID BAILEY (Page 71)

Born between 1745 and 1755, perhaps in Virginia. Married to **David Bailey** in the 1770's in South Carolina. Had sons **Daniel**, **James**, and **William**, and a daughter who married **Wiley Tuttle**. The **Baileys** moved to Hawkins County, Tenn., where the oldest son appeared in the 1830 census and reported he was born in Tennessee. There was a **James Tuttle** in the 1830 Campbell County census but no **Wiley Tuttle** (but **Wiley Bailey** was found instead). **Martin Rice**, the poet, had never seen **Patsy Rice Bailey**. No record of date or place of death has been found for her. Many of the **Bailey** descendants went to Missouri and settled around Cass and Jackson Counties near **James Rice's** descendants.

CHAPTER IX. MOLLY RICE - NATHAN WATSON (Page 114)

Born about 1755-57 in Virginia or South Carolina, **Molly** was in Tennessee in 1777 when her son **Martin Rice** was born. She later married **Nathan Watson** between 1780 and 1790, as her oldest daughter **Nancy** was 40-50 years old in 1830. **Martin Rice** married in 1798 and went to Preble County, Ohio, in 1805. **Molly Rice Watson** and her husband **Nathan Watson** probably died before 1830.

CHAPTER X. ANNA RICE - AUGUSTUS WILSON (Page 131)

Born about 1764 in South Carolina, married **Augustus Wilson** before 1784 at age about 21. Had sons **James**, **Isaac**, **Amos**, **Sampson**, and **George Wilson**. Died before 1815 in Knox County, Tenn. Her husband **Augustus Wilson** remarried, and the family removed to Campbell County and later Anderson County. There were numerous **Wilson** descendants from both **Anna** and the second wife, **Barbara May**. The son, **Isaac Wilson**, was living next to **George Rice**, son of **James**, in Campbell County (then Union) in 1860.

CHAPTER XI. ROSA RICE - JAMES SPENCE - ALEXANDER MORROW (Page 182)

Born about 1770 and married **James Spence**, who died before 1809, after having two or more children. As **Rosanna Spence** she married **Alexander Morrow** in 1809 when about 40 years old, then had four more children. She apparently died after 1840, which was her last appearance in the Knox County, Tenn., census. In 1840 she had some grandchildren living with her. **Alexander** may have died prior to 1830, as he is not listed in that census. A **Charles Morrow** was in the 1850 and 1860 census schedules of Knox County.

CHAPTER XII.   LAVINA RICE - LEWIS BRIM (Page 223)

Born 1770-1775 in South Carolina, married **Lewis Brim** about 1795.   Had sons **Henry, Joseph, William, James, John**(?) and **Daniel**, and daughters **Rose, Betsy, and Lavina**.   The **Brims** moved to Lincoln County, Tenn., about 1825.   **Lavina Brims** was head of the household in 1830 (age 50-60).   Descendants (many) moved farther west, to Missouri and other states.

CHAPTER XIII.   ELIZABETH RICE - DAVID SMITH (Page 244)

Born in South Carolina about 1775, the youngest child of **Henry Rice**, died probably before 1830.   Her father **Henry** died at her home at Lost Creek in 1818.   **Elizabeth** married **David Smith** in 1801 with **Henry Rice** being the bondsman (Grainger County, Tenn.).   In the 1810 Grainger County census there was a **David Smith** whose wife was over 45 years old and who had a male child 10-16 years old.   This would indicate that either **Elizabeth** was **David's** second wife or this was a different **David Smith**.   The daughter **Rachel**, the second wife of **Edmund Chisslers**, supposedly had gone to Missouri, but **Edmund** was not found in the census schedules.   **Edmund's** first wife was **Mary Rice**, a daughter of **Levi**, who was **Elizabeth's** older brother.

CONTENTS

CONTENTS (Continued)

CONTENTS (Continued)

INTRODUCTION

A. COLONIAL ORIGINS

The following information comes from reference (1)a/(page 2):

"When **Henry Rice** died in 1818 at the home of his daughter, **Elizabeth Rice Smith**, he was 101 years old. **Henry** had 'six' sons:

William		
John		
James	m.	Rebecca Miller
Daniel	m.	Anny Ray
Levi	m.	Jane Simmons
Charles		

and 'six' daughters:

Martha (Patsy)	m.	David Bailey
Molly	m.	Nathan Watson
Anna	m.	Augustus Wilson
Rosa	m.	(1) James Spence
		(2) Alexander Morrow
Lavina	m.	Lewis Brim
Elizabeth	m.	David Smith"

For those seeking membership in the Sons of the American Revolution, one member has been accepted on **Henry Rice's** war record with the Cherokees at **Rice's** Mill in Tennessee: **Melvin Weaver Little**, Arlington, Va., National Number 103857, Virginia State Number 3206. Probably there are others. Several women have been accepted in the Daughters of the American Revolution on the same basis. Examples are **Clara Belle Gutzmann**, Fresno, Ca. (No. 463639); **Susan Leigh Sharp**, Manhattan Kansas (No. 587578); and **Ruby Rice Little**, Arlington, Va. (No. 572713).

The pioneer **Henry Rice** had six sons: **Charles, Daniel, James, John, Levi,** and **William**, listed in alphabetical order. **Henry** may have named one son for his father (**Mrs. Nan Shute** believes his father was **James**, son of **Thomas**); there is no son **Henry**. I would list the children by age, but I have no birth records; however some approximations of ages can be reached

---

a/Numbers in parentheses refer to references listed in the Sources and Bibliography (page 251).

by counting backward from census records. Nor do I know where they were born. This also applies to **Henry's** six daughters: **Martha (Patsy) Bailey, Lavina Brim, Elizabeth Smith** (probably the youngest), **Rosa Spence Morrow, Molly Watson,** and **Ann (Anna) Wilson.** The name of his wife (or wives) is still unknown; she may have died before **Henry** built his gristmill in 1775 in the Watauga Settlement--or at least remained in South Carolina with his younger children.

Alva Silas Turnbow and **Maude Ina Turnbow** compiled an excellent record of **Henry Rice** (2). The **Turnbows** quoted (pages 6-7) from the poet **Martin Rice,** a great-grandson of **Henry Rice,** as follows:

> "**Martin Rice....**wrote his account of his remembrance of his great-grandfather and his descendants....The said **Henry** lived to a great age and had a large family. His sons were **William, John, James, Daniel** and **Levi.** His daughters were **Martha Bailey, Molly Watson, Ann Wilson, Rosa Spence, Lavina Brim,** and **Elizabeth Smith.** Some of these the writer has seen and remembers, and some were unknown even to the writer's father." (The compilation of **Martin Rice** is **The Descendants of Henry Rice, Pioneer to Tennessee**.)

Henry Rice did also have a son **Charles,** not mentioned by **Martin Rice**; this is proved by records of land indentures from **Henry** to his son **Charles,** found in Pendleton County, SC, and in Grainger County, TN.

B. EUROPEAN ORIGIN OF THE FAMILY

Henry Rice's parents, and even the name of his wife, have remained a mystery for over one hundred years. By tradition the Southern **Rices** are of British origin, and English at that, but no actual connection with a British ancestor has been established. Another of my Revolutionary War ancestors was **Johan Nicholas Gibbs, Jr.,** two of whose daughters married descendants of **Henry Rice.**

> "The grandfather of **Nicholas Gibbs** left England because of religious and political reasons to save his head when his king, Charles I, lost his in 1649. He married a woman in Amsterdam and never went back to London [Letter from **Charles N. Gibbs,** November 14, 1913], but sought refuge along the Rhine River in Germany, and it was in the village of Wallruth near the town of Krumbach, Duchy of Baden, that **Nicholas** was born Sept. 29, 1973." (3).

2

Then when religious persecution arose in Germany, many families again emigrated, this time to the English colonies in America. In the German passenger lists (**Pennsylvania German Pioneers. Original Lists of Arrivals in the Port of Philadelphia from 1727 to 1808**, by R. B. Strassburger, edited by **W. J. Hincke**) there are many names, such as **Sharps, Graves, Efland, Albright, Snoderly, Loy, Miller, Tillman**, and **Rice**. Many of these immigrants therefore were of German birth, but could have been, like **Nicholas Gibbs**, and possibly including **Henry Rice's** ancestor, of English descent.

Mrs. Nan Rice Shute, the author of **Rice Trails 1717-1977** (1), believes that **Henry Rice's** link with "the old country" is through **James**, son of **Thomas Rice**. This **Thomas Rice** was the father of **David Rice** and the grandfather of **Reverend David Rice**. Other children of **Thomas Rice** included **James, Thomas**, six other sons and three daughters. Some more children are listed in baptismal records, but still most names are unknown. [The son **James** may have died young and **Henry** may not have had brothers and sisters.]

The following quotation is cited regarding the **Rev. David Rice** line (4, page 13). (The **Rev. David Rice** was born in Hanover County, VA, on the 28th day of December, 1733.) (See p. 5 this book.)

"[**Rev. David Rice's**] grandfather, **Thomas Rice**, was an Englishman by birth, of Welsh extraction [to this compiler, the origin was either English or Welsh, but not both]....In the latter part of what is now called Hanover County [Virginia]. Here he left his wife, with nine sons and three daughters and [in 1695] went to England, to receive a con- siderable estate which had been left to him, but returned no more. The sailors reported that he died on [or at] sea. It was supposed that he was assassinated. No return was ever made of the property after which he had gone, and his family were left destitute in a strange land."

Page 14 mentions "His father **David Rice**"; on pages 32 and 33 "my **Aunt Mary Rice** was married to a **John Symms**....my Uncle **James Rice**...."

There is much more data on this line from **Thomas Rice** through **Rev. David Rice**. There are, also, records of other **Rices** in the Commonwealth of Virginia, including other **Henry Rices**.

It is believed that there is <u>no</u> connection between **Henry Rice** and the English **Deacon Edmund Rice** of Sudbury, Massachusetts. The Deacon settled in the year 1638 and named the town for Sudbury,

3

England. There are two authors who claim that **Edmund Rice** was
descended from a Welsh line of kings, which can be traced back to
Charlemagne. The books do not give sufficient proof, and the link
to the kings has been rejected by the <u>Deacon **Edmund Rice** Associa-
tion</u>. These books have been studied, as well as **John Burke** and
John Bernard Burke peerages and books on royal lineage, and there
is agreement with the above Association on this point.

In the 1800's a missionary's daughter came to the southern
states stating that the **Rices** in the South were descended from the
Deacon Edmund Rice. The previously mentioned Association also
disclaims this "connection."

Lastly, there is another possible origin of **Henry Rice's**
ancestors, directly from the "old country" into South Carolina,
but because of the Civil War no records remain of individual
names. **Henry Rice**, his sons **Charles** and **James**, and other **Rices**
had land in South Carolina, in 96 District (Pendleton County,
present Pickens County). This is really the first firm record of
Henry Rice to my knowledge.

In a book on the history of South Carolina (5, pages 86-87),
there are nine townships and national origins. The State of South
Carolina was first divided into 1) "Purrysburgh, on the east bank
of the Savannah River"; 2) "Orangeburg, north of the Edisto
River"; 3) "Amelia in modern Calhoun County"` 4) "Saxegotha in the
lower part of Lexington County"; 5) "New Windsor, across the
Savannah from Augusta, where the town of Hamburg later developed";
6) Williamsburg, with modern Kingstree at its center; 7) King-
ston; 8) "Queensborough"; and [9]"Frederickstown."

Then the same author (**Wright**) wrote just about origins, but
without giving specific names:

"The settlers were a mixed lot: Germans, English, Welsh,
Ulster Scots, Lowland Scots, and an occasional Highlander
....Records show the arrival of many `poor Irish Protest-
ants,` meaning Ulster Scots or Scotch-Irish, as they also
were called. As early as the autumn of 1732, Ulster Scots
were being directed to Williamsburg and settling around what
became Kingstree. Beginning in the 1730's, many German-
Swiss and Rhineland Germans came to Orangeburgh and Amelia.
By 1750 Saxe-gotha was filling up with Swiss and Germans of
the Reformed faith. A few Lutheran Germans were among the
immigrants. Although the Germans were inclined to create
close-knit enclaves, both English and Scots settled in the

same townships. In time many of the Germans anglicized their names, and a man named Miller might have begun as Mueller." [umlaut over "u" - or "Müller."]

Wright also pointed out that indentured servants were in Charleston, and when they became free many went west in the State. Also, "increasing numbers drifted down from Pennsylvania, Maryland and Virginia."

Many people settled in parts of South Carolina still claimed by Indians and lived there as "squatters" for several years in pre-Revolutionary war times, so that their existence may never have been recorded in any official documents--certainly not as landowners. 96 District was one of those areas.

Thus, **Henry** could have taken any one of many routes to his 96 District home where we first can positively pinpoint his residence. My grandfather **Marcellus Moss Rice** has said many times that **Henry** and **James** came from "Big Sandy" in South Carolina--but was unable to say whether "Big Sandy" was a river or other geographical entity. The old maps of South Carolina show more than one possible "Big Sandy" location.

The chart below shows the possible origin and relationships of "Pioneer Gristmiller" **Henry Rice** as discussed on page 3.

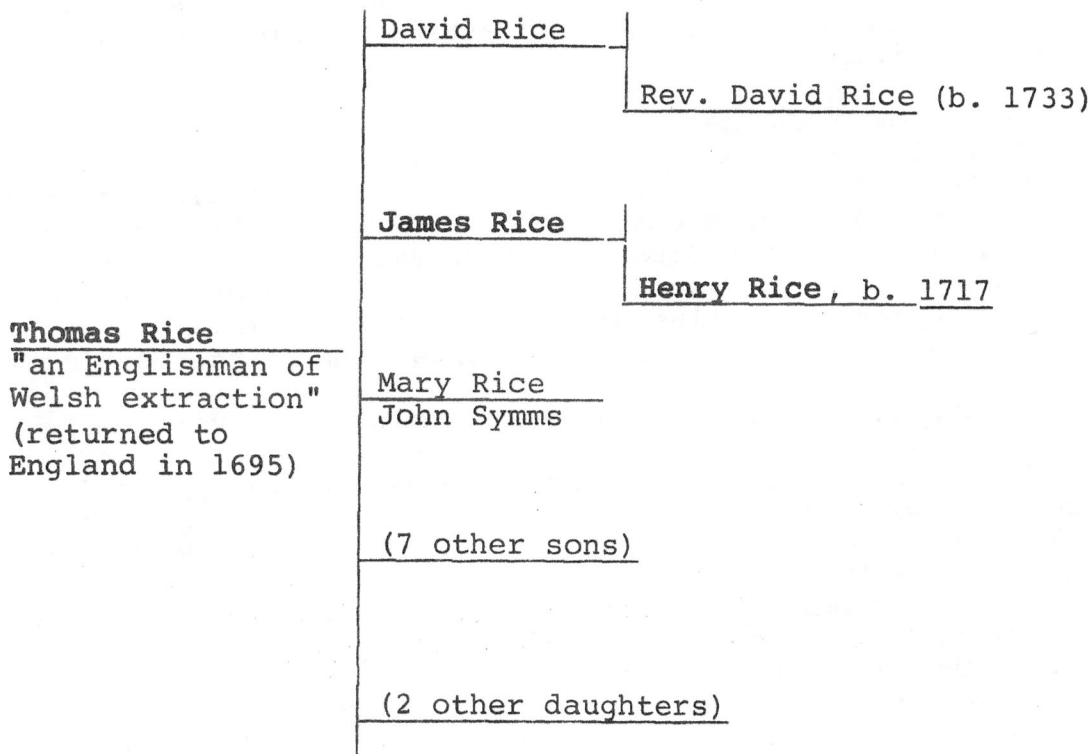

```
                          | David Rice      |
                          |                 |
                          |                 | Rev. David Rice (b. 1733)
                          |
                          |
                          |
                          | James Rice      |
                          |                 |
                          |                 | Henry Rice, b. 1717
Thomas Rice               |
"an Englishman of         |
Welsh extraction"         | Mary Rice
(returned to              | John Symms
England in 1695)          |
                          |
                          |
                          | (7 other sons)
                          |
                          |
                          |
                          | (2 other daughters)
                          |
```

5

CHAPTER I. HENRY RICE

Chapter summary on page v

A. HENRY RICE IN REVOLUTIONARY WAR TIMES

Henry Rice was born in 1717(?) in Hanover County, Va., lived in Virginia, South Carolina, and East Tennessee, and died in 1818 at Lost Creek, Tenn. (Campbell County, now Union). Name(s) of wife or wives unknown. He had at least six sons and six daughters, some born in Virginia and some in South Carolina. **Henry Rice** may have been the son of **James Rice**, son of the **Thomas Rice** who in 1695 returned to England for an inheritance but was presumed lost at sea. If so related, **Henry** was a cousin of the **Rev. David Rice** of Kenrucky. Near the middle of the century the family moved to the "96 District" of South Carolina and settled on land known as Indian Territory. Since those lands were not at the disposal of the State, no records of ownership such as deeds were made. After the Revolutionary War the settlers were granted titles to the lands they had possessed. After several years at Rice's Creek and Twelve Mile River in South Carolina, **Henry** traveled with some of his older children to Watauga Settlement, East Tennessee, where he built and fortified a large grist mill. He spent the rest of his 101 years at Lost Creek.

Henry Rice is mentioned in a book (6) by **Lewis Preston Summers**, along with **Abraham, James, Thomas,** and **William Rice.** Southwestern Virginia was occupied only by American Indians until about 1769. **Mr. Summers** also wrote an earlier history book (7) on Southwestern Virginia.

The first book contains court records of Washington County and other Virginia counties (Washington County, Virginia, included part of East Tennessee back in the 1780's). Your compiler has not connected all of the above **Rices. David Rice** was in Botetourt County, **James Rice** in Wythe County, and **Thomas Rice** in Montgomery County. **Abraham Rice,** in Washington County, was one of three men appointed to estimate the value of the "Estate of **William Cole** Deceased" on August 17, 1779. [I have **Coles** on my father's side.]

I now quote the references to **Henry Rice** as follows:

From (6) (page 980), "At a Court continued and held for Washington County March 18th 1778...." (page 983) "A Jury sworn to try the cause between the Commonwealth of Virginia Plaintiff and **Isaac Lebo** defendant Viz. **Alexander Barnett, Wm. Cowan, William Elli, John Patterson, Adam Keer, John King, John Vance, Robert Coyle, John Carmack,** Henry Rice, **James Kelly & Matthew Dean** returned verdict for Plaintiff and assess the Damage to Seventy five pounds and three months imprisonment his expenses to be discharged by the County which is ordered to be recorded."

(Page 984) "At a Court continued and held for Washington
County March 20, 1778....Be it remembred that **Joseph Calvitt,
James Shelby, Evan Shelby Jun.** and **Elijah Robinson** severally
acknowledged themselves indebted to the Commonwealth of
Virginia in the Sum of one thousand pounds current money
that is to say the said **Joseph Calvitt** in the Sum of Two
Hundred pounds each of their respective goods and chattles
lands and tenements to be levied and to the said Commonwealth
rendred yet upon this condition that if the said **Joseph Calvitt**
shall personally appear at the next Grand Jury Court to be
held the 3rd Tuesday in May to the complaint of <u>Henry Rice</u>
exhibited against him then this obligation to be void else
to remain in full force and virtue."

(Page 985) "Be it remembred that <u>Henry Rice</u> this day in court
acknowledged himself indebted to the Commonwealth of Virginia
in the Sum of five Hundred pounds current money of his lands
and tenements goods & chattles to be levied and to the said
Commonwealth rendred yet upon this condition that if the said
<u>Henry Rice</u> shall appear at the next Grand Jury Court to be
the 3rd Tuesday in May next to prosecute the exhibited
against **Joseph Calvitt** then this recognizance to be void
otherwise to remain in full force and virtue."

It seems that **Henry Rice** owed 500 pounds to the State, and
that **Joseph Calvitt** owed 200 pounds also to the State. Also **Henry**
had a "complaint" against **Joseph Calvitt** - but if both showed up
in court no one would pay anything. (I am no law student.)

I believe that this **Joseph Calvitt** was related to the **Frederick Calvatt** whose name appears on the **Henry Rice** Mill Marker
near Church Hill, Tennessee. The late Professor **W. H. Thomas**
wrote that the **Calverts** were from Maryland; the name **Calvitt** was
originally **Calvert**. (See pages 8-9 for the Mill Marker.)

(Page 1006) "At a Court continued and held for Washington
County November 18th 1778...." (p. 1007) "Ordered that <u>Henry
Rice</u> be overseer of the road from the North Fork to the
lower fork of **Ranfros** Creek and that **John Coulter Gent.** give
him a list of Tithables and that **William Rosebrough** be surveyor of the road from thence to **Capt. James Robinson** and
that **Thomas Caldwell Gent.** give him a list of Tithables and
the said surveyor is to cut the road as it will be laid off
to them by **Robert Patterson, William McBroom & John King.**"

From **Mr. Summers'** second book (7, page 37), the following is
quoted:

"Thus East Tennessee began to be permanently settled in the
winter of 1768-9. Ten families of these settlers came from
the neighborhood of the place where Raleigh now stands, in
North-Carolina, and settled on Watauga. This was the first
settlement in East Tennessee. Soon afterwards it was

7

augmented, by settlers from the hollows in North Carolina, and from Virginia....The trade of the country was in the hands of Scotch merchants, who came in shoals to get rich, and to get consequence. The people of the country were clothed in the goods they imported, and to be dressed otherwise was scouted as a sign of barbarity and poverty. The poor man was treated with disdain, because unable to contribute to their emoluments (i.e. advantage)."

Henry Rice may have been considered a poor man, being a miller. In a book on water mills (8) page 198, first paragraph, we read:

"4. Caustic Criticism   4. At the early part of the present century the water miller was by no means free from that.... one form or other had dogged his craft, from the days of Chaucer....In tracing century by century the fortunes and vicissitudes (i.e. changes) of the much-maligned miller of old--ideally a man...but actually a very hard-working, and often greatly worried, tradesman--we have found much reason to question the popular vote of censure...in the eyes of his fellow countrymen...."

(Page 199) "At the present moment, however, we are concerned solely with the water miller of the early part of the present century, who, as we say, was not..." free "...of popular abuse...,"

Also, all of **Henry's** deeds and land transfers were written in the hand of a court recorder, with a seal at the right of a deed; this means, I was told, that **Henry** could not read nor write.

On page 20 of **Tennessee Historical Markers**, a pamphlet listing historical markers erected by the Tennessee Historical Commission, 6th Edition, 1972, we find markers (a) **1B--15 First Settlers**, (b) **1B--14 Patterson's Mill** and (c) **1B--16 Rice's Mill**. These markers fit in with the settlement of what became Tennessee.

"(U S 11 W) Hawkins Co., 3 miles west of Sullivan County line 1B--15 First Settlers. About 1-1/2 miles west and north of here, in Carter's Valley, **Joseph Kinkead** and **John Long,** first known pioneers to what later became Hawkins County, settled in 1769-70. The valley is named for **Col. John Carter,** who first settled here and later became a prominent member of the Watauga Settlement."

"(U S 11 W) Hawkins Co., in Church Hill. 1B--14 **Patterson's** Mill. On the site of this mill **Robert Patterson** built a fort about 1775, shortly thereafter a mill. It was one of two stations at which the settlers took refuge during the Cherokee raid under **The Raven** in 1776."

"(U S 11 W) Hawkins Co., 2 miles west of Church Hill. 1B--16 **Rice's Mill.** On the site of this mill, **Henry Rice** built and fortified a mill in 1775. Here, in 1776, the settlers took refuge from warring Cherokee. In April, 1777, **Capt. James Robertson** and eight other pioneers had a fight with 30 or 40 Cherokee near here, in which **Frederick Calvatt** was scalped."

In **Summers' History** cited above (7, pages 54-55), the **Rice** and **Patterson** mills are mentioned as follows:

"On the 31st March, 1777 **Colonel Arthur Campbell**, of Fort Patrick Henry, directed **Captain Robertson**, on account of the weakness of the settlements below the fort, and on account of the danger to which they might soon be exposed, to assemble the settlers in one or two places, and not more; and he recommended **Rice's** and **Patten's** [sic] mills, as the most proper ones. Let your company be at **Rice's**, said he, and **Captain Christian's** may come to the other mill. He reuested a list of settlers names, that he might know their strength, and give such further orders as should be necessary ....In May, 1777, at the Long island of Holston, a treaty was held with the Indians, by commissioners on the part of North Carolina and Virginia...."

Henry Rice and his sons may have attended this treaty session. Long Island is near Kingsport. These comments on the Cherokee hostilities come from **Charles Rice, His Ancestors and Descendants** (2, page 3):

"The previous year, on August 1, 1776, Virginia had sent an expedition against the Cherokee at the request of South Carolina. British agents had stirred up the tribes on the western frontiers. This band of patriots was under the command of **Colonel Christian** Among those listed as serving in this expedition we find the names of **Henry Rice** and three of his sons: **John Rice** (the old preacher), **William Rice** and **Charles Rice.**"

"A **William** and **Benjamin**, who may have been grandsons of **Henry**, are also listed. His son-in-law **David Smith**, who married **Elizabeth Rice**, was a private in this expedition." [Quoted from **Summers**, (7, pp. 237-40).]

I believe that the **Rice** mill (at the Historical Marker 1-B 16 above) was used as a fortification. Mrs. **Nan Rice Shute**, my collaborator, and my mother saw the mill in May 1978, and observed that the stone cellar or bottom story has holes in the stonework

which certainly could have been used as portholes. Later, my
mother and I visited the mill and found a large stone fireplace at
one corner, which would have been used for cooking and heating for
settlers assembled there during the hostilities--also for making
bullets.

On the other hand, judging by the construction of the base of
his mill with its huge stones (the upper part has been rebuilt
several times), **Henry** must have had a wealth of ability and
friends and relatives, without which the erection of such a
structure in those days would have been so much harder.

Also, I have copies of maps of the area showing present
Church Hill, and other maps from the 1790's and 1800's showing the
sites of **Rice's** and **Patterson's** mills. The **Rice's** mill described
above is also known as **Hord's** mill. The present topographical map
(Appendix No. 6) shows three distinct mills: **Rice's, Patterson's,**
and **Hord's (Hoard's, or Hard's)** mills. It seems that **William
Hord,** who bought **Rice's** mill land and **Rice's** Island from **Daniel
Rice** in 1813, built another mill upstream in 1840, not on the
foundation of **Henry's** original mill. **Rice's** Island and **Rice's**
Creek (shown on the 1832 map) are now known as **Hord's** Island and
Hord's Creek. There is also a **Hord** cemetery today. Certainly the
upper floors of **Henry Rice's** mill have been rebuilt, for almost
200 years have passed and the present structure is wooden. Also
machinery of a later period has been installed and obviously used.

The Long Island of the Holston River is not **Rice's** Island.
Long Island (also called Big Island, and Great Island) is
southwest of Kingsport in the South Fork of the Holston River just
next to the town. Below the island and the town, the North and
South Forks of the Holston River combine; then a short distance
farther down the meanders of the river is the town of Church Hill.

Kingsport used to be called Old Fort; **Ross's** Ironworks, later
Rossville, was on the other side of the Holston River, downriver
from the juncture of the North and South Forks.

Church Hill is on the maps with Alexander Creek, still so
named today. This is the site of the **Patterson** mill.

A number of maps were consulted, to bridge the gap between
place names of the Revolutionary War times and those of the
present:

Tennessee (1795-1796 1:1,715,000 from **Carey's General
Atlas, 1818**, showing Great Island and Rossville (Appendix 7).

Big Island and Kingsport are on **Tennessee (Holston River Headwaters Area) 18--?, Draper ms. 6C65 (Z6621.W79)** (Appendix 8).

An 1832 map (**Tennessee 1832 1:450,000, Rhea Trails Bibl. 180**) has **Rice's** Creek, Alexander Creek, Ross, Kingsport, and Long Island (Appendix 9).

The map, **Tennessee 1839-1841-deposited** (Appendix 10), has New Canton in Powell County, which County does not appear on the 1842 map (Appendix 11). The county was short-lived, but there is still a valley and river named for the **Powells** who settled there.

New Canton and Bull Run Creek are on the map, **Tennessee-Eastern (1842)** (Photostat from Smith's **"A State Hist. & Desc...."**). New Canton is just on the western edge of what was then Sullivan County (Appendix 11).

New Canton and Church Hill are listed as postal locations, with Hard Creek, on the map **Tennessee Hawkins Co. 1914 P.O. Dept. Rural Delivery Service** (Appendix 12).

Two topographical maps from the late 19th Century show Lost Creek and the Bull Run Creek area on one map; Clinton and Lone Mountain appear on the other. The "Maynardville Quadrangle," surveyed in 1892-95, has Halls Cross Roads, Copper Ridge, Bull Run Creek, Black Oak Ridge, Bull Run Ridge, Sharps Chapel, Loyston, and Lost Creek (Appendix 13). The "Tennessee Briceville" sheet, surveyed from 1888-1891, has Clinton, Lone Mountain, Andersonville, Hinds Creek and Buffalo Creek (Appendix 14).

The latest topographical maps published by the U.S. Geological Survey show that many former landmarks no longer exist because they were erased from the map by the numerous artificial lakes; but some places dear to your compiler can yet be found: The Powder Springs Quadrangle (road crossing the Clinch River), Maynardville Quadrangle (Sharps Chapel and Big White Oak Tree), the White Hollow Quadrangle (Lost Creek, site of **James Rice's** log cabin and the Lost Creek Cemetery), and the Big Ridge Park Quadrangle (**Marcellus Moss Rice's** land on Bull Run Creek).

B. HENRY RICE IN SOUTH CAROLINA

The South Carolina land that **Henry**, **Charles** and **James Rice** had in Pendleton District must have been acquired by "squatter" and "hatchet" rights before 1785. Maybe **Henry** had this land before he settled in the Watauga area. There is no record of any grant or purchase until 1787, when he was given title to land in both Pendleton District and in the Watauga area. But he settled, I believe, on the lands long before the State governments gave him the titles as land grants.

The **Rice** lands and **Rice's** Creek in South Carolina were near the present town of Pickens, the County Seat of Pickens County. Pickens, Oconee, and Anderson Counties were formed from the old Pendleton County. All of western South Carolina in 1787 was called 96 District.

When the **Rices** were given title to their South Carolina land, the land was first surveyed, and then it was granted. The State plats were made by the surveyor.

I will list first the plats, then the grants, for the **Henry Rice** land, followed by the descriptions (I do have South Carolina State plats for the **Charles Rice** land). Photostats and descriptions for the **James Rice** land will be found in the **James Rice** chapter, and descriptions of **Charles Rice** plats in the **Charles Rice** chapter.

(9) South Carolina Department of Archives and History
South Carolina State Plats, 96 District

Charles Rice	96 District	200 acres	6 April 1785
Charles Rice	96 District	200 acres	No date
Henry Rice	96 District	468 acres	23 March 1787
James Rice	96 District	292 acres	7 April 1785
James Rice	96 District	48 acres	5 December 1791
James Rice	96 District	28 acres	24 November 1793

South Carolina State Grants, 96 District

Charles Rice	96 District	200 acres	1 January 1787
Charles Rice	96 District	200 acres	1 January 1787
Henry Rice	96 District	468 acres	5 November 1787
James Rice	96 District	28 acres	3 December 1792
James Rice	96 District	292 acres	1 January 1787
James Rice	96 District	48 acres	2 January 1792

Henry Rice's plat reads: "Warrant to **Henry Rice** for 468 acres on branches of Wolf and Rice Creeks of 12 Mile River and is adjacent to vacant land. Surveyed 23 March 1787. **John Young, Jr. D.S.**" (vol. 20 q - 269.) (Appendix 15.)

The Pendleton District map shows Twelve Mile River, Rice's Creek, Wolf Creek, and Golden Creek (Appendix 15). There is a modern topographical map of the same area where the **Rices** had their land. Rice, Wolf, and Golden Creeks are shown on this map (Appendix 16).

In order to sell the 468 acres, **Henry Rice** gave to **Charles Rice** a power of attorney: "On the 29 May 1800 **Henry Rice** of Granger County, Tenn. do appoint my son **Charles Rice** of Pendleton District to sell a tract of 460 odd acres granted to me and is on waters of Rice and Wolf Creek. Wit: **William Steele, James Wood. Michael Dickson, J.Q.**" (Anderson County, S.C. Deeds, Book E, page 246.)

Then "On the 15 August 1805 **Charles Rice** of Walton County, Georgia the lawful Attorney of my father - **Henry Rice** of Tenn. sells to **Jesse Tatum** 468 acres that was granted to **Henry Rice** on the 5 November 1787. Wit: **Thomas W. Farrar, William Hamilton. M. Hammond** - Deputy Clerk." (Anderson County, S.C. Deeds, Book H, page 213.)

Henry Rice's 468 acres is mentioned in a deed from **Jesse Tatum** to **William Cox** (Book O, page 361): "On the 24 March 1818 **Jesse Tatum** sells to **William Cox** 688 acres. Part of this tract was....and 468 acres was granted to **Henry Rice**...."

C. HENRY RICE IN TENNESSEE

The old gristmiller appears to have sold to his son **Charles** 200 acres in Grainger County in 1803, but there is no record on the selling of this land. Nor is there any other record in Georgia of **Charles Rice** other than that written above and in the description of the 1805 land indenture.

The land at Lost Creek, where **Henry Rice** was when he died, I believe was at one time part of Greene County. Greene County was formed in 1783 out of Washington County. Knox County was formed out of Greene and Hawkins Counties in 1792. Grainger County was formed in 1796 (the year Tennessee became a State) out of Hawkins and Knox Counties. Claiborne County was formed in 1801 out of Grainger and Hawkins. Then Campbell County was formed in 1806 out of Anderson and Claiborne. Union County, where Lost Creek is located in today's map, was formed in 1857 taking in parts of Anderson, Campbell, Claiborne, Grainger, and Knox Counties. This makes it very hard to know where to look for records of deeds. (Can't you imagine the squabbles accompanying all those changes in county boundaries?)

Henry Rice had two major land grants in Tennessee (10). Following is a list of land grants to **Henry**, his sons **John** and **Daniel**, and some possible relatives.

Page	Number	Grantee	Acres	Date	County	
3	95	John Rice	177	1782	Washington	(a)
	83	Thomas Baker	100	1782	"	(b)
7	255	Charles Gentery	250	1782	"	(c)
	263	Isaac Wilson	350	1782	"	(d)
9	333	John Rice	74	1782	"	(e)
29	1313	Henry Rice	643	1784	Sullivan	(f)
43	2019	Henry Rice	640	1787	Greene	(g)
50	2371	Daniel Rice	200	1790	Greene	(h)

These land locations were described as follows:

(a) **(John Rice)** "on the south side of Holston River foot of Bays Mountain."

(b) **(Thomas Baker)** "on the north side of the Nolachucky R."

(c) **(Charles Gentery)** "on an East Branch of Big Limestone."

(d) **(Isaac Wilson)** "on the north side Nolachucky below the mouth of Limestone."

(e) **(John Rice)** "on South side Holstein River."

(f) **(Henry Rice)** "on the north side Holstein river."

(g) **(Henry Rice)** "on both sides Loss Creek in Bold Valley."

(h) **(Daniel Rice)** "on Big Creek South side Nolachucky."

The mill land of **Henry Rice**, given above as located in Sullivan County, is now in Hawkins; while the other grant on Loss (Lost) Creek, then in Greene County, is now in Union; it was in Campbell County until 1857.

The mill land and others had duplicate surveys, which vary as far as acreage is concerned. **Henry** tried to get some land in grants on the south side of the Holston.

These land grants were originally made by North Carolina, so Tennessee made copies of the records. N.C. State Plats and Tennessee duplicates:

1. N.C. Washington County No. 1755, Sept. 30, 1779. 600 acres north side of Holston River above mouth of **Rice's** Creek where said **Rice** lives and a grist mill.

2. N.C. Sullivan County, 20th November 1782. 643 acres north side of Holston River. Tenn. Sullivan County No. 468, 643 acres, Grant No. 347 issued 10 Nov. 1784. Entry No. 1755 Entered 30 Sept. 1779. North side of Holstein River.

3. N.C. March 17, 1780, Sullivan County No. 324. Tenn. Greene Co. No. 488. 640 acres north side of Holston River, his mill and where he now lives.

There are three different entries of the Church Hill land, all for the same land, due to the County changes. This has been very confusing for several years to your compiler.

4. N.C. Eastern District No. 779, Dec. 25, 1778. March 25, 1786, surveyed for **Henry Rice** north side of Clinch River in Bald Valley on both sides of Loss Creek 600 acres.

5. Tenn. Eastern District No. 021. 640 acres. Entry No. 799 Entered 25 Feb. 1778, north side of Clinch River.

Henry had a survey which mentions **Ann Rice**, who may have been **Henry's** daughter. This plat was not granted.

6. N.C. Washington Co., Dec. 25, 1778, No. 779, surveyor to measure 640 acres south side of Holston River joining **Ann Rice's** land. No. 779 not granted. [This survey had the same number as No. 4 above, which was granted.]

I think there are three entries for the same land next to **John Rice**, even though the acres do vary. This was on the south side of the Holston. **The Preacher John Rice** does show up in Knox County, especially in connection with his daughter marrying "**Little**" **Harpe**. There will be more on this son of **Henry** later.

1. N.C. Washington County No. 126, February 26, 1778. To surveyor of Sullivan County measure 300 acres **Woolsey** Bottom running down Holston River.

2. N.C. Washington County February 26, 1778, No. 126 surveyed for **Henry Rice** 260 acres South side of Holston River joining above a survey of 177 acres made for **John Rice**.

3. Tenn. Hawkins County No. 814, **Rice, Henry,** 200 acres Grant No. 650 6th January 1795, Entry No. 126. South side of Holston River.

The last of the plats has the name of **Henry's** son-in-law **Nathan Watson.**

4. N.C. Sullivan County Aug. 24, 1780, No. 680 surveyor to measure for **Henry Rice** 200 acres on **Rice's** Mill Creek.

5. Tn. Hawkins County 200 acres Grant No. 599 issued 12 July 1794 North side of Holston River on Sinking Spring surveyed for **Nathan Watson Henry Rice.** [**Nathan's** name was crossed out with a line through it, but **Henry** did sell to him the same 200 acres. This is in Hawkins County Deed Book 2, page 307. See Hawkins Deeds.]

The above North Carolina records are from (11) Department of Cultural Resources, Division of Archives and History, Archives and Records Section, 109 East Jones Street, Raleigh, NC 27611. The Tennessee records (12) are from the Tennessee State Archives and Library, Nashville, TN.

HENRY RICE DEEDS IN TENNESSEE

I will give deeds, indentures, and/or grants in order by the following Counties--Knox, Hawkins, Grainger, Campbell, and Claiborne--for **Henry Rice.** My first cousin, **John Rice Irwin,** had in his **Notes** (14) that **Henry,** the old pioneer, in 1775 got 200 acres in the Watauga Purchase. This was then considered part of North Carolina, then it was part of the "Lost State of Franklin," and now is in Hawkins County, Tennessee.

I have a photocopy of a deed in Hawkins County from **Henry Rice** to **Jane Evans** for 200 acres. This record is in Hawkins Deed Book 1, p. 114. This is probably one of the State grants that **Henry** got from North Carolina and the above Watauga Purchase.

Knox County Deed Book - Reverse Index

Grantee, **Henry Rice;** Grantor, **Ingles, Thomas;** Instrument, Warranty Deed; Book, C 1; Page, 275; Recorded, 1795 June 9; Dated, 1795, Apr 27; Acres, 420.

Hawkins County Deed Books

Grantor	Grantee	
		Book 1, page 114
		200 acres 65 lbs. Virginia money
Rice, Henry	**Jane Evans**	Dated 7 March 1790
		Recorded 12 July 1792
		2 acres surveyed 28 Aug. 1733
		Transcribed from Liver [Book] E page 95
		Book 2, page 274.
Rice, Henry	**Jessee Maxwell**	236 acres 200 lbs.
		Territory South of Ohio River
		South side of Holston River
		16th Dec. 1795
Rice, Henry	**Nathan Watson**	Deed Book 2 page 307
		200 acres $200
		North side of Holston on Sinking
		Springs
		Mrs. Jane Evans line
		2 Augt. 1797
North Carolina Grant	**Henry Rice**	Deed Book 3, pp. 406-08
		(This is his 643 acres, where he
		built his mill. It is "State of
		North Carolina Sullivan County 20th
		November 1782," as before.)
		(I have a typed description of the
		N.C. grant.)
Rice, Henry	**George Maxwell**	Deed Book 4, pp. 195-96
		24 acres 6 lbs. Va. money
		Territory South of River Ohio
		South side of Holston River
		John Rice's Creek
		John Rice's corner

In the presence of :		
Nathan Watson	:	3rd June 1795
Daniel Rice	:	

Rice, Henry	**Daniel Rice**	Deed Book 6, pp. 357-58
		643 acres $3000
		North side of Holston River
		Robert Youngs line

```
Nathan Watson        :
Thomas Lockart       :    5th March 1811
Levi Rice            :
```

[This mill land **Daniel** sold in 1813
to **William Hard** with Rice Island; in
Grainger deeds.   Deed will be under
Daniel Rice.]

Grainger County Deed Books

Grantor	Grantee	
		Deed Book A, p. 56
		200 acres, 25 lbs. Virginia money
Rhoades, Christian	Henry Rice	North side of Holston River
		Gilmore's corner

```
in presence of us    :
Thomas Smith         :    7 Feb. 1798
John Gilmore         :
```

Rice, Henry	Charles **Rice** of Pendleton County, SC	Deed Book A, p. 307
		Rhodes's Big Survey
		Henry Rice's Corner, **Rice's** line
		David Ray's line
		16 August 1803

Rice, Henry	Levi Rice	Book C, pp. 151-52
		210 acres - valuable consideration
		Formerly County of Knox, Buffalo Creek
		north side of Holston River
		part of 420 acre tract
		Sold and surveyed to **Henry Rice** by **Thomas Ingles** 27 day April 1795

```
in presence of us    :
James Rice           :    7 January
David Smith          :    1812
Joseph Brim          :
```

Grantor	Grantee	
Rice, Levi	Henry Rice	Deed Book C, pp. 293-94 210 acres, $210 28 March 1814 **(Levi Rice** sold the same land back to his father, which **Henry** had previously bought from **Thomas Ingles.)**
Rice, Henry	David Smith	Book D, pp. 462-63 This deed really is from **Henry Rice, David Smith,** and **Levi Rice** (grantors) to **James Richison.** This is the same .210 acres of land as the 2 deeds above; $1100. **Benjamin Austin** was one of the attestors.

Claiborne County Deed Books

Rice, Henry	James Rice	Deed Book A-1, p. 235-1/2 Copied from Book A, p. 300. 400 acres, north side at Lost Creek, in the big valley on Lost Creek in Claiborne County, it being part of survey of 640 acres to the said **Henry Rice.**

in the presents of	:	
David Smith	:	10 January
Josiah Grimmel	:	1805

Claiborne County March Term 1806
oath of **David Smith**
attest of **Walter Evans** Clerk

HENRY RICE IN TAX LISTS

Henry Rice was in two tax lists in Grainger County court records:

1. "Tax List 1799 Grainger County.
   Rice, Henry   620 A   1 pole white tax   90 cents."
2. "1810 August Term
   Henry Rice   1 poll tax   1811 when taxed
   Amount of state tax 12-1/2 cents"

HENRY RICE IN CENSUS RECORDS

1810 Grainger County Tennessee Census

"**Henry Rice** - - - - 1 / - 1 - - 1" (13, p.11)
    (1 male 45 or over; 1 female 10 to 16; 1 female 45 or over

    Henry was elderly in 1810 and was living with his daughter
Elizabeth Rice Smith. The girl could be her daughter **Rachael**.
However, **David Smith** is not under **Henry Rice** in this census, but
there is a **David Smith** on the same census page as **Evan Smith**,
Henry Rice, and **Levi Rice**.

    Henry Rice was bondsman for marriage of his daughter
Elizabeth to **David Smith**, Dec. 23, 1801 in Grainger County
marriage records.

HENRY RICE IN OTHER RECORDS

    The old pioneer is listed in the Family Bible of his great
grandson, **Henry Rice**. He died in 1818, believed to be 101 years
old (tradition). **Henry Rice** was the second person to be buried in
the cemetery grounds now known as Lost Creek Cemetery. This
cemetery became the resting place of his son **James Rice** and wife
Rebecca Miller. The stones marking their graves were diamond-
shaped limestones, without inscriptions. My grandfather,
Marcellus Moss Rice, once showed the stones to my mother so that
the graves would be known to coming generations. A lovely stone
has recently been erected to commemorate **Henry Rice**, thanks to
Mrs. Nan Rice Shute.

    There was a Revolutionary War veteran who was the first to be
buried in Lost Creek Cemetery. From **John Rice Irwin's** notes I
found the name of **John Lipscomb** who, I was thinking, might be this
person. However, the journal quoted below says that **John Lipscomb**
visited **Mr. Rice (Henry)**. However, **Lipscomb** "settled in
Williamson County, where he died in 1820" (14, p. 270).

    John Rice Irwin also had in his notes some comments from
Early Travels in Tennessee 1540-1800 (15) about a journal kept by
John Lipscomb when he was on the way to the Cumberland
settlements. "It is full of human interest, but some of the
language is so ribald that....unfit to print. **Lipscomb** mentions
his nights spent at the home of **Mr. Rice (Rise)**, but he seemed to

like to stay with **Thomas Amis** better because that man had good whiskey." From the same book we learn that **Lipscomb** made three trips "through Cumberland Gap to the Cumberland Country...." "The spring of the year (1784) following...began a rush of officers and soldiers to the Cumberland Country to explore...locations favorable for land grants." The "Cumberland Country" was around Nashville, with the Cumberland River running through the Tennessee State capital.

The East Tennessee Historical Society at the McClung Historical Room of the Lawson McGee Library in Knoxville, Tennessee, has **"Lipscomb's** Account of the Journey" "...but it is badly dog-eared and torn, and well-nigh illegible from frequent thumbing. It has never been printed, and, seemingly, no transcript of the original has ever been made."

Mrs. Nan (Frances) Rice Shute, in 1977, had a lovely new headstone erected at **Henry's** grave, with all of his children listed. It also has her descent from our Revolutionary ancestor. (The first name of the son-in-law **Watson** is mis-stated as **Augustus**; it should be **Nathan.**)

Apparently **Henry Rice** deeded out his lands before his death, instead of making a last will and testament. Nor did **James Rice** make a will, but the **James Rice** estate sold his land, after his death, to his descendants. The estate deeds will be given under **James Rice.**

CHAPTER II. HENRY'S SON WILLIAM RICE

Chapter summary on page v

```
                                            ┌──────────────
                                            │  Charles
                                            │
                                            ├──────────────
                                            │  Susanna
                                            │
                          William           ├──────────────
                          (first wife)      │  Sarah
                          (Name unknown)    │
                                            ├──────────────
                                            │  Esther
                                            │
                                            ├──────────────
Henry Rice                                  │  Rebecca
(Name of wife
not known)
                                            ┌──────────────
                                            │  Nathaniel
                                            │
                          William           ├──────────────
                          Esther, second wife  James
                                            │
                                            ├──────────────
                                            │  Thomas
                                            │
                                            ├──────────────
                                            │  Henry
```

HENRY'S SON WILLIAM RICE

Martin Rice, the poet of Lone Jack, Missouri, in his recollections, wrote, "Of **William's** sons, **Charles** only is known to have had an existence..." (2, page 7). I have not found any sons of **William** other than **Charles**.

The **Turnbows** wrote that **William** was one of **Henry's** sons in a military campaign, and that two of **Henry's** grandsons, **William** and **Benjamin**, were also listed in the campaign (2, page 3). Maybe the last two **Rices** were sons of **William**; I have not found any record of birth for any of **Henry's** children, nor for any of the children of **William**, including **Charles**.

I have found **William Rice** in the same records of Washington County, Virginia, which later became part of East Tennessee:

"At a Court continued and held for Washington County, May 20th, 1779." (6, page 1027) - "**Jaiah Ramsey** against **William Rice**, Att. continued." (**Ibid.**, page 1028.)

"Brief of Deeds - Washington County, Records of Deeds No. 1" (**Ibid.**, page 1273) "

"Page 208, May 17, 1791. **Arthur Neel** to **Wm. Rice**. 100 pounds. 207 acres in Poor Valley on both sides of the Laurel Fork, a branch of the Holston River." (**Ibid.**, page 1291)

"Page 23, April 21, 1792. **William Rice** to **Jacob Carper** of the County of Botetourt. 100 pounds. 207 acres on both sides of Laurel Fork, a branch of the North Fork of Holston River." (**Ibid.**, page 1322)

William Rice had two deed conveyances in Hawkins County. They are first listed in the Deed Index, then summarized, each with the most important data.

Hawkins County Index to Deeds 1788-1861

Conveyor	Year	Book	Page	Conveyee
Rice, William	1796	3	119	William Stamps
Rice, William	1805	4	119	Hazel Harrold

Hawkins County Deeds

(1) **William Rice** to **William Stamps**, Book 3, p. 119.
Dated 8 October 1795
Territory South of the Ohio
50 lbs.   213 acres.

In presence of	:
Gaberal Phillips	:
Lazarus Dodson	:

Registered 25 Aug. 1796

(2) **William Rice** to **Hazel Harrold**, Book 4, pp. 119-20.
Dated 18 May 1805
William Rice of Sumner County
Hazel Harrold of Hawkins County
$430   100 acres
Gravelly Valley middle fork of Renfrees Creek.

There is a **William Rice** in the tax list of Hawkins County.
Maybe this is one of **Henry's** grandsons--although there is no proof
of sonship.

1836 Hawkins County Tax List, District 7

48 acres - old granted land - 1 white poll tax $0.56'
                state tax, $0.12| - total tax $0.56'

Mrs. Shute's discussion of **William Rice** is quoted (1, p. 7):

"2.1 WILLIAM RICE b. 6 April 1743 d. 29 Nov. 18-- in Wilson
Co., TN. He fought with his father, against the British
during the Revolutionary War. He also fought in the war of
1812, and applied in Wilson County on October   1850 for a
Bounty Land Warrant. The pension file is No. 18184 for 80
acres of land in 1850 and No. 43087 for 80 acres in 1855."

"**SARAH HARPER RICE**, his wife stated in her pension
application that she was married to **WILLIAM** in Nottaway
County, Virginia on 13 May 1806.

"The application of **WILLIAM** states that he was a private in
Captain McCulley's Company 3rd Regiment, 1st Battalion, and
Private in **Captain Ezekill Bass'** Company in **Major Workfolk's**
Regt. He participated in the Kings Mountain Campaign. He is
buried in Wilson County, TN."

Your compiler believes that the above **William Rice** facts refer to more than one **William Rice**. If born in 1743, his age age would have been 70 in 1812, 107 in 1850, and 112 in 1855 at the time of his second pension application. In fact, **Henry's** son **William** apparently died in 1831 (see below).

A **William Rice**, as shown earlier, sold Hawkins County land from Sumner County. To me this means he had moved to a county just northeast of Davidson County. Nashville is the county seat of Davidson County, and Wilson County is just east of Davidson.

A **William Rice** left a will in Wilson County, dated 12 March 1818 and recorded December 1831 (**Wilson County Will Book, 1830-1832**, pages 292-293) (12). This will mentions wife **Esther Rice**, then his first [unnamed] wife's children: daughters Susanna, **Sarah**, **Esther** and **Rebecca**. His sons were **Nathaniel, James, Thomas** and **Henry** (apparently through his second wife **Esther**). This **William Rice** died a few months before December 1831, when the will was recorded. Maybe these are **Henry's** son and grandchildren, and with possibly a grandson **Charles** having stayed in Hawkins County.

The sale of the estate of **William Rice** deceased was ordered in December Court Term 1831 and recorded the 10th of March 1832. This estate record is very hard to read. **James, Thomas, Nathaniel** and **Esther** were the **Rices** who bought parts of the estate. The total of the assessment was $736.70 with a grand total of $841.23. The grand total was recorded on 14 March 1832 (**Ibid**, pages 338-347) (12).

There were nine **William Rices** who served in the war of 1812 from the State of Tennessee. Only four of these received pensions for their military service. Pensions were in the form of bounty land, and were usually not granted unless the person was in need of the land to subsist. The bounty land was made available in 1850 and 1855 by Acts of Congress.

A **Charles Rice**, assumed son of **William Rice**, was in the War of 1812, serving with **Chiles'** Battalion, Mounted Gunmen, of East Tennessee Volunteers. He was a private under **Captain James Cumming's** Company of **Major John Chiles'** Battalion. He was "mustered into service at Rogersville," for a term of six months commencing on the 8th October, 1814 (War of 1812).

William Rice had a brother **Levi Rice**. **Levi** had a grandson **Calvin Harper Rice**, but no study has been made on the **Harper** name as of this time, by your compiler.

The military record gives a description of **Charles Rice** as follows: "Roll dated Oct. 8, 1814; age, 23; height, 5 feet 10 inches; complexion, fair; hair, fair; eyes, gray; County, Hawkins."

Charles Rice "appears on Company Muster Roll for Oct. 8, 1814, when mustered into service at Rogersville....For what period of time, 6 months, 26 days. Present or absent, present...." (War of 1812 Service Record.)

He is on the "Company Pay Roll for Oct. 8, 1814 to May 3, 1815....Term of service charged, 6 months, 27 days. Pay per month, 8 dollars ____ cents. Amount of pay 54 dollars, 96 cents. [Allowance of pay for horse, &c., at 40 cents per day*] 208 days; 83 dollars, 20 cents. Total amount, 138 dollars, 16 cents."

[The asterisk (*) is unexplained.]

  Charles Rice employed an attorney, **Arthur G. Armstrong**, who <u>paid</u> **Charles** $140 for his War of 1812 military service. Then the attorney was to collect the money--"all such sums of money as have accrued or may be due or coming to me for my services, back rations, or on any other account whatever, as a private.... IN WITNESS WHEREOF, I have hereunto set my hand, and affixed my seal, this 19th day of June 1815.

Witness		his
Wm. Armstrong Jun.	**Charles** X **Rice**	SEAL"
H. C. F. Caldwell	mark	

The above military service record for **Charles Rice** is shown on the next pages. Since **Charles** was 23 years of age in 1814, he was born in 1791.

I have looked up the census schedules on **Rices** for Wilson County for the years 1820 through 1840. None of the three **William Rices** who were listed in the 1820 census showed up in the 1830 census.

Pages 26a and 26b, which follow, show the above records.

Card 1:

R 1 | Chiles' Battalion, | E. Tenn. Vols. Mounted Gunmen

Charles Rice

Pvt., { Capt. James Cumming's Co., Major John Chiles' Batt'n, (Vol. Mtd. Infantry, East Tennessee)

(War of 1812.)

Appears on

Company Pay Roll

for Oct 8, 1814 to May 3, 1815.

Roll dated May 3, 1815.

Commencement of service or of this settlement, Oct 8, 1814.

Expiration of service or of this settlement, May 3, 1815.

Term of service charged, 6 months, 27 days.

Pay per month, 8 dollars, cents.

Amount of pay, 54 dollars, 96 cents.

[Allowance of pay for horse, &c., at 40 cents per day,*] 208 days; 83 dollars, 20 cents.

Total amount, 138 dollars, 16 cents.

Remarks:

*From rolls of other companies in same regiment.

Hamilton, Copyist.

(672)

Card 2:

R 1 | Chiles' Battalion, | E. Tenn. Vols. Mounted Gunmen

Charles Rice

Pvt., { Capt. James Cumming's Co. of Vol. Mtd. Gunmen from East Tennessee, Major John Chiles' Battalion.

(War of 1812.)

Appears on

Company Muster Roll

for Oct 8, 1814, when mustered into service at Rogersville, to May 3, 1815, when mustered out of service at Rogersville.

Roll dated Rogersville, May 3, 1815.

When entered into service, Oct 8, 1814.

For what period of time, 6 months, 26 days.

Present or absent, present.

Remarks:

Hamilton, Copyist.

(666)

Card 3:

R 1 | Chiles' Battalion, | E. Tenn. Vols. Mounted Gunmen

Charles Rice

Appears with the rank of _____ on

Muster Roll and Descriptive List

of Capt. James Cumming's Company of Mounted Gunmen mustered in East Tennessee Volunteers, and mustered into service at Rogersville, Tenn., for a term of six months, commencing on the 8th October, 1814,

(War of 1812.)

for Oct 8, 181_.

Roll dated Oct 8, 1814.

Age, 23; height, 5 feet, 7 inches.

Complexion, fair.

Hair, fair; eyes, grey.

County, Hawkins.

Remarks:

Hamilton, Copyist.

(690)

KNOW all men by these presents, That I *Charles Rice*
of *Hawkins* County, and State of Tennessee, for divers good causes and considerations me thereunto moving—and also, in consideration of the Sum of *One Hundred and forty Dollars* to me in hand paid, the receipt whereof is hereby acknowledged, hath, and by THESE PRESENTS, doth nominate, constitute and appoint *Arthur G. Armstrong* of the County of Hawkins, and State aforesaid, my true and lawful ATTORNEY, irrevocably, for me, and in my name, but for his own proper use and benefit, to ask, demand and receive, of, and from the Pay-Master for the United States, all such Sums of Money as have accrued, or may be due or coming to me for my services, back rations, or on any other account whatever, as a *private* in Captain *James Cuming's* ~~volunteer mounted gun men~~ Company of East Tennessee Militia, from *the 8th day of October 1814* to *the third day of May 1815* in a Regiment commanded by agreeably to the annexed discharge or certificate, dated the *3d* day of *May 1815* and signed by *James Cuming* And I do further authorize and empower the said *Arthur G. Armstrong* for me, and in my name, to give proper acquittances and receipts, if required; and to do, or procure to be done, all lawful acts and things, thereunto belonging, as fully in every respect, as I might or could do, was I personally present at the doing thereof.

IN WITNESS WHEREOF, I have hereunto set my hand, and affixed my seal, this *19th* day of *June 1815*

Charles X Rice (SEAL)
his
mark

Witness
Benj. Armstrong
H. H. Caldwell

<table>
<tr><td>Duty</td><td></td></tr>
<tr><td>Discharge from Service</td><td></td></tr>
<tr><td>Discharge from Hosp'l</td><td></td></tr>
<tr><td>Description</td><td></td></tr>
<tr><td>Death or Effects</td><td></td></tr>
<tr><td>Contracts</td><td></td></tr>
<tr><td>Confinement</td><td></td></tr>
<tr><td>Casualty Sheet</td><td></td></tr>
<tr><td>Admission to Hosp'l</td><td></td></tr>
<tr><td>Transportation</td><td></td></tr>
<tr><td>Transfer to V. R. C.</td><td></td></tr>
<tr><td>Transfer to Hosp'l</td><td></td></tr>
<tr><td>Rank</td><td></td></tr>
<tr><td>Personal Reports</td><td></td></tr>
<tr><td>Pay or Clothing</td><td></td></tr>
<tr><td>Misc. Information</td><td></td></tr>
<tr><td>Med. Examination</td><td></td></tr>
<tr><td>Furlough or L. of A.</td><td></td></tr>
</table>

Other papers relating to—

Pension Warrant
Discharge Certificates
Descriptive Lists
C. M. Charges
Certs. of Dis. for Discharge
Subsistence accounts
Pay accounts
Resignations
Pris. of War Record
Orders
Med. Des. Lists
Med. Certificates
Furloughs or L. of A.
Final Statements

(War of 1812.)

1 Inclosure.

Ch. Bible, E Tenn. Mil d. Inf.
Pvt. Capt. *Cumings* Co.

Charles Price

Tennessee 1820 Census Index, Accelerated Indexing Systems (16)

Head of Family	County	State	Page	Age Categories*
Rice, Thomas	Wilson	TN	394	000100-10100
Rice, William	Wilson	TN	383	010001-10001
Rice, William	Wilson	TN	386	300010-41010
Rice, William	Wilson	TN	394	000101-01201

*The age categories for the 1820 census are:
Free White Males. Under 10; 10-16; 16-18; 18-26; 26-45;
45 and over.
Free White Females. Under 10; 10-16; 16-26; 26-45; 45
and over.

1830 Census Middle Tennessee
(17, pages 274-275)

There are several **Rices** in the 1830 Wilson County census, but there is no **William**. WI is the county abbreviation for Wilson County.

Head of Family	County	Microfilm Page	Age Categories*	Page
Rice, Benjamin	WI	114	101002-0001101	208
Rice, Henry	WI	149	100001-11002	213
Rice, James	WI	108	110001-21001	207
Rice, John	WI	120	02110011-302121	209
Rice, Nathaniel	WI	113	1001001-110001	207
Rice, Thomas	WI	108	120001-111001	207

The age categories for 1830 and 1840 are:

Free White Males. Under 5; 5-10; 10-15; 15-20; 20-30; 30-40;
40-50; 50-60; 60-70; 70-80; 80-90; 90-100; over 100.
Free White Females. Under 5; 5-10; 10-15; 15-20; 20-30;
30-40; 40-50; 50-60; 60-70; 70-80; 80-90; 90-100;
over 100.

For the 1840 census there is an index book, but it only tells the page on the microfilm. You have to look up the microfilm to get the ages, slaves, free colored and foreigners not naturalized. "Wils" is the abbreviation for Wilson County in the 1840 census. "No TWP L" stands for NO TOWNSHIP LISTED.

Tennessee 1840 Census Index
(18, page 195)

Head of Family	County	Microfilm Page	Township	Age categories
Rice, Ann	Wils	302	No TWP L	0001-120200001
Rice, Benjamin	Wils	302	No TWP L	001010111-11000011
Rice, James	Wils	227	No TWP L	200001-21001
Rice, John	Wils	313	No TWP L	000010001-10001001
Rice, John	Wils	216	No TWP L	101000001-2000101
Rice, John	Wils	223	No TWP L	20001-12001
Rice, Nathaniel	Wils	261	No TWP L	100100001-0010101
Rice, Sarah*	Wils	346	No TWP L	1221-000101
Rice, William	Wils	225	No TWP L	00001-10001

* I did not find **Sarah** in Wilson County, but in Warren County; Warren County is on the same microfilm with Wilson and other counties.

Ann, Benjamin, two of the three **John Rices** and **Nathaniel** were 60 to 70.

CHAPTER III. CHARLES RICE

Chapter summary on page v

Henry Rice's son **Charles** had two South Carolina land grants. The land areas were first surveyed, plats were made, then later the grants were made.

S.C. State Plats - 96 District (9)

Charles Rice...96 District...200 acres...6 April 1785
Charles Rice...96 District...200 acres...no date

S.C. State Grants - 96 District

Charles Rice...96 District...200 acres...1 January 1787
Charles Rice...96 District...200 acres...1 January 1787

Copies of these plats and grants are shown in the Appendix, courtesy of **Mrs. Nan Rice Shute**.

S.C. State Plats

Vol. 15 q - p. 106. To **Charles Rice** for 200 acres
Vol. 15 q - p. 106. To **Charles Rice** for 200 acres
Vol. AA   - p. 73.   Cert. for **Ferdinand Hopkins** for 2,782 acres

Some South Carolina records were destroyed by fire, so this may be the reason why there is no record of **Charles** selling his two land grants. However, records were found that **Henry** and **James** sold their grants, and Charles' land was in close proximity.

Next, your compiler gives one of the two references to the sale of **Henry's** land by his son **Charles Rice**.

Anderson County, S.C., Deeds

Book E, p. 246. "On the 29 May 1800 **Henry Rice** of Granger County, Tenn. do appoint my son **Charles Rice** of Pendleton District to sell a tract of 460 odd acres granted to me and is on waters of Rice and Wolf Creek." (See p. 13.)

Other references to power of attorney from **Henry Rice** to his son **Charles** are:

"On 29 May 1800, **Henry Rice** of Grainger County, Tenn., gave a power of attorney to his son **Charles Rice** of Pendleton District, which was witnessed by **William T. Steele**." (19, p. 50.)

and "**Henry Rice** of Grainger County, Tenn., 29 May 1800, gave a power of attorney to his son **Charles Rice** of Pendleton, to sell 460 acres on Wolf Creek branch of Twelve-Mile Creek. **Charles Rice** was enumerated in Pendleton in 1790 but **Henry** was not found there in 1790 or 1800." (19, p. 53.)

The Anderson County, S.C., deed dated 1805 of **Charles Rice** selling **Henry's** land is the last record I found on him. He is not in the 1810, 1820, nor 1830 Walton County, Georgia, census. **Charles Rice** must have moved, maybe to Alabama or even to Mississippi. Maybe his descendants are trying to find out who his father was. He could have been in the Claiborne County census in 1830.

I do have a deed whereby **Henry Rice** sold to his son **Charles Rice** 200 acres in 1803 in Grainger County (see p. 18). (The County might have changed.) However, I find no instrument for the sale of this 200 acres by **Charles**. This land was, I believe, next to **Henry's** Lost Creek land.

1790 Census of S.C., 96 District (20, p. 81)

Charles Rice.....Pendleton County.....1 - 2 - 3*
*First column = Free white males including heads of family.
*Second column = Free white males under 16.
*Third column = Free white females including heads of family.

The 1790 census is also on microfilm, having microcopy #637 roll #11.

My records give no information about who he married, nor the names of any of his children.

1800 Census of Pendleton District, S.C.
(19, p. 27, No. 483, **Charles Rice**)

Males: 2 under 10; 2 age 10-16; 1 age 26-45 **(Charles)**
Females: 2 under 10; 1 age 10-16; 1 age 26-45

Harold DeLorme, Jr., a Columbia, S.C. genealogist, supplied me with a lot of data on Rices. He wrote, "Stewart has a different version of the females. It appears the above may be correct....The above Charles Rice appears to be about 35 to 40 years old since he had seven children under 16 years of age."

To your compiler, this seems to mean the same thing.

There are three census books on Pendleton District in 1800. Another is (21) South Carolina 1800 Census, page 446:

Rice, Charles, Pendleton Dist. S.C. - 27 - 22010-21010-00.

The third is (22) Index to the 1800 Census of South Carolina, page 199:

Rice, Charles - Pen. 130.

This is all the records so far on Charles Rice, the son of pioneer Henry Rice.

CHAPTER IV – JAMES RICE

Chapter summary on page v

1. Tabitha Rice	b. 4-28-1789; d. 4-25-1868[a]	
George Snodderly	b. 9-17-1787; d. 8-20-1852[b]	
2. Enoch Rice	b. 1-23-1791; d. 7-25-1851	
Mary Young	b. 3-16-1792; d. 3-11-1881	
	m. 12- -1813	
3. Susannah Rice	b. 1792; never married	
4. **George Rice**	b. 3-27-1794; d. 11-30-1869	
Sarah Snodderly	b. 5-5-1794; d. 10-21-1855[b]	
	m. circa 1821	
5. Mary Rice (Polly)	b. 1796, m. 1811, d. 1852[b]	
Thomas Jackson		

James Rice
Rebecca Miller

6. Charles Rice	b. 12-5-1797; d. 6-26-1883	
Sarah Lett	d. 1845[b]	
7. Elizabeth Rice	b. 1800; d. 1856	
Absalom Powell	b. 3-27-1803; d. 4-28-1851	
8. Anna Rice	b. 1802	
Jonathan Powell	b. 3-14-1795; d. 1851	
9. James Rice	b. 1804; d. 1842	
Elizabeth Lett		
10. Rebecca Rice	b. 1807[a] or 10-4-1803, d.	
Eli Sharp	2-5-1871[b]	
	b. 2-7-1798; d. 6-2-1886;	
	m. 8-21-1831[b]	

---

[a]/Information from **Turnbows** (2, pages 21-22).
[b]/Information from **Shute** (1).

32

CHAPTER IV. JAMES RICE
Third Son of Henry Rice

A. JAMES RICE

James Rice, my third great grandfather, was a gristmiller and a gunsmith. He must have learned about building and operating gristmills from his father Henry. At the home of my aunt and uncle, Ruth Annette Rice and Glenn Gatewood Irwin, is a rifle that James Rice fashioned. Charles (Chuck) Sharp, son of Lorene Rogers Sharp and William Foster Sharp, has made a replica of the same rifle.

My first cousin, "Rice" Irwin, wrote in his book, The Story of Marcellus Moss Rice etc., (23, p. 30):

"It is believed that James Rice, Henry's...son, did not leave South Carolina until about 1795. Perhaps some of Henry's ... children had accompanied him from South Carolina some twenty years earlier."

[Note by Ruby Rice Little: Henry appears to have left for parts west when James was about 8-10 years old, and left a considerable family in South Carolina during his early Tennessee years--his wife and some younger children. Since James was the third son, many of the older children must have been daughters. Also, it seems that Henry was 46 years old when James was born. Elizabeth must have been one of the youngest.]

Alva Silas and Maude Ina Turnbow wrote (2, p. 11):

"James Rice, the third son of Henry Rice, was believed to have been born in (South Carolina) about the year 1763, and died at Lost Creek, Union County, Tennessee, in 1829...." "Although James lived in South Carolina, and came from there to East Tennessee, we have no record of...his life before that time, except his marriage to Rebecca Miller in Newberry County, South Carolina, in 1787." [The Newberry Courthouse had a fire that destroyed this marriage and other county records.]

The poet Martin Rice's remembrance of his grandfather is given next.

"**James**, my grandfather, was, I think, the third son of his father **Henry**. He came to what is now Union County, about the year 1796 or `97 and settled on Lost Creek in what is known as Big Valley, and built the first water mill in that vicinity. He had four sons and six daughters. My father **Enoch**, the oldest son, followed by my uncles **George**, **Charles**, and **James**. **Tabitha** was the oldest daughter and the oldest child, and my other aunts were **Susannah**, **Polly**, **Elizabeth**, **Anna** and **Rebecca**. My grandmother's name before marriage was **Rebecca Miller**, and I have very little knowledge of her family, but I have heard her and others speak of her brothers **Jacob** and **Morris Miller**, living in Kentucky, and I think she had a sister who married a **Mr. Paul**, and another who married **John Stephens**, and one who married a **Mr. Duncan**." (2, p. 11.) (See page 47 for more on **Rebecca's** family.)

All of the above children of **James Rice** will be further mentioned with the records of each.

The first records we have of **James Rice** are South Carolina Surveyor Plats for the State Grants. **Benjamin**, **Hezekiah**, **Ezekiah**, **Othniel** and **Stephen Rice** were other **Rices** who also acquired land from the State.

1. State Plats, vol 15, p. 99 (9)
(see page 35)

"South Carolina I have caused to be admeasured and laid out unto **James Rice** a tract of Land containing Two hundred and ninety two acres situated in the District of Ninety Six West of the ancient Boundary on Goldings Creek of Twelve Mile River & hath such form & marks, buttings & boundings as the above."

2. State Plats, vol 31, p. 110 (9)
(see page 36)

"South Carolina I do hereby certify for **Ja^s Rice** a tract of land containing Twenty eight acres. (Surveyed for him the 2^d of Septr 1790). Situate in the District of 96 on both sides of Wolf Creek of 12 Mile River and hath such form marks buttings & boundings as the above plat represents."

RICE, JAMES

Description	Reference - S. C. Archives
Plat for James Rice 48 A. - 96 Dist. Dec. 15, 1791	State Plats Vol. 27, p. 507

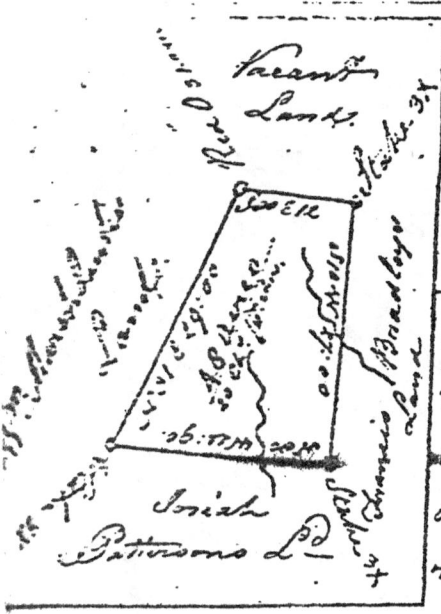

SOUTH CAROLINA

I do hereby certify for JAMES RICE, a tract of land containing Forty-eight acres (surveyed for him the 2nd day of September 1790) situated in the District of Ninety six on two small branches of Wolk Creek a branch of 12 Mile River and hath such form and marks buttings and boundries as the above plat represents

Given under my hand this 15th day of December 1791

BREMAR SWOR, Gen C.

35

Description	Reference - S. C. Archives
Plat for James Rice 28 A. - 96 Dist. Sept. 2, 1790	State Plats Vol. 31, p. 110

SOUTH CAROLINA

I do hereby certify for JAMES RICE a tract of land containing Twenty-eight acres (Surveyed for him the 2nd of Sept 1790) situated in the District of 96 on both sides of Wolk Creek of 12 Mile River and hath such form marks buttings and bound#ings as the above plat represents

Given under my hand this 24th of November 1793

I. WHITMORE, D. S.

F. BREMARD, Swor Gen

Plat for James Rice
292 A. - 96 Dist.
Apr. 7, 1785

Reference - S. C. Archives
State Plats
Vol. 15, p. 99

SOUTH CAROLINA

I have caused to be admeasured and laid out unto JAMES RICE a tract of Land containing Two hundred and ninety two acres situated in the District of Ninety Six West of the ancient Boundary on Goolding's Creek of Twelve Mile River & hath such form & marks, buttings & boundings as the above.

Plat Represents Certified for the 7th day of April 1785
WM BENSON D.S. EPHRAIM MITCHELL S. Gen.

3. State Plats, vol 27, p. 507 (9)
(see page 37)

"South Carolina I do hereby certify for **James Rice** a tract of Lands containing Forty-eight acres (Surveyed for him the 2^d day of September 1790). Situate in the District of Ninety six on two small branches of Wolf Creek a branch of 12 Mile River and hath such form & marks buttings & boundings as the above plat represents."

Later, in Anderson County, South Carolina, **James Rice** (Book G reference page 471) sold his land. Book R, page 238, mentions **James Rice.**

Anderson County, S.C. Deeds, Book G, p. 471 (9)

"On the 29 October 1803 **James Rice** of Claborn County, Tenn. sells to **John Tatum** of Pendleton District 300 acres on both sides of Wolf Creek waters of Twelve Mile River and is part of several tracts of land granted to (1) **James Rice**, (2) **Josiah Patterson**, and (3) **James Henderson**. Wit/**James Jett, Nath. Tatum**. **John Cochran** J.P. (Justice of the Peace)."

Anderson County, S.C. Deeds, Book R, p. 238 (9)

"On the 8 October 1823 **John Tatum** of Pendleton County sells to **Jeremiah Field** of Pendleton County 300 acres of land on both sides of Wolf Creek of 12 Mile River and is part of several tracts of land (1) land granted to **James Rice**, (2) land granted to **Josiah Patterson**, (3) land granted to **James Henderson**. Wit/**Lewis Gilstrap, William (X) Tatum. Bailey Barton**, J.Q."

Then **James Rice** is in the 1790 census schedule for South Carolina. The 1800 through 1820 census schedules for Big Valley were destroyed, except for 1810 Grainger County, **Henry** and **Levi Rice**, and **David Smith** were in this census schedule and tax list.

1790 South Carolina Census
96 District Pendleton County, p. 83 (20)

(**James Rice**):
Free white males over 16, including heads of families: 2.
Free white males under 16: 1.
Free white females: 2.

[James would have been about 27 years old in 1790; the second "male over 16" could not have been his child. Presumably one of the "free white females" was his wife Rebecca Miller. Tabitha, James' oldest child, and Enoch, the oldest son, were born respectively Apr. 28, 1789, and Jan. 23, 1791, so the second male over 16 and male under 16 were perhaps brother and/or nephew or other relative.* The second female could be Tabitha.] *(unless they were children who later died)

James is not found in any census for Tennessee, the 1800, 1810 and 1820 records having been lost in a fire. Only Rebecca was found in the 1830 census.

1830 Census, Campbell County, Tennessee
FM 19 Roll 178

Rebecca Rice: 1 male 10-15; 1 male 20-30.
1 female 10-15; 1 female 15-20; 1 female 30-40; 1 female 60-70.

[See page 34 for children of James and Rebecca Rice.]

The 18th century gristmiller "came to East Tennessee about 1796 and settled on the upper part of his father Henry Rice's old Land Grant 490." (2, p. 11.) He was involved in land transactions in Claiborne and Campbell Counties, Tennessee.

General Index to Deeds Claiborne County

Grantor	Grantee	Instrument	Date	Book	Pages	Amount
Rice, Martin*	Rice, James	W.D.**	1805	A	18-19	$450.00
Rice, Henry	Rice, James	D	1805	A	253-1/2	1.00
Rice, James	Simmons, John***	D	1824	H		
Rice, James	Simmons, John***	D	1828	I	32	150.00

  * The son of Molly Rice Watson.
 ** Warranty deed.
*** John Simmons could be the brother of Jane Simmons, who married Levi Rice. This is the only reference to this transaction.

Summary of the deed, **Martin Rice** to **James Rice** (from **Claiborne County Deed Book A,** p. 17).

Deed to **James Rice**, 28 September 1805.
$400 - 100 acres be the same more or less in the county of Claiborne, on the waters of Lost Creek - Beginning on **Henry Rice's** corner **Hill's** branch...to the low grounds on the Lost Creek, **Alexander McNuts** line, to **Henry Rice's** line.

In the presents of	:	
his		
Coonrod X Sharpe	:	**Martin Rice** Seal
mark	:	
Joshua Broct	:	

The summary of the deed between **Henry** and **James Rice** can be seen on page 19 of the section on **Henry Rice**.

General Index to Deeds Campbell County

Grantors	Grantees	Ins.	Date	Book	Page	Loc.
Glasgow, James	Rice, James	P.A.	12-21-1811	B	269	*
Moser, Jacob	Rice, James	W	10-12-1812	B	196	**
Rice, James	Wilson, Elizabeth	W	2-19-1825	E	2	*
Rice, James heirs	Jackson,Thos.	Will	10-13-1830	E	222	***
Rice, James heirs	Rice, Susannah	"	10-13-1830	E	230	***
Rice, James heirs	Rice, Enoch	"	10-30-1830	E	232	***
Rice, James heirs	Rice, Charles	"	10-13-1830	F	14	***
Rice, James heirs	Snoderly, George	"	10-30-1830	F	42	***

* Campbell County; ** Anderson County; *** Lost Creek.

The deeds are summarized below:

1. Book B, pages 269-270, 21 December 1811.
   Glasgow, James, by his attorney **John Adair** of the County
   Knox to **James Rice** of the county of Campbell - $40 - 80
   acres. Being part of an Original Grant to **King, James** &
   Donaldson, Stokely of No. 641 registered in Hawkins
   County.

In presence of	:	Signed
David Smith	:	**James Glasgow**
Thomas Jackson	:	by his attorney
John Casey	:	**John Adair**

State of Tennessee)	(December Sessions 1813. This
Campbell County)	(Deed was proven in open court
)	(of the oaths of **David Smith**
)	(and **Thomas Jackson**,
)	(Witnesses.

2. Book B, pages 196-197, 12 October 1812.
   Moser, Jacob of Knox County to **James Rice** of Campbell
   County - $175 - 250 acres - land in Anderson County.

In presents of	:	Signed
Elisha Chambers	:	**Jacob Moser**
Robert X White	:	**Pleasant McBride**

3. Book E, pages 2-3, 19 February 1825.
   Rice, James to **Elizabeth Wilson**, both of Campbell County
   $175 - 80 acres - **Henderson and Company** line.

In the presents of	:	Signed
George Snodderly	:	**James Rice**
George Rice	:	

State of Tennessee)	(Court of pleas and quarter
Campbell County)	(Session 13th June 1825

The Execution of the within Deed Conveyance was this
day proven in Open Court by **George Rice** and **George
Snodderly** witnesses.

I believe that **Elizabeth Wilson** might be a daughter of **Anna
(Rice)** and **Augustus Wilson**, or the wife of a **David Wilson** who is,
at this time, an unconnected **Wilson**. See Chapter X.

4. Book E, pages 222-223, 13th October 1830.
   Rice, James, estate Deed to **Thomas Jackson**
   $375 - 100 acres more or less.

		Signed
In presence of	:	her
William Ussary	:	**Rebecca X Rice**
Jacob Snoderly	:	mark
James Arwine	:	**George Snoderly**
		Enoch Rice
		Susanna Rice
		George Rice
		James Rice
		Charles Rice
		Jonathan Powell
		Absalom Powell
		Eli Sharp

State of Tennessee)   (Court of Pleas and Quarter
Campbell County   )   (Sessions, 13th June 1831

The Execution of the foregoing deed of conveyance was this
day proven in open court by the oaths of **William Ussary**
and **James Arwine**, Witnesses.

5. Book E, pages 230-231, 13th October 1830.
   Rice, James Estate Deed to **Susanna Rice**
   $250 - no number of acres mentioned. Beginning near Loss
   Creek, **Isaac Wilson's** corner, **G. Snoderly's** line.

		Signed
In presence of	:	her
William Ussary	:	**Rebecca X Rice**
Jacob Snodderly	:	mark
James Arwine	:	**George Snodderly**
		Enoch Rice
		Thomas Jackson
		Charles Rice
		George Rice
		James Rice
		Jonathan Powell
		Absalom Powell
		Eli Sharp

State of Tennessee)   (Court of Pleas and Quarter
Campbell County   )   (Sessions 13th June 1831.

The Execution of the foregoing deed of conveyance was this day proven in open court by the oaths of **William Ussary** and **James Arwine** witnesses.

6. Book E, pages 232-233, 30th October 1830.
   Rice, James Estate Deed to **Enoch Rice**
   $375 - 100 acres.

Signed

In presence of :
William Ussary :
Jacob Snoderly :
James Arwine :

Signed

Rebecca   her X   Rice   mark

George Snoderly

Susanna   her X   Rice   mark

Jonathan Powell

Absalom Powell

James Rice

Charles Rice

Thomas Jackson

George Rice

Eli Sharp

State of Tennessee)   (Court of Pleas and Quarter
Campbell County   )   (Sessions 13th June 1831

The execution of the foregoing deed of conveyance was this day proven in open court by the oaths of **William Ussary** and **James Arwine** witnesses.

7. Book F, pages 14-15, 13 October 1830.
   Rice, James Estate Deed to **Charles Rice**
   $500 - 100 acres more or less
   near Loss Creek being part of tract of land granted to **Henry Rice** by the State of North Carolina. Valley Road, **Isaac Wilson's** corner on said **Wilson's** line.

in presence of :
William Usrey :
Jacob Snoderly :
James Arvine :

Signed:
Rebecca Rice
Enoch Rice
Susanna Rice
Thomas Jackson
George Snoderly

[The deed should continue to Book F, page 16, which was not copied. Page 16 could have more names and the presentation to the court to be registered in the deed book.]

8. Book F, pages 42-43, 30 October 1830.
   Rice, James Estate Deed to **George Snoderly**.
   $250 - 50 acres more or less. **Hydes** Branch thence down
   said branch to the low grounds of Loss Creek.

in presence of	:	Signed
William Ussary	:	**Rebecca Rice** (Seal)
Jacob Snoderly	:	**Enoch Rice**
James Arwine	:	**Susanna Rice**
		Thomas Jackson
		Charles Rice
		George Rice
		James Rice
		Absalom Powel
		Jonathan Powel
		Eli Sharp

State of Tennessee)   (Court of Pleas and Quarter
Campbell County   )   (Sessions 13 June 1831

The Execution of the within Deed of conveyance was this
day proven in open court by the oaths of **William Ussary**
and **James Arwine,** witnesses thereto.

James Rice, the gristmill builder and gunsmith, is in the
1827 Campbell County Tax List.

The **Turnbows** (2, page 14) gave the sale of **James Rice's**
estate (other than the land). He did not leave a will, and his
property was sold by his heirs.

"In the Inventory of Articles of the Estate of **James Rice**,
filed in Campbell County, Tennessee, on September 15th, 1829,
Enoch Rice and **Thomas Jackson**, Administrators, list the
following:

"`Sixteen heads of cattle, ten head of hogs, twelve head of
sheep, three head of horses, one set of blacksmith's tools,
two beds, and furniture, farming tools, ploughs, etc., one
rifle gun, one old still and some copper, some rye, corn,
etc.`"

Since **James** had a still, he must have made some whiskey--
probably for medicinal purposes.

Following are names of the people who bought articles from **James Rice's** estate: **Rebecca Rice** (his widow), **George Snoderly, Susannah Rice, Enoch Rice, James Rice, Thomas Jackson, Charles Rice, George Rice, William Usrey, William Oaks, Thomas Woreham, Joseph Rice, Isaac Sharp, John Brook, Nicholas Sharp, James Erwin, James Lett, John Brook, Jr., Absalom Parrott, John Archer, Jonathan Powell, Isaac Archey, Richard Malone, John Albright, Abraham Powell, Thomas Nations, John Campbell, Isaac Rice, John Sharp, James Arvine, John Lett, James Marlow, William York, John Snoderly, Sr., John Snoderly, Dave Pritchard, Elijah Craven** and **Peter Loy.** The estate sold for $493.53. At that time there were half-cents, but no fourth-cents. Many of the prices included fractions of cents.

James Rice was appointed judge of voter registration and elections. "June 8, 1815, **Robert Smith, George Baker, Senior,** and **Isaac White-Cotton** were appointed judges of elections at **George Baker's; James Rice, James Fulkerson** and **Robert Glenn** at **Robert Glenn's;** and **Spencer Graham, David Cunningham** and **Isaac Chrisman** at Jacksboro." (24, page 42.)

James Rice did not give five acres of land to the Lost Creek Church, as has been believed. His son **George Rice** donated this land, by deed dated Nov. 8, 1859, in Union County and recorded March 19, 1866. The Church was established in 1834, after **James'** death, but the five acres was a part of the land originally owned by **Henry,** then his son **James Rice.** A summary of this land transaction is "from **George Rice** to **Isaac Sharp** and **Joseph Oaks,** Deacons of Old United Baptist Church at Lost Creek and their successors....grant and give and bestow 5 acres...."

Attest: **William Shelby**   **George Rice**   (Seal)
        William Bridges

State of Tennessee   )   (Personally appeared before me
Union County   )   (**Wm. Colvin** Clerk of the County
                              (Court the within named bargain-
                              (or with whom I am personally
acquainted....in Maynardville this 5th day of June 1865.

                                      Wm. Colvin Clerk

State of Tennessee   )   (I **Isaac Snodderly** Register do
Union County   )   (certify that the foregoing deed
                              (was....duly registered in Book
C at page 39 witness my hand at office this 19 day of March 1866.

B. THE JAMES RICE GRISTMILL

My first cousin, **John Rice Irwin**, wrote (23, pages 35-36):
"Soon after constructing a dwelling, **James Rice**, following in
the footsteps of his father, built a water-powered gristmill
on Lost Creek in Big Valley. The intricate cogs and shafts
were skillfully hewn from hickory and oak; and the
millstones, which usually were transported from France, were
also fashioned by **James** from native stone."

One of the original wooden cogs is now in **John Rice Irwin's**
"Museum of Appalachia," along with keys to the mill.

John Rice Irwin wrote further (23), "**James Rice** built the
mill for utilitarian reasons--to grind corn meal for his
neighbors and his own family." And, "although one-eighth
of all meal ground was the `toll` for grinding corn meal
for as long as the mill stood in Union County, **James Rice**
started the practice of grinding `free meal` for the poor
families from the ridge country."

The **Turnbows** wrote about the **James Rice** mill (2, page 11):

James Rice "in 1798 started work in building the famous old
Rice mill on Lost Creek. The valley where this mill was
located was flooded by the Tennessee Valley Authority in the
building of Norris Dam....The old mill was carefully
dismantled and moved to its present location about one mile
below the dam...."

In the booklet "**18th Century Gristmill**," first published in
1949 but followed by several later editions, **John Rice Irwin** wrote
(25, pages 6-7) about the location of the Lost Creek mill site.

"This particular location had been the home of a small tribe
of Indians who, however, had moved away a season before the
white men arrived at Lost Creek. There were found many
implements of war and signs of a battle in a nearby woods;
therefore it was concluded that the natives had been driven
out by an enemy, most likely another tribe of Indians....This
region, with its stately virgin timber and beautiful mountain
streams, had provided a most picturesque home for the
Indians." And further (page 9), "The mill was located at a
swift place in the creek near where the old Indian camp had
previously stood"

In the magazine **Cooperative Farmer** for 1952, (26, page 14), is
an article entitled "**Rice's Mill - A Symbol of Cooperation**"

46

featuring this artifact of our treasured ancestry. "Old water-powered grist mills have about passed from the American farm scene, but some remain even today as reminders of progress and advances of agriculture." Under the caption, "Signs of Our Times," they state, "Cooperation among peoples is not uncommon ....Signs of our times are cooperatives; among the signs of pioneer days were barn raisings, corn huskings and mills operated collectively for the good of all."

This mill, in its present location, is pictured in the World Book Encyclopedia, 1959 edition, in an article entitled "Industrial Revolution" - but without being identified.

C. THE MILLER FAMILY

My collatorator, **Nan Rice Shute**, wrote that **Rebecca Miller**, wife of **James Rice** was born "in Newberry Co., S.C. (b. 1767, dau of **John Miller**. She was the sister of Captain `Racoon` John Miller, a Revolutionary War Hero." (1, page 303.)

Eve Whitener Miller, John's wife (**Rebecca's** sister-in-law), applied for a pension, which received the number R-7187. The "R" means "rejected." She could not give his military unit nor the length of his service. She said he served under **Col. Joseph Martin** in the Virginia State Line. I could not find a **Captain John Miller**, nor a **Col. Joseph Martin**, although there were many soldiers having both last names, especially privates. **Eve Whitener Miller** could not remember when she married **John Miller**. A DAR descendant of "**Racoon**" gave the date of marriage as March 1, 1776, in Sullivan County.

There is a record of his service payment, which I include (page 50); it does not give his unit nor muster roll. He was paid 143 pounds, 7 shillings, and 6 pence on November 17, 1783, for service in Virginia.

I do have a service record for a **Captain John Miller** who was in charge of infantry under **Col. R. Maj. Hunter**.

Another source states,

"**Captain Racoon Miller** led troops against the Chickamauga Indians in 1779, the Militia being commanded by General **Evan Shelby**. They embarked in boats near Chattanooga, returning through the forests to their homes. These troops at this time evidently found suitable lands for settlement and later moved from the Upper Holston to the valleys between Holston and Clinch Rivers, for in 1793 Captain **Miller** sold his lands up there and moved to Racoon Valley, near present Maynards-ville." (2, page 14.)

"`There were a vast number of German names in Union County, TN, many so anglicized as to have lost their Deutschland flavor, for these people appeared to want to forget their Teutonic origin. Many of the **Millers** were known originally as **Muellers** [ umlaut over "u"]....`" (**Thomas, Professor W. H.**, quoted by **Mrs. Shute**, (1) page 303.) **Mrs. Shute** wrote that the Captain "was of German stock, perhaps born in Germany on 17 Dec. 1754. The Ship Neptune arrived at Philadelphia and among the passengers were a **HOHAN HENRICH WEIDENER** and **ADAM MULLER**. **Captain Miller** was born in 1747 and died in 1832...."His wife **Eve** lived to be 102, and died near Maynardsville in 1851."

Another name for **Eve** was **Lucy**. "**Alfred Miller** stated that **Racoon** married a German girl named **Lucy Weidner** (b. Jan. 31, 1751, d. Aug.12, 1853, at the age of 102 years), and sett-led first in what was Hawkins County, Tenn."(27, p.188.)

John Miller, Rebecca`s father, "was killed in action at the Battle of Alamance in the uprising of 16 May 1771." (1, page 303) "The Alamance" refers to an uprising against heavy taxation and cruel treatment by the British. Your compiler studied two cases in which a person was deported to America simply because he was caught stealing bread, while another stole clothes.

Further comments on the Alamance affair are taken from **Haywood`s Civil and Political History of Tennessee**, 1891, (28, Page 68): "The extortions of clerks, lawyers, and tax gatherers fell with intolerable weight upon the people. Sheriffs in the collection of taxes, exacted more than was due, and appropriated the surplus to their own use. The offenders were the men in power, who were appointed by the law to redress the wrongs of the people. Those who were injured met and petitioned the legislature for relief, and made representations of mal-practices....Their petitions were rejected, and treated with disdain. Driven by oppression to desperation and madness, the people rose in bodies, under the title of Regulators." The British, without relent, sent an army against the Regulators, "killing above two hundred...some of them...hanged; others took the oath of allegiance...others fled to Holston...full streams of emigration began to flow in various directions from the misgoverned province of North Carolina.".

48

"From the application of a descendant of **John Miller** who became a member of the DAR, it was learned that the marriage date of **John Miller** to **Eve Whitener** was Mar. 1, 1776 in Sullivan County and that **Eve Whitener** was born Jan. 31, 1751." (27, page 189.) "**Racoon**" **Miller** got his nickname from the place where he settled. "Their Racoon Valley home was about 8 miles south of Lost Creek where **James** and **Rebecca Miller Rice** had settled." (2, page 14.) Maybe there were racoons there too.

Many letters were sent to the Bureau of Pensions from descendants of **John Miller** because the widow's application had been rejected, and in search of the service record. More records are found in **Mrs. Peters'** book (27, page 188).

John Rice Irwin wrote (23, page 36), "**Miller** is reported to have purchased the present site of Middlesboro, Kentucky, from the Indians for a few jugs of whiskey. Interestingly, `**Racoon**` **Miller** was the first man to introduce the silk worm in the state of Tennessee--in Hawkins County in 1791." Middlesboro, KY, is at Cumberland Gap in Bell County, with the County Seat at Pineville. Your compiler has not checked Bell County records to see about the land deal, or about "**Racoon's**" brothers and sisters.

[The following comments were added by **Ruby Rice Little**. Some of the information quoted by **Mrs. Peters** (27, page 189) is at variance with poet **Martin Rice's** Remembrance of his grandmother **Rebecca Miller Rice** (see page 31). **Mrs. Peters** quoted from an unpublished history of the **Miller** family by **Alfred Miller**: "...descendants of `**Racoon**` **Miller** believe...(he) came from Newberry County, South Carolina, and was one of 4 children, the other 3 being girls....Rebecca, wife of **James Rice**...may have been a sister of `**Racoon**` **Miller**." It seems likely that more than one line of **Millers** may have been confused.]

John Miller
Capt. Inf.

Appears in a

Book

under the following heading:

"A List of State and Navy Officers who have received Certificates for the balance of their full pay, &c."

(Revolutionary War.)

By whom received Col. R. Maj Hunter

Day when drawn November 17, 1783.

Sum £145 57 D 6.

Remarks:

Vol. 175; page

(547)

J. W. Wilkinson

Copyist.

Va.

Miller, John

Virginia.

(Revolutionary War.)

Captain Inf.

CARD NUMBER

1	39161856	20	
2		21	
3		22	
4		23	
5		24	
6		25	
7		26	
8		27	
9		28	
10		29	
11		30	
12		31	
13		32	
14		33	
15		34	
16		35	
17		36	
18		37	
19		38	

Number of personal papers herein _____

BOOK MARK: _____

D. TABITHA RICE SNODDERLY

Tabitha was the oldest child of **James Rice** and **Rebecca Miller**, according to the list published by the **Turnbows**.

"1. **Tabitha Rice** born April 28, 1789 in Pendleton District, South Carolina. Died at Lost Creek, Tennessee, April 25 1868. Married **George Snoderly**, who was born in Orange County, North Carolina." (2, page 21.)

Mrs. Shute gives a long list of **Snodderly** descendants. Regarding **Tabitha**, she wrote:

"2.3=3.1 **TABITHA RICE** b. 28 Apr 1789 in the Pendleton District, S.C., d. 2 Apr 1868 in Lost Creek, TN, m. **GEORGE SNODDERLY** (b. 17 Sep. 1787, son of **JOHN** and **ELIZABETH [GIBBS] SNODDERLY**....**GEORGE** was the brother of **SARAH SNODDERLY RICE** who married **GEORGE RICE**." **Tabitha** and **George** "lived and died on the farm of **HENRY RICE** who d. in 1818. **GEORGE [Snodderly]** d. on 20 Aug. 1852 in Campbell Co. TN." (1, page 304.)

I quote at length from **Mrs. Peters** (27, pages 202-203):

"It was probably about 1785-6 that **John Snodderly** married **Elizabeth Gibbs**, born about 1765 in North Carolina, oldest daughter of **Nicholas** and **Mary Efland Gibbs**. Sometime after that they moved to East Tennessee and settled in Campbell County....Their children:5/

1. **George**, b. Sept. 17, 1787, in N.C.; gunsmith and farmer; m. **Tabitha Rice**, b. Apr. 28, 1789, in Pendleton District, S.C., daughter of **James** and **Rebecca (Miller?) Rice**. Their children were:6/

(These footnotes are those of **Mrs. Peters** (27):

5/ Records of **J. Crit Sharp**. The birthdates were taken from the **George Snodderly** Bible now owned by **Gaines Snodderly**, New Market, Tenn. [1953]

6/ Records of **W. H. Thomas**, Athens, Tenn. (now deceased).

(1) **Jacob**, b. Mar. 5, 1810; d. in 1889; buried in Franklin Butte Cemetery, near Scio, Oregon. Children: **George W.; A. H.; James Hugh; John W.; Elizabeth Curl; Susannah Ray; Laura Frost; America Coshow; Nancy Smith** and **Sarah Smith**[5].

(2) **Rebecca**, b. Sept. 19, 1811; m. **George Sharp**, son of **Henry** and **Elizabeth (Black) Sharp**; moved to Nodaway County, Mo.

(3) **Isaac**, b. June 2, 1812; m. (1) **Mary Sharp**, daughter of **Henry** and **Elizabeth Black Sharp**; (2) **Sarah Baker**. Children: **George C.; Henry; Nancy; Daniel C.; Rebecca; Alvis; Jacob; John; Lewis; Rice**, m. **Charlotte Baker; Tabitha; Phoebe** and **William**.[1]

(4) **Elizabeth**, b. Nov. 14, 1814; m. **William Sharp**, son of **Conrad**.

(5) **Lee Roy**, b. Feb. 17, 1816; settled in Polk Township, Nodaway County.

(6) **John**, b. Jan. 18, 1819; m. **Eliza Sharp**, daughter of **Isaac** and **Nancy Heath Sharp**, on Feb. 18, 1846, in Campbell County, Tenn.

(7) **Huldah**, b. Dec. 16, 1820; m. **Simpson Albright**, son of **John** and **Elizabeth Sharp Albright**.

(8) **George**, b. July 16, 1823.

(9) **Mary**, b. Dec. 25, 1825.

(10) **Anna**, b. Aug. 4, 1827; m. **Colson Sharp**, son of **Isaac** and **Nancy Heath Sharp**.

(11) **Phoebe**, b. Aug. 4, 1829; m. (1) **Lewis Duke**; (2) **Jack Brock**.

(12) **Henry Rice**, b. Apr. 19, 1832; m. (1) **Lucy Irwin**, Mar. 5, 1855;[2] (2) **Mary Love Petree**.

(**Mrs. Peters** [27] footnotes):

[1] 1850 Census of Campbell County, Tenn.

[2] Campbell County - Marriage Records.

2. **Elizabeth**, b. 1791 in Tenn.; d. 1868; m. **Reuben Craig**, born in N.C. in 1792, who died of smallpox in 1864.

3. **Sarah**, b. Nov. (Mar.) 5, 1794; d. Oct. 21, 1855; m. **George Rice**, b. Mar. 27, 1794; d. Nov. 30, 1869.

4. **Mary**, m. **Morris Bridges**.

5. **Phoebe**, b. 1800 in Tenn.; m. **William Ussary** in 1837; d. 1846 in Platte County, Mo.—3/ Children: **John**; **Elizabeth**; **James**; **Louisa**, m. **J. C.** [**John Calvin**] **Sharp**, son of John and Rebecca Sharp; **Rebecca**; **Henderson**; **Nancy Jane**; **Zeba Annie**; and **William**.

6. **Huldah**, m. **Isaac Wilson**. [Gibbs book has **Gabriel Nelson** as Huldah's husband.]

7. **John** [**Mahala Nelson?**]

8. **Nicholas**, b. about 1806; d. Feb. 18, 1899, near Clarinda, Iowa; m. in October 1834 (Court record) **Mahala Hill**, b. May 13, 1815, in Tenn.; d. Aug. 9, 1905, in Clarinda, Iowa; daughter of **Matthew Hill**, went to Platte County, Mo. Children: **John**; **Elizabeth**; **Henry**, b. Apr. 18, 1842, in Platte County; **William**; **Malinda**; **Mary**.

9. **Jacob**. [**Margaret (Peggy) Burton**] **Gibbs**.

10. **Henry**, a gunsmith, went to Clarinda, Iowa."

[Mrs. Peters' (27) footnote]:
3/ Annals of Platte County, Mo.

Footnote 5 above mentions the **George Snodderly** Bible. Their children are in this Bible, but **Mrs. Peters** does not have the date of marriage of **George** and **Tabitha**.

The **Turnbows** wrote (2, pages 19-20) about the two wives of the late **William (Willie) Henderson Thomas**--(a) **Maude Hill** and (b) **Lucy Snodderly**; both descended from **George Snodderly**, **Maude** from **Henry Rice Snodderly**'s second wife and **Lucy** from **Henry Rice Snodderly**'s first wife.

"Among their sons was **Henry Rice Snoderly**, who was born at Lost Creek, Tennessee on April 19, 1831, and died there February 12, 1901. **Henry Rice Snoderly** was married twice: First to **Lucy Irwin** in 1850. Second to **Mary Love Petrie**.

His first wife **Lucy Irwin** was born at Forkvale, Tennessee, in 1836. She died at Lost Creek in 1879. By this marriage there were 11 children. Their daughter **Elizabeth Snoderly** was born March 5, 1859 and died August 3, 1942 at Philadelphia, Tennessee. She married, in 1880, **Ferrin Hill**, a son of **Terry Hill** and **Jane (Sharp) Hill** who was a great-granddaughter of old **Henry Sharp**. Their daughter **Maude Hill** was born at Lost Creek on May 20, 1885, died June 23, 1928, and is buried in Cedar Grove Cemetery, Athens, Tennessee. She was married December 18, 1904 to **William Henderson Thomas**, of Riceville Pike, Athens, Tennessee. **Mr. Thomas** was married secondly to **Lucy Snoderly**, the daughter of **Henry Rice Snoderly** and **Rice Snoderly's** second wife **Mary Love Petrie**, by whom there were seven children."

The late **Professor Thomas** wrote in his book (29, pages 16 and 29) about the **Snodderly-Sharp** connections, concerning the tenth child of **Conrad "Coonrod" Sharp** and **Sarah Gibbs Sharp**:

"**William Sharp**, youngest son of **Conrad**, was born in 1814. He, along with his mother, inherited land last owned by the **Ferrin Hill** estate and lands adjoining to the north and west. **William** married **Betsey Snodderly**, daughter of **George** and **Tabitha (Rice) Snodderly**. They migrated to Andrew County, Missouri...."

"Another of the sons of **George** and **Tabitha (Rice) Snoderly** was **Jacob H. Snoderly**, who came to Oregon in the **Joab Powell** wagon train, arriving in Oregon Territory on October 1, 1852. His wife died on this trip across the plains and is buried at Ash Hollow, Nebraska. **Jacob H.** was born in Campbell County, Tennessee in 1810....**Jacob H. Snoderly** settled on a donation land claim near Scio, Linn County, Oregon, but relinquished part of this claim to his cousin **Francis M. Rice**, son of James and **Elizabeth (Lett) Rice**. He later lived in Princeville, Crook County, Oregon and died in 1889. He is buried near his daughter **Susannah Ray** in the Franklin Butte Cemetery near Scio, Oregon. Old Linn County records show that he was a Justice of the Peace, and also a Notary Public. His daughters were **Elizabeth Curl**, **Susannah Ray**, **Laura Frost**, **America Coshow**, **Nancy Smith** and **Sarah Smith**. Biographical Sketch of Jacob H. Snoderly, by Maude Turnbow (1956), on file at Oregon State Library, Salem, Oregon." (2, page 20)

Sketch of the Lost Creek Primitive Baptist Church drawn from a photograph taken in 1924. Featured are separate entrances for ladies (left) and gentlemen (right), and the "upping block" for mounting horses and carriages. Since ladies rode sidesaddle, the upping block was a convenience for them in mounting their horses. The upping block can still be seen, as well as foundations of this building and an earlier one, at the Lost Creek Cemetery. Photograph published in Norris Reservoir Scrapbook 1934-1939 (Photo no. 15).

CHAPTER V - DANIEL RICE THE GUNSMITH

Chapter summary on page vi

Martin Rice in his remembrance wrote about Daniel: "Daniel Rice, I believe the fourth son, lived and died in Claiborne County, Tennessee, not far from the Cumberland Gap. His sons were Henry, Lewis, Thomas, and Jefferson, and his daughters were Temperance and Patience. Some of these I have seen and remember but have no knowledge of them or their descendants for 50 years past. Daniel was a gunsmith, and his son Henry was a militia Colonel in 1832 or about that time." (2, pages 6-8.)

There is a Daniel Rice in the 1779 Tax List of Orange County, North Carolina, with a Thomas Rice. This Thomas had a daughter Susannah, and could be another Thomas, not Daniel's son.

Henry Rice's son Daniel had two Claiborne County deed conveyances.

Claiborne County, Tenn. Index to Deeds

Grantor	Grantee	Instrument	Date	Book	Page	Amount
Daniel Rice	John Baker	D(eed)	1818	F	5	100.00
Daniel Rice	Absolom Robinson	D	1820	F	123	350.00

Hawkins County, Tenn., Index to Deeds
Conveyor-Conveyee 1788-1861

Date	Conveyors	Book	Page	Conveyees
1813	Rice, Daniel	3	240	William Hord*
1813	Rice, Daniel	3	269-270	William Hord*
1814	Rice, Daniel	3	284	William Bradley
1812	Rice, Daniel	6	380	William Bradley
1812	Rice, Daniel	15	486	Bradley & Joseph McMinn
1834	Rice, Daniel	15	15	Levi Rice*
1835	Rice, Daniel	15	293	Wm. Cape
1835	Rice, Daniel	15	306	Nancy S. Miller
1835	Rice, Daniel	15	307	Joel Rice
1836	Rice, Daniel	15	380	Joel Rice
1836	Rice, Daniel	15	461,465, 466	John Seal

*The star means that I have a copy of the deed; the rest are just references as they appear in the Index.

The Hawkins County deeds of **Daniel Rice** to **William Hord** are summarized below, except for the indenture to **Levi** which is given in the section on **Daniel's** brother **Levi Rice**.

Hawkins County Deed Books (12)
Microfilm Roll #34 Hawkins Co. Book 3, page 240

Grantor		Grantee

Rice, Daniel   to   **William Hord**
        date - 27 February 1813
Hawkins Co.   Claiborne Co.
$5000   643 acres

North side of Holston River, **Robert Young's** line, **Beard's** Creek, **William Engle's** line. Grant from State of North Carolina #347 dated 10th November 1784.

in presence of	:		
John Young	:	**Dan[l] Rice**	Seal
George Wright	:		
Wm. Weaver	:		

August Sessions 1813
Registered 9 September 1813

Hawkins County Deed Books (12)
Microfilm Roll #34 Book 3 pp. 269-270

Grantor		Grantee

Rice, Daniel   to   **William Hord**
        date - 28 February 1814
Hawkins Co.   Hawkins Co.
$500   10 acres

"Island on Holston River oposite to the mouth of **Rices** Mill Creek known by the name of **Rices** Island...."

in the presents of	:		
Hugh Graham	:	**Dan[l] Rice**	Seal
William Young	:		

Campbell County Deeds

Grantor	Grantee	Instrument	Date	Book	Page	Amount
Hord, Wm.	Rice, Daniel	Deed	1813	D	183	1400.00
Rice, Daniel	Robinson, Absalom	Deed	1820	F	123	350.00
Hord, William	Rice, Daniel	Deed	1819	G	4	1.00
Hord, William	Rice, ------	Bond	1827	H	348	

Daniel Rice, the gunsmith, had a land grant from the glorious State of Tennessee:

> Tennessee State Grant No. 5999 (12)
> 15 acres, 11/2/1818, Greene Co.
> Location East Tenn. District
> Book 5, page 374

Daniel was in 4 tax lists:

Hawkins Co. Tax List 1809-1812

McWilliams Company, 1809
Rice, Dannel...640 acres...1 white poll...1 black poll

Hawkins Co. 1836 Tax List

Dist. 2, land 135, value 350, tax .78-3/4, state tax
    17-1/2, total .78-3/4
Dist. 1, land 100, 1 white poll tax .56-1/4, state tax
    .12-1/2, total .56-1/4

1833 Claiborne List of Males

Daniel Rice 196

1837 Anderson County Tax List

1st Dist., **Rice, Daniel,** 1 white tax .12-1/2, state tax
    .12-1/2, total .62-1/2

Daniel Rice was married to **Anny Ray** on July 17, 1821. The bondsman was **Edward Cheshire**. On the next day, July 18, 1821, the marriage was solemnized by **John Moore**, J.P. This in on page 130 of Grainger County Marriages, Volume I, 1796-1837. **Anny Ray** could have been a second wife of **Daniel**.*

The pioneer **Henry Rice** had, through his son **Daniel**, 4 grandsons and 2 granddaughters (see page 56).

Henry Rice the son of **Daniel** appears in the 1833 Claiborne County list of males. The other reference states that he was a military colonel in 1832 (page 56).

Daniel's son **Lewis Rice** is in the following records:

(1)   Hawkins County Tenn. Index to Deeds
           Conveyor—Conveyee 1788-1861

Date	Conveyor	Book	Page	Conveyee
1812	**Rice, Lewis**	6	425	Gabriel Phillips

(2)   1830 Claiborne County Census
               F M 19 Roll #180

Rice, Lewis: 1 male 30 to 40; 2 females un. 5, 1 f. 20 to 30

(3)   1805 Greene County List of Free Taxable Inhabitants.

Thomas Rice, the third son of **Daniel**, is with the fourth son, **Jefferson Rice** in the 1833 Claiborne County List of Males. **Thomas** had a grant from the State of Tennessee:

        Tennessee State Grant No. 4075 (12)
        100 acres ... November 28, 1816
        Granger Co. East Tennessee District
        Book 4, volume 2, page 527

---

*Daniel's sons were all adults in the 1830 census and the 1833 tax lists.

Claiborne County Index to Deeds

Conveyor		Conveyee
Barnes, Levi	to	Thomas Rice
Rice, Thomas et al	to	Rice, Susanah
Rice, Thomas	to	Isaiah Jones

Lucylle Rice Davis, (30) gives **Jefferson Rice**, instead of **Henry**, as a militia colonel in 1831. I have not found a military record for either, but I might have overlooked it.

Maybe someone can trace **Daniel's** descendants further. Perhaps they went to Kentucky and westward, and are trying to connect back to **Henry**, the gristmiller.

There was a different **Thomas Rice** in Hawkins County, who was from Virginia. In the **Roster of Soldiers and Patriots of the American Revolution Buried in Tennessee**, 1974 (31, page 336) we find:

"**Rice, Thomas,** Hawkins Co., Va. Mil., 1834"

The **Susannah Rice** who was daughter of the Revolutionary War **Thomas Rice** was in the 1830 Claiborne County census and the 1850 Hawkins County census schedule (see above Claiborne Deed Index.)

Even though the **Thomas Rice** died in 1834, he is not in the following census:

1830 Claiborne County Census
F M 19 Roll #180

Susannah Rice   1 male 5-10; 2 m. 15-20; 2 m. 20-30; 1 m. 30-40
1 female under 5; 2 f. 15-20; 1 f. 50-60

1850 Hawkins County Census
page 429, line 113

Sousannah, 75	Birthplace, Tennessee
Elizabeth, 38	Fathers birthplace, Va.
Daniel P., 36	Mothers birthplace, Tenn.

CHAPTER **VI. JOHN RICE, THE OLD PREACHER**

Chapter summary on page vi

Your compiler believes that there were at least three different **John Rices** in Hawkins County. I have been told that there could have been up to sixteen **John Rices** in Virginia, North Carolina, South Carolina and Tennessee. However, there was only one son of pioneer **Henry** named **John Rice**, a preacher, who had a daughter married to a man that later became an outlaw.

In his recollections, the Bard of Lone Jack wrote that **William** had the daughter who married "**Little Harpe**," but this was corrected by **Alva** and **Maude Turnbow** to be the daughter of **John**; I think is Henry's son **John**. The two other **John Rices**, who will be mentioned later, did not become preachers and did not have any outlaw connections that I know of.

"....of **William's** sons, **Charles**, only is known to have an existence, and one daughter is said to have been the wife of **Little Harpe**, the noted bandit and robber, in the early settlement of Kentucky...." (2, page 7.)

At the bottom of the same page:

"**Sarah (Sally) Rice** was the daughter of the second son, **John Rice**. She married **Wylie (Willie) Harpe** in 1797, according to **Jeanette Acklin's Abstracts of Marriages**. [32] See also [33] `The Outlaw Years` by **Robert M. Coates**, 1930, pp. 17-18; and `The Outlaws of Cave In-Rock,` by **Otto A. Rothert**, 1924, p. 63." [34]

I have seen both the marriage record and the Outlaw books, and further information on what happened and about **John Rice** with family being seen leaving Tennessee in 1820.

There is in the **Knox County Tennessee Marriages**, bond June 1, 1797, which is written in the following references:

"**Willie Harp** x, Knox County, married **Sarah Rice** Oct. 5, 1797." (2)

"1797 Oct. 5, **Harp, Willie** (x) to **Sarah Rice**." (32)

Some excerpts from writings on **Sally Rice Harpe** are quoted:

"Such was the welcome the **Harpes** received, among those who came down to the frolic were **John Rice**, a minister living a few miles to the northward, and his daughter **Sally**...."

"**Sally Rice** had a frail blond beauty; she was not yet twenty years old: **Little Harpe** was smitten with her at once. Through the summer, he haunted the **Rice's** cabin, paying his court in his hang-dog fashion. Before the setting-in of Fall he had married her. Her father performed the ceremony." (33, page 28)

"Obeying the principle that birds of a feather flock together, the **Harpes**, it seems, were attracted toward the new settlement of Knoxville. In March, 1798, **James Weir**, ... to Kentucky, spent a few days in the town...

"Under this feint of honest occupation they experienced no difficulty in gaining the confidence of their neighbors. In fact, so easily had they made a favorable impression that within a few weeks after their arrival **Little Harpe** married **Sarah** or **Sally Rice**, a daughter of **John Rice**, a preacher living about four miles north of the **Harpe** hut." (34, pages 62-63)

"The spies traced them as far as the Green River crossing: here, they found, the women had traded their mare for a canoe, and vanished....Then **Susan**, **Betsey**, and even the frail **Sally Rice**, the preacher's daughter, so soon accustomed to bloodshed--they were off to join their murderous masters at some preconcerted rendezvous." (33, page 40)

"The **Harpes** evidently had arranged to meet their three women associates....in December, 1798, they entered Kentucky --the 'dark and bloody ground'...." (34, page 66)

"When **Sally Rice** was tried, her father, **Parson Rice**, was present, a man of fine, irreproachable character, and took his prodigal daughter home near Knoxville. It was said, and doubtless truly, that **Sally** was thought a fine girl until she married **Wiley Harpe**. In 1820 **Major Stewart** was at **Ford's** Ferry on the Ohio--(a few miles above Cave-in-Rock) and saw **Parson Rice**, his family, **Sally** and her (second) husband moving to Illinois. He did not recognize them, but thought he knew them, particularly **Sally**, who eyed him closely and, after a little, went to one side, sat down and with her face in her hands, had a weeping spell, doubtlessly recounting her **Harpe** adventures, prompted by the presence of one of the few persons who had treated her with civility and kindness in her wayward career. After he left them, **Major Stewart** recollected hearing the old gentleman called **Rice** and the identity flashed upon his mind. **Sally Harpe's** daughter had then grown to womanhood and was a fine young lady. (12 F)

The girl referred to by **Stewart** as **Sally Harpe**'s daughter was, in all probability, not a daughter of **Harpe**." (33, pages 155-156)

Your compiler has searched the many **Rice** names in the Illinois census schedules through 1850 for **Rices**. They could have gone to another State. Also **Sally** must have remarried, for both **Harpe** brothers, **Micajah** or **"Big" Harpe** and **"Little" Harpe** were killed, before she was tried in court. The above are all the records that have been found, having **Sally Rice** with second spouse and child and including their travel to begin life anew. The preacher could have passed away before 1830, or the family could have moved farther west.

Under the section on **Henry**, **John Rice** was mentioned as fighting the Cherokee Indians with **Henry Rice**. (See <u>Charles Rice</u> etc. (2, page 3); also page 9 of this book.) I also showed that **Henry** received two land grants in Tennessee from North Carolina. **John Rice** had two grants as well. (See page 14.)

Lewis Brim sold land to **John Rice** in Knox County:

<u>Knox County Deeds, Reverse Index, p. 125</u>

<u>Grantee</u>	<u>Grantor</u>	<u>Book</u>	<u>Page</u>	<u>Date</u>	<u>Location</u>
Rice, John	**Brim, Lewis**	E vol.1	401	Oct.12 1798	Tenn. R. 102 A.

This deed reference proves that the preacher was **Henry**'s son, in two ways. First, **Lewis Brim** was a brother-in-law of **John** and son-in-law of **Henry**. Second, this land was in Knox County, where the preacher was, when **Sally** married **"Little Harpe."**

There are many Hawkins County Deed references for **John Rices**, one a **John Rice Senior**, from 1792 through 1811. There were at least three different **John Rices** in this county: (1) the preacher; (2) **John Rice Senior**; and (3) **Isaac Rice**'s son John. The second stayed in Hawkins, while both **Isaac** and his son **John** moved to Roane County. Your compiler believes that the latter two are different. The preacher [(1) above] moved first to Knox County, then moved away (to Illinois?) in 1820, while the others left wills in Hawkins County **(John Rice Senior)** (1811) and in Roane County (1815). **Isaac Rice** left a will in 1818 in Roane County. (This **Isaac Rice** married **Margery Walden** and is the father of the 1815 **John Rice**.) In the **John Rice Senior** will (1811) there is a son **John**, but no mention of any **Henry**. The only **Henry Rice** in Roane County was a Reverend Henry Rice. The Rev. Rice was a grandson of the 1815 John and son of Isaac Rice and Martha Lucinda Matlock, one of two wives of Isaac. This Isaac Rice is the grandson of the Isaac Rice who married Margery Walden. Much has been studied on these John Rices, but little is given here, for the preacher has been separated from the other two John Rices.

The Hawkins County deed references from the Index Book that I have for John Rices, are from 1792 through 1811. Since the preacher was in Knox County in 1798, the later references, and maybe some of the earlier ones, have to do with different John Rices. I have not studied the actual deeds for locations in order to separate them, except the first one.

Hawkins County Tenn. Index to Deeds

Conveyors	Year	Book	Page	Conveyees
Rice, Jno. Senior	1792	1	118	Wm. Stubblefield 300 A Stanley Valley
Rice, Jno.	1792	1	127	Thos. Poteet
Rice, Jno.	1793	2	99	Ben Green
Rice, Jno.	1794	2	165	Jos. Barttel
Rice, Jno.	1795	2	233	Moses Johnson
Rice, Jno.	1795	2	259	Jno. Walling
Rice, Jno.	1795	2	265	Wm. Walling
Rice, Jno.	1799	2	488	Daniel Jones
Rice, Jno.	1802	3	36	J. Thimprin et al
Rice, Jno.	1803	3	75	Lewis Christian
Rice, Jno.	1809	6	193	Robert Keyle
Rice, Jno.	1811	6	324	James Johnston

Conveyees	Year	Book	Page	Conveyors
Rice, Jno.	1795	2	225	Elijah Chimm
Rice, Jno.	1796	3	139	Wm. Stubblefield

The preacher John Rice went west in 1820. Maybe this was a spark for westward migration, for most of Henry's descendants, especially those of his son James's except for George, moved to the fertile areas of the Plains.

CHAPTER VII.   LEVI RICE

Chapter summary on page vi

Levi Rice was another preacher, besides **John.**

"**Levi Rice** was my grandfather's younger brother (quoting from the remembrances of **Martin Rice**). He lived and died in Hawkins County. He was a third rate Baptist or Dunkard preacher. I remember seeing the old man and hearing him preach when I was a small boy. I also remember his sons, **James** and **Joel.** His son **John** was a Baptist minister and died about two years ago in Texas County, Missouri; and his grandson **James** is a Baptist minister living in Licking, in that County now (1891)." (2, page 8)

"**Levi,** youngest son of the pioneer **Henry,** married **Mary C. Mitchell,** daughter of **Isaac** and **Mary Williams Mitchell,** and granddaughter of **Ursula Henderson** and **Daniel Williams.** Isaac **Mitchell** had removed with wife and children to Newberry District, South Carolina, and later to Abbeyville District where he died. His will signed June 23, 1789, probated Oct. 6, 1789, named his wife and children, **Ursula, Mary Catherine, Sarah** and **Isaac Jr.**   **Levi Rice** signed for his wife...." (30, page 76)

Lucylle Rice Davis wrote a big list of **Levi Rice's** descendants in her book (30, pages 76-105).

Levi Rice may have had a second wife, for he is listed in the Grainger County marriages:

Grainger County Marriages
Vol. I, 1796-1837, p. 130

Levi Rice to **Jane Simmons,** Dec. 4, 1801. Bondsman **Jeremiah Chamberlain.** Bond only.

The preacher **Levi Rice** was on the same page of the census (page 11) with his father, **Henry Rice,** in the 1810 census schedule for the same county.

1810 Grainger County, Tennessee Census (13)

Page 11: "**Levi Rice**   3 - - 1 - / 2 - 1 - -"

This means that **Levi** had 3 sons under 10, with himself being between 26 and 45 years old. There were 2 daughters under 10, and his wife was between 16 and 26.

In "**A List of Polls and Taxable Property** Returned to Court by **William Clay** Esquire in the bounds of **Richard Cotses** Company for the Year 1810" (13), we find:

	(Column 1)	(Column 2, BW)	(Column 3)
"**Rice, Levi**	700	–	1"

The figure 700 refers to acres. The second column means Black and White poll. Column 3 is males 21 years of age and above.

1830 Census East Tennessee Index (35)

"**Rice, Levi**   Ha - 85." - "0 0 0 1 0 0 0 1 - 2 0 0 1 0 0 1"

The person first is looked up under the last name; **Rice, Levi** is on page 85 under Hawkins County (Ha). **Levi** had a son 15-20, with **Levi** himself being 50-60. There were 2 daughters under 5, one 15-20, and his wife was 40-50.

1837 Anderson County Tax List

"7th Dist. **Rice, Levi**	School land 100 acres	val $.25	tax" .1-1/4

Hawkins County Index to Deeds
Conveyor-Conveyee 1788-1861

Conveyor	Year	Book	Page	Conveyee
Rice, Levi	1833	13	282	John Cantrell
Rice, Levi	1834	15	15	Daniel Rice*
Rice, Levi	1834	15	60	Joel Rice
Rice, Levi	1834	15	95	John Cantrell
Rice, Levi	1834	15	96	James Rice**
Rice, Levi	1834	15	170	Joel Rice***
Rice, Joel & Levi	1835	15	303	Daniel Greene

* This is the only deed I have looked up. This deed is summarized next.
** This **James Rice** could be **Levi's** nephew, son of **Levi's** brother **James Rice**, or probably is **Levi's** son **James S. Rice**.
*** The **Joel** is **Levi's** son.

Levi Rice to **Daniel Rice**
12th day September 1832
both Hawkins County (residents)
Reg. April 30, 1834
$800 - number of acres not given
(being the son* of **Levi Rice**)
Book 15 page 15
Deed proven 6th day May 1834

in the presence of us	:	
Joel Rice	:	Levi Rice Seal
One of two testators	:	

* This is a deed between brothers, not between father and
  son. **Joel** is **Levi's** son.

Grainger County Deeds

Book C, pp. 151-52	**Henry Rice** to **Levi Rice***
Book C, pp. 293-94	**Levi Rice** to **Henry Rice****
Book E, pp. 186-87	**Levi Rice** to **Henry Alsup**
Book E, p. 628	**Levi Rice** to **Henry Alsup**

  * See page 18.   ** See page 19.

  The first two listings refer to the same land.

Levi Rice to **Henry Alsup**
22nd May 1819
both Grainger County
$530 - 80 acres
James Richison's line
original line of **Rice's** Old Survey
Richisons corner

Isaac Harris	:	
Asbery Shamness	:	Levi Rice Seal
Daniel Rice	:	

May Session 1821
Grainger County Book E, pp. 186-87

Levi Rice to Henry Alsup
6 March 1824
County of Hawkins
$900   159 acres
being in County of Grainger
Aquilla Mitchell's line
Michael Massingill's line
80 acres tract part of Thomas Ingles

in presence of us	:		
Aquilla Mitchell	:	Levi Rice	Seal
James R. Alsup	:		
Martin Cleveland	:		

Nov. Term 1827
Grainger County Book E p. 628

There are deed references on sons **Joel** and **James Rice** under each of them respectively.

There is no record for the death of **Levi Rice**. He does not show up in the 1840 Hawkins County Census Schedule. His son **James** "was a stone mason and made many tombstones for the community. One is still standing in the cemetery at the Big Springs Primitive Baptist Church, Springdale, Tennessee. It is at the grave of his first wife, in his handwriting the inscription still legible (1960), `Francis Rice, beloved wife of **James S. Rice**, Died June 14, 1841.`" (30, page 78.)

This **James Rice** lived in Claiborne County, after he was in Hawkins. I have checked the 1840 Claiborne census. Springdale is in this county and has been seen on a recent topographical map, southeast of Tazewell. It is not on highway maps.

Joel Rice, son of **Levi**, bought and sold land in Hawkins County.

Hawkins Co. Index to Deeds
Conveyor to Conveyee, 1788-1861

Conveyor	Year	Book	Page	Conveyee
Rice, Joel	1814	3	284	Wm. Bradley & Joseph McMinn
Rice, Joel & Levi	1835	15	303	Daniel Greene
Rice, Joel	1835	15	305	Daniel Greene
Rice, Joel	1836	15	370	Wm. Tucker

Hawkins Co. Index to Deeds
Conveyee-Conveyor 1788-1861

Rice, Joel	1834	15	60	Levi Rice
Rice, James	1834	15	96	Levi Rice
Rice, Joel	1834	15	170	Levi Rice
Rice, Joel	1835	15	206	James Rice
Rice, Joel	1835	15	307	Daniel Rice
Rice, Joel	1836	15	380	Daniel Rice

All these are just deed references. This **James Rice** is Levi's son.

Joel Rice is in the Claiborne County census with his brother **John** in 1840:

Tennessee 1840 Census Index Book (18)
page 195

Rice, James A.	Clai.	201	NO TWP L	(No township listed)
Rice, Joel	Clai.	201	NO TWP L	
Rice, John	Clai.	244	NO TWP L	

They give the first four letters of the County; next is the page, and whether there is a township or not.

James Rice, son of **Levi,** sold three tracts of land in Hawkins County:

Hawkins County Index to Deeds
Conveyor to Conveyee, 1788-1861

Conveyor	Year	Book	Page	Conveyee
Rice, James	1834	15	94	Parntt Cantrell
Rice, James	1835	15	206	Joel Rice
Rice, James	1835	15	208	John Cantrell

James Rice, according to this data from Index books, received one deed conveyance from his father (see conveyees in list above).

James and John are both in the 1830 Hawkins County census (F M 19 Roll #178):

James Rice   3 m un. 5; 1 m 20-30; 1 f 20-30
John Rice   1 m un. 5; 1 m 20-30; 1 f 20-30

James had three sons under 5, while he was between 20 and 30 years old and so was his wife. John's census data is the same, except that he had only one son.

1850 Tennessee Census Index Book (36, page 200) (Vol. 6)

"Rice, Harper 21, Eliza 19, Calvin 1, T T Cl - 683-572."

The two T's mean that Harper Rice and wife were both born in Tennessee. "Cl" stands for Claiborne County, TN. The numbers refer to page number and microfilm roll number.

Calvin Harper Rice was the son of James Samuel Rice, and grandson of Levi.

Harper Rice had two purchases of land:

Claiborne County Deeds

Grantor	Grantee	Warranty	Year	Book	Page	Amount
Hurst, Simpson	Rice, Harper	Deed	1854	W	406	400.00
Hurst, Simpson	Rice, Harper	Deed	1857	Y	144	400.00

Mrs. Charles A. Rice (Ila M. Rice) of Pittsburg, Kansas, submitted a letter with the 1860 Dallas County, Missouri census on Rhoadman Hickory Rice, son of James Samuel Rice and grandson of Levi Rice. The letter was published in The Epistle (37), Vol. IV, No. 2, Aug. 1977, page 45. The Dallas County record is:

Aug. 29, 1860, Urbana Twp. (Greene), Dallas Co., Mo:

Rice, Roaderman	age 23	born Tennessee
Rice, Virginai	age 24	born Tennessee
Rice, Westley W.	age 6 mo.	born Tennessee
Rice, Westley S.	age 26	born Tennessee

Westley S. is a brother of Rhoadman Rice.

CHAPTER VIII - MARTHA or PATSY RICE - DAVID BAILEY
Chapter summary on page vii

```
                                          | Pleasant F. Bailey
                                          |
                                          | Wiley Bailey
                                          |
                                          | James B. Bailey
                      James Bailey        |
                      Mary                |
                                          | William Bailey
                                          |
                                          | Elizabeth C. Bailey
                                          |
                                          | 2 more sons
                                          |
                                          | 2 more daughters
  Martha or
  Patsy Rice
  David Bailey
                      William Bailey (Continued next page)
                      Wife not known
                                          | 2 unnamed daughters
                                          |
                      Daniel Bailey       |
                      Sarah
                      A daughter
                      Wiley Tuttle
```

	Sarah Matilda Bailey
	Isaac L. Rice
	William P. Bailey
	Madona or Madera
	George M. Bailey
William J. R. Bailey *	
Elizabeth Storey	
	Mary Jane Bailey
	Jacob Marion Myers
	Andrew J. Bailey
	4 other children

* Son of William Bailey, page 71.

MARTHA or PATSY RICE - DAVID BAILEY

The names **Baile, Baily, Bailey, Baley, Baly, Baylie, Bayley** go back to the 1600's in the Virginia passenger lists. Then the **Baileys** show up in the first census of South Carolina, the 1810 Grainger County census, the 1830 Hawkins County census, and in various Hawkins County records.

A. MARTHA or PATSY RICE

1. **Martin Rice's** recollections.

The poet wrote, "**Martha**, or as she was called **Patsy Bailey**, wife of **David Bailey**, I never saw, but two of her sons, **James** and **William**, came to Missouri after I did and I knew them here. Their descendants, or some of them, are here yet, living in Cass and other Counties. I think she had a son **Daniel** and a daughter who married **Wiley Tuttle**." (2, pages 8-9.)

Patsy Rice Bailey must have been elderly before **Martin** was born, around 1813, for in the 1830 Hawkins County census **Daniel Bailey** was 50-60; **James Bailey** was 40-50; and **William** 30-40. For example, **Daniel** was born between 1770 and 1780, and **Patsy** possibly was 18 when she married in the 1770's. Therefore she could have been born in the late 1740's to middle 1750's.

B. DAVID BAILEY

David, husband of **Patsy** and son-in-law of the pioneer Henry Rice, might have been from South Carolina. There are two persons of this name in the 1790 South Carolina census, but your compiler has not found a record of their moving to East Tennessee. The **Rices** certainly moved, and the **Baileys** could have moved with them.

1790 South Carolina Census (20)

One **David Bailey** is in the 96th District, Laurens County, while the second is in Orangeburgh District South Part:

Name	Free white males 16 & over, incl. heads of families	f.w.m. under 16	f.w.f. incl. heads of families	All other free	Slaves
David Bailey	1	1	3	–	–

Orangeburgh District South Part (20)
1790 South Carolina Census page 99

David Bailey	1	–	2	–	–

The above census is also on microfilm, microcopy 637 Roll 11.

David Bailey is not in the 1810 Grainger County census, but a **John Bailey** is. David's sons **James** and **William** are in the 1830 Hawkins County census. **James** and **William Bailey** are in Van Buren County in Missouri in the 1840 census. In the same decade the name of the county was changed to Cass. Some are in Jackson County, Mo., in 1880. The 1850, 1860, 1870, and 1880 census records were seen by your compiler, as well as the 1900 census, for both Cass and Jackson County.

The oldest son, **Daniel**, is in Hawkins in 1830 and 1840, and Greene County in 1850, and there was an unnamed daughter who married **Wiley Tuttle**. There was a **James Tuttle** in Grainger in 1830. The tax lists for early Tennessee also were checked for **Baileys.**

C. DANIEL BAILEY

This grandson of the pioneer **Henry Rice** was in the census, as well as in three Hawkins County deed references.

1830 Hawkins County Census
FM 19 Roll No. 178.

Daniel Bailey. 1 male 50-60; 1 female 15-20; 1 f. 50-60.

Since he was 50 to 60 in 1830, **Daniel** was born between 1770 and 1780. His wife was in the same age category. The daughter was born between 1810 and 1815.

Tennessee 1840 Census Index
(Reference 18, 1976, page 9)

Bailey, Daniel. Hawk. 261. No township listed.

1840 Hawkins County Census
Microcopy 704, roll 526, page 261.

Daniel Bailey. 1 male 60-70; 1 female 10-15;
1 female 30-40; 1 female 60-70.

Tennessee 1850 Census Index
(Reference 38, 1977, page 15)

Bailey, Daniel. Gree. 573. No TWP L.

1850 Tennessee Census Index (39)
(Vol. 1, page 62)

"**Bailey, Daniel,** 72, **Sarah** 57, T, T, GE-2230-573." Both
Daniel and **Sarah** were born in Tennessee and lived in Greene
County. He was 50 to 60 twenty years earlier. **Sarah** must be a
second wife. **Daniel** was not found in Greene County after the 1850
census.

Hawkins County Tennessee Index to Deeds
Conveyor to Conveyee - 1788 to 1861

Conveyor	Year	Conveyee		Book	Page
Thomas Bailey	1833	Bailey,	Daniel	13	230
Ned Murphy	1833	Bailey,	Daniel	14	260
Ned Murphy	1834	Bailey,	Daniel	14	403

Register of Deeds, Deed Index, Hawkins County
Tennessee State Library and Archives (12)
Microfilm Roll No. 32, EX 13759, Title Register's
Deed Index, vol. 1-2, 1788-1906.

Year	Conveyors	Book	Page	Conveyee
1818	Bailey, Dan'l	7	153	Jno Bailey
1826	Bailey, Daniel	11	350	John Tunnell
1833	Bailey, Daniel	13	250	Thomas Bailey
1833	Bailey, Daniel	14	260	Ned Murphy

These are just references; the actual deeds for the above were not seen. There were other **Baileys** on the microfilm, which will be given later. The **John** and **Thomas Bailey** could both be related.

D. JAMES BAILEY AND HIS BROTHER WILLIAM

The second son, **James**, was in Hawkins County in 1830. He was in Van Buren County, Missouri, in 1840 and in Cass County in 1850, with **James B. Bailey**. **James B.** and other **Baileys** were in Cass and Jackson Counties in 1880; the in-between years are included in this chapter, too.

James is not in the Hawkins County land indentures. There was a **James** son of **William Bailey**, Senior, in his 1828 will. There was also a **James B. Bailey** who was the son of **David Bailey** in a 1879 will. Also, besides **William, Sr.**, there were two other **William Baileys** in 1830 in this county census. Maybe the **William Sr.** was the brother of **Henry's** son-in-law **David Bailey**. All of these **Williams** will be discussed under the **William Bailey** part of this chapter. Since **James** and **William** are together on page 36 of the census below, they are assumed to be brothers.

1830 Hawkins County Census
Microcopy FM 19 Roll No. 178, page 36

James Bailey. 1 male under 5; 1 m. 5-10; 2 m. 10-15; 2 m. 15-20; 1 m. 40-50.
1 female under 5; 1 f. 5-10; 1 f. 30-40.

William Bailey. 2 males under 5; 1 m. 5-10; 1 male 10-15; 1 m. 30-40.
1 female under 5; 1 f. 5-10; 2 f. 10-15; 1 f. 30-40.

There was one **James Bailey** in the 1840 census, but he was 20-30 years of age and was in Henderson County:

James Bailey. 1 m. under 5; 1 m. 20-30; 1 f. 15-20.

Then **James** and his brother **William** show up in Van Buren County, Missouri, census for 1840. **Robert** and **Pleasant F. Bailey** also were in the 1840 Van Buren County census. Van Buren was formed on 14 September 1835, and the name was changed to Cass on 19 February 1849. Part of the families settled in Van Buren, while other families were in Jackson County just to the north. **Martin Rice, Charles Rice, Elizabeth Lynch,** two **Ousleys, Theopholus Powell, William Jackson, Hiram Jackson, David Powell, Elijah Lynch, William Lynch, Elijah Jackson, Thomas Jackson** (living next to **James Bailey**), and **James C. Jackson** were in Van Buren in 1840, while the following were in Jackson County: **William Rice, Louis Rice, William Rice, Absalom Powel, John Powel, Joab Powel, Adkins Powel, Thomas Pilcher, John Dealy, Enoch Rice, David Dealy, William Linch, William Dealy, James Snow, John Snow, Archibald Rice** and **Michael Rice** (**Tates** were skipped.)

1840 Van Buren County Census
Microcopy 704 Roll 232, pages 131, 138, 146

				Township
Robert Bailey	01110010 - 1112001	P. 131		Deep Water
James Bailey	01110001 - 1010001	P. 138		Mt. Pleasant
William Bailey	00110010 - 1020001	P. 138		" "
Pleasant F. Bailey	10002000 - 1000100	P. 146		" "

The age categories for 1830 and 1840 census years are:
Under 5; 5-10; 10-15; 15-20; 20-30; 30-40; 40-50; 50-60; 60-70; 70-80; 80-90; 90-100; 100 and up.

The **Robert Bailey**, who is unknown to the compiler, had sons 5 to 10, 10 to 15, and 15 to 20; while his daughters were under 5, 5 to 10, 10 to 15, (2) 15 to 20. **Robert** and his wife were 40 to 50 years of age.

James Bailey, the son of **Patsy** and **David Bailey**, was 50 to 60, while his wife was 40 to 50. **James'** sons were 5 to 10; 10 to 15; 15 to 20; and his daughters were under 5, and 10 to 15.

The **William Bailey**, the brother of **James** had sons 10 to 15 and 15 to 20; while his daughters were under 5 and (2) 10 to 15. **William** and his wife were 40 to 50.

The **Pleasant F. Bailey** is, maybe, a son of **James**. He had a son and a daughter both under 5, and another male 20 to 30, and **Pleasant's** wife was also 20 to 30.

James and **Pleasant F. Bailey** are in the 1850 Cass census with **Wiley, James B., Wm. J. R.** and **Moses Bailey**. **Moses** was mentioned by the poet **Martin Rice** in <u>Rural</u> <u>Rhymes</u> and <u>Talks</u> and <u>Tales</u> <u>of</u> <u>Olden</u> <u>Times</u> (47). The **Wm. J. R.** is the son of **William**, in a biographical sketch (48) of **Mrs. Elizabeth Bailey**, the wife of **Wm. J. R. Bailey**.

<u>1850</u> <u>Cass</u> <u>County</u> <u>Missouri</u> <u>Census</u>
<u>Missouri</u> <u>1850</u> <u>Census</u> <u>Index</u> (40)
Accelerated Indexing System, Inc., 1976, page 13

<u>Name</u>	<u>County</u>	<u>Page</u>	<u>District</u>
Bailey, Pleasant F.	Cass	080	Being* 16
Bailey, Wiley	Cass	080	Being 16
Bailey, William J. R.	Cass	083	Being 16
Story, Mary J.	Cass	083	Being 16
Bailey, (M)oses	Cass	097	Being 16
Bailey, James	Cass	105	Being 16
Bailey, James B.	Cass	105	Being 16

* It was the 16th district; the word "in" had been crossed out and the word "being" written in.

<u>1850</u> <u>Cass</u> <u>County</u> <u>Missouri</u> <u>Census</u>
Microcopy No. 432, roll 395, Sixteenth District

<u>Name</u>			<u>Real</u> <u>Estate</u>	<u>Where</u> <u>Born</u>

(a) Page 80, line 35, household 307, family 307

Name	Age/Sex	Occupation	Real Estate	Where Born
Pleasant F. Bailey	39 M	Farmer	400	Tenn.
Janetty Bailey	36 F			Tenn.
Mary Jan Bailey	14 F			Tenn.
Owen M. Bailey	10 M		school	Mo.
Margaret C. Bailey	2 F			Mo.
Charlotte Rector	12 F		school	Tenn.

Name				Real Estate	Where Born

(b) Page 80, line 31, household 306, family 306:

Name				Real Estate	Where Born
Wiley Bailey	30	M	Farmer	1250	Tenn.
Nancy Bailey	25	F			Mo.
Elizabeth J. Bailey	3	F			Mo.
Nancy N. Williams	20	F			Ill.

(c) Page 83, line 12, household 344, family 344, 14th day of Sept. 1850:

Name				Real Estate	Where Born
Wm. J. R. Baily	25	M	Farmer	360	Tenn.
Elizabeth Baily	23	F			Ark.
Sarah M. Baily	3	F			Mo.
Wm. P. Baily	8/12	M			Mo.
Mary J. Story	12	F		school	Mo.
James P. Story	7	M			Mo.

(d) Page 97, line 38, household 534, family 538, 4th day of Oct. 1850:

Name				Real Estate	Where Born
Moses Bailey	33	M	Farmer	600	Tenn.
Mahala Bailey	32	F			Ky.
Mary E. Bailey	8	F		school	Mo.
Nancy M. Bailey	6	F		school	Mo.
Jeremiah Bailey	4	M			Mo.

(e) Page 105, line 46, household 649, family 654:

Name				Real Estate	Where Born
James Bailey	65	M	Farmer	400	N.C.
Mary Bailey	53	F			Tenn.
William Bailey	22	M	Farmer		Tenn.
Elizabeth C. Bailey	16	F			Tenn.

(f) Page 105, line 20, household 650, family 655:

Name				Real Estate	Where Born
James B. Bailey	24	M	Farmer	250	Tenn.
Elizabeth A. Bailey	26	F			Tenn.
Mary Bailey	3	F			Mo.

Pleasant F. Bailey's son Owen, was born in Missouri. Charlotte Rector, under Pleasant Bailey, was 12 and born in Tennessee. After the census schedules, the biographical sketch of Mrs. Elizabeth Bailey will be given. The sketch gives her maiden name as Storey, and that "....W. J. R. Bailey, who was born in Tennessee in 1825. He moved to Missouri with his father, William, in 1840."

Later the church and cemetery records on **Baileys** will be given. There are records also for **Rices** and many families; however, just the **Bailey** name will be included.

The Cass and Jackson County Court records have not been seen, but a **Wiley Bailey** married in Cass County in 1852: "Cass (Van Buren) County. **Mary Jane Rice** and **Wiley Bailey** were married 28 Nov. 1852." [37, vol. III, No. 3, September 1976, page 49, No. 616, "Reader Contributes List of **Rice** Marriages in Missouri," contributed by **Mrs. Doris Parker**, Pawhuska, Oklahoma.]

The **James Bailey** above, age 65, was the son of **Patsy Rice** and **David Bailey**; the **James B. Bailey** living next to him would be his son. Maybe **Pleasant F., Wiley**, and **Moses** also were sons of **James, William**, and/or **Robert Bailey**. **William** and **Robert Bailey** do not show up in the 1850 census reports above.

1860 Cass County Missouri Census
Microcopy 653, roll 612

Dolan Township, P. O. Morristown, 16th day of Aug. 1860

(a) Pages 108-109, line 36, line 1, household 757, family 757:

Name				Value of Real Estate	Value of Pers. Est.	Where Born
W. J. R. Baily	35	M	Farmer	1800	1000	Tenn.
Elizabeth	33	F				Ark.
Matilda	13	F		school		Mo.
Wm. P.	10	M		school		Mo.
Geo. M.	8	M		school		Mo.
Mary J.	4	F				Mo.
Sarah Baily	11	F		school		Mo.

(b) Page 109, line 10, household 759, family 759:

Jas. Correthers	33	M	Farmer	1400	400	Ind.
(wife and five children; on line 17 was:)						
S. C. Baily	17	M		school		Mo.

Mount Pleasant Township, P.O. Morristown, 17th day of Aug. 1860

(c) Page 110, line 31, household 766, family 766:

William Baily	32	M	Farmer	2200	500	Tenn.
Margaret	23	F	Wife			Mo.
Mary A.	5	F		school		Mo.
Florence J.	2	F				Mo.

(d) Page 110, line 35, household 767, family 767:

Name			Value of Real Estate	Value of Pers. Est.	Where Born
James Bayley	76 M	Farmer	1500	100	Tenn.
Mary	66 F	Wife	(cnrw)		Tenn.

(e) Page 111, line 4, household 769, family 769:

James B. Bailey	36 M	Farmer	2250	580	Tenn.
Caroline	28 F	Wife			Tenn.
Mary H.	12 F		school		Mo.
Clementine	10 F		school		Mo.
Abigail	8 F		school		Mo.
Darius	5 M		school		Mo.
Anna	3 F				Mo.

Big Creek Township, P.O. Pleasant Hill, 6th day of Sept. 1860

(f) Page 193, line 1, household 1355, family 1355:

N. Bayley	40 M	Farmer	10,000	2840	Tenn.
Mary J.	33 F				Tenn.
Mary A.	12 F		school		Mo.
E. Jane	13 F		school		Mo.
Wm. H.	9 M		school		Mo.
Geo. T.	6 M		school		Mo.
Eliza E.	5 M				Mo.
Chas. C.	1 M				Mo.

Big Creek Township, P.O. Pleasant Hill, 12th day of Sept. 1860

(g) Page 187, line 22, household 1586, family 1586:

Moses Baily	45 M	Farmer	4300	800	Tenn.
Mehaly	40 F				Mo.
Mary	17 F		school		Mo.
Margaret	15 F				Mo.
Jeremiah	12 M				Mo.
J. D. Skaggs	49 M	Farmer	5000	5000	Ky.
Mary	50 F		(cnrw)		Ky.
Jno.	15 M		school		Mo.
Maggie	12 F		school		Mo.

Pleasant Hill Township, P.O. Pleasant Hill,
15th day of Sept. 1860

(h) Page 221, line 19, household 1699, family 1699

Name				Value of Real Estate	Value of Pers. Est.	Where Born
Green E. Story	55	M	Farmer	18,000	3300	Ky.
Edy	48	F	Wife			Tenn.
Sarah M.	7	F		school		Tenn.
Nancy B.	4	F				Tenn.
Thomas Rice ?	2	M				Tenn.

The census takers spelled the surname **Bailey** here as **Baily**, and **Bayley**. The last part of this **Bailey** chapter has even more different spellings.

At the bottom of page 80 is a **William Baily**, who is 32. He is living next door to his father **James Bayley** and mother **Mary**. There is a **William**, 22, in the 1850 census under **James** and **Mary Bailey**. The daughter, **Elizabeth C.**, 16, in 1850, is gone.

James B. Bailey is still living next to the elder **James**. Now there are children, **Clementine**, 10, **Abigail**, 8, **Darius**, 5, and **Anna**, 3, with **Mary H.**, 12, who was **Mary**, 3, in the 1850 census. The wife of **James B. Bailey** is now **Caroline**, 28, instead of **Elizabeth A.** ten years earlier. This **James B. Bailey** is in the 1870 Jackson County census, which will be given later.

Both **N.** and his wife **Mary J. Bayley** were born in Tennessee. **N. Bayley** is 40, while **James B.** is 40 and **Moses** is 45.

Moses Bailey is believed to have gone farther west, for he is not found in the census for Cass and Jackson Counties after 1860. **Moses** is with **Pleasant F. Bailey** and **Pleasant's** wife **Jeanette**, as among the first members of Union Baptist Church, now Greenwood Baptist Church, in 1837. However, **Pleasant** and his family are not found in the census of Cass and Jackson in 1860 nor later. **Rev. Joab Powell**, one of the founders of this church and a relative of the **Rices**, went to Oregon in 1851. **Charles Rice**, the son of **James Rice** (grandson of **Henry**), also went to Oregon in another wagon train. So **Pleasant F. Bailey** may have gotten the "western spirit" along with other **Bailey** families later.

The family of **Green Storey** is related, for **W. (Wm.) J. R. Bailey** married **Elizabeth Storey** in 1844, March 17. **W. J. R. Bailey** is in the above Cass County 1860 census, and he is the son of **William** and grandson of **Patsy Rice** and **David Bailey**. One can see the transcript of the biographical sketch of **Mrs. Elizabeth Bailey** later in this chapter.

The **W. J. R. Bailey's** three children, **Matilda Rice, William P. Bailey,** and **Mary J. Myers** are in the 1880 census with the latter in the 1900 census as well. However, **W. J. R.**, who died March 15, 1880, was not found in the 1870 census for Cass nor Bates County, Missouri; nor was his wife found in the 1880 census, even though the sketch was written in 1883. Bates County was checked for 1870, because he lived in that County between 1853 and 1858 according to this sketch. **W. J. R.** moved back to Cass County and is in the 1860 census above; he moved around in the county to different townships.

Next is the 1860 Jackson County Census Schedule. Jackson County was named for **Andrew Jackson**, who visited the county when he was Governor of Tennessee in 1844. Then in 1845 **Andrew Jackson**, the seventh President of the United States, died. He served as President from 1829 to 1837. **James B. Bailey** is also in the Jackson County census in 1870 and 1880.

1860 Jackson County Missouri Census
Microcopy 653, Roll 625
Township of Blue, 13th June 1860, p. 71
P.O. Independence, line 13, household 551, family 492

Name				Value of Real Estate	Value of Pers. Est.	Where Born
William Baily	31	M	Farmer	(cnrw)		Mo.
Sarah	30	F		"		Mo.
William H.	9	M				Mo.
Thomas M.	5	M				Mo.
James A.	11/12	M				Mo.

This **William** has not been connected at this time with the rest of the **Baileys**. The **Baileys** below are related, except for **Una**.

1870 Cass County Missouri Census
Microcopy 593, Roll 767

(a) Pleasant Hill Township, 23 & 25 day July 1870, Page 18,
P.O. Pleasant Hill, line 6, household 111, family 111

					Value of Real Estate	Value of Per. Est	Where Born
Bailey, Wily	49	M	W	Farmer	15,000	1500	Tenn.
Bailey, Mary J.	43	F	W	Keeps House			Tenn.
Bailey, Thomas	16	M	W	At home	School		Mo.
" Ellie	12	F	W	" "	"		Mo.
" Charles S.	11	M	W	" "	"	(cnrw)	Mo.
" Wm. Henry	19	M	W	" "	"		Mo.
Adams, Mary	22	F	W	" "			Mo.

(b) Page 13, Township 45, Range 32, P.O Harrisonville, 21 Sept.
1870, line 24, household 104, family 104

Baily, William	41	M	W	Farmer	5000	1000	*		Mo.
" Eliza	26	F	W	Keeping House			*		Tenn.
" Mary	15	F	W	At Home	School				Mo.
" Jane	12	F	W		School				Mo.
" Columbus	9	M	W		School				Mo.
" Anna	6	F	W		School				Mo.
" Edward	2	M	W						Mo.
" Mary	74	F	W						

* Married within the year. This **William Baily** is in the Cass
County Census for 1860, with wife **Margaret** (page 80).

(c) Page 2, Township 45 Range 33, P.O. Harrisonville, 26 Sept.
1870, line 32, household 15, family 15

Bailey, Una	30	M	W	Farmer	6000	1000	Mo.
" Amanda	27	F	W	Keeping House			--

84

1870 Jackson County Missouri Census
Microcopy 593, Roll 781

(a) Page 109, p. 71 of Township 47 Range 31, P.O. Lee Summit,
1 July 1870, line 7, household 542, family 557:

						Value of Real Estate	Value of Pers. Est.	Where Born
Bailey,	**Jas. B.**	46	M	W	Farmer	4500	1100	Tenn.
"	**Mary C.**	36	F	W	Keeping House			Mo.
"	**Abby**	17	F	W	At School			Mo.
"	**Colman**	14	M	W	" "			Mo.
"	**Annie**	12	F	W	" "			Mo.
"	**Willie**	9	M	W	" "			Mo.
"	**Belle**	2	F	W				Mo.

(b) P. 40 of Township 47 Range 31, P.O. Lee Summit, 22 June 1870,
line 21, household 314, family 325:

							Value of Pers. Est.	Where Born
Bailey,	**C. C.**	28	M	W	Farmer	--	1000	Mo.
"	**Lee**	24	F	W	Keeping House			Ind.
"	**Emma**	4	F	W				Ill.
"	**Luella**	3	F	W				Ill.
"	**Libby**	10/12	F	W		(Aug.)		Mo.

William Bailey and **Una Bailey** were heads of families in 1870
in Cass County, with **Wily Bailey**. **Wiley** was 30 in 1850 in Cass
County; now he is 49 in 1870. He was not found in 1860.

William was 32 in 1860, with a daughter **Mary A.** age 5, and
Florence J., age 2. Now he has a daughter **Mary** 15, while daughter
Jane is 12 in 1870. This **William** appears to be the **William** age 22
in 1850 in Cass County under **James** and **Mary** Bailey. The **Mary** age
74 under **William** is his mother. This **William** is continued in the
1880 and 1900 censuses.

The **Una Bailey** in Cass County in 1870 is not connected as of
now. And the above **C. C. Bailey** also probably is unrelated
because his wife was born in Indiana and two of his children were
born in Illinois.

The **James B. Bailey** is assumed to be an older son of **James**
and **Mary**, and a brother of **William**. But it takes documents such
as wills, marriage licenses, Bible records, deeds, etc., to really
prove relationships. This **James** is continued in the 1880 Jackson
County census.

1880 Soundex Code System
and
1880 Census for Cass and Jackson Counties

a. **Cass County**. Your compiler found **Baileys** in Cass County in 1880, but not all were from Tennessee. Those that apply are given here.

1880 Soundex Code System
Microcopy T-758, roll 7, code for **Bailey**, B-400
B-400 through B-425

Name			Age	B.P.**	Vol.	E.D.*	Sheet	Line
Bailey, C.M.	W	M	40	MO	7	76	10	13
Bailey, J.A.	Wife		39	NC				
Reid, Mary	N.R.+		9	MO				

** = Birthplace; * = Enumeration District; + = "not reported."

(Cass County, District West Peculiar)

Bailey, Wm.	W	M	57	TN	7	83	6	2
Bailey, Eliza	Wife		36	MO				
Bailey, Edward	Son		12	MO				
Bailey, Frank	Son		9	MO				
Bailey, Vewter ?	Son		7	MO				
Bailey, Clara	Dau		5	MO				
Bailey, Lillia	Dau		3	MO				
Bailey, Julia	Dau		1	MO				
Bailey, Clementine	Dau		19	MO				
Bailey, Annie D.	Dau		16	MO				
Ross, Melanie	M*		56	KY				

* "M" is short for Mother, as will be seen in the regular census. **James Bailey** had a son **William**, age 22, in 1850.

Cass County, City Pleasant Hill
District Pleasant Hill

Bailey, George T.	W	M	26	MO	7	88	8	25
Bailey, Hattie	Wife		23	NY				
Bailey, Ella	G.D.*		1	MO				

* The "G.D." stands for granddaughter--which seems most unlikely in this instance.

There is a **George T. Bayley** in the 1860 census, under **N. Bayley**.

Next are the Soundex data for the families of **William P. Bailey**, **Isaac L. Rice**, and **Jacob Marion Myers**, all being children of **Wm. J. R. Bailey** and **Elizabeth Storey Bailey** and grandchildren of **William**, and great-grandchildren of **Patsy Rice** and **David Bailey**.

1880 Soundex Code System
same as above

(Cass County, East Dolan)

Bailey, Wm. P.	W M	30	MO	7	78	15	43
Bailey, Madona	Wife	25	KY				
Bailey, Gertrude	Dau	4	MO				
Bailey, Laura B.	Dau	2	MO				

1880 Soundex Code System
Microcopy T-758, roll 83; code for **Rice**, R-200
R-152 through R-200 I

(Cass County, Peculiar)

Rice, Isaac L.	W M	33	MO	7	84	5	46
Rice, Matilda	Wife	31	MO				
Rice, Charles	Son	9	MO				
Rice, George M.	Son	6	MO				
Rice, Walter	Son	3	MO				

1880 Soundex Code System
Microcopy T-758, roll 72; code for **Myers**, M-620
M-612, through M-625

(Cass County, West Dolan)

Myers, Jacob M.	W M	29	IN	7	77	7	20
Myers, (Mary) Jane	Wife	25	MO				
Myers, Jessee J.	Son	6	MO				
Myers, Bettie A.	Dau	4	MO				
Myers, Harry J.	Son	1	MO				

Then following the Soundex Code is the regular census, which has marital status, occupation, school and birthplaces of the mother and father; all besides given above in the Soundex.

1880 Cass County Census
Microcopy T-9, Roll 679, E.D. 76, Sheet 10
Line 13, household 93, family 93

Bailey, C. M.	W	M		40	Married	Farmer	MO	TN	TN*
Bailey, J.C.A.	W	F	Wife	37	Married	Keeping House	NC	NC	NC
Reid, Mary	W	F		9		School	MO	KY	-

* State of birth of (a) head of family, (b) father, (c) mother.

E.D. 83, sheet 6, line 2, household 39, family 45

Wm. Bailey	White,	Male		57	Married	Farmer	TN	TN	TN
Eliza	W	F		36	Wife, married, house-keeping		MO	KY	KY
Edward	W	M		12	Son	At school	MO	TN	MO
Frank	W	M		9	Son	At school	MO	TN	MO
Varotee ?	W	M		7	Son	At school	MO	TN	MO
Clara	W	F		5	Dau		MO	TN	MO
Lillie	W	F		3	Dau		MO	TN	MO
Julia	W	F		1	Dau		MO	TN	MO
Clementine	W	F		19	Dau	Single	MO	TN	MO
Annie	W	F		16	Dau	At school	KS	TN	MO
Melvina Ross	W	F		56	Mother, widowed		KY	KY	VA

This **William Bailey** seems to be the grandson of **Patsy Rice** and **David Bailey**, through **James Bailey**, and he was in Cass County in 1900. **William's** first wife was **Margaret**, with **Eliza** being the second. There were older children still. Please, do check the earlier census reports. But the children from **Edward** down to **Lillie** are gone, with **Julia** (age 21) still at home. Other children of **William Bailey** were in the 1900 census.

Then next are the census reports of **William P. Bailey, Isaac L. Rice** and **Jacob Marion Myers**, which are the families of descendants of **William Bailey**, son of **Patsy Rice** and **David Bailey** through **William J. R. Bailey** and **Elizabeth Storey**

E.D. 78, sheet 15, line 43, household 140, family 141
East Dolan Township, 16th day of June, 1880

Wm. P. Bailey	W	M		30		Married	Farmer	MO	ARK	IN
Madera Bailey	W	F		25	Wife	Married		KY	KY	KY
Gertrude Bailey	W	F		4	Dau	Single		MO	MO	KY
Laura B. Bailey	W	F		2	Dau	Single		MO	MO	KY

88

E.D. 84, sheet 5, line 46, household 40, family 41
Peculiar Township, 7th day of June, 1880

Isaac L. Rice	W	M	33		Married	Farmer	MO	MO	MO
Matilda Rice	W	F	31	Wife	Married	Keeping House	MO	MO	MO
Charles Rice	W	M	9	Son	Single		MO	MO	MO
George M. Rice	W	M	6	Son	Single		MO	MO	MO
Walter Rice	W	M	3	Son	Single		MO	MO	MO

1880 Cass County Census
E.D. 77, sheet 7, line 20, household 62, family 65
West Dolan Township, 1st day of June 1880

Jacob M. Myers	W	M	29		Married	Farmer		IN	KY	KY
Jane Myers	W	F	25	Wife	Married	Keeping House		MO	MO	AR
Jessee J. Myers	W	M	6	Son	Single	School		MO	IN	IN
Bettie A. Myers	W	F	4	Dau	Single			MO	IN	MO
Harry J. Myers	W	M	1	Son	Single			MO	IN	MO

1880 Soundex Code System
Microcopy T-758, roll 7; code for Bailey, B-400;
B-400, through B-425

Name			Age	B.P.**	Vol.	E.D.*	Sheet	Line
(Jackson County, District Washington)								
Bailey, James B.	White Male		55	TN	17	38	10	27
Bailey, Mary C.		Wife	45	TN				
Bailey, Abby L.		Dau	24	MO				
Bailey, Darious		Son	22	MO				
Bailey, Annie		Dau	21	MO				
Bailey, Dora B.		Dau	10	MO				
Bailey, Laura		Dau	7	MO				
(Jackson County, Lone Jack)								
Bailey, William	White Male		31	TN	17	38	9	23
Bailey, Mary M.		Wife	27	VA				
Bailey, Alice		Dau	2	MO				

** = Birthplace; * = Enumeration District.

No census seen from Soundex.

1880 Jackson County Census
Microcopy T-9, Roll 694, E.D. 38, sheet 10
line 27, household 117, family 118

Name	Color	Sex	Age	Rel.	Marital Status	Occupation	Birthplaces*		
Bailey, James B.	W	M	55		Married	Farmer	TN	TN	TN
Bailey, Mary C.	W	F	45	Wife	Married	Keeping House	TN	TN	TN
Bailey, Abby L.	W	F	24	Dau	Single		MO	TN	TN
Darious	W	M	22	Son	Single	Farming	MO	TN	TN
Annie	W	F	21	Dau	Single		MO	TN	TN
Dora B.	W	F	10	Dau			MO	TN	TN
Laura	W	F	7	Dau			MO	TN	TN

* See note on page 85.

This descendant was living near the poet **Martin Rice**, as **Martin** stated in his family "recollections." The **James B. Bailey** and a **William Bailey**, 31, who was residing in Lone Jack, were living in Jackson County outside of Kansas City.

1900 Soundex Code System
Microcopy T-1055, rolls 17 and 18; Code for **Bailey**, B-400
which appears on both rolls

Not all **Baileys** in the 1900 Soundex were noted--only those who were in the 1880 records and who were born in Tennessee or Missouri. **Baileys** born in Missouri were checked to see whether the parents were both born in Tennessee.

Baileys in Cass County

Name	Col.	Rel.	Birthdate	Age	BP.	Vol.	E.D.	sht.	line
(a)									
(Cass County, Pleasant Hill Township, Pleasant Hill Town)									
Bailey, Chas.	W		May 1859	41	MO	18	38	6	21
Bailey, Nannie		Wife	Dec 1861	38	MO				
Bailey, Ethel May		Dau	Sep 1881	18	MO				
Bailey, Lizzie		Dau	Jan 1883	16	MO				
Bailey, Ernest		Son	Nov 1890	9	MO				

According to this census record, a **William G. Rice** was living next door with a son **Martin Rice**, 2 years old.

Baileys in Cass County
Continued

Name	Col.	Rel.	Birthdate	Age	BP.	Vol.	E.D.	sht.	line
(b) (Cass County, Mt. Pleasant Township, Belton Town)									
Bailey, Ewing M.	W		May 1840	60	MO	12	35	12	1
Bailey, Arminda		Wife	Feb 1843	57	NC				
(c) (Cass County, Pleasant Hill Township, Pleasant Hill Town)									
Bailey, Thomas	W		Mar 1854	46	MO	18	38	15	21
Bailey, Hattie		Wife	Nov 1856	45	NY				
Bailey, Ella Grace		Dau	Jun 1879	20	MO				
Bailey, Edwin		Son	Feb 1888	12	MO				

There is a **Thomas Bailey**, 16, under father **Wily** in the 1870 Jackson County census.

Name	Col.	Rel.	Birthdate	Age	BP.	Vol.	E.D.	sht.	line
(d) (Cass County, Pleasant Hill Township, Pleasant Hill Town)									
Bailey, Wiley	W		Jul 1820	79	TN	18	38	4	6
Bailey, Mary J.		Wife	Nov 1826	73	TN				

This **Wiley Bailey** was in the 1850 Cass County census, and also in the 1880 Cass County census; he is assumed to be a son of **James Bailey**.

Name	Col.	Rel.	Birthdate	Age	BP.	Vol.	E.D.	sht.	line
(e) (Cass County, West Peculiar Township)									
Bailey, Wiley F.	W		–	–	MO	18	43	2	78
Bailey, Ada B.		Wife	Sep 1875	24	MO				

According to the corresponding census, this **Wiley F. Bailey** was living next to a Tennessee-born **William J. Powell** and family. The **Powell** could be a **Rice** relative, for two of **James Rice's** daughters married **Powells**.

Name	Col.	Rel.	Birthdate	Age	BP.	Vol.	E.D.	sht.	line
(f) (Cass County, West Peculiar Township)									
Bailey, William	W		Jun 1828	72	TN	18	43	3	11
Bailey, Eliza M.		Wife	Jul 1844	55	MO				
Bailey, Julia		Dau	Jan 1879	21	MO				
Bailey, Birtha A.		Dau	Oct 1881	18	MO				
Dempsey, Bailey**		G.S.*	Jan 1898	2	KS				
Dempsey, Frankline		GS	Apr 1899	1	MO				

** **Dempey** was the name used here, but **Dempsey** was in the 1900 census.

* G.S. = Grandson.

91

Name	Col.	Rel.	Birthdate	Age	BP	Vol	E.D.	sht.	line
(g)	(Cass County, Peculiar Township)								
Myers, Jacob Marion	W		Mar 1851	49	IN	18	36	2	77
Myers, Mary Jane		Wife	Jan 1856	44	MO				
Myers, James		Son	Aug 1881	18	MO				
Myers, Lucy Matilda		Dau	Mar 1884	16	MO				
Myers, Beula May		Dau	Jun 1886	13	MO				
Myers, Chas. Elliot		Son	Oct 1889	11	MO				
Myers, Mary Ellen		Dau	Mar 1891	9	MO				
Myers, John Lee		Son	Nov 1895	4	MO				
Myers, Carl		Son	Aug 1899	9/12	MO				
Myers, Harry Jackson		Son	Mar 1879	21	MO				

Mary Jane, the wife of **Jacob Myers**, is a daughter of **Wm. J. R. Bailey** and **Elizabeth Storey Bailey**.

1900 Cass County Census Schedule
Microcopy T-623, roll 846, vols 17-18 complete,
Carroll and Cass Counties
Cass County E.D.s 25 to 43

Name	Rel.	1.	2.	Birthdate	Age	Status	3.	4.	5.	Birthpl.*
(a)	E.D. 38, sheet 6, line 21 (Pleasant Hill Township & Town)									
	6 or 7 June 1900. Household 135, family 135									
Bailey, Chas.	Head	W	M	May 1859	41	Married	20			MO TN MO[a]
Bailey, Nannie	Wife	W	F	Dec 1861	38	Married	20	4	4	MO OH KY
Bailey, Ethel May	Dau	W	F	Sep 1881	18	Single				MO MO MO
Bailey, Lizzie	Dau	W	F	Jan 1883	17	Single				MO MO MO[b]
Bailey, Chas.W.	Son	W	M	Sep 1887	12	Single				MO MO MO[b]
Bailey, Ernest	Son	W	M	Nov 1890	9	Single				MO MO MO[b]

Explanation of columns:
   1 = color; 2 = sex; 3 = years married; 4 = children
   born; 5 = children living.
Other Notes:
   * = Birthplaces: State where person was born; state
      where father was born; state where mother was born.
   a = no occupation given; b = at school.
   There is a **Chas. C. Bayley** under **N. Bayley**. **Chas.** was
      one year old in the 1860 census.

1900 Cass County Census Schedule
Continued

Name	Rel.	1.	2.	Birthdate	Age	Status	3.	4.	5.	Birthpl.*

(b)   E.D. 38, sheet 6, line 27, household 136, family 136

Name	Rel.	1.	2.	Birthdate	Age	Status	3.	4.	5.	Birthpl.*
Rice, Wm. G.	Head	W	M	Feb 1861	39	Married 11				MO TN MO^c
Rice, Lucy J.	Wife	W	F	Apr 1876	24	Married 11	5	4		MO MO MO
Rice, Ethel M.	Dau	W	F	Jan 1893	7	Single				MO MO MO^b
Rice, Chester	Son	W	M	Apr 1896	4	Single				MO MO MO
Rice, Martin	Son	W	M	Nov 1897	2	Single				MO MO MO
Rice, George	Son	W	M	May 1900	0/12					MO MO MO

[The four children had their fathers' birthplace (center column) as Tennessee, but **William's** father (their grandfather) was the one born in Tennessee.]

(c)   E.D. 35, sheet 12, line 1, Pleasant Hill Township & Town
12 June 1900. Household 244, family 246.

Name	Rel.	1.	2.	Birthdate	Age	Status	3.	4.	5.	Birthpl.*
Bailey, Ewing M.	Head	W	M	May 1840	60	Married 40				MO TN TN^d
Bailey, Arminda	Wife	W	F	Apr 1876	24	Married 40	0	0		NC NC NC

(d)   E.D. 38, sheet 15, line 21, Pleasant Hill Township & Town
18 June 1900. Household 348, family 348.

Name	Rel.	1.	2.	Birthdate	Age	Status	3.	4.	5.	Birthpl.*
Bailey, Thomas	Head	W	M	Mar 1854	46	Married 23				MO TN TN^e
Bailey, Hattie	Wife	W	F	Nov 1856	43	Married 23	3	2		NY Can NY
- Ella Grace	Dau	W	F	Jun 1879	20	Single				MO MO NY^f
- Edwin	Son	W	M	Feb 1888	12	Single				MO MO NY^b

(e)   E.D. 38, sheet 4, line 6, Pleasant Hill Township & Town
5 June 1900. Household 83, family 83.

Name	Rel.	1.	2.	Birthdate	Age	Status	3.	4.	5.	Birthpl.*
Bailey, Wiley	Head	W	M	Jul 1820	79	Married 47				TN TN TN^g
- Mary J.	Wife	W	F	Nov 1826	73	Married 43	4	3		TN TN TN

Notes: See notes for the previous families.
c = photographer; d = landlord; e = corn grower;
f = teacher; g = retired.

1900 Cass County Census Schedule
(Continued)

Name	Rel.	1.	2.	Birthdate	Age	Status	3.	4.	5.	Birthpl.*

(f) E.D. 43, sheet 2, line 77, West Peculiar Township 7 June 1900. Household 42, family 43.

Name	Rel.	1.	2.	Birthdate	Age	Status	3.	4.	5.	Birthpl.
Bailey, Wiley F.	Head	W	M	Oct 1870	29	Married	6			MO TN MO[h]
- Ada P.	Wife	W	F	Sep 1875	24	Married	6	1	0	MO NC MO

(g) E.D. 43, sheet 2, line 79, household 43, family 44.

Name	Rel.	1.	2.	Birthdate	Age	Status	3.	4.	5.	Birthpl.
Powell, Wm. J.	Head	W	F	May 1863	37	Married	10			MO TN TN[h]
- Fannie E.	Wife	W	F	Apr.1869	31	Married	10	2	2	MO NC MO
- Ada P.	Dau	W	F	Sep.1890	9	Single				KS MO MO
- Josie J.	Dau	W	F	Apr.1892	8	Single				MO MO MO

(h) E.D. 43, sheet 3, line 11, West Peculiar Township, 8 June 1900, household 51, family 52.

Name	Rel.	1.	2.	Birthdate	Age	Status	3.	4.	5.	Birthpl.
Bailey, William	Head	W	M	Jun 1828	71	married	32			TN TN TN[h]
Bailey, Eliza	Wife	W	F	Jul 1844	55	married	32	7	6	MO KY KY
Bailey, Julia	Dau	W	F	Jan 1879	21	single				MO TN MO
- Birtha A.	Dau	W	F	Oct 1881	18	single				MO TN MO
Dempsey, Bailey	G.S.	W	M	Jan 1898	2	single				MO MO MO
- Frankline	G.S.	W	M	Apr 1899	1	single				MO MO MO
Pitts, Edward	Boarder	W	M	Nov 1876	19	single				MO KY KY[i]

(i) E.D. 36, sheet 2, line 77, Peculiar Township household 37, family 37.

Name	Rel.	1.	2.	Birthdate	Age	Status	3.	4.	5.	Birthpl.
Myers, Jacob Marion	Head	W	M	Nov 1851	49	married	27			IN KY IN[h]
Myers, Mary Jane	Wife	W	F	Jan 1856	44	married	27	10	10	MO IN AR
Myers, James	Son	W	M	Aug 1881	18	single				MO IN MO[i]
Myers, Lucy Matilda	D	W	F	Mar 1884	16	single				MO IN MO
Myers, Beula May	Dau	W	F	Jun 1886	13	single				MO IN MO
Myers, Chas.Elliot	S	W	M	Oct 1889	10	single				MO IN MO
Myers, Mary Ellen	D	W	F	Mar 1891	9	single				MO IN MO
Myers, John Lee	Son	W	M	Nov 1895	4	single				MO IN MO
Myers, Earl	Son	W	M	Aug 1899	9/12	single				MO IN MO
Myers, Harry Jackson	Son	W	M	Mar 1879	21	single				MO IN MO[h]

Notes: See notes for previous families.
h = farmer; i = farm laborer.

94

1900 Jackson County Census
Microcopy T-623, rolls 860-865

Name	Rel.	1.	2.	Birthdate	Age	Status	3.	4.	5.	Birthpl.*

(a)   Roll 864, E.D. 134, sheet 1, lines 82 and 83.

Bailey, David H. (He was under **Phoebe Johnson** as a boarder.)

	Boarder	W	M	Jul 1874	25	married	2			MO TN TN[j]
- Lillian	Boarder	W	F	Feb 1880	20	married	2	0	0	MO KY MO

William Bailey, son of **James** (not **James B.**) **Bailey** had a son
David, but that David's parents were both born in Tennessee.

(b)   Roll 865, vol. 47, E.D. 144, sheet 1, line 53
Jackson County, Kansas City, household 12, family 12.

Jones, Anna Bailey

Name	Rel.			Birthdate	Age	Status				Birthpl.
Jones, T. F.	Head	W	M	Aug 1860	39	married 13				KY KY KY[h]
- Anna	Wife	W	F	Aug 1862	37	married 13				MO TN TN
Bailey, Laura	SIL+	W	F	Apr 1876	24	single				MO TN TN

Notes: + - Sister-in-law. **Anna** could be **Annie**, 21, and
Laura could be **Laura**, age 7, both listed as daughters
of **James B. Bailey** in the 1880 records.

(c)   Vol. 47, E.D. 144, sheet 14, line 21, Washington Township.
28 and 29 June 1900, household 296, family 298.

Name	Rel.			Birthdate	Age	Status				Birthpl.
Bailey, D. C.	Head	W	M	Jan 1860	40	married	6			MO TN TN[i]
- Pearl	Wife	W	F	May 1874	26	married	6	4	4	MO MO MO
- James	Son	W	M	May 1884	16	single				MO MO MO[i]
- Corrie	Dau	W	F	Jun 1882	17	single				MO MO MO
- Lizzie	Dau	W	F	Oct 1886	13	single				MO MO MO
- Willie	Son	W	M	Oct 1888	11	single				MO MO MO
Stubblefield,-	Sist	W	F	Sep 1874	25	widowed				MO MO MO
- Hugh	Nephew	W	M	Nov 1896	5	single				MO NE MO

Notes: See notes for previous families.
j - groceryman.

95

1900 Jackson County Census
Microcopy T-623, continued

| Name | Rel. | 1. 2. Birthdate | Age | Status | 3. | 4. | 5. | Birthpl.* |

(d) Roll 860, vol. 41, Jackson County, Kansas City.
E.D. 20, sheet 6, line 49, Walnut Street, house 562.

Bailey, Susan Lodger W F Jul 1874 25 widowed 5 2 2 MO TN TN

[**Susan's** parents were both born in Tennessee; she is
widowed but was married 5 years and has 2 children. The
children were not living with her.]

(e) Roll 860, vol. 41, Jackson County, Kansas City
E.D. 20, sheet 6, line 49, Walnut Street, house 562

Bailey, Sadie

Lake, John H.	Head W M	Mar.1857	43	married	10			*Canada^k
Lake, Mary	Wife W F	May 1870	30	married	10	1	1	MO TN TN
Bailey, Sadie	STD**W F	Oct.1883	16	single				MO MO MO

Notes: * **John Lake** and his parents were all French
Canadians, with 1881 as the year of immigration to
the U.S.; 19 years in the U.S. and naturalized.
** Stepdaughter.

(f) E.D. 88, sheet 8, line 24, household 55, family 56

Bailey, George T.

Musselman, Parm H.	W M		28	single				KY KY KY^1
Bailey, George T.	W M		26	married				MO TN TN^1
— **Hattie E.**	Wife W F		23	married				KY NY NY^m
— **Ella G.**	Dau W F		1	single				MO MO KY

Notes: See notes for previous families.
k = hack driver; l = clerk in store;
m = keeping house.

96

E.   BIOGRAPHICAL SKETCH OF MRS. ELIZABETH BAILEY, PECULIAR
TOWNSHIP, CASS COUNTY, MISSOURI

In a rare book at the Library of Congress that has been put
on microfilm, there is a biographical sketch of **Mrs. Elizabeth
Bailey**, wife of **W. (Wm.) J. R. Bailey**, son of **William** and grandson
of **Patsy Rice** and **David Bailey**. The book is entitled The History
of Cass and Bates Counties, Missouri, etc. (41).

"MRS. ELIZABETH BAILEY

was born in St. Francis County, Arkansas, December 1827.
Her parents were **Green Storey**, a native of Illinois, and
Matilda (Hensley) Storey, a Kentuckian by birth. In 1837
the former moved his family to Missouri, and bought land
and located in Cass County. He was a thrifty farmer and
at one time the heaviest tax payer in this county. **Mrs.
Bailey** was married at her home in Cass County March 7, 1844,
when in her seventeenth year, to **W. J. R. Bailey**, who was
born in Tennessee in 1825. He moved to Missouri with his
father, **William**, in 1840. **W. J. R. Bailey** entered land and
improved a farm in Cass County directly after his marriage.
In 1853 he sold out and went to Bates County where he
improved another farm, on which he resided five years. In
1858 he sold his Bates County property and returned to Cass
County, cultivating a place in Grand River Township. In
1868 he disposed of this and bought the land now occupied
by his family and where he died March 15, 1880. This farm
consists of 100 acres of land, with a fair house and orchard
with a fine selection of fruits, and is located in section
14. **Mrs. Bailey** has five children living: **Matilda** (now the
wife of **Isaac L. Rice**), **William P.**, **George M.**, **Mary J** (now
Mrs. Jacob Myers) and **Andrew J.** Four are deceased. **Mrs.
Bailey** is a member of the Missionary Baptist Church, as was
her husband."

Peculiar Township is in the middle of Cass County. The
W. J. R. Bailey is according to the census **Wm. J. R. Bailey**. Even
though this biographical sketch was published in 1883, and **W. J.
R.** died in March 1880, **Mrs. Elizabeth Bailey** was not found in the
1880 census. **Matilda Rice**, **William P. Bailey**, and **Mary J. Myers**
were found in the 1880 Cass County census. The latter family was
found twenty years later.

F. BAILEY CHURCH AND CEMETERY RECORDS IN JACKSON COUNTY, MO.

The information here was compiled in 1933 and 1934 by the National Society of Daughters of the American Revolution, Kansas City, MO (42). There are many records on related names, but most of the data given here is on the Bailey name. These records are from 1826 until 1876.

From page 14:

"SIX MILE BAPTIST CHURCH
Section 7, Township 50, Range 30W
On the Blue Mills Road
It is also known that one of the early pastors was Rev. Joab Powell to whom Mr. Martin Rice in his `Rural Rhymes of Olden Times` pays tribute as an earnest and sincere preacher. His belief was of the Hardshell type...."

In Jackson County, at Greenwood, Missouri, Pleasant, and Pleasant's wife Jeanette Bailey were among the first members of Union Baptist Church, which later became Greenwood Baptist Church.

From page 33:

"UNION BAPTIST CHURCH
Now known as the Greenwood Baptist Church
Greenwood, Missouri
Union church was organized on the Saturday before the third Sunday in October, 1837 by John Jackson, Joab Powell and James Savage. The first members were Jerry Farmer, Eliza Farmer, Pleasant Bailey, Moses Bailey, Jeannette Bailey, and Mary Williams."

From page 43:

"WESTPORT BAPTIST CHURCH
Formerly called Big Blue Baptist Church
Minute Book II"

From page 47: November 5, 1874. Bro. Hiram Bailey elected
Treasurer."

From page 58:

THE BLUE SPRINGS BAPTIST CHURCH
Section 35, Township 49, Range 31 W

From page 63: (membership list)
"1867
James B. Bayley, by letter
Mary Bailey (James), by letter
Elizabeth Bailey (Shelton), by letter
Carolin Shelton (Bailey), by baptism"

According to the previous census schedules, James B. Bailey had a wife Elizabeth A. Bailey, 26, in 1850 in Cass County. Then in the same County in 1860, his wife was Caroline, 28. Then in Jackson County in 1870, James' wife is Mary C., age 36.

From page 70:   "THE FIRST BAPTIST CHURCH
                    Kansas City, Missouri
                    Organized 1855"
From Page 72:   "List of all members received
                    Elizabeth (Holmes) Bailey
                    Wm. Bailey
From page 73:   George W. Bailey
From Page 75:   Clara Bailey
Page 81   Deceased
                    Jan. 1869, Melissa Bailey"

Page 82   OFFICERS OF SUNDAY SCHOOL
                    Superintendent, W. H. Powell

Page 83   "Dismissed by letter
                    Miss Clara Bailey, Nov. 30, 1873, Statesville,
                    N.C."

Page 146   CONGREGATIONAL CHURCH GREENWOOD, MISSOURI
Page 148   REGISTER OF FAMILIES AND INDIVIDUALS IN THE PARISH
Page 149   Parents: Jesse W. Bailey, b. Oct. 5, 1827;
                             Mary Jane Bailey, b. May 31, 1829;
                    Children: Jesse W. Bailey, Jr., b. Dec. 28, 1853;
                             Mary E. Bailey, b. Jan. 6, 1857;
                             Alice Bailey, b. Oct. 3, 1858;
                             John Mark Bailey, b. Aug. 21, 1860."

Page 200   THE FIRST PRESBYTERIAN CHURCH, Kansas City,
                    Missouri

Page 201   "The first presbyterian church of Kansas City,
                    Missouri, was incorporated August 1, 1873, the
                    members being: Mrs. E. D. Bailey...."

            "Frank Taylor and **Fannie Bailey**
            July 4, 1872, by **Rev. W. Schenk"**

    "Holmes Cemetery, Kansas City, Missouri
Contributed by **Mrs. Mattie Stevenson,** daughter of
Silas Holmes; Silas Holmes came to Kansas City
in 1844 from Kentucky. He died August 15, 1855,
and was the first one buried in this plot on his
farm.
        Bailey, Alfred
        Bailey, Betsey, wife of **Alfred Bailey**
        Bailey, Alice, AGE 2-1/2 year
        Bailey, William, AGE 2 years....
These remains were removed to Elmwood Cemetery."

                "UNION CEMETERY
      LIST OF LOTS SOLD IN UNION CEMETERY
                1858 - 1873
    1869, Jan. 15, **M. Bailey,** block 55, lot 5
    1870, Sept. 17, **B. A. Bailey,** block 19, S 1/2
           lot 11"

                "UNION CEMETERY
     Copied from the tombstones by
      Mrs. Max A. Christopher and
         Mrs. Hale Houts

Bailey, Eddie, son of **Joseph** and **Emma Bailey,**
b. July 3, 1872, d. Nov. 1876."

           "LONE JACK CEMETERY
       SE Quarter Section _____
         Township 47, Range 29
    Bailey, Moses E. (father), born December 25, 1814,
      died May 1, 1897
Bailey, Mahala, wife of **Moses Bailey,** born May 6,
      1818, died January 19, 1868
Bailey, Oscar, born February 20, 1845, died
      November 11, 1890"

Page 394   "LEE'S SUMMIT CEMETERY
           Bailey, Jesse W., Sr., born October 5, 1817,
                died July 30, 1905
           Bailey, John Mark (father), born 1860, died 1929
           Bailey, Mary F. (mother), born May 31, 1829
                died November 18, 1914
           Bailey, Alice, daughter of **J. W.** and **Mary J.**
                Bailey, died August 31, 1877; age, 18 years,
                11 months, 3 days"

These are all the **Baileys** that were recorded for the years 1826 through 1876. Some of the **Baileys** might have gone west with **Rices** and **Powells.** But a lot of them did stay in Cass and Jackson Counties, as previously listed in the census schedules in this chapter.

G.   OTHER WILLIAM BAILEYS

There were three **William Baileys** in the 1830 Hawkins County census, but your compiler assumes that the one on page 36 of the census with **James Bailey** is the correct **William.** One of the **William Baileys** was a Senior. He was in Hawkins County in 1840 and 1850 census schedules. See subchapter D. for **William** son of **Patsy** and **David Bailey.**

1830 Hawkins County Census
FM 19 roll 178

Page 31, **William Bailey,**   2 1 0 0 0 1 - 2 0 0 0 1
         (2 males under 5; 1 male 5-10; 1 male 30-40;
         2 females under 5; 1 female 20-30)

Page 31, **William Bailey,** 0 0 0 0 0 0 0 0 1 - 1 0 0 0 0 0 0 0 1
         (1 male 60-70; 1 female under 5; 1 female 60-70)

1840 Hawkins County Census
Microcopy 704, roll 526

Page 258, **William Bailey,** 3 2 2 0 0 0 1 - 0 1 2 0 0 1
         (3 males under 5; 2 males 5-10; 2 m. 10-15; 1 m.
         40-50; 1 female 5-10; 2 f. 10-15; 1 f. 30-40)

Page 259, **William Bailey Senr.,** 0000000001 - 0100000001
         (1 male 70-80; 1 female 5-10; 1 female 70-80)

1840 Hawkins County Census (Continued)

Page 266, **William Bailey,** 0 0 0 0 1 - 0 0 0 0 1
(1 male 20-30; 1 female 20-30)

The **William Bailey** on page 266 could be a fourth **Bailey** with the same first name. Other **Baileys** in the 1830 and 1840 census schedules will be given later.

1850 Tennessee Census Index (39)
Vol. 1, **Aaron** through **Childress,** edited by
Byron and **Barbara Sistler,** Evanston, IL, page 64

"**Bailey, William,** 52, Sarah 48, Mary 21, Andrew 20, William 18, **Nancy** 16, **Robert** 14, Charles 12, Alfred 10, Chahaley 9, Louisa 5, T T, HW 159-809." This **William Bailey** and his wife **Sarah** were both born in Tennessee, living in Hawkins County. (Microfilm page 159, household No. 809.) This **William** is the only one in Hawkins County in 1850. This is the **William Bailey** who was 40-50 ten years before.

Hawkins County Deed Index
Register of Deeds, Deed Index - General - Vol. 1 (A-W),
1788-1884; Tenn. State Library & Archives, Hawkins Co. (12)
Roll 32, EX 13759, Title Register's Deed Index
Vol. 1-1, date 1788-1906

Year	Conveyors	Book	Page	Conveyees
1796	Bailey, Wm.	1	191	Jno McCarver
1795	Bailey, Wm.	2	221	Needham Lee
1792	Bailey, Wm.	2	62	Jos. Evans
1797	Bailey, Wm.	3	173	Ephraim Andrews
1818	Bailey, Jno.	8	1	Wm. Bailey
1821	Bailey, William	10	205	Carr Bailey
1823	Bailey, Wm.	10	323	John Ball
1819	Barnard, Jona	9	77	Wm. Bailey
1819	Bailey, Carr	9	164	Wm. Bailey
1836	Bailey, Elisha	15	439	Wm. Bailey
1836	Bailey, Wm.	15	441	Wesley Ball
1841	Bailey, Wm.	18	8	Thos. Ainis

There were **Baileys** in this deed index after 1841, as well.

H.   DAUGHTER BAILEY - WILEY TUTTLE

The first name of this daughter is unknown to the compiler. Although the name **Wiley Tuttle** was given by the poet **Martin Rice** as having married a **Bailey** daughter, **Wiley** is not listed with other **Tuttles** in the 1830 to 1850 census schedules. For **Wiley Tuttle** to have married a daughter of **David** and **Patsy Bailey**, he would have to be older and maybe the oldest son of **James Tuttle**.

1830 Census East Tennessee (35)
Transcribed and indexed by **Byron** and **Barbara Sistler**, 1969, Evanston, IL   page 144 index, page 33

Tuttle, James .... G - 365.
    [G = Grainger County; 365 is the page of the original census and microfilm.]
Tuttle, James, 0 0 0 0 1 0 0 0 1 - 0 0 0 0 2 0 0 1"
    [The younger son was 20-30, while **James** was 60-70. There were three women, two 20-30 and the oldest 50-60.]

1840 Grainger County Census
Microcopy 704, roll 525

Page 141, James Tuttle, 3 2 0 0 0 1 - 0 0 0 0 1
    [3 males under 5; 2 m. 5-10; 1 m. 30-40; 1 female 20-30]

Maybe the **James Tuttle** listed in 1840 is the son of the **James** listed in 1830, for the older **James** had a son age 20-30, and the 1840 **James** is 10 years older.

1850 Tennessee Census (36)
Transcribed and indexed by **Byron** and **Barbara Sistler**, 1974, vol. 6, page 255

"**Tuttle, James,** 45, **Mary A.** 39, **Thomas** 12, **John** 11, **Joseph** 10, **William** 9, **George** 6, **Sarah A.** 5, **Elizabeth J.** 3, **Rebecca C.** 1, T NC Cl*-800-589."

    *Cl = Claiborne County.

There were other **Tuttles** in 1850, mostly in Sumner County, but still no **Wiley Tuttle**. There were no **Tuttles** listed in Missouri in 1850, nor has the name been sought in 1860 for any state.

I.   OTHER BAILEY CENSUS RECORDS

1830 East Tennessee Census (35)
Byron and Barbara Sistler, 1969, pages 31 and 36

Hawkins County

Page 31,	Thomas Bailey,	0 0 1 2 0 0 0 1 - 1 0 0 0 1 0 0 0 0
Page 36,	Carr Bailey	0 0 0 0 0 0 0 1 - 0 0 0 0 1 0 0 1 0
	John Bailey	1 1 0 0 1 0 0 0 - 0 0 0 0 1
	Carr Bailey	1 1 1 0 0 1 0 0 - 1 1 0 0 0 1
	Thomas Bailey	0 0 0 1 0 0 0 0 - 0 0 0 0 1 0 1

The age categories for 1830 and 1840 (below) are: Under 5; 5-10; 10-15; 15-20; 20-30; 30-40; 40-50 (etc., all the way up to 90-100); 100 and over.

1840 Hawkins County Census
Microcopy 704, roll 526

Page 262	Lawson Bailey	0 0 0 0 1 0 0 0 0 - 2 0 0 0 1
	Andrew Bailey	3 0 0 0 0 1 0 0 0 - 0 0 0 0 1
Page 265	Stephen Bailey	2 1 1 0 0 1 0 0 0 - 2 0 1 0 0 1
Page 266	Samuel Bailey	0 0 1 1 2 0 0 0 1 - 0 0 0 1 0 0 0 1
Page 267	Stephen Bailey	1 0 0 0 0 1 0 0 0 - 0 2 1 0 0 1

1840 Anderson County Census
Microcopy 704, roll 517

Page 17,	Jesse Bailey	0 0 0 1 0 0 0 - 0 0 0 1
Page 16,	Thos. Bailey	2 1 2 1 0 0 1 - 1 0 0 0 0 1
	Sib. Bailey	1 2 1 0 0 0 1 - 1 0 0 0 0 1

There were many **Baileys** in the 1850 census, including **Sib Bailey** and others listed above. Also there were many **Bailys**.

J.   OTHER BAILEYS IN ABSTRACT OF TAXES (43)

There were **Baileys** and **Bailys** in nearby counties, as follows:

Bailey, Christopher	K - 1799 (Knox)
- Claudius	Ge - 1805 (Greene)
- Ezekiel	C - 1823 (Campbell)
- James	Ge - 1805 (Greene)
- Robert	A - 1805 (Anderson)

K. OTHER BAILEYS, DEEDS

Register of Deeds (12)
Deed Index - General, Vol. 1 (A-W) 1788-1884
Tennessee State Library & Archives, Hawkins roll 32
EX13759, Title Register's Deed Index, vol. 1-2, 1788-1906

Year	Conveyors	Book	Page	Conveyees
1797	Bailey, Thos.	1	211	Jos. Martin
1797	Bailey, Jno	2	312	Geo. Mattock
1805	Bailey, Thos.	4	75	J. Carter & Isham Lawson
1806	Bailey, Jno.	4	178	Jno. Gatlin
1818	Bailey, Jno.	8	11	James Tunnell
1817	Bailey, Carr	7	84	Ruben Barnard
1836	Conner, Wm.	15	454	Samuel Bailey
1836	Luster, S. D.	15	440	Elisha Bailey
1841	Jones, Dankel K.	17	529	S. Bailey & E. Jones

There were more **Baileys** after 1841, but I did not record them in Nashville. **William Bailey** left a will, which will covered in the next section. Nothing has been done to connect the various **Bailey** families with each other.

L. BAILEY WILLS

Hawkins County Wills (12)
Hawkins Roll 31 EX13758, Wills, vols. 1-2
Nov. 1797 - Aug. 1880, pages 42-43 and 517-518

Abstract of **William Bailey's** will, May 30, 1828, gives the following names:

Son, **William Bailey, Jr.** (100 acres of land, south side of Beed Creek
Daughter, **Franakey Luster**, wife of **S. D. Luster**
Son **James Bailey**
Granddaughter, **Jude Harman**
Aggy, Stacy, and **Betsy**, 3 heirs of **John Bailey**
Christian, Polly, Fields, heirs of **Thomas Bailey**

James Bailey Executor)
Witnessed by **Jno A. Rogers**)   **William Bailey** (Seal)
            Atn. Long   )
            Robt. Miller   )

Abstract of **David Bailey's** will, 6th day of July, 1879, lists the following names:

Son **James B. Bailey**
Son **John B. Bailey**
Daughter **Elizabeth J. Bailey**
Daughter **Rosaicah**
Daughter **Julia Ann**
Son **William K. Bailey**
Daughter **Sarah Willoughby**
Son **Francis M. Bailey**, Executor

Farm joining lands of **Joseph Bailey** and wife **Nancy**

Attest: **Branch Tucker**   )   **David Bailey** (Seal)
         Joseph Bailey   )

These two wills are the only **Bailey** wills in Hawkins County. Most **Baileys** in the Deed Index are connected with these **Baileys**, but there is no will of **Henry Rice's** son-in-law **David Bailey**.

M.   ELIZA BAILEY

Campbell County Marriage Register
Book B, 1868-1881, pages 46-47

In Campbell County an **Eliza Bailey** married **Jacob Weaver**. **Timothy Weaver**, a great-great grandfather on my mother's side, had a son **Jacob Weaver**.

"**Jacob Weaver** to **Eliza Bailey** - Issued 18th Oct. 1871. I solemnized the rites of matrimony between the above named parties the 19th Oct. 1871. **Ph. Shosshan, J.P.**"

N.   BAILEY PASSENGER LISTS

There are two books containing passenger lists; the first is by **John Camden Hotten** (44), and the second by **George Cabell Greer** (45) is the update of the first.

<u>1</u>. The names **Baley** and variations, listed by **Hotten**, follow:

Page 512,   **Baily**: John, Mary, Temperance, William.
                Baley: Ann, Lewis, Mary, Nicholas (2)
                          Temperance, Thomas, William (2)
Pages 513-514, **Bayley**: Ann, Charles, George, Henry, John (4)
                          Margaret, Richard, Wm.

<u>2</u>. **George Cabell Greer's** book has the names that follow:

Page 17:   **Baile, Matthew** 1656, by **Wm. Justice**, Charles City Co.
            Bailey, Anthony, 1656, by **Vincent Stanford**, _____ Co.
            Baily, John, 1643, by **Walter Aston**, Gent., Charles City
                Co.
Page 19:   **Baley, Wm.**, 1653, by **John Medston**.
            Baly, Richard, 1636, by **Robert Ho**.

Hotten's book has a "List of Immigration, 1623 of the Living and Dead in Virginia, Persons Mustered as Settlers, and Lists of Criminals."

The "Licenses to Go Beyond the Seas" for **Baileys** are cited next, with your compiler's abbreviations. Each list had date, place of destination, name of ship, name of the ship's master, oath of allegiance to the Church of England, names of the transported, and years:

Pages 82-83, 28 May 1635, "to Virginia, **Speedwell** of London, **Jo. Chappell** Mr. [Master], **Richard Baylie**, 22."

Pages 85-87, x Junii, 1635, "to Bormoodes [Bermuda] or Somer Islands, **Truelove** of London, **Robert Dennis**, Mr., **Jo. Baylie**, 18."

Pages 116-117, Ultimo July, 1635, "to Virginea, ye **Merchant's Hope**, **Hugh Weston**, Mr., **Henry Baylie**, 18."

Pages 119-121, 7 August, 1635, "to Virginea, **Globe** of London, **Jeremy Blackman**, Mr., **Margaret Bailie**, 20."

Pages 127-129, 2 September, 1635, "to Saint Christopher's, **William and John**, **Rowland Langram**, Mr., **Wm. Bailie**, 23."

The next part of **Hotten's** book is "The Living and Dead in Virginia," originally written by **Governor William Berkeley** in the 1690's.

Page 162, "A List of Names of the LIVING in Virginia, February the 16th, 1623."

Page 170, "Att West and Shirlow Hundred [Island]. **Nicholas Baley, Ann Baley**."

Page 171, "at Jordan's Jorney, **Temperance Baylife**."

Pages 179-180, "at the Plantation over against James Cittie, Lewis
      Baley, George Bayley."

Pages 189-190, "A List of the NAMES of the DEAD in Virginia since
      APRIL Last, February 16, 1623."   "...at James Cittie,
      John Bayley."

      The "Muster Rolls of Settlers in Virginia 1624" begins at
page 201.

Page 205, "William Bayley's Muster - William Bayley, aged 41
      years, in the Prosperous, in May 1610. Mary, his
      wife, aged 24 years, in the George, 1617. Thomas, his
      sonn, aged 4 years."

Page 216, "The MUSTER of Nicholas Baly. Nicholas Baly arrived in
      the Jonathan, 1620. Ann, his wife, in the Mameluke,
      1621."

      The final part of Hotten's book is "Patents Granted to
Settlers in Virginia."

Pages 270-271, "The Corporacon of James Cittie, In Hog Island,
      Mary Bailey, 500 acres, planted (by Pattent).

Pages 267-268, "The Corporacon of Charles Cittie, William Baly,
      100 acres by patent.:

Page 269, "The Territory of Great Weyonoke,
      William Bailey, 50 acres   )
      Temperance Baily, 200 acres)   by Pattent."
      Temperance Baily 200 planted)

O.   BAILEY MILITARY RECORDS

Since the **Bailey** name is numerous, many of that name and closely related spellings served in the early wars of this country. The French and Indian War or Seven Years War was not seen, but three **David Baileys** served in the American Revolution.

A.   Revolutionary War--Index to Military Service
Microcopy 860, roll 2 ANGI - BALLAN

1. **Bailey, David**
    Hazen's Regiment, Continental Troops
    Private   ¦   Private

2. **Bailey, David**
    Sherburne's Reg't, Continental Troops
    Private   ¦   Private
              Reference card
        Original filed under **Baley, David**

3. **Bailey, David**
    Clark's Illinois Regiment
    Virginia State Troops

These three were checked in the service records, without searching the units, to determine the states of origin, but these records did not give such data as states.

Revolutionary War Service
Hazen's Reg't, Continental Troops
A-Bi

Private; **Satterlee's Co.**
Col. Moses Hazen's Regiment
Enlisted Dec. 23, 1776
Casualties Des^d Apl. 17. 77"

The above **David Bailey** deserted on April 17, 1777. The other records were seen, but they were not believed necessary.

The DAR Magazine for May 1982 page 370 (vol. 116, No. 5) has the following "New Ancestor Record": "Bailey, **Thomas**: b c 1760 d a 1-12-1824 m (1) **Mildred Clark** (2) **Temperance Bailey** PS VA". To determine whether this **Bailey**, who served in the Revolutionary War from Virginia, is related to **Baileys** in South Carolina, the first step is to see the Ancestor Record at the DAR headquarters in Washington.

B. War of 1812 Service Records

David Bailey was determined to be too old to serve in the War of 1812. A **David Bailey** served as a private in "**Russell's** Separate Battalion" of mounted gunmen from Sept. 28, 1814 to Mar. 27, 1815. He joined up at Murfreesborough, but he appointed a lawyer in Madison County, Mississippi, to receive his pay.

A **James Harrison** served in the same above unit as a substitute for a **James Bailey**.

Since **David** had sons **Daniel**, **James** and **William**, they were checked. No **Daniel Bailey** served from the State of Tennessee.

A **James** and a **William Bailey** both served in the same unit. These may be the sons of **David**. There were several persons of each name who were in this war from Tennessee.

War of 1812 Index to Military Service
MC 602 roll 8, B-Bai

1. **James Bailey**
   3 Reg't (**Johnson's**) E. Tennessee Militia
   | Corporal | Sergeant |

2. **William Bailey**
   3 Reg't (**Johnson's**) E. Tennessee Militia
   | Private | Private |

The two were under "**Capt. Elihu Millikan's** Co. of East Tennessee Militia, Regiment commanded by **Col. William Johnson**." They served from "Sept. 20, 1814 to May 3, 1815" with service ending May 5, 1815." They served "7 months and 16 days." The Company Muster Rolls were dated Knoxville. **James** received $11 per month, while **William** received $8. The **William** was from Rhea County, while **James** was from Jefferson County. **James** received $82.86 ($82 and 86 cents), while **William** received $60 and 26 cents. Both were present and given 2 days travelling allowance of pay." Both men appointed attorneys to receive their payments for services.

"Know all men by these presence that I **James Bailey** of the County of Jefferson & State of Tennessee doth make constitute & appoint **James Buckhannon**....of the firm of **Buckhannon & Martin** my true and lawfull attorny for me...as may be due me from the United States for a term of duty performed... commencing on the 17th day of Sept. 1814 and ending on the 3rd day of May 1815...**Col. Johnson** Regt and in **Capt. Milliken** Company...."

110

The **William** appointed **Humes & Tryan** as his attorney from Knoxville, although **William Bailey** was of Jefferson County. The **Buckhannon** above was from Jefferson, also. Both of these documents for both soldiers were signed and witnessed by other people.

C. Mexican War

A **William Bailey**, who was 21, served from the state of Missouri. He was in "Co. I, 3 Reg't Missouri Mounted Infantry **(Rall's)**. Private ¦ Private." The private was in "**Capt. Lane's** Co., Mo. Mounted Vols." on the Company Muster-in Roll," which was dated "Jefferson BKS MO, June 12, 1847." "Joined for duty and enrolled: When, May 28, 1847; Where, Fredericktown MO." The horse was valued at $70 while the horse equipments were valued at $16 and 3/4 of 100.

Later he was in "**Capt. Haley's** Co., 3 Reg't **(Rall's)** Missouri Mounted Infantry."

The "Co. Muster-out Roll, dated Independence, MO, Oct. 20, 1848; with last paid to June 30, 1848."

This **William** could be related. **Wm. J. R. Bailey** was born in 1825 and was a little older. Independence is in one of two Missouri counties where the **Baileys** settled in the above census schedules.

D. Union Service Record for Civil War

Five soldiers with the names **James** and **William Bailey** were seen in "Index to Compiled Services Records of Vol. Union Soldiers Who Served in Organs from Missouri:" (Microcopy 390, roll 112, As-Bar." The names were written **Bailey, Baily,** or **Baley**.

1. **Union 1 or First Cavalry Missouri**
A-Ba, Microcopy 405 Roll 1

Baley, James
Co. M, 1 Missouri Cavalry
Pri ¦ Pri

This name was written **Bailey** in the service record. James "joined for duty and enrolled: When, Aug. 1, 1861; where: Bunkerhill Ills.; period: 3 years. Absent sick in hospital at Memphis, Tenn., April 21, 1863."

2. Union Missouri 8th State Militia, Cavalry
A-Bl, Microcopy 405 roll 198

Bailey, James B.
Co. G, 8 Reg't Mo. State Mil. Cav.
21 years, 5'11"
Muster-in Roll:
Born Marion Co., KY.
Enlistment Feb. 23, 1862.
Linn Creek; period, war.
Lt. Col. McClury   Muster-out Roll
Springfield, MO. Apr. 13, 1865
[Sick and absent as scout]

3. Union Missouri 9th State Mil., Cav.
A-Bo, Microcopy 405 roll 213

Bailey, William J.
Pvt, Co. K, 9 Reg't Mo.
State Militia Cav.
Age 23; Muster-in-Roll
Mexico, MO; July 10, 1863
When: June 11, 1863
Where: Mt. Pleasant, Mo.
Period: War.
Co. Muster-out Roll
Benton Rushes, MO.
July 13, 1865
Last paid to Aug. 31, 1863.
Clothing account.
Last settled: never.
Remarks: Discharged Nov. 27, 1864 on Surgeon certificate of
     disability.

4. Union Missouri Home Guards
B-Bo, Microcopy 405 roll 706

Bailey, James
Organization and duration of service
When: Aug. 5, 1861
Where: Lexington
Date of discharge: Oct. 19, 1861
Period allowed for 2 months 14 days
Total amount due and to be paid $40 69/100
Paid Aug. 29, 1865
Remarks: Taken prisoner at Battle of Lexington Sept. 19,
     1861.

5. Union Mo. Second Cavalry (Merrill's Horse)
A-Barl, Microcopy 405 Roll 33

Bailey, James
Where born: Canada
Mustered in: St. Louis

Since this **James** was born in Canada, his record is not given here.

Some of the above soldiers could be related. The Confederate service records have not been consulted, because the areas of Cass and Jackson Counties signed a statement that they were for the Union side in order to stop looting and other violence by the soldiers. The statement did not stop these ravages.

This is the conclusion, for now, of the military records and the **Bailey** chapter.

CHAPTER IX. MOLLY RICE - NATHAN WATSON
Chapter summary on page vii

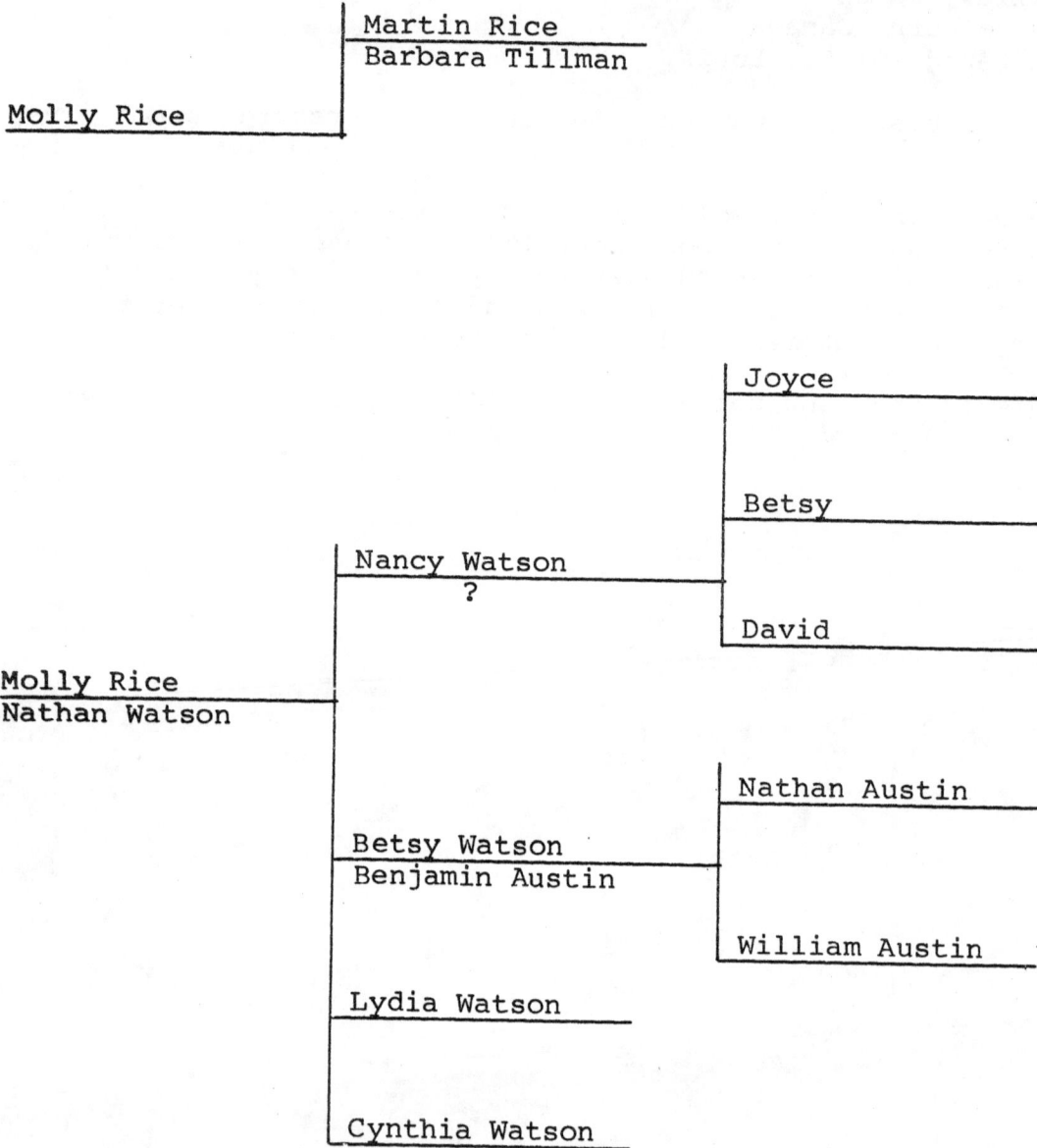

```
                         | Martin Rice
                         | Barbara Tillman
                         |
Molly Rice               |


                                              | Joyce
                                              |
                                              |
                                              | Betsy
                                              |
                         | Nancy Watson        |
                         |      ?              | David
                         |                     |
Molly Rice               |
Nathan Watson            |
                         |                     | Nathan Austin
                         |                     |
                         | Betsy Watson        |
                         | Benjamin Austin     |
                         |                     | William Austin
                         |
                         | Lydia Watson
                         |
                         |
                         | Cynthia Watson
```

114

CHAPTER IX. MOLLY RICE - NATHAN WATSON

Chapter summary on page vii

Molly Rice married **Nathan Watson**, but before she married, she had a child, **Martin Rice**. **Mrs. Nan Rice Shute**, a descendant of **Molly** through this **Martin Rice**, believes the father was a land speculator, in 1777. The father could have been **John Liscomb**, who made three trips through the Cumberland region. He wrote a journal with bad language, and stayed with **Henry Rice** during his travels. There was information in his journal about an expedition of officers and soldiers going through to the Cumberland Plateau in 1784. Most of the journal was not printed (15, pages 17-18).

The poet **Martin Rice**, in his recollections, put down the following about this **Rice** line:

"**Molly Watson's** only son and oldest child, **Martin Rice**, after whom I was named, was born before marriage and came to Campbell County at an early age. Married there, and about the year 1805 migrated to Preble County, Ohio, where he died, and some of his descendants are there yet."

The poet continues, "After marriage, **Molly** had four daughters: **Nancy Watson, Betsy, Lydia,** and **Cynthia**. **Betsy** married **Benjamin Austin**, and their sons **Nathan** and **William** were my schoolmates and playfellows. I was also well acquainted with **Nancy** and her children **Joyce, Betsy** and **David. Lydia** and **Cynthia** I never knew." (2, page 8).

A. NATHAN WATSON

Even though there are no legal documents on **Molly**, there are documents on **Nathan Watson**.

First, his name definitely was **Nathan**; this name is in the land deeds of **Henry Rice** as conveyee from **Henry**, and as a witness to several other deeds.

1. Tennessee Grant No. 599. This was a land plat and grant with the name of **Nathan Watson** on the plat. This grant is in the list of **Henry Rice's** deeds (see page 14).

2. This 200 acres was then sold by the pioneer gristmiller to son-in-law **Nathan Watson**. See the third deed on page 15.

Hawkins County, Tenn., Index to Deeds
Conveyor - Conveyee 1788-1861
Tenn. State Library & Archives (12),
Hawkins Co., roll 32, EX 13759
Title Register's Deed Index
Vol. 1-2 date 1788-1906; vol. 1 (A-W) 1788-1884

Conveyor	Year	Conveyee	Book	Page
Rice, Henry	1797	Nathan Watson	2	307
Watson, Nathan	1800	*	4	489

* When the second deed was looked up several years ago,
through an oversight the conveyee's name was left out.

3. Attestor of Deeds. **Nathan Watson** was the witness of two
Henry Rice deeds. One is from **Henry Rice** to **George
Maxwell**, in 1795. The second was to **Daniel Rice** in 1811.
The first deed was also attested by **Daniel Rice**. The
second deed was the mill land, and the second witness
was **Levi Rice** (see page 15).

Nathan Watson must have died before 1830, for his daughter,
Nancy, was head of the family in the Campbell County census for
1830, with five younger females listed in the family. **Molly** died
before then, as well.

B. MARTIN RICE

Two major books contain information about **Martin Rice**, son of
Molly. They are:

Rice Trails, 1717-1975 (46 , compiled by **Nan (Frances) Rice
Shute**, Bethesda, MD, 1975 (updated each year, but the 1975
    edition has the most information about descendants of
    Martin Rice).

Know Your Relatives (27), by **Genevieve E. Peters**, 1957 and
    updated 1972.

Nan Rice Shute's 1975 information will be summarized here.

"2.6 **MOLLY RICE**

= 3.1 **MARTIN RICE** b. June 18, [1777] in TN. d. Oct. 24, 1849 in Preble County, OHIO. **MARTIN** was the oldest child of **MOLLY** and was adopted by his grandfather, **HENRY RICE**. He m. **BARBARA TILLMAN** daughter of **TOBIAS** and **CATHERINE (SHARP) TILLMAN** on 16 November 1798 in TN. He went to Campbell County, TN at an early age, and about 1805 moved with **TOBIAS TILLMAN** and other members of the **TILLMAN** families to Harrison Township, near Lewisburg in Preble County, OH."

"The **TILLMAN/RICE** history cannot be separated so data and information has been extracted from the **History and Program of Lewisburg Area** for the sesquicentennial celebration, authored by **Seth S. SCHLOTTERBECK** of Lewisburg, in 1968." (46, page 75.)

Gordon Rice Little, fraternal twin of MWL, lives now in Kettering, OH, a suburb of Dayton in Montgomery County, just east of Preble County.

The **Turnbows** (2, pages 12-13) wrote:

"Adjoining and to the south of Land Grant No. 490 lived **Martin Rice**, the son of **James Rice's** sister **Molly** who later married [**Nathan**] **Watson**. **Martin** was a man of some merit and ability." They "lived at the present site of **Hord's** Mill, near Church Hill, in Hawkins County [TN]....From **Jeanette Acklin's 'Abstracts of Marriages,'**[1]/we learn that on November 16, 1798, Martin married **Barbara Tillman**, in Knox County." [Footnote [1]/ **Marriage Records of Knox County, Tennessee**, by **Jeanette Acklin]** (32)

Mrs. Peters, a **Sharp** cousin, gave the children of **Tobias** and **Catherine Sharp Tillman**, with the second child below: (27, pages 206-207.)

"2. **Barbara**, b. Oct. 29, 1778, d. Dec. 18, 1865; m. Nov. 16, 1798, in Knox County, Tenn., **Martin Rice,**[2]/ b. June 15, 1776, d. Oct. 21, 1849, in Preble County, O. **Martin Rice** is believed to have been the [grand]son of **Henry Rice** of South Carolina, one of the pioneer settlers in Big Valley, Tenn. **Daniel Sharp**, son of **Henry, Sr.**, was bondsman for the marriage. Their children were: (Quoted from Records of a Descendant, **Mrs. G. H. Savage**, Monticello, Indiana.)

(1) **Elizabeth**, b. Feb. 20, 1800, d. Darke County, O., Oct. 28, 1872, m. **John Nealeigh** on Dec. 19, 1816, in Preble County, O.
(2) **Tillman**, b. Jan. 24, 1802, m. **Mary Meroney** Dec. 27, 1827.
(3) **Nancy**, m. **William Gunder**, Aug. 2, 1821.
(4) **Henry**, m. **Sarah Lemon**.
(5) **Dicy**, b. 1809, Preble County, O., m. **John Collville**.
(6) **Temperance**, m. **Jesse Ozias**.
(7) **Jesse**, m. **Eliza Hapner**.
(8) **Hulda**, m. **Angie Tullos**, July 29, 1832.
    [These are all **Rices**.]

MWL's collaborator, **Nan Rice Shute**, had a list of the thirty people who went to Preble County in 1805 (46, 1975, page 76).

John Tillman, Sr. (age 101).
Tobias Tillman, son of **John Tillman, Sr.**
Catharine (Sharpe) Tillman, wife of **Tobias Tillman**.
Henry Sharpe and **Rebecca Sharpe**, aunt and uncle of
        Catharine Sharpe Tillman.
Frederick Miller and wife, **Elizabeth Sharpe**.
Alexander McNutt, son of **James** and **Mary (Sharpe) McNutt**.
Elizabeth (Tillman) McNutt, with children John McNutt,
        Eli McNutt, and Hiram McNutt.
*Martin Rice
*Barbara Tillman Rice, wife of Martin Rice, with children
        Elizabeth Rice, Tillman Rice and Nancy Rice.
Jacob Loy.
Phebe (Tillman) Loy, wife of **Jacob Loy**, with child **Job Loy.**
James Abbott.
Catharine (Tillman) Abbott, wife of **James Abbott**
John Tillman, Jr.
Nancy (Harless) Tillman, wife of **John Tillman, Jr.**
Many Tillman (later m. **John Simonton**).
Margaret (Peggy) Tillman (later m. **Isaac Nation**).
Jacob Tillman (later m. **Lydia Rinehart**).
Rachael Tillman (later m. **Moses Huffman**).
Henry Tillman (later m. **Permelia House**).
George Harless, brother of **Nancy Tillman**.
Harvey Medlam.
William Myers.
Labrechts.

There are many other records of **Martin Rice**, such as:

"The first election in Harrison Township was in 1816, at which time **Martin Rice**, son-in-law of **Tobias Tillman**, was made Treasurer and **Tobias** Overseer of the Poor, with **John Lock, Sr.**" (27, page 206.)

Also, **Tillman Rice** and other families appear in the 1850 Preble County, Ohio, census, given in the same book, pages 210 and 211.

Lastly, **Martin Rice** had three deeds in Claiborne County:

Claiborne County Index to Deeds

Grantor	Grantee	Instrument	Date	Book	Pages	Amount
Rice, Martin	Rice, James	Warranty Deed	1805	A	18-19	$450.00
Donaldson, Stokely	Rice, Martin	Deed	1800	A	184	20.00
Gibbs, David	Rice, Martin	Deed	1805	A	205	215.00

1. Claiborne County Deed Book A, p. 17.
   Rice, Martin, deed to **James Rice**
   28 September 1805
   $400 - 100 acres more or less
   in the county of Claiborne
   on the waters of Lost Creek
   Beginning on **Henry Rice's** corner
   Hill's branch to the low grounds
     on the lost creek
   Alexander McNuts line
   to **Henry Rices** line

In the presents of	:	
his	:	
Coonrod X Sharpe	:	**Martin Rice** (Seal)
mark	:	
Joshua Broct	:	

2. Claiborne County Book A, p. 215, Grainger County, 17
      October 1800.
   Deed from **Stockley Donelson** (to **Martin Rice**)
   $20 - 150 acres
   beginning on **James Rices** line

in presents of	:	**Stockley Donelseon**
James Rice	:	by his attorney
		James Adair

3. Claiborne County Book A, p. 205.
   Rice, Martin, Deed from **David Gibbs**
   27 December 1805 - $215
   100 acres be the same more or less
   North side of the River Clinch
   in Bold Valley on both sides of
   Lost Creek joining **Henry Rice's** survey
   Said **Rices** corner.

in the presents of	:	
Jesse Martin	:	**David Gibbs**
Alexander McNut	:	

Thus are summarized the three deeds; one was from **Martin's** uncle **James Rice**. **David Gibbs** is the son of **Johan Nicholas Gibbs II**, who is another revolutionary war ancestor of MWL. **Stockley Donaldson** was a land speculator who bought thousands of acres and sold for a profit. **David Gibbs** and **Alexander McNutt** are brothers-in-law of **Martin Rice**, for **David** married **Sarah Tillman**, the oldest child, while **Alexander** married the third child, **Elizabeth**. The **Coonrod** or **Conrad Sharp(e)** is an ancestor of MWL.

C. NANCY WATSON

Nancy Watson was the first of four daughters of **Molly Rice** and **Nathan Watson**. According to the poet, **Nancy's** children were named **Joyce**, **Betsey**, and **David**.

Nancy Watson was in the 1830 census of Campbell County.

1830 Campbell County Tennessee Census
F.M. 19, roll 178

P. 233. **Nancy Watson.** No males - 0 1 2 2 0 0 1.
(1 female 5-10; 2 females 10-15; 2 females 15-20;
1 female 40-50.)

The poet recalled that **Molly Rice Watson** had four daughters:
Nancy, Betsy, Lydia and **Cynthia.** Three of the five females under
Nancy could be her sisters, **Betsy, Lydia** and **Cynthia.** The other
two would be her own daughters **Joyce** and **Betsy.** However, **Nancy's**
son **David** is missing. Maybe **Nancy** and **David** are in Gibson County
in 1840. **Nancy** is the only **Nancy Watson** in 1840 in the entire
state of Tennessee.

1840 Gibson County Census
Microcopy 704, Roll 521

Page 205. **Nancy Watson,** no males; 1 female 50-60.
Page 207. **David Watson,** 1 male 20-30; 1 female under 5;
1 female 20-30.

There were eight **David Watsons** in 1850, but only one in
Gibson County. **Nancy** is not in the 1850 census.

1850 Gibson County Census
1850 Tennessee Census Index
Vol. 7, Walland through Zumbro, page 17
Byron and **Barbara Sistler,** 1975. Evanston, Ill. (47)

"**Watson, David,** 34, **Catherine** 45, **Margaret** 14, **Emeline** 9,
Peter 6, **Henry** 3, **Pinkney** 6/12, T NC, G-2281-577." [The
number 2281 is the household, while 577 is the microfilm
page.]

At this time the **Watsons** have to be researched in the court
records of Gibson County at the Tennessee State Library and
Archives. This is necessary to be sure that the names are in the
marriage register, etc., in order to trace them to Gibson County
and to and beyond the 1850 census schedules.

D. OTHER WATSON AND AUSTIN DOCUMENTS

1. There was a **William Watson** who had land granted to him in the Watauga Purchase. **William** could be the father of **Nathan Watson**, for he had land with **Henry Rice** on Sinking Creek.

     a. Tennessee Land Grant Office
       Watauga Settlement.
       Watson, William - N.C. Grant 152
       300 A, Oct. 24, 1782
       Watauga Book pp. 492-93.
       On Sinking Creek
       Robert Young's line
       Joseph Denton's line.

     b. 1805 Anderson County Tax List (43, pages 205, 206-207).

       William Watson.

Other **Watson** names appearing in the tax lists in eastern Tennessee counties were:

Watson, Andrew	Gr - 1821 (Grainger)	
Watson, Archibald	Su - 1797, 1812 (Sullivan)	
Watson, David	Gr - 1804, 1805, 1821	
Watson, Elijah	Su - 1812	
Watson, James	Bo - 1800, 1801 (Blount)	
Watson, John	Su - 1797	
Watson, Mary joining **Baker**, Su - 1812		

["Joining Baker" may mean that a **Mr. Baker** lived next door.]

Watson, Robert	Gr - 1804, 1805	
Watson, Samuel, Rev.	Wa - 1819 (Washington)	
Watson, Thomas	Gr - 1805	
	Ge - 1805, 1812 (Greene)	

Then there were the following **Austins** in the same early tax list.

Austin, Archibald	Je - 1800, 1822 (Jefferson)	
Austin, Benjamin	Wa - 1819 (Washington)	
Austin, Benjamin	Ca - 1823 (Campbell)	
Austin, John	Cl - 1803 (Claiborne)	
Austin, Joseph	Je - 1822	
Austin, Landers	Gr - 1799	

```
Austin, Nathaniel,          Ge - 1812, Cl - 1802
Austin, Nathaniel, Gen.     Cl - 1802
Austin, Robert              Gr - 1799, Gr - 1821
Austin, Samuel              Wa - 1819
Austin, Stephen             Gr - 1799
Austin, Thomas              Cl - 1803
Austin, William             Je - 1822
Auston, Nathaniel           Gr - 1799 (2)
Auston, William, Jr.        Gr - 1799
```

The **Benjamin Austin** in Campbell County could be the one who married **Betsy**, daughter of **Nathan** and **Molly Watson**. There were also, in 1799 in Grainger, two **Nathaniel Austons**, and one **William, Jr.**, in the same tax list.

     c. **Watson** Land Indentures.

The deed indices have been seen for Claiborne and Knox Counties for **Watsons** but not for **Austins**.

Claiborne County Deed Index

Grantor	Grantee	Book	Page	Date	Description
Yancy, Robert	James Watson	A-1	391		17,895 acres

Knox County Deed Index

Grantor	Grantee	Book	Page	Date	Description
Watson, Josiah	John Love	A-1	342	1795	
Watson, Josiah	John Love	A-1	366	1795	
Watson, Josiah	James Watson	E-1	193	1798	
Watson, Josiah	William Cobb	F-1	201	1799 (1800)	[several tracts *[Big Valley
Watson, Josiah	William Cobb	F-1	203	1799 (1800)	[Little Buffalo [Creek
Watson, Josiah	Robert Burton et al	F-1	257	1798 (1800)	
Watson, Josiah (by atty.)	Robert Houston	F-1 (vol.2)	167	1800 (1801)	

Watson, James	Jonas Potts et al	L-1	82	1802 (1805)	
Watson, Josiah and Jane	Walter S. Chandler	L-1	111	1800 (1805)	
Watson, Josiah and Jane	Robert Burton	E-2 (vol.1)	289	1808 (1823)*	
Burton, Robert	Josiah Watson	E (vol.1)	200	1796 (1798)	190,000 A. Powells Valley & Clinch River
Burton, Robert	Josiah Watson	E (vol.1)	203	1798 (1798)	190,000 A. Clinch River

* The first date is the written date, and the second is the date when recorded in court records.

1810 Grainger County Census
McClung Historical Collection Special Studies
No. 1, Grainger County, Tennessee Federal
Census Population Schedule (Third Census
and County Tax Lists for 1810)
Pollyanna Creekmore, 1956 (13)

Page 6. **David Watson**, 2 males under 5; 1 male 5-10; 1 male 15-20 1 male 20-30; 3 females under 5; 1 female 10-15.
Page 6. **Robert Watson**, 1 male 15-20, 1 female 5-10.
Page 13, **William Watson**, 2 males under 5; 1 male 15-20; 1 female under 5; 1 female 10-15.

An older **William Watson** had land in the Watauga Settlement and is assumed to be **Nathan's** father. Maybe, all the above are brothers of **Nathan**.

The David Watson, above, could be the son of **Nancy** and grandson of **Nathan** and **Molly Watson**.

E. OTHER WATSONS IN THE 1830 and 1840 CENSUS SCHEDULES

1830 Census East Tennessee
(Byron Sistler, pages 199-200) (35)

Page 15,	Watson, Eliazear,	Carter Co.,	10001-1001
Page 115,	Watson, Azariah,	Claiborne Co.,	001001-00100001
Page 370,	Watson, David	Grainger Co.	00020001-00212001
	Watson, William	"	10101-10001
Page 385,	Watson, Samuel	"	10001-00001
Page 389,	Watson, Sarah	"	1011-0110001
Page 395,	Watson, Andrew	"	210001-10000101
Page 400,	Watson, Thomas	"	000100001-00000101
	Watson, Thomas	"	00001-00001
Page 184,	Watson, Washington,	Greene Co.	10011-10001
Page 337,	Watson, James	Knox Co.	20032-10001
Page 226,	Watson, Catherine,	Washington Co.	0-000000001
Page 256,	Watson, Christianna,	"	00022-00010001

1840 Census East Tennessee Counties
Microcopy 704, rolls as footnoted

Page 124,	Watson, James	Blount Co.	10001-10001[1]/
Page 172	Watson, Elizor	Carter Co.	101001-120001[2]/
Page 302,	Watson, William	Campbell Co.	10001-0001[2]/
Page 239,	Watson, William	Claiborne Co.	10001-0001[2]/
Page 217,	Watson, Asariah	"	0000001-000000001[2]/
Page 101,	Watson, Thomas	Grainger Co.	000000001-0000001010[3]/
	Watson, Thomas Jr.	"	210001-120001
Page 102,	Watson, Godwin	"	00001-30001
Page 105,	Watson, Harden	"	20001-1001
	Watson, Sarah	"	001-0001001
	Watson, Samuel	"	011001-110001
Page 110,	Watson, David	"	000000001-10001
Page 226,	Watson, Pleasant	"	10001-00001
	Watson, Robert W.	"	01001-20101
	Watson, William	"	111001-101011
Page 297,	Watson, Andrew	Jefferson Co.	2111001-0110010010[4]/
Page 003	Watson, John	Knox Co.	00001-00001[5]/
Page 236,	Watson, Isaac	Washington Co.	00001-201010[6]/

[1]/ Roll 517. [2]/ Roll 518.
[3]/ Roll 525. [4]/ Roll 526.
[5]/ Roll 527. [6]/ Roll 535.

The age categories for both 1830 and 1840 censuses are:

"un. 5; 5-10; 10-15; 15-20; 20-30; 30-40; 40-50; 50-60; 60-70; 70-80; 80-90; 90-100; 100+."

Lastly, there are many **Watsons** in the 1850 census schedule, so it is not feasible to list them here.

F. THE WATSON ORIGIN IN THE VIRGINIA PASSENGER LISTS

There were many **Watsons** who came over to Virginia, and probably to other states.

a. The Original Lists of Persons of Quality, edited by **John Camden Hotten** (44). [This list also had oaths of allegiance to the Crown and the Church of England, which are not included here. The abbreviation "Mr." refers to the "Master" of each ship, and the name of the ship is underlined.]

Page 36, "(Secundo Januarii, 1634), to Virginia, Secundo Januarii, ye Mercht. Bonaventure, **James Ricoste**, Mr., **Jo. Watson**."

Page 50, "Licenses to Go Beyond the Seas, 3 April 1635, at Gravesend, transported to St. Christophus, Paul, of London, **Jo. Acklin**, Mr., **Tho. Watson, Abram Watson**."

Pages 73-74, "2 May, 1635, ye Barbadoes, Alexander, **Capt. Burke**, and **Gilbert Grimes**, Mr., **Nicholas Watson**, 26."

Page 80, "21 May 1635, to St. Christophers, Mathew of London, **Richard Goodladd**, Mr., **Christopher Watson**, 31."

Pages 82-83, "28 May, 1635, to Virginea, Speedwell, of London, **Jo. Chappell**, Mr., **Jo. Watson**, 22."

Pages 85-87, "X Junii, 1635, to Bormoodes or Somer Islands, Truelove of London, **Robert Dennis**, Mr., **Francis Watson**, 16."

Pages 101-103, "4 July 1635, to Virginea, Transport of London, **Edward Walker**, Mr., **Wm. Watson**, 24, **Margaret Watson**, 18."

Pages 119-21, "7 August 1635, to Virginea, Globe of London, **Jeremy Blackman**, Mr. **Abram Watson**, 16."

Pages 121-22, "10 August, 1635, to Virginea, Safety, John Graunt, Mr., **Nicho. Watson**, 16."

Page 124, "21 August, -- , to Virginea, George, **Jo. Severne**, Mr., **Alice Watson**, 30."

Page 169, "**The Living and Dead in Virginia. A List of Names of the LIVING in Virginia, February the 16th, 1623.** Living att ye Colledg Land, **John Wattson.**"

Page 172, "The rest at West and Shirlow Hundred Island, **James Wattson.**"

Page 201, "**Muster Rolls of Settlers in Virginia.** 1624. The MUSTER of Inhabitants of the Colledge Land in Virginia, taken the 23rd of January, 1624, **John Watson** came in the William and Thomas."

Page 207, "The MUSTER of **Mrs. Mary Maddison**, a widow. **James Watson**, aged 20 years, in the George, 1623."

Page 256, "**Mr. Stockton**, his MUSTER. Servants, **John Watson**, aged 24, in the Swan, 1624."

b. **George Cabell Greer** listed a number of **Watsons** in his **Early Virginia Immigrants** (45, pages 346-347).

Watson, Marg., 1653, by **Corbet Piddle**, Northumberland Co.
Watson, Art., 1653, by **Robert Woodey**, Lower Norfolk Co.
Watson, Nicho., 1653, by **Capt. Robt. Abrahal**, York Co.
Watson, Ann, 1653, by **Francis Hale**, _____ Co.
Watson, Alexander, 1653, by **Mr. Wm. Hoccoday**, York Co.
Watson, Joane, 1651, by **Robert Holt**, James City Co.
Watson, Tho., 1653, by **Tho. Keene**, Northumberland Co.
Watson, John, 1652, by **Littleton Scarburg**, _____ Co.
Watson, Andrew, 1653, by **Joseph Hogkinson**, Lower Norfolk Co.
Watson, James, 1653, by **Wm. Knott**, Surry Co.
Watson, Geo., 1653, by **John King**, Surry Co.
Watson, Mary, by **James Watson** (her husband), Isle of Wight Co.
Watson, Richard, 1652, by **John Wareham**, Northumberland Co.
Watson, Alice, 1654, by **John Watson** and **John Bognall**, Westmoreland Co.
Watson, Eliz., 1654, by **Robert Hubard**, Westmoreland Co.
Watson, Samuel, 1635, by **Christopher Stoakes**, Elizabeth Co.
Watson, Isaac, 1656, by **Tho. Merredith**, New Kent Co.
Watson, Richard, 1649, by **Edmund Scarburgh, Jr.**, Northampton Co.

Watson, Jeffery, 1649, by **Tho. Dale**, _____ Co.
Watson, John, 1648, by **James Mason**, James City Co.
Watson, Arthur, 1649, by **John Sibsey**, Lower Norfolk Co.
Watson, Henry, 1645, by **Mr. Robt. Eyers**, _____ Co.
Watson, Richard, 1649, by **Capt. Ralph Wormeley**, _____ Co.
Watson, Alin, 1655, by **George Truett**, Northampton Co.
Watson, Abraham, 1650, by **Tho. Tilsley**, James City Co.
Watson, Eliz., 1635, by **Jon. Watson** (her husband), _____ Co.
Wattson, **Wm.**, 1654, by **Col. Hump. Higgenson, Esq.**, and
        Abraham Moone, Westmoreland Co.
Wattson, Nicholas, 1640, by **Thomas Causey**, _____ Co.

G. BETSY WATSON - BENJAMIN AUSTIN

The poet **Martin Rice** wrote that, after they were married **Benjamin** and **Betsy Austin** had sons **Nathan** and **William Austin**.

Austin is still a name that is very common. **Austins** are in the abstracted tax lists, census schedules, and early passenger lists.

Betsy Watson, **Nancy Watson's** sister, married **Benjamin Austin** after 1830, for she appears to be one of five females under **Nancy Watson** at that time. The courthouse marriage register has not been seen for the date, and there is only one **Benjamin Austin** in Tennessee in the 1840 and 1850 Hardin County census; **Benjamin Austin** was 63 in 1850. Then the **Nancy Watson** who was in Gibson County in 1840 by herself, was 40-50. Or, the family could have moved to another state.

Benjamin Austin was in the 1823 tax list of Campbell County, and a **Benjamin Austin** was in Washington County four years earlier, in 1819. See Part D of this chapter for tax lists.

H. AUSTINS IN THE 1830 AND 1840 CENSUSES IN EAST TENNESSEE

1830 Census, East Tennessee Index
(Sistler, 35, Page 7)

Page 29,	Austin, Edward	Carter Co.		1000100001-000200001
	Austin, Joseph	"		01001-40001
Page 20,	Austin, Clisbe	Hawkins Co.		11001-12001
Page 282,	Austin, Champness W.,	Jefferson Co.		100001-10001
	Austin, William	"		000001-20001

```
Page 288,  Austin, Archabald, Jr. Jefferson Co.     10001-11001
           Austin, Archey Sr.          "          000000001-00001001
Page 293,  Austin, Joseph              "            1011001-221001
Page 104,  Austin, Nathaniel   Sevier Co.           000001-0
```

1840 East Tennessee Counties
Microcopy 704, rolls 525[1] and 527[2]

```
Page 104,  Austin, William   Grainger Co. [1]      110101-1020001
Page 141,  Austin, Elisha          "          0111010001-3211010001
Page 5,    Austin, Mary     Knox Co. [2]              0-00001
```

The age categories for both 1830 and 1840 are: "un. 5; 5-10; 10-15; 15-20; 20-30; 30-40; 40-50; 50-60; 60-70; 70-80; 80-90; 90-100; 100+."

I. AUSTIN PASSENGER LISTS

a. **John Camden Hotten** edited a passenger book in 1874 (44) that has early settlers. Here are the names **Austin** and **Austine**; the entries have been summarized, leaving off here the oaths of allegiance to the Crown and the Church. The word "Mr." is an abbreviation for the "Master" of each ship below.

Pages 82-83, "28 May, 1635. Theis under written names are to be transported to Virginea, imbarqued in the Speedwell, of London, **Jo. Chappell**, Mr., **Edward Austin**."

Pages 117-118, "1 August, 1635, Elizabeth of London, **Christopher Browne**, Mr., **Jo. Austin**."

Pages 169, 173-4, "The Living and Dead in Virginia. A List of Names of the LIVING in Virginia, February the 16th, 1623." "Living at James Citie, and with the corporation thereof, **Robert Austine**."

Page 364, "Tickets Granted, August 2[d], 1679, **Katherine Davies**, a servant belonging to **John Austin**, in the Ship Young William, for Virginia, **Thomas Cornish**, Comander."

In **Hotten's** book there were mentioned, also, **Austin** and **Austine** as prisoners deported to Bermuda and St. Christophers, with other people transported to the same islands; also baptismal records of **Austins** in Bermuda. However, since these records did not have to do with Virginia, they are not included here. But some of these persons later came to the continent.

b. **George Cabell Greer**, (45, page 16) listed one **Austen** and wife, several **Austins** and **Austines**, and two **Austons**:

Austen, Tho., and wife, 1654, by **Wm. Lea**, Charles River Co.
Austin, Richard, 1638, by **John Watkins**, James Cittie Co.
Austin, James, 1650, by **Mrs. Frances Townsland** (widow), Northumberland Co.
Austin, Richard, 1654, by **Wm. Lea**, Charles City Co.
Austin, John, 1654, by **Wm. Lea**, Charles City Co.
Austin, Thos., wife and two children, 1642, **Bertram Hobert**, _____ Co.
Austin, Geo., 1643, by **Capt. Samuell Mathews**, Esq., _____ Co.
Austin, Geo., 1643, by **Capt. Samuell Mathews**, Esq., _____ Co.
Austin, Wm., 1637, by **Francis Osborne**, _____ Co.
Austine, Tho., 1652, by **Mr. Tho. Gutheridge**, Lower Norfolk Co.
Austine, James, 1652, by **Robt. Bauldry**, York Co.
Austine, Tho., 1650, by **Mrs. Francis Townslend** (widdow), Northumberland Co.
Auston, Jno., 1654, by **John Drayton**, Westmoreland Co.
Auston, Rich., 1648, by **Wm. Ewen** James City Co.

CHAPTER X – ANNA RICE – AUGUSTUS WILSON

Chapter summary on page vii

Anna Rice
(1st wife)
Augustus Wilson

James Wilson 2/	
Betsey Simpson 4/	
Amos Wilson 2/	
Barbara James 4/	
Isaac Wilson 2/	(This line continues on the next page)
1. Hulda or Mary Snodderly*	
2. Jemima Evans 3/	(This line continues on the next page)
Sampson Wilson 1/	
George Wilson 1/	

Barbara May
(2nd wife)
Augustus Wilson

John Wilson 2/	(See page 136)
Lydia (daughter of Isaac) 1/	
Martha 2/	
David Wilson 5/	(Connection with **Augustus Wilson** not clear)
Elizabeth Winslow	

1/ **D. Maynard Wilson** manuscript (48).   2/ Census records.
3/ Pension letter.   4/ Marriage records.
5/ Estate.   * Discrepancy, explained in the chapter.

Isaac Wilson	John	
Rosanna Wilhoit**	Elizabeth Wilson	
(or...Snodderly)	Lydia Wilson	
(first wife)	Bettie (Bets) Wilson	
	Isabelle (Ibby)	(See page after
	John Graves	**Caswell Wilson**)
	2 other sons	
	2 other daughters	

	Sharpe (Squire)*	
	George Wilson*	
	Caswell Wilson*	(see next page)
Isaac Wilson	Parlia Sharp	
Jemima Evans	Catherine Wilson*	
(second wife)	John Wilson*	
	Sarah Wilson*	
	Nancy Evans*	(**Isaac Wilson's** stepdaughter)

---

* Children of the second wife.
** One source gives the name of **Huldah Snodderly;** another source gives **Mary Snodderly.** **Rosanna Wilhoit** was the bride of one of the two **Isaac Wilsons.** Your compiler is inclined to believe the bride of this **Isaac Wilson** was a **Snodderly.**

132

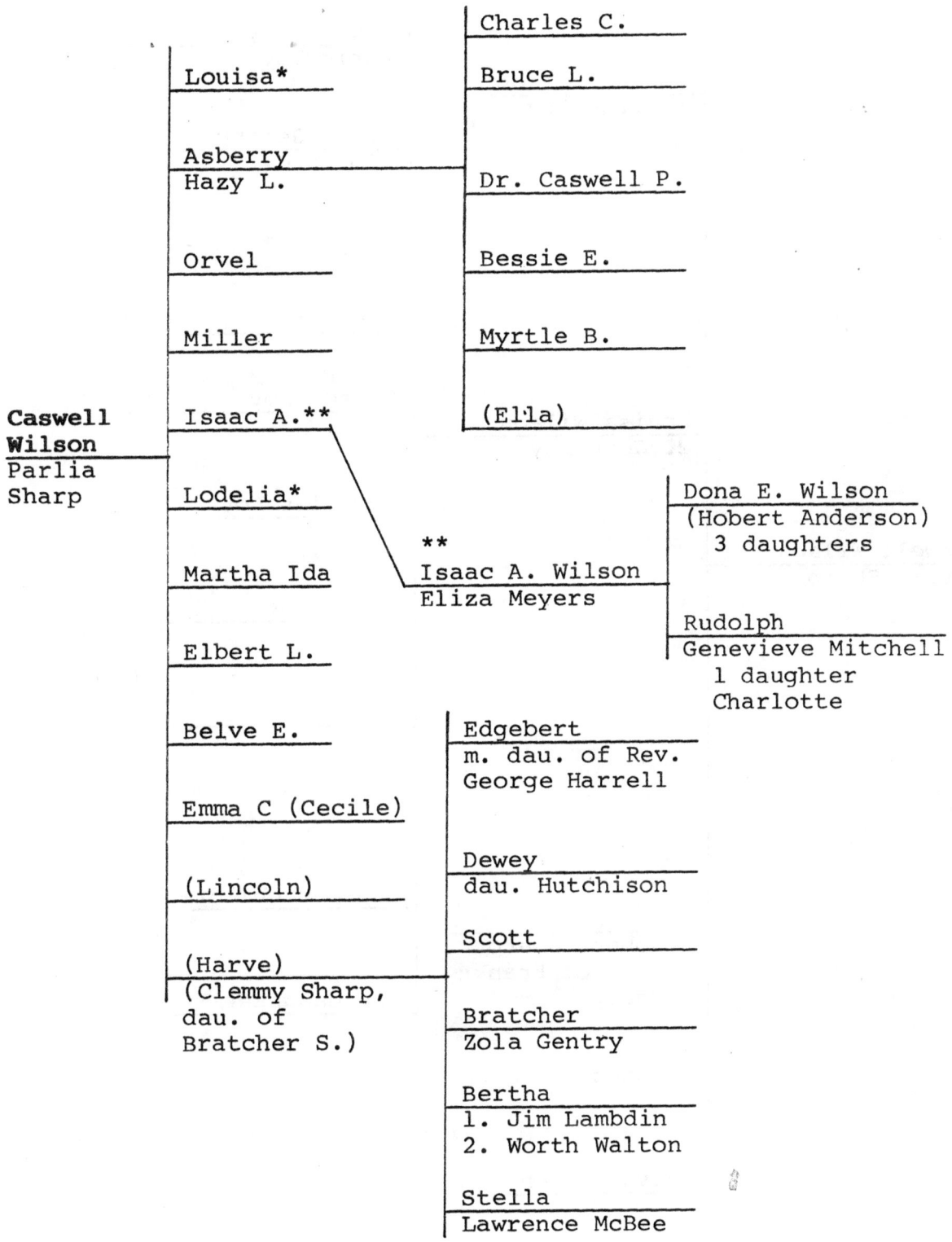

```
                              Charles C.

            Louisa*            Bruce L.


            Asberry
            Hazy L.            Dr. Caswell P.


            Orvel              Bessie E.


            Miller             Myrtle B.


Caswell     Isaac A.**         (Ella)
Wilson
Parlia
Sharp       Lodelia*                      Dona E. Wilson
                          **              (Hobert Anderson)
            Martha Ida    Isaac A. Wilson    3 daughters
                          Eliza Meyers

            Elbert L.                     Rudolph
                                          Genevieve Mitchell
                                            1 daughter
            Belve E.           Edgebert       Charlotte
                               m. dau. of Rev.
                               George Harrell

            Emma C (Cecile)
                               Dewey
                               dau. Hutchison
            (Lincoln)
                               Scott

            (Harve)
            (Clemmy Sharp,
            dau. of           Bratcher
            Bratcher S.)      Zola Gentry

                              Bertha
                              1. Jim Lambdin
                              2. Worth Walton

                              Stella
                              Lawrence McBee
```

*See page 134.

```
                                                │ Ida Gentry
                                                │ Paris Loy
                        Louisa Wilson          ─┤
                        .1....Gentry
                        .                       │ Ethel Gentry
                        .                       │ Jim Ford
                        .
                        .
                        .
                        .
                        .                       │ Will Loy
                        .
                        .
                        .                         Gibson Loy
                        .
                        Louisa Wilson          ─┤
                        2. John Loy
                                                  Hercules Loy

Caswell Wilson    ──────┤
Parlia Sharp
                                                  Haley Loy


                                                  Ola Loy



                                                  Unnamed children

                        Lodelia                ─┤
                        1.Robert Sharp
                          (son of Frank
                          Sharp)                  One daughter


                        2.Isaac Bridges



                        Belva Wilson
```

```
                                                                    ┌─ (son)
                                            ┌─ Cisero ──────────────┘
                                            │  (wife)
                                            │
                                            │  Greene _____
                                            │
                                            │  John _____
                                            │
                                            │  Raymer _____
                                            │  Maggie Sharp
                        ┌─ Preston          │
                        │  ....Miller ──────┤  Wannie _____
                        │                   │  Lela Sharp
                        │                   │
                        │                   │  Dorothy _____
                        │                   │
                        │                   │  Clara _____
                        │                   │
                        │                   │  Genevieve ────────────┐
                        │                   └─ Charlie Ousley        │
                        │                                            └─ Ruby
  Isabelle (Ibby)       │
  Wilson ───────────────┤                      Europe _____
  John Graves           │                   ┌─
                        │                   │  Earnest _____
                        │                   │
                        │  Patrick          │  Myrtle _____
                        ├─ ....Irwin ───────┤
                        │                   │  Elva _____
                        │                   │
                        │  Greene           │  Dora _____
                        │  (never           │
                        │  married)         │  Lassie _____
                        │                   └─ Edd Sharp
                        │
                        │                   ┌─ Crit _____
                        │                   │  Laura Nash
                        │  Ellen            │
                        ├─ Alfred Ousley ───┤  J. Milus Ousley, M.D. _
                        │                   │  Myrtle Longmire
                        │  Daughter         │
                        │                   │  Gertie _____
                        │                   │  Shade Irwin
                        │                   │
                        └─ Daughter         │  Daughter _____
                                            └─ Elbert Dyer
```

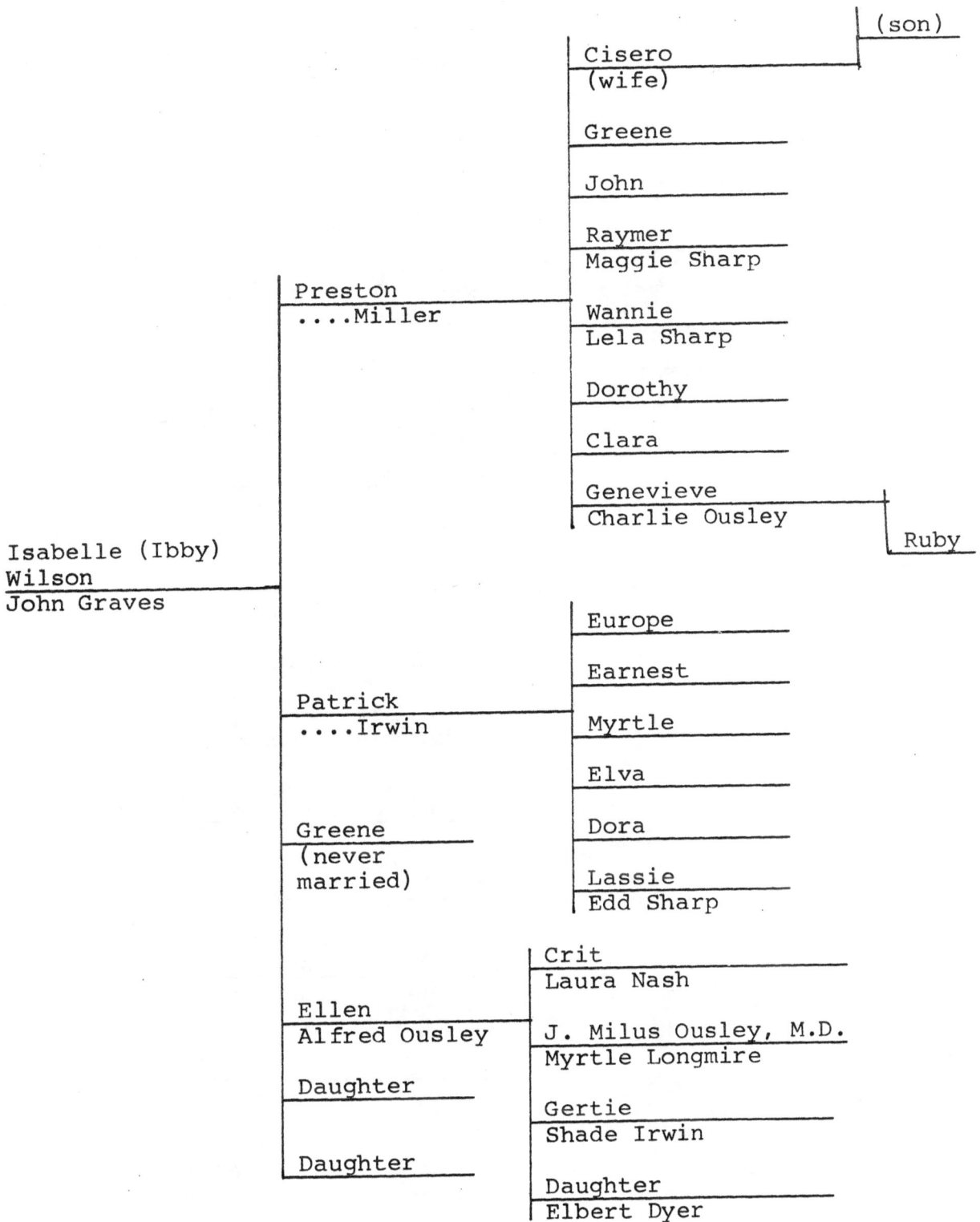

(Based on **The Wilson Generation** (48); not verified by your compiler.)

```
                              (Stepson)
                              Dr. Isaac Alvis Wilson   (See page 137)
                              1. Martha J. Graves
                              2. Nancy
                              3. Esther


                              James F.
                              _____

                              Elizabeth Jane Wilson
                              ....Johnson
                              _____

                              William
                              _____

                              Gusta (son)
John Wilson                   _____
Lydia Wilson
                              Levi W.
                              _____

                              Frederick B.
                              _____

                              Washington W.
                              _____

                              Christopher C. (a "blind idiot")
                              _____

                              Walhai
                              _____

                              Martha A. Wilson
                              ....Auston
                              _____

                              Mary B.
```

(Based on 1850, 1860, and 1870 census schedules and 1898 pension papers; **John** was alive in 1898, but he was not found in 1880 nor 1900 census schedules.)

	James R. Wilson*	Nassaw D. (son)
	Sarah E.	Daniel M.
	Henry Scott Wilson* (See page 138)	
	Lucy Jane Beeler	
	Samuel S.*	
	Lyddia M.*	
Dr. Isaac Alvis Wilson	Parris L.*	
1. Martha J. Graves	Charley B.	
2. Nancy (1880 census)		
3. Esther (1900 census)	Coram C.	
	Fredrick B.	
	Alvis S.	
	Clauda C. (grandson)	

*Information from the 1880 census.

Information from the 1900 census shows:
Appe? Wilson (widowed mother and family, two households away (see page 8). Elvin White (brother-in-law). **James E. White** (family next door. **Francis M. White** family lived next door to Henry Scott Wilson). Also, in the 1900 census for **Isaac** was **Elvin White**, a **brother-in-law of this Dr. Wilson.**

Based on 1880 and 1900 census schedules, and on **Fred R. Gibson's** lineage chart. (**Isaac** not found in 1860 and 1870 census reports.)

Birtha E.

Eliza R.
(Rosie Lyzoria)
Alvis Fletcher Weaver

Henry Scott Wilson
Lucy Jane Beeler
(see Fred Randolph
Gibson lineage
charts)

Dora Ethel

Alvis H.

{ **Alvis Weaver**, son of
{ Mynatt Weaver, grand-
{ son of **John Bradford**
{ **Weaver**, and great-
{ grandson of **Timothy**
{ **Weaver** and **Emily**
{ **Brantly.*** Your com-
{ piler is descended
{ from **Timothy Weaver**
{ through Elder **Thomas**
{ **Weaver**, a younger
{ brother of **John B.**
{ **Weaver**.

*Daughter of **Thomas
Brantley**

Phillip S. (twin)
Sherman E. (twin)

Appe?

....Wilson

Mertie V

Virginia T. Wilson
(sister to Appe)

Isaac L. Wilson (nephew to Appe)

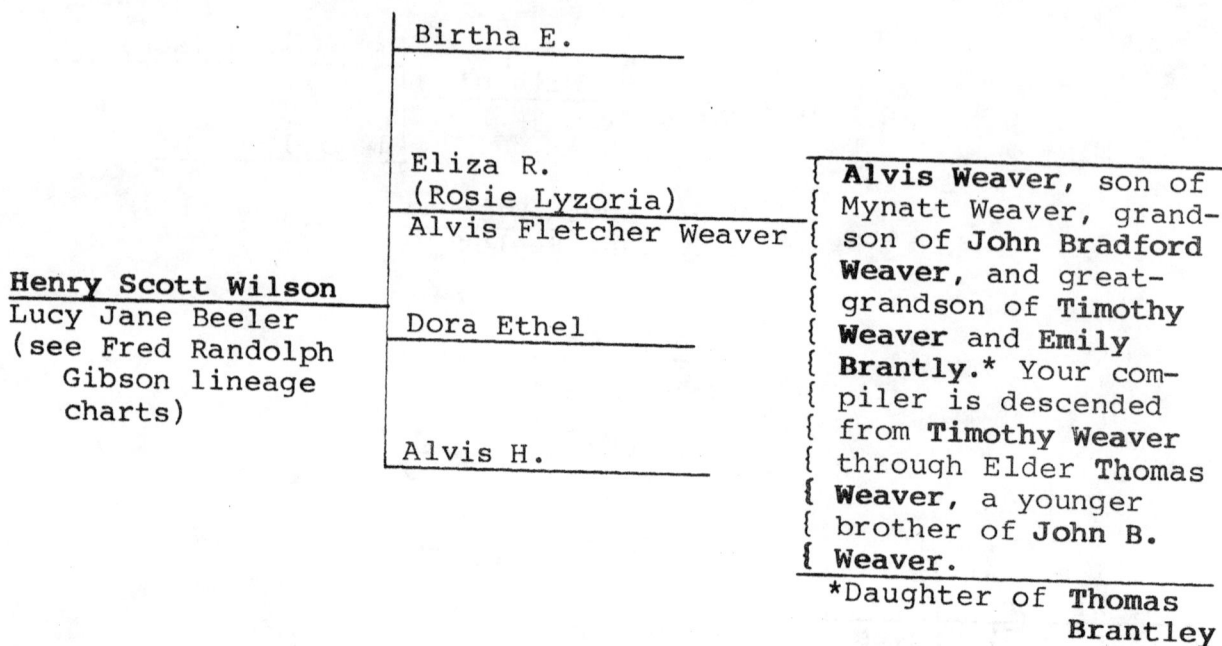

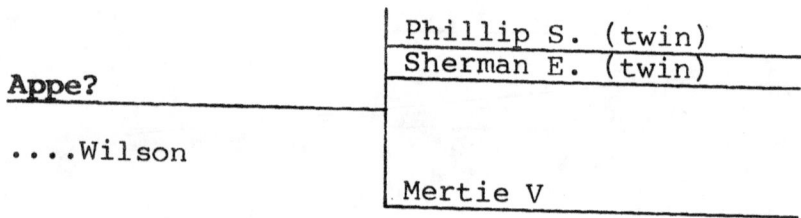

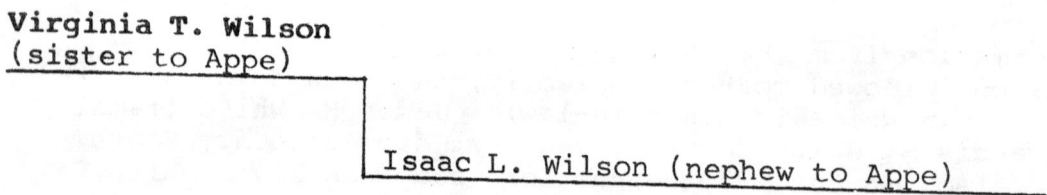

The family next door to **Appe Wilson** was **John E. White**. Under
John E. White was son-in-law (or sister-in-law?) with parents born
in Virginia, **Surhmer? E. Wilson**).

138

CHAPTER X - ANNA RICE - AUGUSTUS WILSON
Chapter summary on page vii

A. ANNA RICE

Henry Rice, our pioneer ancestor, had six daughters, which matches the number of sons. The poet **Martin Rice,** son of **Enoch Rice,** wrote about **Henry's** lady offspring--quoted from <u>Charles Rice</u> (2, page 8), as follows:

"Of my grandfather's sisters, I may say that I knew some of them in my boyhood, and of others I speak only by hearsay by my father and others...." About **Anna, Martin** wrote, "**Anna Rice** married **Augustus Wilson.** Their sons were **James,** Isaac and **Amos.** Isaac and **Amos** I knew in my boyhood, living in Campbell County, where some of **Isaac's** children still live."

Your compiler thinks that **Anna** and **Augustus** might have married before 1786, for their son **Isaac** was 64 years old in 1850. But **James** could have been the oldest son, for he was 26-45 in the 1810 Grainger County census, and subtracting 26 from 1810 one would come to 1784.

D. Maynard Wilson (48, pages 2-3) wrote: "This, Hawkins County, is more likely where **Augustus** met and married **Anne Rice,** daughter of **Henry Rice.** They began their drifting southwest; it seemed this was the general direction of most of the people from that (area) were headed."

D. Maynard Wilson was one of the Lost Creek Reunion Emeritus, with the late **Professor William H. Thomas, Obie D. Longmire,** and Wm. Browning. In a letter to **Messrs. Wm. D. Browning, Obie D. Longmire** and **D. Maynard Wilson,** the late **Professor Thomas** wanted the three men to form a committee and "**Maynard** will, perhaps, consent to act as chairman for the [Lost Creek] reunion" for Sunday, May 28, 1967. This letter is dated April 22, 1967, and is included in the late **Professor Thomas'** book (29).

Later in the same source, there is the following: "Announcing the Annual Lost Creek Reunion...Sunday, May 19, 1968.... The working, Saturday, May 4, 1968."

The same announcement gave names and addresses of officers and members of the Maintenance Committee:

President: **Wm. H. Taylor,** Rte 13, Knoxville, Tenn., 37918.
Sec'y-Treas: **Carl E. Bledsoe,** First Farmers Bank, Englewood, Tenn., 37329.
Mrs. Irwin Longmire, Andersonville, Tenn., 37705

John Rice Irwin, Norris, Tenn., 37828.
Earl Snodderly, P.O. Box 431, Johnson City, Tenn., 37601.
J. Clondis Wilson, Piney Grove Ch. Rd., Knoxville, Tenn.,
    37900.
Mrs. Louvernia Wells, Cunningham Rd., Knoxville, Tenn.,
    37900.
Wm. C. Sharp, Jr., Andersonville, Tenn., 37705.
Mrs. M. A. Norton, Crescent Dr., Knoxville, Tenn., 37900.
Wm. Rice Thomas, 4 Foch St., Maryville, Tenn., 37801.
Mrs. Joe Palmer, Rte. 13, Knoxville, Tenn., 37918.
Miss Emma Dunn, Corryton, Tenn., 37721.
L. O. Petree, 2228 W. Woodrow Dr., Knoxville, Tenn., 37900.
Mrs. Baylor L. Johnson, Lake Shore Dr., Knoxville, Tenn.,
    37920.

Members Emeritus:

O. D. Longmire, Route 13, Knoxville, Tenn., 37918.
D. Maynard Wilson, Old Andersonville Rd., Knoxville, Tenn.,
    37900.
Wm. Browning, 4421 Buffat Rd., Knoxville, Tenn., 37900.
Wm. H. Thomas, 203 Kilore St., Athens, Tenn., 37303.

D. Maynard Wilson is listed as a Member Emeritus several
times, while J. Wm. C. Sharp, Clondis Wilson, along with John Rice
Irwin, and others, are among the members above.

Anna Rice could have been born in the 1750's or 1760's, and
the place of her birth could be in the present Pickens County,
South Carolina. She was the first wife of Augustus Wilson; his
second wife was Barbara May. There will be a subchapter on
Augustus Wilson's offspring through Barbara May.

Still unverified except by remembrances of the poet Martin
Rice, and through D. Maynard Wilson's compilation, Anne and
Augustus Wilson had sons James, Amos, Isaac, Sampson and George.
Augustus Wilson had two more children by his second wife--John and
Martha. This John Wilson, not Captain John Wilson, married
Isaac's daughter Lydia (source Fred R. Gibson, who descended from
Thomas Weaver's brother John Bradford Weaver; their father Timothy
Weaver is also one of my ancestors). (Fred Gibson is descended,
also, through John and Lydia Wilson.) (According to the census,
Amos had a son Sampson.)

Maynard Wilson also wrote that Augustus and his wife Anne
Rice lived in the present Foundain City area of Knoxville:
"Augustus, and his wife, Anne, lived in Knox County on the Grassy
Valley Farm, and that is where Fountain City now covers--the
Harrill Hills section of Fountain City." (48, page 2.)

Lastly, **D. Maynard Wilson** wrote about **Anne Rice's** death and burial. **"Augustus'** wife, **Anne**, died before they moved from Knox County....(the following has not been verified) we are pretty sure from some of the brief notes from **Isaac's** possessions that they took her back to Virginia to bury her." (48, page 3.)

B. EARLY WILSON INFORMATION

According to **The Wilson Generation** (48), page 1, the **Wilsons** came from "North Ireland and sailed for the New Country to Philadelphia, Pennsylvania, with the following families: 'the **Jacksons, Finleys, Crockets, Wilsons, McKinleys** and **Polks.**'"

Part of **The Wilson Generation** included here has not been verified as yet, but will be checked when this book is updated. The author states that the settlement was called "the Nottingham, or Knottingham, Colony. This name might have been from the English shire Nottingham, famous for being the area of **Robin of Loxley,** or **"Robin Hood."** The author further states that **Augustus** was born in Cecil County in the year 1759." **Goodspeed's History of Tennessee** says that he was "born in the Potomac Valley, Md., May 4, 1759, and died February 28, 1851...." (49, page 1151.)

This subject will be pursued to learn whether **Augustus'** father was **"Isaac or Augustus."** There was an early **Isaac Wilson** who settled in East Tennessee and later in Big or Bold Valley.

My first cousin **John Rice Irwin** wrote, "Other prominent families who pioneered the settlement in Big Valley were the **Ousleys, Smiths, Wilsons, Kecks, Loys, Stooksburys, Longmires, Dukes, Irwins** and **Stiners** (23, page 30).

C. THE EARLY ISAAC WILSONS

Although not verified, there apparently were two other **Isaac Wilsons** who, according to land indentures and two early marriage records, make it seem possible that one **Isaac** could have been the father of **Augustus,** and the other his brother. Early Pennsylvania and Maryland records should be checked to establish the **Wilson** history before they came south.

The elder **Isaac** had two land purchases in the Watauga Settlement, which is in present Greene County.

North Carolina Land Grants in Tennessee 1778-1791,
compiled by Betty Goff Cook Cartwright and
Lillian Johnson Gardiner, 1958, (10), page 7.

Grant No. 263 reads: "**Wilson, Isaac,** Land Indenture from
Jacob Brown, 350 acres, April 18, 1776, Watauga Purchase
Book pages 91-92, North side of Nolichucky River."

Grant No.256 reads: "**Wilson, Isaac,** N.C. Grant No. 256, 350
acres, Oct. 24, 1782, Washington County, Watauga Book p. 415.
North side of Nolichucky River Below mouth of Little Limestone
Creek."

Marriage Records
(from Greene County Tennessee Marriages)

"**Wilson, Isaac** to **Rosanna Wilhoit** (389), 16 Jan. 1796,
Conrad Wilhoit second."

"**Wilson, Isaac** to **Jane Williams** (1443), 15 July 1811, **Thomas
Wilson** second."

The name of **Isaac Wilson`s** first wife will be discussed under
that part of this chapter entitled "**Augustus` son Isaac Wilson.**"
The oldest children of **Isaac Wilson** in the 1830 Campbell County
Census were two daughters 15-20 years of age, which fits with the
1811 marriage record above.

D. AUGUSTUS WILSON

Augustus Wilson had two deeds recorded in Knox County:

Knox County Deeds Reverse Index

Grantee	Grantor	Acres	Book	Date	Location	Page
Wilson, Augustus	Beaird, Joseph	400	C Vol.1	Aug 6 1794	*	32
Wilson, Augusta	N.C. State of, Grant	300	C2	Jan 21 1797	**	99

* White`s Creek Grassy Valley
** Eastern District Grassy Valley Headquarters Whites Mill
Creek.

Additional information on this grant follows.

The names **Augustus** and **Augusta** are believed to mean the same person, for the location of White's Creek and Grassy Valley agree.

Regarding the second grant above, the following data came from the Tennessee State Archives and Library, Nashville: (12.)

```
Grantee: Wilson, Augustus.
Grant No.:  182.
No. Acres:  300.
County:
Location:  Eastern District--Grassey Valley.
Book:      9.
```

Hawkins County, Tennessee, Index to Deeds
Conveyor-Conveyee 1788-1861

Conveyors	Year	Conveyees	Book	Page
Thos. Armstrong	1817	Wilson, Augustus	7	88

1830 Anderson County Census
FM 19 Roll 175, page 191

Augustus Wilson: 1 male 10-15; 1 male 70-80; 1 female 50-60.

Augustus is the male 70-80 (born May 4, 1759), while the only female is 50-60 and must be his second wife, **Barbara May**. The male 10-15 (son?) could be either **Sampson** or **George Wilson**.

1837 Anderson County Tax List

Augustus Wilson is shown as follows:

Land	Value	Tax	State Tax	Total
213	$365	$.18-1/4	$.18-1/4	$.91-1/4

[It does not add up.]

1840 Anderson County Census
Microcopy 704, roll 517, page 4

Augustus Wilson: 1 male 80-90; 1 female 70-80.

On the same page there was the son of **Augustus, John Wilson.** On page 20 there was another **John Wilson.** The census record for **John Wilson** will be given under himself. **Barbara** is under **John** in the 1850 Anderson County census. **John Wilson** is also in the 1860 Anderson County census, and in the 1870 Union County census. According to his pension papers, **John** was alive in 1898, but your compiler could not find him in the census past 1870.

The Wilson Generation (48, page 3) states that the sons of **Augustus, "Amos, Sampson** and **George**....seem to have been men when they moved to Anderson County...."

"**Augustus Wilson** moved from Knox County to Anderson County to the mouth of Buffalo Creek. Incidentally, Buffalo Creek ran through the place we know as Loyston and emptied into the Clinch River....Their home was where the creek empties into the river."

The topographical map "Norris, Tenn., 1973" published by the U.S. Geological Survey, Washington, D.C., shows Buffalo creek running down Big Valley in Anderson County just north of Andersonville, and then southeast of Norris to the Museum of Appalachia, a replica pioneer village operated by my first cousin **John Rice Irwin.** Then Buffalo Creek winds past Bethel Church and joins Hinds Creek, which meanders down to join the Clinch River. (A portion of the map is shown in the Appendix.)

The above 1830 Anderson County census, 1837 Anderson County tax list, and 1840 Anderson County census, show that **Augustus** was in this county. Your compiler has not looked to see if **Augustus** had a land indenture for the Buffalo Creek acreage.

According to this same source, "**Augustus** lived at this location (Anderson County) until his death at age 92, in 1851, and he was taken back to Virginia. That is one of the notes in **Isaac's** book." (48, page 2.) This may mean that he was taken back to Staunton, Virginia, where the Wilsons lived between the time they were in Cecil County, Maryland (previously Cecil County, Pennsylvania), and East Tennessee. (The book is probably in the McClung Room, Lawson-McGhee Library, in Knoxville, Tennessee.)

Lastly, **Augustus Wilson** applied for a pension, which has been photocopied from microfilm (see the next several pages). The pension was rejected. The essentials of the application and transcript of a pension letter are given here.

The pension letter was from **Alfred Sharp**, Anderson County, Justice of the Peace, and was attested to by **John Key**, County Clerk. **Alfred Sharp** and **Augustus Wilson**, 89, were in court on January 27, 1848. They sought a pension for **Augustus** under the June 7, 1832 Act of Congress.

Following are excerpts from **Augustus Wilson's** statement in support of his pension application.

"I lived in what was then cal(1)ed North Carolina near the line of Virginia and now Sullivan County, Tennessee. I was drafted to go to meet the British under **Capt. Robert Kile** and Hired a Substitute to go in my place by the name....in the year of 1780 or 1781 the date I cannot recollect."

"I think in the year seventeen hundred and ninety I volunteered under **Joseph Martin** for three months for the purpose of guarding the Key Cave fort....(something like (also)) called Curtiss Station and served three months and ....started on first of January and was discharged the third of April same year. I rec'd a discharge at the time from my Capt. which has long since....lost so that I cannot now produce it."

"I was in no particular battles during my services but there was eight men kil(1)ed out of the company....**Jacob Boughman, John Benton, Sigh Benton, Daniel Benton, Jessee Benton, Burrell Sevier, John Mason, Robert Bowman** (these men were not checked in the service index)."

"I again volunteered in the year seventeen hundred and ninety four under **Capt. Henry Clark** to go against the Cherokee Indians to a place cal(1)ed the Chickamauga town but was not in any regular battles but in general scrimmages one of the lookout mountain when we killed one or____ Indians, or likely more we was then in the service for about three months I do not recollect of getting any discharge."

William Sharp, Robert Stukesbury, Jacob Stukesbury, Jacob **Loy, Lewis Miller, Pleasant M. Rogers**, George Miller, Adam McCoy, **Reuben Craig** were listed by **Augustus Wilson** after mentioning getting a discharge from **Capt. Joseph Martin**.

Also, **William Sharp** and **Pleasant M. Rogers** swore to have known **Augustus Wilson** and that he had been a soldier.

John Key wrote that he, as county clerk, upheld **Alfred Sharp** and his testimony above on January 29, 1848, which was two days later.

Pension Denied.

The reason **Augustus Wilson** did not receive a pension was that the June 7, 1832, Act of Congress had only to do with the years of the American Revolution, and only for actual service. Since **Augustus** hired a substitute, he had not served during the fight to secure independence.

There were pensions granted for service after the American Revolution, but no **Augustus Wilson** was found.

The letters that were sent about a pension for **Augustus** are as follows:

On February 10, 1848, **John Baker** sent a letter to the pension office.

"Newmarket
Jefferson County Tennessee
Feby 10th -48.

Dear Sir

I here with enclose you this declaration of **Augustus Wilson** who is making application for a pension you will do him the favor to have it attended to as early as practicable

Yours with Report [Respect?]

John Baker

A. L. Edwards
Commissioners of pensions"

The reply was dated September 15, 1848, from the Pension Office:

"Pension Office
September 15, 1848

"Sir:

The papers in the Case of **Augustus Wilson** have been examined and ____ under the Act of 7 June 1832.

In his declaration claimant states that in 1780 or 1781 he was drafted to go to meet the British under **Capt. Rolle**, and that he hired a substitute. The act above refered to provides for actual service only rendered during the Revolutionary War. He rendered it appears from his own declaration no actual service, during that war, and as that rendered in 1790 or subsequently to the conclusion of peace in 1783....he has no claim whatever to a stipent, this application is therefore rejected....

John Baker, Esq.
New Market
Jefferson Co. Tenn.

Since **Augustus Wilson** said in his pension application that he served in the years 1790 and 1794, the Index to Compiled Service Records of Voluntary Soldiers who Served from 1784 to 1811 was checked for **Augustus Wilson** (and **Augustus Willson**). This microfilm roll was for names T-Z under Microcopy 694, roll 9. No pension was found.

Lastly, **Augustus Wilson**, sometimes written **Augusta**, is in Mortality Schedule Tennessee 1850 (71). The data for Augusta Wilson and other **Wilsons** are as follows:

Page	Name	County	State	Age	Sex	Month of Death	Place of Birth	Cause of Death
106	**Wilson, Augusta**	Anderson	TN.	100	M	Feb	MA	old age 00
107	**Wilson, Samuel**	Claiborne	TN	38	M	Feb	TN	Fever 00
	Wilson, Smith	Claiborne	TN	9 mo	M	Sep	KY	Cholera
	Wilson, Susan	Claiborne	TN	17	F	Feb	TN	Fever 00
	Wilson, Upias	Knox	TN	50	F	May	TN	Consumption 00

Code for occupation - 00 = farmer.

1. James Wilson
===============
1. <u>James Wilson</u>

   James Wilson was in Greene County, and was married there.

Greene County Marriages

"Wilson, James to Betsy Simpson (957). 13 Aug. 1804. Even Evans, Second."

Since **James** was listed first by the poet **Martin Rice**, probably he was the oldest. There was one **James Wilson** in the 1810 census, and two in the 1830 census. The **James Wilson** in 1810 was 26-45, living by himself with 3 slaves. The two **James Wilsons** in 1830 are below:

1830 Grainger County Census
FM 19, roll 180

Page 376.   **James Wilson.**   1 male 5 to 10; 1 male 30 to 40;
                                2 females under 5; 1 female 5 to 10;
                                3 females 10 to 15; 1 female 30 to 40.

Page 382.   **James Wilson.**   1 male 10 to 15; 1 male 15 to 20; 1 male
                                   40 to 50;
                                2 females under 5; 3 females 5 to 10;
                                   1 female 15 to 20; 1 female 30 to 40.

One **James Wilson** had a land grant from the State of Tennessee as follows:

> "Grantee: **Wilson, James.**
> Grant No. 2506
> No. Acres: 246, 3 rods and 2 chains.
> Date of Grant: August 3, 1812.
> County: Sevier
> Location: East Tennessee District.
> Book 4, volume 1, page: 40-41." (12)

From the **Grainger County Deed Index**, James Wilson sold eight deeds and bought four land plats. This could have been either, or both, of the persons named **James Wilson**. The locations of the plats might give clues as to the identity of the respective buyers and sellers.

Grainger County Index to Deeds (12)
Vol. 2, 1797-1855 N-Z
(Tennessee State Library & Archives
Microcopy EX20094, Grainger County Roll 35

Year	Conveyor	Book	Page	Conveyee
1807	**Wilson, James**	B	49	Francis Mayberry
1810	**Wilson, James**	C	1	Robert Blain
1812	**Wilson, James**	C	136	Robert Blain
1829	**Wilson, James**	F	90	James Gilmore
1834	**Wilson, James**	F	513	William Gilmore
1836	**Wilson, James**	G	414	Henry Allsus
1837	**Wilson, James**	G	416	Henry Allsus
1837	**Wilson, James**	G	430	Juble Nutchell

Grainger County Index to Deeds
Vol. 4, N-Z

Year	Conveyee	Book	Page	Conveyor
1824	**Wilson, James**	E	447	James Richerson
1824	**Wilson, James**	E	449	Michael Massengill
1829	**Wilson, James**	F	83	Thomas Whitlock
1837	**Wilson, James**	G	403	James Whitlock

Your compiler has a **James Wilson** buying two land deeds in Campbell County in 1855 and 1858, respectively. Since **Augustus** was born May 4, 1759, this is probably not **Henry Rice`s** grandson **James Wilson**. This latter **James Wilson** left a will in Campbell County in 1884, being written in 1878.

In the same book with the 1810 Grainger County Census (**Grainger County, Tennessee Federal Census of 1810, Population Schedule (Third Census) and County Tax Lists for 1810** (13, page 23) there is also tax information. "The following rates had been set in 1809:

1. on each one hundred acres of land	12-1/2 cents	
2. on each town lot	25	"
3. on each free poll	12-1/2	"
4. on each black poll	25	"
5. on each retail store	$5.00	
6. ?		

"The original manuscript book from which the following lists were taken is now in the McClung Historical Collection. The amount of tax is omitted in this copy."

149

"A list of poles and taxable property in the bounds of
Capt. Thomas Sharp's Company Returned to Court by
Mathew Campbell Esqr. for the year 1810."

Page 38:(Referring to the tax rates above)

Column: 1 2 3 4 5 6 (referring to tax rates above)
Wilson, James   1 1

This **James Wilson** was a free white poll "between the age of
twenty one and fifty years" while a black poll was "between the
age of twelve and fifty years." (Page 36). There was a **John
Wilson** or **Willson** in the same pages with **James Wilson** in the 1810
census and tax records. That data will be given later.

James Wilson served in the War of 1812: "**Wilson, James.**

1 Reg't (**Wear's**) East Tennessee Volunteers." (Compiled Service
Index for War of 1812, Microcopy 602, roll 229, Wilm-Wilz.)
The "Company Pay Roll" has "**Capt. Daniel Price's** Co. of Inf., **Col.
Samuel Wear's** Reg't, and East Tennessee Militia." **James Wilson**
enlisted at Knoxville and served for three months and nine days
from Sept. 23, 1813, to Jan. 1, 1814. His brother, **Amos Wilson**,
also was a private under **Col. Samuel Wear**, but served under **Capt.
Morgan's** Co. of Inf. **Col. Samuel Wear's** Reg't, East Tennessee
Militia."

George Rice and **George Snodderly** (who married each others'
sisters) were in the "1 Reg't (**Wear's**) East Tennessee Volunteers";
however, they were serving under "**Capt. Robert Doak's** Co. of
Infantry." **George Rice** and **James Wilson** were first cousins.

2. Amos Wilson

This grandson of **Henry Rice** moved to Campbell County with his
brother **Isaac Wilson**. He was in the Anderson County Census
Schedules in 1830 and paid tax in 1837. He was also listed in the
Campbell County tax list in 1837. This might indicate there was
another **Amos Wilson**.

1830 Anderson County Census
FM 19, Roll 175

Amos Wilson.   "2 males un. 5; 1 male 10 to 15; 1 male 30 to 40*;
                2 females un. 5; 2 females 5 to 10; 2 females 15 to
                20; 1 female 30 to 40."

    * = Discrepancy.

1837 Anderson County Tax List

	Land	Value	Tax	State Tax	Total
Amos Wilson	400	$400	$.20	$.14	$.70
			1 white tax		
			$.12-1/2		

1840 Campbell County Census
Microcopy 704, roll 518

Amos Wilson "1 male 10 to 15; 1 male 60 to 70.*
1 female 15 to 20; 1 female 50 to 60."

* Discrepancy.

1837 Campbell County Tax List, 10th District

	School Land	Value	Tax	White Poll	Total Tax
Amos Wilson	100 acres	$15	$.75	None	$.75

Amos Wilson married Barbara James on May 26, 1812, with bondsman Hugh Gilmore, while on August 12, 1806, Robert Willson and Nancey Hayes were married with just a bond, Thomas Copeland. (Grainger County Microcopy Roll No. 20, Marriages, EX 20081, vol. 1, 1796-1837, pages 163 and 130.)

Amos Wilson was in the 1850 Anderson County census report, but not in 1860.

1850 Anderson County Census
16th Subdivision, 16 October 1850
Microcopy 432, roll 869
Page 59, line 19, household 824, family 828

Amos Wilson	59	M	Farmer	300	Tenn.	CNRW
Barbry Wilson	59	F			"	"
Laraney	19	F			"	-
John	17	M	Farmer		"	School
Sampson	16	M	Farmer		"	School

Augustus might have had a son Sampson. This son of Amos has been found in two census schedules after 1850--1870 and 1900 Campbell County census schedules.

Amos Wilson was living very close to John and Lydia Wilson. John was at Household 822/824, while Louisa Wilson was at Household 820/824 and could be a daughter, daughter-in-law, or other relative of Augustus Wilson.

This John Wilson, according to new sources, was Amos' half brother. The father of both was Augustus, but the mother of John was Augustus' second wife Barbara May, while Amos' mother was Anne Rice. Also, this John married Lydia Wilson, the daughter of Amos' brother Isaac Wilson--his own half niece. More information will be given under Augustus' second wife Barbara May. Lydia must have had a previous husband, name unknown.

Amos Wilson received a land grant from the State of Tennessee (Campbell Co. Roll 27 EX 17485 Registers Deed Index, Vol. 1, Direct and Reverse Vol. 1, 1804-1890.)

"Grantee: Wilson, Amos (12)
Grant No: 20700
No. Acres: 100
Date of Grant: April 24, 1837
County: Campbell
Location: East Tenn. District
Book: 21, page: 175."

Grantee	Grantor	Book	Page	Grant No.	Date
Wilson, Amos	State of Tennessee	G	268	20027	Mch.7, 1828

Location: Beech F. of B. C."

As more than a coincidence, Amos Wilson served in the War of 1812 in the same regiment as his first cousin once removed (or second cousin), George Rice, and George's brother-in-law George Snodderly (1st Regiment, Wear's) East Tennessee Volunteers (War of 1812)). Amos served under "Capt. Rufus Morgan's Co. of Inf., Col. Samuel Wear's Reg't, East Tennessee Militia" from Sept. 23 to Dec. 31, 1813, and enlisted at Knoxville. He served one day less than James Wilson, George Rice and George Snodderly. Amos was a private.

3. Isaac Wilson (Augustus Wilson's Son)

This son of Anna Rice and Augustus Wilson was last in the list by the poet Martin Rice. There were two Isaac Wilsons in Greene County Tennessee Marriages. Perhaps the first was an uncle. The marriages are on page 142.

Mrs. Peters (27, pages 202-203) states that the sixth child of **John Snodderly** and **Elizabeth Gibbs**...

"6. Huldah, m. Isaac Wilson."

However, the **Nicholas Gibbs** book (ref. 7, page i of this book) says that Huldah Snodderly married Gabriel Nelson. (See Section VIII, **ELIZABETH GIBBS-JOHN SNODDERLY**, page 71.)

In **Isaac Wilson's** pension papers, when his widow **Jamima Evans** applied in 1878, she wrote, "**Isaac** was previously married to **Mary Snodderly**. She died about 1834 or 5." (WO 33795 and WC 24822). The correct name must have been **Huldah** because **Mrs. Peters** says "**Mary (Snodderly) m. Morris Bridges.**" **Mrs. Peters** further states that **Jamima** "was also previously married to one **Wm. Evans** and who also died about 1834....in Ala. His (**Wm. Evans'**) first wife died in Tennessee. **Isaac** died on June 17, 1874." **Mrs. Peters** could not find any proof of marriage in Claiborne County nor from the family, but **Isaac** gave the date of his marriage as 19th Feby. 1837, when he applied for a pension in 1871 (SO 33795 and SC 24822).

Henry Rice's grandson **Isaac Wilson** served in the War of 1812. He enlisted at Knoxville, as did **Amos** and **James Wilson**, but was in "3 Regiment (**Johnson's**), East Tennessee Militia." He was a Sergeant at the beginning and end of his military obligation. On the "Company Pay Roll" we read, "**Capt. James Stewart's** Company, Reg't East Tennessee Militia commanded by **Col. William Johnson**" from Sept. 20, 1814 to May 3, 1815. Two Company Muster Rolls were in this service record, with one roll from Sept. 20, 1814 to Mar. 20, 1815, and residence Knoxville.

Also, there is one paper in which **Isaac Wilson** "of the county of Knox and the state of Tennessee, do constitute, make and appoint **Wilson Dukes Harwick** of the county and state aforesaid, my true and lawful attornies....to ask, demand and receive....such sum or sums of money as is due me for my services...."

Isaac applied for a pension in 1871, and his widow did the same in 1878. Persons who witnessed some of these papers were **A. A. Snoderly**, **W. H. Snoderly**, **Anthony Graves**, **Caswell Wilson** (**Isaac's** son), and (in 1878) **Henry Rice** and **Rice Snodderly**. Other names were **Isaac M. Gentry**, **Elijah Longmire**, Commissioner **T. W. Baker**, and **John Witt**. (The pension numbers for **Isaac Wilson's** application are SO22178 and SC14301; his widow's numbers are WO33795 and WC24822.) The **Isaac Marion Gentry** is the son of **Addison Gentry** and **Rebecca Rice**, a daughter of **George Rice**

and sister of the above **Henry Rice**. The **Elijah Longmire** is a 3rd great-grandfather of **MWL**. **Thomas Winfield (T. W.) Baker** is also a primitive baptist minister and great-uncle, having been married to **Neva Jane Rice**. **Sarah Elizabeth Longmire** married **Henry Rice**, **Jane's** parents. **Sarah** is **Elijah Longmire's** granddaughter through **Robert Longmire** and **Sarah Sharp**. This **Henry Rice**, 56, is **Rebecca Rice's** older brother and great-grandson of the pioneer gristmiller.

Henry Rice, 56, and **Henry Rice Snoderly**, 46, "Citizens of the Town of Lost Creek P. O., County of Union, State of Tennessee...." made the following affidavit: "That we have known said claimant for at least forty (40) years, and also said `dec'd` Soldier the same time, and we know the said **Isaac Wilson** died at his home at Lost Creek P. O. in Union County, Tennessee on or about the 17th day of June 1874 and that we know the Said **Jamima Wilson** has not remarried since the 17th June 1874 and that she remains the widow of the said **Isaac Wilson** `dec'd` we know the above facts to be true for the reason we have lived close neighbors to her all the above time....We further declare that we have no interest in said case, and are not concerned in its prosecution, and are not related to said applicant."

This **Henry Rice** was the great grandson of the Pioneer **Henry Rice**, through **James Rice** and **James'** son **George Rice**; also this **Henry Rice** is the great grandfather of your compiler through **Marcellus Moss (Sill, Sillas, Cill) Rice** and his daughter **Ruby Rema Rice Little**.

George Rice married **Sarah Snodderly**, and **George Rice's** sister **Tabitha Rice** married **George Snodderly**; **George Snoderly** was the brother of **Hulda Snodderly** .

Possibly they did not consider the relationship important, when making their affidavits, but **George Rice** and **Isaac Wilson** were first cousins; also **Henry Rice** and **Caswell Wilson** were first cousins once removed or second cousins; and **Henry Rice Snodderly** was also a first cousin to both **Henry Rice** and **Caswell Wilson**.

In Jacksboro, Tennessee, the County Seat of Campbell County, your compiler noted a deed from **David Smith** (pioneer **Henry Rice's** son-in-law) to **Isaac Wilson**.

Campbell County Direct Index to Deeds

Grantor	Grantee	Book	Page		Date
Smith, David	Isaac Wilson	C	157	Warranty	June 1 1819

Grantee	Grantor	Book	Page	Date
Wilson, Isaac	P. & J. & Wm. Sharp	K	366	June 9, 1849

Augustus` son **Isaac** was in the census in Campbell County in 1830, 1840, and 1850. He was in the 1860 Union County census, age 74. **Isaac** was found in the 1870 Union County census and died in 1874.

1830 Campbell County Census
FM 19 Roll 178, page 233

Isaac Wilson. 2 males under 5; 1 male 40 to 50;
2 females 5 to 10; 1 female 10 to 15;
2 females 15 to 20; 1 female 40 to 50

1840 Campbell County Census
Microcopy 704, Roll 518, page 298

Isaac Wilson. 1 male under 5; 1 male 5 to 10; 3 males 10 to 15;
1 male 50 to 60;
1 female 5 to 10; 1 female 10 to 15; 2 females
15 to 20; 1 female 30 to 40.

Isaac Wilson. 1 male 5 to 10; 1 male 20 to 30;
1 female under 5; 1 female 20 to 30.

The older of the two is the subject of this section, while the younger could be the elder **Isaac Wilson's** son. **Isaac** had two sons under 5 in 1830, and in 1840 they would have been 10-15; now there are three sons of the 10-15 age group. Also there are two younger sons, one under 5 and the other 5-10. The three oldest daughters are gone by 1840--probably married. Then in that 10-year period another daughter was born. The daughter who was 10-15 in the 1830 census was Lydia, who married her half-uncle **John Wilson** on April 27, 1837.

1850 Campbell County Census

Wilson, Isaac, 64, Jemima 44, Caswell 12, Catherine 8, Sarah 4, Nancy Evans 14, T NC C-662-650 (1850 Tennessee Census Index vol. VI, by Byron and Barbara Sistler, 1974, Evanston, Ill.) (36).

The Jemima Wilson in the 1850 census should be Isaac's second wife, who was 44, while the first wife was 40 to 50 in the year 1830. Also, in 1850 four of Isaac's sons probably had their own families. Nancy Evans would be a daughter of William and Jemima Evans before her marriage to Isaac Wilson.

1860 Union County Census
Microcopy 653 roll 1276, page 124, line 27
Dist. No. 9, household 880, family 880

Isaac Wilson	74	M	Farming	2500*	450**	Tenn.
Jamima Wilson	50	F	Housewife			"
Caswell	22	M	Farmhand			"
Catherine	18	F	Domestic			"
Sarah	14	F				"

* personal estate
** real estate

In 1860 Isaac Wilson is in the census between John Rice and Henry Rice, two of George Rice's sons. There is also a Jesse Wilson in the Union County census; maybe he was related to Isaac Wilson.

1860 Union County Census
Microcopy 653 roll 1276, page 112,
Dist. No. 9, line 32, household 798, family 798

Jesse Wilson	55	M	Farming	1000	500	Tenn.
Matilda Wilson	50	F	Housewife			"
Nancy Wilson	70	F	Serving			N.C.
James M. "	19	M	Farmhand			Tenn.
Calvin "	17	M	Farmhand		School	"
Elizabeth "	14	F			"	"
Always(?) "	11	M			"	"
McHenry "	9	M			"	"
Lewis "	3	M				"

D. **Maynard Wilson** wrote, "**Isaac Wilson** died in 1874 and was buried on a spur extending out from the main body of Clinch Mountain....**Isaac** said he wanted to be buried up there because the valley some day would be covered with water. **Isaac's** wife **Huldah**, who preceded him in death, was buried up there also, I am told...."

"However, as **Isaac** predicted, the water from Norris Dam, some 65 years after he died, covers the valley where his farm was, also the old burying place...." (48, page 5.)

Genealogy charts (pages 131-139) were constructed from **D. Maynard Wilson's** information on the descendants of **Isaac Wilson** given on pages 5 and 6 of the reference above.

Isaac Wilson was a Justice of the Peace. In this capacity, he solemnized the marriages of **George Rice's** daughters, **Anna** to **Henry Wood**, and **Rebecca** to **Addison Gentry**.

Isaac Wilson does appear in the 1870 Union County Census, which is next with his son **Caswell**. He was 85 in 1871, when he applied for a pension. **Jemima** was 71 in the 1880 census under her son **Caswell**. **Isaac** died June 17, 1874; and maybe he left a will in Jacksboro.

1870 Union County, Tennessee Census
Microcopy 593, roll 1567
9th District, 28 July 1870, P.O. Lost Creek
Line 17, household 83, family 83

Wilson,	Caswell	32	M	W	Farm Laborer	-	700	TN	
-	Parley	24	F	W	Keeping House			"	CW
-	Luisey	4	F	W				"	
Fry,	Susan	15	F	W				"	CNRW

The next two lines are 22 and 23, household 84, family 84:

Wilson,	Isaac	84	M	W	Farmer	2000 - 200	TN	
-	Gemima	61	F	W	Keeping House		NC	CW

a. Caswell Wilson

Caswell Wilson was born circa 1838 and was probably the fifth son of **Isaac**. He was the father of **Asberry Wilson** and the grandfather of **Dr. Caswell P. Wilson** (14). **Caswell Wilson** is in the 1880 Soundex Code System and the 1880 census, as well as the 1900 Soundex and census, with **Asberry** being in the 1900 records.

Your compiler thinks it is more than a coincidence that two **Rice** lines were living next to each other. **Caswell's** ancestry goes back to **Henry Rice's** daughter **Anna**. Then in the 1900 census, **Marcellus (Sill) Moss Rice**, now listed as head of the second **Henry Rice** family, was descended through "old" **Henry's** son **James Rice** through **George** and the second **Henry Rice**. Also living in Lost Creek next to **Caswell Wilson** was **James Rufus Rice**, the older brother of **"Sill."**

<u>1880 Soundex Tennessee</u>
(Microcopy T 772 roll 82, W-420 E through W-426 I,
Code for Wilson W-425) Tennessee vol. 33, E.D. 115,
sheet 31, line 16, Dist. 9

Name	Relationship	Age	B.P.	Vol.	E.D.*	Sheet	Line
Wilson, Caswell (white,male) Union		42	Tenn.	33	115	31	16
Wilson, Parlia	Wife	35	Tenn.				
Wilson, Louisa	Dau	14	Tenn.				
Wilson, Asberry	Son	13	Tenn.				
Wilson, Orvel	Son	12	Tenn.				
Wilson, Miller	Son	8	Tenn.				
Wilson, Isaac	Son	6	Tenn.				
Wilson, Eli	Son	4	Tenn.				
Wilson, Lodelia	Dau	2	Tenn.				
Wilson, Martha Ida	Dau	11/12	Tenn.				
Wilson, Jamima	Mother	71	Tenn.				

Footnotes for this and the following census records:
  * Enumeration District
  Note: The <u>format</u> for the above data was changed from <u>Soundex</u>.
After seeing the above **Soundex**, one looks up the regular census.

<u>1880 Union County Census</u>
Microcopy T-9, roll 1283 (E.D. 115,
Supervisor Dist. 1, page 31, line 16, Dist. 9,
Household 68, family 71)

Name	1.	2.	Age	Rel.	Status	Occupat.	Birthplace**		
Wilson, Caswell	W	M	42	Head	Married	Farmer	TN	TN	NC
Wilson, Parlia***	W	F	35	Wife	Married	K.House	TN	TN	TN
Wilson, Louisa***	W	F	14	Dau	Single	At home	TN	TN	TNs
Wilson, Asberry	W	M	13	Son	Single	Farm hd.	TN	TN	TNs
Wilson, Orvel***	W	M	10	Son	Single		TN	TN	TNs

(Continued next page)

158

Wilson, Miller	W	M	8	Son	Single		TN	TN	TN[S]
Wilson, Isaac	W	M	6	Son	Single		TN	TN	TN
Wilson, Eli	W	M	4	Son	Single		TN	TN	TN
Wilson, Lodelia	W	F	2	Dau	Single		TN	TN	TN
Wilson, Martha Ida	W	F	11/12 July	Dau	Single		TN	TN	TN
Walker, John	W	M	19	Serv	Single	Servant	TN	TN	TN
Wilson, Jamima	W	F	71	Mother	Widowed	Boarding	TN	–	–

** Birthplaces (person, father, mother)
***Cannot write.
[S] = School

At line 28, household 68 family 72 is the census for **Rice, Henry**, given under **Henry Rice**.

There is no 1890 census, since they were burned in all but one or two counties. For the whole country, however, there is a special census compiled from the descendants of Civil War veterans for the year 1890, which helps make up for the loss of the regular censuses. In the 1900 <u>Soundex</u> your compiler found, for the entire State, only **Asberry Wilson** among the children of **Caswell**. The sons **Eli** and **Miller** (maybe **V. M.**) died before 1900, while sons **Orvel** and **Isaac** more likely had moved to another state. In fact, all the children had gone, and there were three new ones and a new servant. And **Caswell's** sister **Elizabeth**, 89, was now under his roof. Where she was before 1900 is not known, for she was not even in the 1830 Campbell County census under **Isaac**.

<u>1900 Soundex Tennessee</u>
Mc T 1072, roll 179, W-420M* through W-425 John H.
W-425 Code for Wilson.

Name	Rel.	Birthdate	Age	B.P.	Vol.	E.D.*	Sheet	Line
Wilson, Caswell		Dec. 1837	62	TN	70	162	2	81
Union – 16th Civil Dist.								
Wilson, Parley	W	Feb. 1845	55	TN				
Wilson, Elbert L.	S	Sep. 1881	18	TN				
Wilson, Belve E.	D	Sep. 1885	14	TN				
Wilson, Emma C.	D	July 1888	11	TN				
McCoy, Gibson	Se	May 1883	17	TN				
Wilson, Elizabeth	Si	Sep. 1810	89	TN				

1900 Census Union County
E.D. 152 to 162 complete E.D. 162, sheet 2,
Line 81, household 32, family 32
(Microcopy T-623, roll 1602, vol. 70, E.D. 152 to 162 complete,
Supervisor's District 2)

Name	Rel.	1.	2.	Birthdate	Age	Status	3.	4.	5.	B.P.s**
Wilson,										
Caswell	Head	W	M	Dec. 1837	62	married	36			TN TN NC[a]
" **Parley**	Wife	W	F	Feb. 1845	55	married	36	12	8	TN TN TN
" **Elbert L.**	Son	W	M	Sept.1881	18	single				TN TN TN[b]
" **Belve E.**	Dau	W	F	Sept.1885	14	single				TN TN TN[c]
" **Emma C.**	Dau	W	F	July 1888	11	single				TN TN TN[d]
McCoy,										
Gibson	Sv	W	M	May 1883	17	single				TN TN TN
Wilson,										
Elizabeth	Si	W	F	Sept.1810	89	single				TN TN TN

Other families of interest found here were:
(Line 59, **Snoderly, George**)
(Line 75, **Hankins, Robert**)
(Line 88, household 33, family 33; **Smith, Jacob**)
(Line 95, household 34, family 34, **Rice, James R.**
= **J. Rufus Rice**)

Notes: ** = birthplaces--State where person was born, State where father was born, State where mother was born. 1 = Color. 2 = Sex. 3 = Years married. 4 = Number of children born. 5 = Number of children living. a = Farmer. b = At school (7 months). c = Servant. d = School (3 months). Under Relationship: Sv = Servant, Si = Sister.

Caswell and **Parley** had been married for 36 years and had 12 children, eight of whom were still living; however, only 3 remained at home **Elizabeth** was still single. Except for **Jacob Smith**, all the above families of interest are known to have been related. The census records for **George Snodderly, III**, son of **Henry Rice Snodderly**, **Robert Hankins**, and **James R. (Rufus) Rice** will be given in a later edition.

Caswell's wife, **Parlia** or **Parley** was the daughter of **Alfred Sharp** and **Elizabeth Loy**. **Parlia** was 16 under **Alfred Sharp** in the 1860 Union County Census (27, page 240), as quoted below:

1860 Union County census
Microcopy 653, roll 1276, Page 472

(764)	Alfred Sharp	51	M	Farmer, Tenn.	17,000	12,200
	Elizabeth (Loy)	48	F	"		
	James	18	M	"		
	Parlia	16	F	"		
	Rachel	13	F	"		
	A. B.	10	M	"		
	Lewis M.	5	M	"		

New Loyston Cemetery, Union County

Tombstones at this cemetery mark the resting places for **Caswell, Parlia, Ely,** and **V. M. Wilson. Ely** is a son of **Caswell,** and **V. M.** may be the initials for the son **Miller Wilson.**

Caswell Wilson
Born Dec. 24, 1837
Died May 18, 1918

Parlia Wilson
Born Feb. 21, 1845
Died Nov. 21, 1929

V. M. Wilson
Born Aug. 4, 1872
Died Oct. 31, 1890
 (age 18)

Ely Wilson
Born Dec. 25, 1875
Died Jan. 28, 1891
 (age 16)

Some other **Wilsons** buried in the New Loyston cemetery are:

Maynard O. Wilson
July 5, 1953 - May 31, 1970

Rex P. Wilson
May 6, 1901 - Jan. 7, 1966

Knox L. Wilson
Nov. 13, 1919
Oct. 4, 1961

Sarah E. Wilson
Apr. 1, 1864
Mar. 15, 1909

J. Rosen Wilson
Feb. 17, 1862
June 5, 1938

Caswell Wilson's Children, according to D. Maynard Wilson

On page 6 of his manuscript (48), **Maynard Wilson** wrote:

"**Caswell (Cas)**, married **Parley Sharp**, daughter of **Alfred Sharp.** Their sons were **Asbury, Lincoln, Harve, Isaac, Eli** and **Elbert.** Their daughters were **Louisa, Delia, Belva,** and **Cecile. Asbury** married a **Stooksbury (Hazy L.)**--had **Claude, Bruce, Caswell, Bessie, Myrtle** and **Ella. Isaac** married **Eliza**

Meyers--had one son, **Rudolph**, who married **Genevieve Mitchell**--they have one daughter, **Charlotte**. **Isaac** and **Eliza's** one daughter, **Dona** married **Hobert Anderson** and they had three daughters. **Caswell's** son, **Harve Wilson**, married **Clemmy Sharp**, **Bratcher's (Sharp)** daughter. Their children were **Edgebert** who married **Rev. George Harrell's** daughter --he also was a minister, a Missionary Baptist; **Dewey** and **Scott** who married sisters **Hutchison**; **Bratcher** who married **Zola Gentry**, daughter of **Lucy**, **Susan's** daughter; **Bertha Wilson** who married **Jim Lambdin**, then **Worth Walton**; and **Stella** who married **Lawrence McBee**."

Most of the above has not been verified at this time. The son **Harve** is not in the 1880 nor 1900 Union County census, which follows. **Parley** is under her father **Alfred Sharp** in the 1860 Union County census. **Isaac** is in the 1900 census with wife **Eliza** and daughter **Dona**.

Asbury Wilson is in the 1900 Union County census with his wife **Hazy L.**, and children **Charles C., Bruce L., (Dr.) Caswell P., Bessie E.,** and **Myrtle B. Wilson**. The daughter **Ella** must have been born after 1900.

D. Maynard Wilson did not know about "**Elbert's** children and wife," nor does this compiler at this time.

But, he says, "**Cas'** daughter **Louisa** was first married to a **Gentry**. They had two daughters, **Ida** who married **Paris Loy** and **Ethel** who married **Jim Ford**. After **Gentry's** death, **Louisa** married **John Loy**. Their children were **Will, Gibson, Hercules, Haley** and **Ola**. **Cas'** daughter **Delia Wilson** married **Robert Sharp**, **Frank's** son. They had a number of children whose names I don't know. **Robert** died and **Delia** married **Isaac Bridges**. Their children were **Emma, Ruth, Newman**, and others. **Cas'** daughter **Cecile**, married **Elonzo Hill**. Their two sons were **Esco** and **Clarence**; their daughter, **Lillian**."

D. Maynard Wilson next stated that **Asbury Wilson's** son **Bruce** became a veterinarian, while "**Asbury's** youngest son became a medical doctor."

The **Gentry** and **Loy** families can be tied into the settling families of the early 1800's. Under the **George Rice** chapter of this book will be the name **Adison Gentry**. **Adison Gentry** married **George Rice's** daughter **Rebecca Rice** in 1843. A **Charles Gentery** had a land grant in 1782 in what was then North Carolina, later Washington County, Tenn. (See page 14.)

(1) **Asberry Wilson.** The spelling "Asberry" is very similar to "Asbury." On the **Weaver** side--**Marcellus Moss Rice's** wife **Ibbie Jane Weaver** there is a brother **(William) Asbury Weaver.**

Your compiler did not find out about **Asberry Wilson** until recently and only through the census records. He was 13 in 1880, and 33 in 1900, as follows:

1900 Soundex
Microcopy T-1072, roll 179.
W-425 Code for Wilson

Name	Rel.	Birthdate	Age	B.P.	Vol.	E.D.*	Sheet	Line
Wilson, Asberry		Aug. 1866	33	Tenn.	70	159	9	1
(Union - 8th Civil District)								
Wilson, Hazy L.	Wife	Oct. 1864	35	Tenn.				
" **Charles C.**	Son	Feb. 1885	15	Tenn.				
" **Bruce L.**	Son	July 1888	11	Tenn.				
" **Caswell P.**	Son	Sept.1891	8	Tenn.				
" **Bessie E.**	Dau	Apr. 1894	6	Tenn.				
" **Myrtle B.**	Dau.	Aug. 1897	2	Tenn.				

* = Enumeration District.

The next roll, No. 180, was checked for **Asberry's** brothers **Orvel, Miller,** and **Eli,** and for his sisters. According to the notebook of **John Rice Irwin** (14), **Caswell P. Wilson** is **Dr. C. P. Wilson** of Sevierville, Tennessee, named for his grandfather **Caswell Wilson.** (Also found in **The Descendants of Henry Rice Pioneer to Tennessee,** compiled by **Martin Rice,** quoted by **Willie H. Thomas,** (50, page 3). There should be other records in the courthouse at Jacksboro, Tennessee.

Next is the 1900 Union County census for **Asberry Wilson.**

1900 Census, Union County, Tennessee
Microcopy T-623, roll 1602, Enumeration District 159,
sheet 9, line 1, 8th Civil Dist., 4th June 1900
Household 136, family 137

Name	Rel.	1.	2.	Birthdate	Age	Status	3.	4.	5.	B.P.**
Wilson, Asberry	Head	W	M	Aug. 1866	33	married 18				TN^{ax}
Wilson, Hazy D.	Wife	W	F	Oct. 1864	35	married 18	5	5		TN
(continued on the next page)										

163

Wilson,
Charley C.	Son	W	M	Feb. 1885	15	single	TNb
Wilson, Bruce L.	Son	W	M	July 1888	11	single	TNb

Wilson,
Caswell P.	Son	W	M	Sep. 1891	8	single	TN
Wilson, Bessie E.	Dau	W	F	Apr. 1894	6	single	TN
Wilson, Myrtle B.	Dau	W	F	Aug. 1897	2	single	TN

> a = Farmer   b = Farm laborer
> x = All born in Tennessee--including father and mother of **Asberry** and **Hazy D. Wilson**.

1900 Census, Union County, Tennessee
Enumeration District 159, sheet 9, line 22,
Household 140, family 141

Wilson, Isaac A.	Head	W	M	Mar. 1875	25	married	5			TN
Wilson, Eliza	Wife	W	F	May 1877	23	married	5	1	1	TNx
Wilson, Dona E.	Dau	W	F	Feb. 1899	1	single				TN

Isaac A. Wilson, the son of **Caswell Wilson**, was given as 19 years older than the **Isaac Wilson** who was the son of **Caswell Wilson**, who was 6 in 1880. So this is **Asberry's** brother.

Notes: x = All born in Tennessee, except **Eliza's** father, who was born in Alabama.

b. **Lydia Wilson**. **Fred Randolph Gibson**, a **Weaver** relative of your compiler, furnished the information that **Isaac Wilson** had a daughter **Lydia**, who married her half uncle **John Wilson**--another son of **Augustus** but of the second wife **Barbara May** (personal communication). **Mr. Gibson** also referred me to **John Wilson's** pension papers that say that **Lydia's** son **Dr. Isaac A. Wilson** was **John's** stepson, and born before April 27, 1837 (the date of the marriage of **John** and **Lydia**). Therefore, **Lydia** must have had a previous husband, name unknown as of now.

In **Goodspeed's History of East Tennessee** (49), (1887, reprinted in 1980), there is a biographical sketch on **Capt. John Wilson** under Union County. This sketch says, "April 27, 1837, he married **Lydia**, a daughter of **Isaac Wilson**, and born in Campbell County, in May 1816. They have five sons and two daughters."

More of this sketch will be included under **John Wilson** and his mother, **Barbara May Wilson**. This sketch does not mention that **Isaac** and **John** are half brothers. Census records for 1850 and 1860, Anderson County, and the 1870 Union County listings for **Lydia** will be found under **John Wilson**.

E. AUGUSTUS WILSON'S SECOND WIFE, BARBARA MAY

At the time of this writing, all that is known about Barbara May is from the **Goodspeed** sketch (49) on **Capt. John Wilson**.

> "Capt. John Wilson, farmer and stock dealer, was born in Anderson County, October 28, 1813, the son of **Augustus** and **Barbara (May) Wilson**....while the mother was born in Virginia, and died in the same county. They had two children, our subject and a sister. The former was fairly educated, and remained on the homestead, caring for his parents, until about 1855...."

Barbara was in the 1850 Anderson County census under **John Wilson** with **John's** sister, **Polly**. **Augustus** died on February 28, 1851, according to this sketch, but he did not appear in the 1850 census. Also, the 1850 census gives Maryland for the place of **Barbara's** birth. **John Wilson**, in the 1870 census, had 12 children.

    a. <u>**John Wilson**</u> John Wilson was born October 28, 1813, the son of **Augustus Wilson** and his second wife **Barbara May**. In this section will be included the 1840 and 1850 Anderson County census records, plus the 1860 and 1870 Union County census schedules. According to **D. Maynard Wilson**, John Wilson was 88 when he died in 1901; however, he was not found by your compiler in either the 1880 or the 1900 census schedules for the entire State of Tennnessee.

The military service record and pension application will be included here also.

1840 Anderson County Census
Microcopy 704 Roll 517, page 4

John Wilson was listed on the same page as his father:

John Wilson. 1 male un. 5; 1 male 5-10; 1 male 15-20
              1 female un. 5; 1 female 20-30

John was born in the year 1813, so should have been included in the age category 20-30. Since he married **Lydia** on April 27, 1837, the son 5-10 was born before their marriage and was the stepson, **Isaac A. Wilson**. **Isaac A. Wilson** was 16 in the 1850 census, with **James F.** 14 and **Elizabeth J.** 13. **George**, 11, might have been born just after the 1840 census was recorded.

Next is the 1850 census schedule for Anderson County, Tennessee, for **John** and **Lydia Wilson**. **Louisa Wilson** also is listed here, being two households away from **John**. **Amos Wilson** also was two households away, but his census record will be given under his own section.

<u>1850</u> **Anderson** <u>County</u> Tennessee <u>Census</u>
Microcopy 432, roll 869, 16th subdivision, 16 October 1850
Page 59, line 32, household 820, family 824

Louisa Wilson	23	F	Virginia - Cannot read nor write
			(CNRW)
Squire Wilson	5	M	Tenn
Manervy J.	3	F	Tenn.
Caswell S. Wilson	1	M	Tenn.

Maybe the above **Louisa** was the widow of a son of **Augustus**, and **Polly** (below) could be a sister or half-sister of **John** or **Lydia Wilson**. **Rufus** (below) seems to belong to **Polly**.

<u>1850</u> **Anderson** <u>County</u> <u>Census</u> (Continued)
Page 59, line 41 through second part of
Page 59, line 11, household 822, family 826

John Wilson	39	M	Farmer	700 real estate	Tenn.	
Lydia Wilson	30	F			"	CNRW
Isaac A. Wilson	16	M	Farmer		"	School
James F. Wilson	14	M			"	"
Elizabeth J.	13	F			"	"
George Wilson	11	M			"	"
William Wilson	9	M			"	"
Gusta Wilson	6	M			"	"
Levi W. Wilson	4	M			"	
Frederick	4/12	M			"	
Barbry Wilson	80	F			Md.	CNRW
Polly Wilson	30	F			Tenn.	CNRW
Rufus P. Wilson	6	M			"	School

The ages given for **John** and **Lydia** vary. Since **Lydia** was born in May 1816 in Campbell County, she should have been listed here as age 34.

On page 60, line 17, household 829, family 833 (very near to **John** and **Lydia**, and to **Amos Wilson**, we see:

Hamilton Wilson 24 M Farmer 150 real estate Tenn. CNRW
Matilda Wilson 16 F   "

In 1857 Union County was formed from portions of Anderson, Campbell, and Claiborne Counties. The seventh district land of **John Wilson** thereafter has the post office Raccoon Valley.

1860 Union County Tennessee Census
Microcopy 653, roll 1276, Raccoon Valley,
7th District, 9 July 1860.
Page 82, line 30, household 592, family 592

John Wilson	47	M	Farmer	1500	200	Tenn.
Lidia	42	F	Housewife		200	"
James F.	23	M	Farmhand			"
Elizabeth J.	20	F	Domestic			"
George M.	19	M	Farmhand			"
William S.	17	M	Farmhand			"
John A.	13	M				"
Frederick	10	M				"
Levi W.	11	M				"
Washington W.	8	M				"
Christopher C.	5	M				"

The step-son **Isaac A. Wilson** does not appear in either Anderson nor Union County in 1860, nor later in 1870, but the doctor does show up in Union County in 1880, without his father. But **John** was still living in 1880, for the pension papers are dated 1898. Maybe **Isaac** was receiving his medical training in another county. The 1880 Union County census will be shown under **Isaac A. Wilson**, and an ancestral line through **Isaac A. Wilson's** son **Henry Scott Wilson**.

Gusta, a son who was 6 in the 1850 census, does not show up in 1860. **Levi**, given as 4 years old in 1850 is now 11 (sic) years of age, and **Frederick**, 4/12 in 1850, is now 10. There are two new sons, **Washington W.**, and **Christopher C.** According to a pension letter of 1898, the latest son "was born August the 9th 1854 who is a blind Ediot."

Next is the 1870 Union County census for **John Wilson**, with a new post office Warwicks X Roads, but still in the 7th District.

1870 Union County Tennessee Census
Microcopy 593, roll 1567
Warwicks X Roads, 7th District, 10 July 1870,
Page 17, line 32, household 121, family 121

Wilson, John	55	M	W	Farmer	700	500	Tenn.
(1 male citizen above 21)							
Liddy	53	F	W	Keeping House		"	CNRW
Freddie B.	20	M	W	Farm Laborer		"	
Washington W.	17	M	W	Farm Laborer		"	
Walhai?	16	M	W			"	CNRW
Christopher C.	13	M	W			"	CNRW
Martha A.	11	F	W			"	CNRW
Mary B.	9	F	W			"	

John, according to the sketch, "in 1884 moved to his present farm." However, **John** should still have been in the 1880 census, but he was not on the Soundex code system which covers the entire State of Tennessee.

John Wilson's Military Service Record

When the **Index to Compiled Service Records Voluntary Union Soldiers Who Served from Tennessee** was seen, there were three soldiers. One was **J. Wilson**, who served as a private in Company C, 6 Tennessee Mounted Infantry. This record was not consulted.

The second was **John Wilson**, Co. I, 7 Tennessee Mounted Infantry, Private to Corporal. He was 21, enlisted at Clinton, and was in the same military unit as your compiler's great-grandfather **Elder Thomas Weaver**. It would seem that this **John Wilson** might be a relative somehow.

The third **John Wilson** seen is the right one. His service record is in **Compiled Service Records of Voluntary Union Soldiers Who Served in Organizations from Tennessee Eleventh Cavalry, S-Y**. The envelope containing this service record is labeled "**Wilson, John**, Co. L, 11 Tenn. Cav. Capt." The **Goodspeed** sketch says that **John** was in Company M before he was transferred to Company L. The pension application gives only Company M for 11th Tennessee Cavalry.

The **first card** of the record has "**John Wilson** 9 Cavalry, Capt. Co. L, sub. 9 Tenn. Cav., 11 Reg't Tenn. Cav., Office muster-in, Dated Wash. D.C. Sept. 11, 1875, of the officer as of the grade named above to date, from the 29 day of Mch. 1864, date of assignment to duty & from which paid...."

168

John **Wilson** was changed on the record from Co. L, 9 Tenn. Cavalry to the 11th Regiment Tenn. Cavalry. The record of **John's** service was inscribed after the Civil War.

The second card has the following:"**John Wilson** Capt. Co. L., 11 Reg't Tenn. Cav., appears on COMPANY MUSTER ROLL for Sept. & Oct. 1864, Present. Remarks: Commanding the Co. since Oct. the 1/64 responsibility due since that time (age not given; Enrolled Mch. 29/64, Cumberland Gap Tenn.; Muster In Mch. 29/64 Cumberland Gap Tenn."

Capt. John Wilson was mustered in on March 29, 1864, but there are no records for his service before he became an officer. Your compiler does not know why these records are missing, but they would have given his age. Maybe the above was considered all that was necessary, since **John** became an officer.

The service record continues with the third card as follows: "**John Wilson** Capt. Co. L, 11 Reg't Tenn. Cavalry, Appears on COMPANY MUSTER ROLL from Nov. & Dec. 1864, Present, Remarks: Comd'g Co. since Oct. the 1/64, Responsibility due him since that time."

The fourth card mentioned that there was a special order or enclosure. "**Wilson, John**, Capt. Co. L, 11 Reg't Tenn Cav., 1 Enclosure, 1 Orders."

The special order consisted of two letters. The first was for **John Wilson** to report to the Sergeant in Charge Officers Hospital as follows: "Cumberland Gap Tenn., May 26, 1864, Special Order No. 15; Ordering **Capt. John Wilson**, Co. L, 11 Tenn. Cav. to report to the Sergeant in Charge Officers Hospital for medical treatment. Order: M.D.O. Ohio, Rec'g M.D.O.D.O. July 1, 1864."

The second letter was written ordering **John Wilson** to go to an officer's hospital in Knoxville.

                              "Cumberland Gap Tenn.
                               May 26th 1864

        Special Order   )
        No. 15   )

            Upon the recommendation of Chief Surgeon **John
    R. Robson** in charge of Post Hospital Cumb. Gap Tenn.
    Capt. John Wilson Co. L. 11th Tenn. Cav. will
    proceed to Knoxville Tenn. and there report to the
    Surgeon in charge of Officers Hospital for medical
    treatment.

                              By Command of
                              Col. W. G. Dillard
                              William P. Amos
                              Lieut. and W A A Gen`l."

        According to the pension application, **John Wilson** had a fever
    from exposure to cold in the Kentucky mountains. But he also
    wrote that he was injured before and after the war, and that he
    was worse from the fever. His health was very poor when he
    applied for a pension.

                 Capt. John Wilson`s Pension Application

        His pension papers are extensive because of his injuries
    before, during and after the Civil War. The entire record is
    given here.

        "Certificate No. 275144   Department of the Interior
        Name, **John Wilson**   Bureau of Pensions
                                         Washington, D.C.,
                                         January 15, 1898.

        First. Are you married? If so, please state your wife`s
                full name and her maiden name.

        Answer. No. My wife Departed this life Nov. the 11th day
                1889.

        Second. When, where, and by whom were you married?

        Answer. April the 30th day 1837, by **Isaac Miller** Esq. in
                Anderson County, Tennessee.

    170

Third. What record of marriage exists?

Answer. A Family Record and perhaps a County C. [Circuit] Clk
in Clinton Tenn. Anderson County.

Fourth. Were you previously married? If so, please state the
name of your former wife and the date and place of
her death or divorce.

Answer. No I never had but one wife [Never gives name].

Fifth. Have you any children living? If so, please state
their names and the dates of their birth.

Answer. Yes, I have four children living; **Frederick B. Wilson**
was born December the 29th day 1849; **Martha A. Wilson**
now **Auston** born Sept. the 30th day 1857; **Elizabeth
Jane Wilson** now **Johnson** was born Oct. the 18th day
1838; **Christopher C. Wilson** was born Aug. the 9th
1854 who is a blind Ediot.

Date of reply, May 4th, 1898   John Wilson"

"Invalid Pension - Original
Acts of July 14, 1862, and March 3, 1873

Claimant **John Wilson**   (Rank, Capt.
P.O., Maynardsville   (Company, M.
County, Union   (Regiment, 11 Tenn. Cavl.
State, Tenn.

Attorney, **S. Munson**, Knoxville, Tenn.
Fee, $25.00 contract filed. Material evidence filed since
July 8, 1870.

Enlisted Mch. 29, 1864, Mustered into rank Capt. Mch. 29,
1864

Discharged June 6, 1865; Date of completing proof Oct. 11,
1875; Not in the military or naval service since
discharged June 6, 1865 (filed Mch. 30, 1874.)

Disabled by Spinal Irritation or hyperanthesia of the
spinal column.

Brief for ? Submitted Nov. 6, 1875, **H. D. Smayze** (?),
Examiner.

Declaration filed Mch. 11, 1872, alleging disability from
    liver disease & heart disease, that while in line of
    duty near Cumberland Gap he was sick with fever caused
    by cold & exposure which caused the above disability
    - May 13. 75. Claimant testifies that....on or about
    Mch. 2, 1864 while in line of duty near Cumberland Gap,
    he contracted pneumonia fever from cold and exposure
    and that said fever settled in his liver and has
    affected heart and his whole system since and that he
    afterward (was) discharge(d) on account of the effects
    of said fever.

Board of Ex`g Surgeon,)   Finds Spinal Irritation or
Knoxville, Tenn.   )   Hyperanthesia of the spinal
                              column. No disease of liver."

Next is a letter from **James W. Turner** and **Jacob Beeler**.

"State of Tennessee   )
Union County   )   SS

        In the matter of Invalid Pension Claim No.   of
        John Wilson, late Captain, Co. M. 9th Regt, Tenn.
        Cav. Vols.

    Personally appeared before me a Justice of the Peace in
and for aforesaid County and State **James W. Turner** and **Jacob
Beeler** P. O. address Warwick`s X Roads--Citizens of Union
County State of Tennessee well known to me to be reputable
and entitled to credit who being by me duly sworn declares
in relation to the aforesaid as follows:

    That they have been acquainted with and near neighbors
to **John Wilson**, aforesaid for over 30 years, and that about
20 years ago the said **John Wilson** fell from a house and broke
or in some way injured his shoulder, that prior to and at the
time of his enlistment he had recovered from said injury--
except the shoulder (was) a little stiff--and was as sound
after as before and that he was sound in the shoulder when
he entered the army as though he had never been injuried
....further states since his discharge and before he was
discharged from the army, we saw him suffering from chronic
diorhea, and he yet complains, of a general debility the
effects of exposure while in the army--this debility did not
exist until after he enlisted in the army.

We further declare that we have no interest in the prosecution of this claim are not concerned in its prosecution and are not related to said applicant.

James W. Turner
Jacob Beeler."

The above letter did not help in obtaining a pension.

Fred Randolph Gibson gave to your compiler a chart which shows his line from **Augustus Wilson** down to **Reverend Henry Scott Wilson**, the son of **John Wilson's** step-son **Dr. Isaac A. Wilson**. **Henry Wilson's** mother was **Isaac's** first of three wives, **Martha J. Graves**, and **Henry's** wife was **Lucy Jane Beeler**. **Lucy** was born on March 2, 1870. They were married in the year 1889. Her date of death was July 30, 1964, and Knox County is the place of death.

Maybe **Lucy Jane Beeler** was daughter of **Jacob Beeler**.

The pension application continues with other papers having to do with questions about **John Wilson's** many injuries. The part that follows concerns additional injuries not mentioned before.

"Deposition Ex. "e" Case of **John Wilson**, No. 173151 on this ____ day of November, 1883, at Knoxville, County of Knox State of Tennessee, before....a Special Examiner of the Pension Office, personally appeared **John Wilson....**"

Next are some "Questions by **E. T. Johnson**, Supervising Examiner.

"3. It has come to our knowledge that before you entered the service that you had received another serious injury not mentioned in your former statement nor by any of the witnesses. We desire from you a full history and description of such injury....

"A. Yes, sir: I was injured by my horse falling and throwing me over his head. My left shoulder was broken or dislocated. I don't know which that was in the fall of 1863, just after the seige of Knoxville. During the siege I have been in Knoxville. At the close of the siege the 11th Tennessee Cavalry was stationed at Strawberry Plains. I went there and was with the regiment and was making up my company preparatory to going into service with them. The company was not yet organized and I was not yet enlisted or mustered and have no commission, but was getting my company together. I rode on horseback from the camp at Strawberry Plains to my own home in Union County, where I now live, and for several days was riding around the country gathering up men for my company. It was on one of these trips, and while returning to my house on horseback, after night, that I met with the accident. My horse, in crossing a little log or pole bridge, fell with me and threw me over his head. I fell, head foremost, on my left shoulder, which struck a little stump. My shoulder was either dislocated or broken, I don't know which. I was confined to the house with it about one month before I was able to go back to the regiment. Meantime the regiment had left Strawberry Plains and gone to Maynardsville, about six miles from my house, and I rejoined it there."

Question 4 summarized, asked if any physicians attended him. His answer was no and that he, **John**, did the best he knew how.

"5. In what condition was your shoulder left by that injury?

"A. The dislocation is very pained by the bones of the shoulder on the top sticking up above the shoulder. It has ever since been in a very bad condition. The shoulder joint is very stiff. I can't move my arm backwards nor raise it to a level with the shoulder. A backward or upward motion of the arm causes me intense pain. It hurts powerful bad. I have always suffered since that injury with great pain in my arm between the elbow and shoulder, and that arm is partly perished away on that account, so that it is not nearly as large as the other. The other shoulder was broken in a fall from a house before the war, but this one broken by the fall from my horse has always given me a great deal more trouble than the other.

"6. With both shoulders broken, and the other injuries which you described in your former statement, how did you succeed in passing the necessary medicine examination preceding your muster into service?

"A. There was no medical examination. I got my commission and just went over to the 34th or 24th Kentucky Regiment and was mustered in without examination."

Note: The Index to Compiled Service Records of Voluntary Union Soldiers Who Served In Organizations From Kentucky, We, Microcopy 386, roll 29, was searched, and there was no **John Wilson** in the 24th or 34th Kentucky Infantry. These units were checked as well. Three soldiers were also checked, as follows:

"John W. Wilson, Co. G, 28 Ky Inf. Capt/Capt; John C. Wilson, Co. C, 47 Ky Inf. Capt/Capt; John Wilson, Co. C. A., 8 Ky Inf. Capt/Capt." These are the only John Wilsons who were also captains.

Records to Find

Your compiler has written this subchapter on John Wilson without having seen county court records for marriages, deeds, orders, wills, estate records, tax lists, Bible pages, tombstone inscriptions, etc. All of these should be looked up for John and his children.

F. SAMPSON WILSON

Sampson was a grandson of Augustus Wilson and his first wife Anna Rice. Then Sampson is the son of Augustus' son, Amos and Barbara James. Sampson is under Amos in the 1850 Anderson County Tennessee census as sixteen years of age. However, Sampson was not found in the 1860 and 1880 census schedules for Anderson, Campbell, nor Union County. He is in the 1870 and 1900 Campbell County census reports.

1870 Campbell County Census
Microcopy 593, roll 1516
1st Civil District, 21 July 1870
Post Office Jacksboro, page 13
Line 13, household 98, family 90

Wilson,	Sampson	35	M	W	Farmer		200	275	Tenn.	
"	Eliza	34	F	W	Keeping House				Tenn.	*
"	George	13	M	W	At Home	School			Tenn.	*
"	James	10	M	W	At Home	School			Tenn.	**
"	Nancy	6	F	W					Tenn.	
"	Barbry	84	F	W	At Home				Tenn.	**

Notes: * = Cannot write. ** = Cannot read nor write.

The George, above, who is 13, was then born in 1857, might be the George, who was living two households away from Sampson in 1900. This George had a big family with one of his sons being named Sampson D. Wilson. This family will be given, with the census of Sampson and other closely residing Wilson families.

The Barbry Wilson above is 84 in 1870. Her maiden name is James, and she was the widow of Amos. See the Amos Wilson subchapter, page 151.

Microcopy T-623, Roll 1559, Enumeration District 29,
Supervisor's District 2, 1st Civil District,
4 and 5 June 1900, sheet 3, line 28
Household 42, family 42

Wilson, George	Head	W	M	Feb 1857	40	M	17			TN	TN	TN	Farmer
"	Manervy J.	Wife	W	F			38	M	17	9 8	TN	TN	TN
"	Sampson D	Son	W	M	Nov 1881	18	S			TN	TN	TN	Farm Lb
"	Merry E.	Dau	W	F	Dec 1885	14	S			TN	TN	TN
"	Nancy J.	Dau	W	F	Sep 1887	12	S			TN	TN	TN
"	Ida E.	Dau	W	F	Oct 1889	10	S			TN	TN	TN
"	Cora M.	Dau	W	F	Feb 1893	7	S			TN	TN	TN
"	Pearley	Dau	W	F	Aug 1894	5	S			TN	TN	TN
"	Walter L.	Son	W	M	May 1896	4	S			TN	TN	TN
"	Stella E.	Dau	W	F	Oct 1899	2/12	S			TN	TN	TN

George and **Manervy J. Wilson** had been married for seventeen years, with Manervy being the mother of nine children. Eight of the offspring were still alive in 1900. The M stands for married, while the S stands for single.

Sheet 3, lines 38 through 44
Household 43, family 43
George Baker and family

Sheet 3, line 45, household 44, family 44

Wilson, Sampson	Head	W	M	Feb 1834	66	M	22			TN	TN	NC
"	Mary M.	Wife	W	F	Mch 1845	55	M	22	3 1	TN	VA	TN

Sampson and **Mary M. Wilson** had been married for twenty-two years with one of three children still living. **Mary M.** is a second wife, and her father was born in Virginia. **Sampson** was the father of at least six children. In the 1870 census, above, his children are **George**, 13, **James**, 10, and **Nancy**, 6. The 1900 census says that one of the three offspring of **Mary** was alive.

Next are other **Wilsons**, who were living next to the above families in Campbell County in 1900.

1900 Campbell County Tenn. Census
(Same data as above)
Enumeration District 29, sheet 2, line 89,
Household 36, family 36

Wilson,	Armstead	Head	W	M	Nov 1872	27	M	7		TN	TN	TN	Farmer
"	Maggie	Wife	W	F	Jul 1873	26	M	7 3 3		TN	TN	TN	
"	John	Son	W	M	Aug 1885	14	S			TN	TN	TN	
"	Calvin	Son	W	M	Apr 1888	11	S			TN	TN	TN	
"	Nancy A.	Dau	W	F	Dec 1891	8	S			TN	TN	TN	
"	James	Son	W	M	Apr 1894	6	S			TN	TN	TN	
"	George	Son	W	M	Jul 1896	3	S			TN	TN	TN	
"	Belle	Dau	W	F	Feb 1899	1	S			TN	TN	TN	

Wilson,	Amanda	Head	W	F	Mch 1864	36	WD	10 6	TN	TN	TN	
"	Alfred	Son	W	M	Sep 1883	16	S		TN	TN	TN	
"	Amos	Son	W	M	Oct 1885	14	S		TN	TN	TN	
"	Louisie	Dau	W	F	Jun 1888	11	S		TN	TN	TN	
"	Flora L.	Dau	W	F	Jul 1890	9	S		TN	TN	TN	
"	Matilda	Dau	W	F	Jun 1892	7	S		TN	TN	TN	
"	Dona	Dau	W	F	Jun 1894	5	S		TN	TN	TN	

Since **Augustus Wilson** had a son **George**, and **Sampson** had a brother **George**, there will be next a Subchapter G on even more than these **George Wilsons**.

G. GEORGE WILSON

There is living next to **Isaac Wilson** in 1850 in Campbell County a **George Wilson**, who is believed to be the son of **Augustus**. **Isaac** married secondly **Jemima Evans**. Also, a **John Evans**, with daughter **Jemima**, is living next to **George Wilson**, and his census record will be included here. See the Isaac Wilson Subchapter for **Isaac Wilson's** census data.

1850 Campbell County Tenn. Census
Microcopy 432, roll 872
17th Subdivision, 21 Oct. 1850, page 325, line 28,
Household 660, family 660

John Evans	23	M	Farmer		NC
Minerva	18	F			TN
Jemima	5/12	F			TN

1850 Campbell County, Tenn. Census (continued)
Page 325, line 31, household 661, family 661

George Wilson	23	M	Farmer	TN
Sarah	27	F		TN
Campbell E.	3	M		TN
Mariah Hurst or Hunt	15	F		TN

Isaac was living at household 662 and family 662 on page 325 and lines 35 to 40. This George Wilson was not found in the census after 1850, but there are Georges in the 1880 and 1900 census reports below.

H. OTHER GEORGE WILSONS

In Campbell County in 1880 there are two George Wilsons and a G. W. Wilson. There was a G. W. Wilson also in Knox County, and that census is included here. The George in 1850 was 23 and, therefore, was born in 1827. The two Georges and G. W. are younger. There is in Campbell County a George, who was born in 1837 and 62 years of age in 1900.

1880 Campbell County Tenn. Census
Microcopy T-9, roll 1246, 2nd Civil District
17th & 18th days of June, 1880
Page 19, line 6, household 149, family 156
Enumeration District 119

Wilson,	G. W.	W	M	44		M	Farmer*	Cnw**	TN	TN	TN
"	Mary	W	F	39	Wife	M	Keeping Hs	Cnw	TN	TN	TN
"	Lewis	W	M	15	Son	S	Works on farm	School	TN	TN	TN
"	Jane	W	F	2	Dau	S			TN	TN	TN

Page 19, line 11, household 150, family 157

Wilson, James		W	M	26		M	Farmer		KY	TN	KY
"	M. J.	W	F	36	Wife	M	Keeping Home	Cnrw***	TN	TN	TN
"	Lindsay	W	M	8	Son	S			TN	TN	TN
"	Jno. J.	W	M	5	Son	S			TN	TN	TN
Boshares, Lindsay		W	M	31	Laborer	S	Farm laborer		TN	TN	TN

Notes: * = disability or illness--cancer.
   ** = cannot write.
   *** = cannot read nor write

1880 Campbell County Tenn. Census (Continued)
Page 19, line 16, household 151, family 158

Wilson,	Geo.	W	M	35		M	Farmer	Cnrw	TN	TN TN
"	B. A.	W	F	39	Wife	M	Keeping House	Cw	TN	TN TN
"	S. E.	W	F	13	Dau	S	At home	Cw	IN	TN TN
"	Isaac	W	M	11	Son	S	Works on Farm	Cnrw	IN	TN TN
"	M. J.	W	F	7	Dau	S			KY	TN TN
"	Wm. E.	W	M	5	Son	S			TN	TN TN
"	F. M.	W	M	1	Son	S			TN	TN TN

Page 19, line 21, household 152, family 159

Keith, Nancy	W	F	98		WD	At home	Cnrw	NC	NK* VA
Boshares, Elizabeth	W	F	48	Dau.	M	Keeping House	Cnrw	TN	SC NC
Laine, Sarah	W	F	53	Dau	M	Keeping House	Cnrw	TN	TN TN
" Martha	W	F	14	GD**	S	At Home	Cnrw	TN	TN TN
" Joseph	W	M	12	GS**	S	Works at Home	Cnrw	TN	TN TN

Notes: * = Not known.   ** = Grandson or Granddaughter

The above **G. W. Wilson** had cancer. The census had the
following column: "Is the person (on the day of the Enumerator's
visit) sick or temporary disabled, so as to be unable to attend to
ordinary business or duties? If so, what is the sickness or
disability?"

The last family was given, for the name **Boshares** is in common
with the **Lindsay Boshares** under **James Wilson**.

1880 Campbell County Tenn. Census
2nd Civil District
10th & 12th days of June, 1880
Supervisor District 1, page 12, line 34
Household 98, family 103

Wilson,	Daniel E.	W	M	49		M	Farmer		TN	NK NK
"	Eliza	W	F	50	Wife	M	Keeping House	Cnrw	TN	NC NC

Page 12, line 41, household 99, family 105

Wilson,	Geo.	W	M	32		M	Farmer	Cnrw	TN	TN TN
"	Lindy	W	F	28	Wife	M	Keeping House	CNrw	TN	TN TN
"	Jas. W.	W	M	6	Son	S			TN	TN TN
"	Nancy A.	W	F	4	Dau	S			TN	TN TN
"	Milton	W	M	6/12 S	S	Nov.			TN	TN TN

179

1880 Knox County Tenn. Census
Microcopy T-9, roll 1265, 23 Civil District
Enumeration District 154, Supervisor District 1
17 June, 1880
Page 37, line 33, household 244, family 244

Wilson,	G. W.	W M 33		M Works on Farm	Cnrw	TN TN TN
"	Eveline A.	W F 32	Wife	M Keeps House	Cnrw	TN TN TN
"	Charly A.	W M 10	Son	S Works on Farm	Cw	TN TN TN
"	Martha	W F 9	Dau			TN TN TN
"	Mary	W F 8	Dau	S		TN TN TN
"	Margret	W F 4	Dau	S		TN TN TN
"	Lucy	W F 2	Dau	S		TN TN TN
"	George	W M 5/12	Son	S		TN TN TN

Since **Augustus** and **Anne Rice** lived in Knox County around what is now Fountain City, this **G. W. Wilson** with a son **George** might be related.

1900 Campbell County Tenn. Census
Microcopy T-623, roll 1599, Enumeration District 30
John M. Irwin, Enumerator, Supervisor District 2
4 & 5 day of June, 1900
Sheet 2, line 60, household 29, family 29

Wilson,	Marry	Head W F Aug 1841 58 Wd	3 2	TN TN TN Farm Lab.
"	Martha	Dau W F Mar 1870 29 S		TN TN TN

Sheet 2, line 62, household 30, family 30

Weaver,	Charly	Head W M Nov 1877 22	Wd	TN TN TN Farmer
"	George	Son W M Apr 1900 4/12 S		TN TN TN

Sheet 2, line 64, household 31, family 31

Wilson,	George	Head W M Jul 1837 62 Wd		TN TN TN Farmer
"	Louis	Son W M Dec 1864 35 M	3	TN TN TN Farm Lab.
"	Florence	Wife W F Feb 1873 26 M	3 1 1	TN TN TN
"	Viola	Dau W F Jun 1898 1 S		TN TN TN

The **Marry Wilson** was widowed and living two houses away from **George**. There are **Weavers** in Campbell, Union and Knox Counties in your compilers ancestry. This **George Wilson** was born 10 years later than the one living next to **Isaac** 50 years earlier.

180

13 day of June, 1900
Sheet 7, line 77, household 115, family 117

```
Wilson, James       Head  W M Oct 1843 56 M 10        TN TN TN Farmer
   "    Nellie B.   Wife  W F May 1845 55 M 10  0 0 TN TN TN
   "    Hulda       Mother W F Dec 1820 79 Wd    10 7 TN TN TN
```

Sheet 7, line 85, household 117, family 119

```
Wilson, George      Head  W M Nov 1835 64 M 38        TN TN TN Farmer
   "    Anna        Wife  W F May 1837 63 M 38  7 5 TN TN TN
Patterson, Barbra   Sist  W F Jun 1847 52 Wd    3 3 TN TN TN
```

Sheet 7, line 88, household 118, family 120

```
Wilson, Edgar       Head  W M Apr 1876 24 M  2        TN TN TN
   "    Allice      Wife  W F May 1884 16 M  2  0 0 TN TN TN
```

Not given here, but on the sheet 7, are also families of L. **Wilson** and **Square Wilson** under **Jacob Moser**.

This concludes the **Wilson** chapter.

CHAPTER XI. ROSA RICE – JAMES SPENCE – ALEXANDER MORROW
Chapter summary on page vii

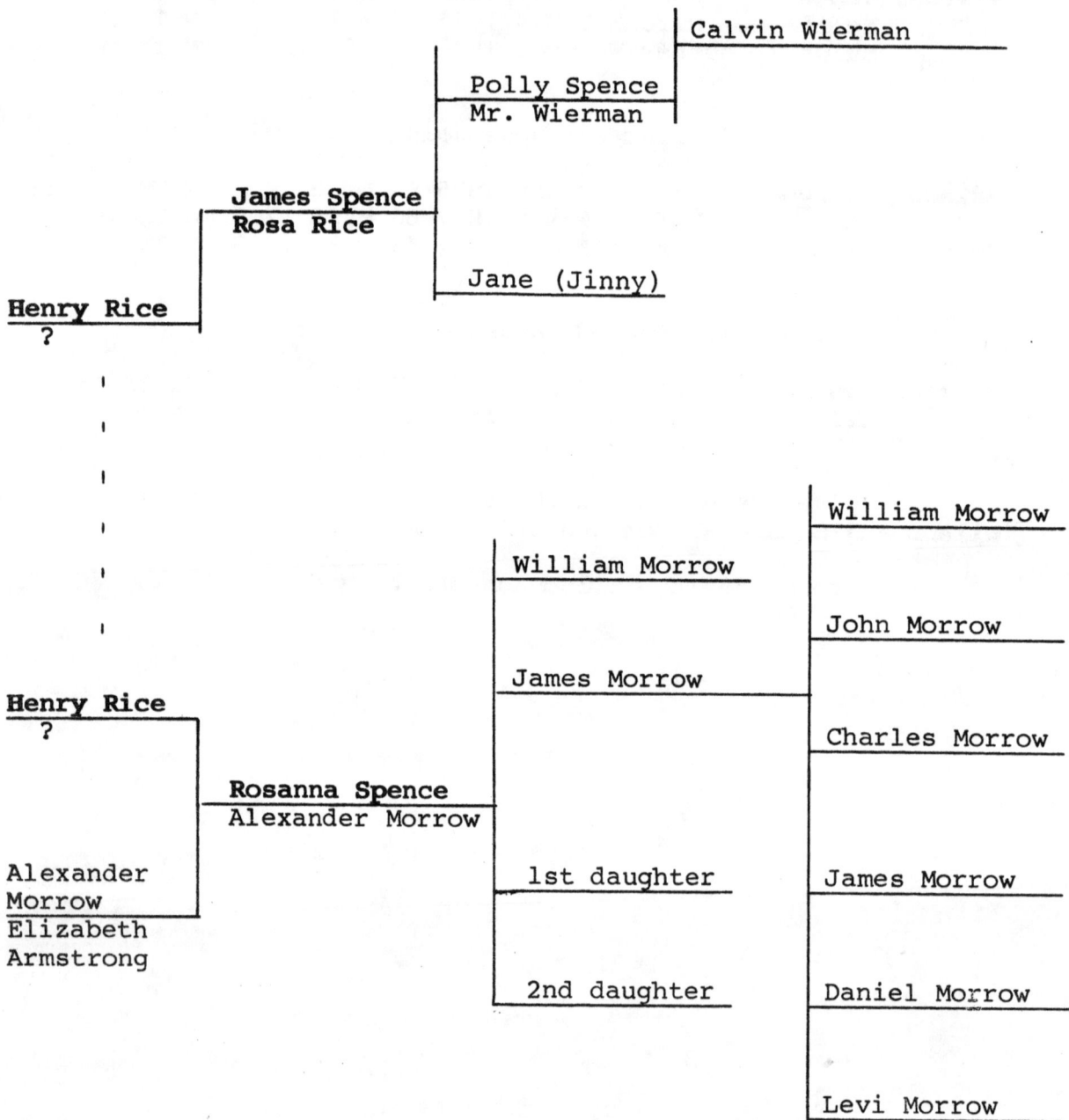

```
                                                  Calvin Wierman
                                            |─────
                                 Polly Spence
                                 Mr. Wierman
                                            |
                  James Spence
                  Rosa Rice  ──────
                                 Jane (Jinny)
                                 ─────────

 Henry Rice ─────
 ?
  ¦
  ¦
  ¦
  ¦
  ¦
  ¦                                               William Morrow
  ¦                                            ───────────────
  ¦                              William Morrow
 Henry Rice                      ───────────────
 ?         ─────                                  John Morrow
                                 James Morrow   ───────────────
                                 ────────────
                                                  Charles Morrow
                 Rosanna Spence                 ───────────────
                 Alexander Morrow ─────
 Alexander                                        James Morrow
 Morrow                          1st daughter   ───────────────
 Elizabeth                       ────────────
 Armstrong                                        Daniel Morrow
                                 2nd daughter   ───────────────
                                 ────────────
                                                  Levi Morrow
                                                ───────────────
```

CHAPTER XI.   ROSA RICE - JAMES SPENCE
ROSANNA SPENCE - ALEXANDER MORROW

Chapter summary on page vii

This daughter of **Henry Rice** had the name **Rosa** in Martin
Rice's recollections. In the Knox County Marriage Records of her
marriage to **Alexander Morrow** her name was given as **Rosanna Spence.**

The probable first name of Rosa's first husband was **James,**
for **James Spence** had a Tennessee State Grant. **James** was in the
Revolutionary War with **Samuel Spence.**

The "Bard of Lone Jack" wrote the following:

"**Rosa Spence** married **Alexander Morrow** in 1809. She had two
sons, **William** and **James,** and two daughters. I remember the
old lady and the two daughters and son **James.** His (**James'**)
sons were **William, John, Charles, James, Daniel** and **Levi.**
Polly Spence married a **Mr. Wierman** and they had a son **Calvin,**
about my age. **Jane,** or **Jinny,** was unmarried when I left that
State in 1833." (2, page 8)

"**Alexander Morrow** married **Rosanna Spence** on Dec. 9, 1809 with
John Wear as a witness or security." ("The Descendants of
Henry Rice, pioneer to Tennessee," compiled by **Martin Rice**
and recorded by **Willie H. Thomas,** page 1, footnote B) (50)

The late Professor **Willie H. Thomas** made additions to **Martin
Rice's** recollections (see **Alexander Morrow** for more on his
marriage).

A. JAMES SPENCE

1. **James Spence** had a grant in Hawkins County, Tennessee
(then in North Carolina).

> "**Tennessee State Grant 583**
> July 7, 1794   200 acres
> Hawkins County   Location N.C.
> Grant Book 9   Page 289."

[Note by **RRL:** The above quotation from the "Bard of Lone
Jack"does not make clear which of **Rosa's** children listed were
Spences and which were **Morrows,** except for **Polly Spence.**]

Although there is no birth, marriage, nor death record for **James Spence**, it is believed, from other evidence available, that **James** is the first name of the **Spence** who was **Rosa's** first husband.

2. **Revolutionary War Records.** **James** and **Samuel Spence** were in the 1st Regiment North Carolina Militia. This Militia regiment was distinct from the service unit having the name "1st Regiment North Carolina," which was not a militia unit.

Both **James** and **Samuel Spence** are mentioned in **The Colonial Records of North Carolina**, vol. XVII, 1781-'85, with another **James Spence**, **Insell Spence**, and **Jabez Spence**. (**The State Records of North Carolina**, Vol. XVII, 1781-'85, collected and edited by **Walter Clark**, one of the Justices of the Supreme Court of N.C., Nash Brothers, Book and Job Printers, Goldsboro, N.C., 1899, pages 246, 247, 1054.) The military records of **James** and **Samuel** are on the following pages. The above is source 51.

Abstract - The Army Accounts of the North Carolina Line
Page 246 "S"

Number	Name & Rank	Amount	By Whom Received	Remarks
959 (p.247)	James Spence Drag.(Dragon)*	65 pounds 1 shilling 4 pence	Arch. Lytte	None
1100 (p.248)	Insell Spence	27 pounds 16 shillings 1 pence	B. McCulloch	
2026	Jabez Spence	Warrenton 117 pounds 3 shillings 6 pence	B. McCulloch	For Selby Harney

* **Webster's New Collegiate Dictionary**, 1977 ed., has this definition: "dragon 4a: a short musket formerly carried to a soldier's belt; also: a soldier carrying such a musket. b: an artillery tractor."

184

Pay Roll of Capt. Alexander Whitehall's Company
of the 1st North Carolina Regiment of Militia
Commanded by Col. Sam'l Jarvis. June 2, 1780
Page 1054

Number	Names	Ranks	Commencement of Payment
34	James Spence	Private*	
35	Samuel Spence	Private*	

* These two service records will be next in this book but the
company payroll was not dated, nor was there a company
muster roll for this regiment to give place of muster.
There is no service record for No. 959 **James Spence** in the
"**Rev. War Index to Military Service** Sousl-Steward."
(Microcopy 860 Roll 49.) There is a service index for
North Carolina other than all states, but there are no
Spences on that roll. (Microcopy 881 Roll 783, "Compiled
Service Records of Soldiers Who Served in the American
Army During the Revolutionary War, North Carolina First
Regiment, Militia.")

James Spence and **Samuel Spence** could have been from
Pasquotank County, N.C., for there are **Spences**, including **James
Spence**, drummer, in the muster roll for the aforesaid county in
1755.

Before the 1755 muster roll is given, the **Incell Spence** and
Jabez Spence are in the "Roster of the Continental Line from North
Carolina 1783" (Vol. XVI, The State Records of North Carolina
1782-'83, **Walter Clark**, ed., pages 1002, 1157 and 1161), and
Jabez is in "List of Such Soldiers" in Camden December 21st
1786." (Same, vol. XVIII....1786 with supplement, 1779, Walter
Clark, ed., etc. except 1900, pages 796-797.) (52)

Roster of the Continental Line from North Carolina 1783
Vol XVI, 1782-'83. (52)

Page	7th Regiment	Company	Date of Commissions & Enlistments	Periods of Service
1157	Spence, Jabez pt. [private]	Pointers	1777	3 yrs.

"Occurence omtd. Oct., 1777."

1161   10th Regiment (continued)

Spence, Incell   Bradley's   20 July, 78   9 mo.
pt.   No occurrences

(53) Vol XVIII, 1786

796   "Col. Selby Harney to Gov. Caswell"
797   (From Executive Letter Book) "Endorsed is a List of such Soldiers as I have signed for chiefly for these three lower counties....Jabiz Spence." Camden, December 21st, 1786.

(54) The State Records of North Carolina
Vol. XXII, Miscellaneous, ed. by Walter Clark, 1907
1755 Spence Muster Rolls

Page 345   "Pasquotank County, 1755.
North Carolina - Pasquotank County, An Exact Muster Roll of the Regiment of s'd County, commanded by Coll. Robert Murden.
Page 346   In Captain Jos. Nash's, Being ye Second.
Page 347   Robert Spence
             Truman Spence.
         In Captain Nehemiah Jones' Company, Being ye Third.

             Greves Spence, Drummer
             James Spence, Drummer
             Alexander Spence
             James Spence
Page 348   In Captain Griffen Jones' Company
Page 349   David Spence
Page 352   In Capt. William Abercrombie's, Deceased, Company
             Alexander Spence
             Joseph Spence, Drummer
         In Capt. Henry Delon's Company
Page 353   Simon Spence."

3. **Other Spence Colonial Records**. There are North Carolina Colonial records (Vol. I, pages 487-88 of **State Records of North Carolina** ed. by **Walter Clark**) showing that **Spences** go back to the year 1697. (55)

> "At a Court Holden for the precinct of piquemons (Perquimans) at the Hous"e" of **Thomas Blunt** y[e] Second Monday in October 1697 pr.Sent **Capt. Ralph Ffletcher, Mr. John Whedby** y[e] 18th day psent **Caleb Calleway Samual Nicholson.**
> The Court is Rejorned till Monday next being y[e] 18th da. **John Spence** proved three Rits for three psons transported Into this County whoes names are under wrettan vis him Selfe **Cattern** his wife **Robert Spence.**
> **Alexander Spence** proved Rits for five psons transported Into this County hoes names are under wretten vis himselfe **Dorety Spence John Spence Daved Spence James Spence.**"

Pages 836, 837-838, "**Journal of the Virginia Council**:

> At a Council held at the Capitol the 20th day of February 1711(12). A letter from men 'to the **Honble Alexander Spotswood** her majestys Lieutenant & Governor General of Virginia' of grievance....**Elaxander Spence.**"

(56) Vol. II, **1713 to 1728**, Raleigh
P. M. Hale, Printer to the State, 1886
Pages 80, 89, 208, 522-23

Records of General Court, North Carolina State Society:

Page 80 - "At a Genll Court holden for the province afsd on Tuesday 31 March Anno Dmi 1713....**(page 89) Mr Alex Spence** one of jury that brought fine of five pounds. 'ordered that **Wm. Willson** pay unto **Joseph Jordan** ye Sume of five pounds with Costs als Exa.'"

Page 208 - "And Be It Further Enacted by the authority aforesaid precincts and parishes consisting of the ministers of the parish, when any such shall be there resident, & Twelve men whose names are hereafter mentioned....No East, Parish Pasquotank....**Thomas Miller, Esq., Mr. Jno Bell, Mr. Alex[r] Spence.**"

Page 522 - North Carolina S S "At a Council held at Edenton April the 9th Anno Dom 1724

Page 523 - "Read the petition of **Alexander Spence** shewing that **Griffen Jones** in the year 1716 obtained a patent for 74 Acres of Land lying Pasquotank which is not cultivated as the Law directs he prays a Lapse patent for the same &c."

[Edenton is the present county seat of Chowan, N.C.]

3. <u>Other</u> <u>North</u> <u>Carolina</u> <u>Spence</u> records:

<u>Vol. XXV</u>
<u>The</u> <u>State</u> <u>Records</u> <u>of</u> <u>North</u> <u>Carolina</u>
<u>Laws</u> <u>1789-1790</u> and supplement <u>Omitted</u> <u>Laws</u> <u>1699-1783</u>
with index to Vols. XXIII, XXIV, XXV, 1906
Walter Clark, ed. (57)

(58) <u>Vol. XXV</u>, page <u>187</u>

"Laws of North Carolina - 1723. A List of Jurymen in Pasquotank Precinct.
James Spence, Jn`r	121
Jam. Spence Sen`r.	142
Alex. Spence, Sen`r.	143
Jno. Spence	145"

(59) <u>Vol. XXIII</u>, <u>1904</u>, pages <u>6-7</u>

"That there shall be a vestry No. East Parish of Pasquotank.
Mr. Alexr. Spence."

<u>Vol. XXII</u>, pages <u>248</u> and <u>250</u>

By Whom Paid	No. of Yrs. Pd.	No. of Acres	Quit Rent Res'd	Amt. in Sterling Money Lb S D	Currency at seven for one Lb S D	Total Currency
Spence, Alexander		318			5 11 3-3/4	
Spence, James		300			5 5 0	
Spence, Alexander		200			3 10 0	
Spence, John Senr		400			7 0 0	

Two **James** and one **John Spence** were deported as criminals, while **William** and **Elizabeth Spence** were in the Parish Register of Barbadoes.

5. Two Origins of Spences

It appears that **Spences** came much earlier and separately to Virginia than to North Carolina. Therefore the connection between the **Spences** must be back in England. There are sources on Virginia **Spences**, such as the book compiled by **Clayton Torrence**, Virginia Wills and Administrations 1632-1800, the William Byrd Press, Inc., Printers, Richmond, VA.

Also, three volumes of the book, Cavaliers and Pioneers Abstracts of Virginia Land Patents and Grants, Vol. I: 1623-1666, Virginia Land Office, Richmond, VA, Genealogical Publishing Company, Inc., Baltimore, MD, 1963; Vol. II: 1666-1695, Virginia State Library, Richmond, VA, 1977; and Vol. III: 1695-1732, Virginia State Library, Richmond, VA, 1979, abstracted and indexed by **Nell Marion Nugent**. (Ref. 67)

This is but a few of the sources on early records of Virginia. The Central Library of Arlington County has a large "Virginiana Collection," which I have used and appreciate. Also, microfilm has been ordered from the Virginia State Library and Archives, on county records such as deeds, wills, marriage registers, orders, guardian accounts, etc.

The **Thomas Spence** was 50 to 60, having a son 15 to 20. The females under **Thomas** were one 15 to 20; one 20 to 30; and two 50 to 60.

Robert Spence had two males under 5 and one 5 to 10, while he was 40 to 50. The females were 5 to 10 and 30 to 40.

Rachel Spence was head of the household and age 70 to 80, with a female under her in the age category of 30 to 40.

The **Stephen Spence**, who resided in Blount County, was 20 to 30, with two males 5 to 10. The females were, three under 5 years old, and one 20 to 30.

B. The Tennessee census schedules for 1840 for **Spences** are much more wide spread for the whole state. Only a **William M. Spence** is in Blount County, and only a **John Spence** in Roane County. The rest of the **Spence** families are listed in alphabetical order by county: Bedford Co., **Wricker Spence**; Davisdon Co., **Brent Spence, James Spence, Richard Spence** and **William Spence**; Dyer Co., **Mark Spence** and **W. Spence**; Henderson Co., **John Spence** and **William W. Spence**; Henry Co., **William G. Spence**; Hickman Co., **John L. Spence**; Fayette Co., **John C. Spence**; Lincoln Co., **Hugh Spence** and **M. G. Spence**; Marshall Co., **Jane Spence**; Maury Co., **William H. Spence**; Rutherford Co., **Jane Spence** and **Mannaw Spence**; Weakley Co., **Elizabeth Spence, Levy Spence, James Spence** and **William Spence**; and Williamson Co., **Bartholomew Spence** and **Joseph Spence**.

1840 Roane County Census
Microcopy 704 Roll 535

Page 90, **John Spence**, 210001-00011

1840 Blount County Census
Microcopy 704 Roll 517

Page 131, **William M. Spence**, 010111-110001

The **John Spence** in Roane County was 30 to 40, with two males under 5 and one male 5 to 10. Two females were 15 to 20 and 20 to 30.

Then the **William M. Spence** in Blount County was 30 to 40, with other males being ages as follows: one male 5 to 10; one 15 to 20; and one 20 to 30. The females were one under 5; one 5 to 10; and one 30 to 40.

When one sees the **Sistler** index for 1850 (36), one finds out that some of the **Spences** in the 1840 list on page 190 are from Ireland. Also, in the 1850 census there are **Spences** from Hawkins and Rhea Counties.

Spences in the Census Schedules for Tennessee:

1840 Bedford County Census
Microcopy 704 Roll 519

Page 39   **Wricker Spence**   2222001-1111

1840 Davidson County Census
Microcopy 704 Roll 520

Page 346	Spence, Brent	1100001-012
Civil District 12	Spence, Richard	00000001-000100001
Civil District 14		
Page 348	Spence, James	010010001-10001
Civil District 22		
Page 362	Spence, William	110101-1110010001

1840 Dyer County Census
Microcopy 704, Roll 521

Page 95	**W. Spence**	120011-100011
Page 101	**Mark Spence**	2002001-0211011

1840 Fayette County Census
Microcopy 704, Roll 521

Page 108   **John C. Spence**   10101-20001

1840 Henderson County Census
Microcopy 704 Roll 522

Page 334	**William W. Spence**	100001-0200101
Page 365	**John Spence**	021001-100001

1840 Henry County Census
Microcopy 704 Roll 522

Page 439   **William G. Spence**   100001-000001

1840 Hickman County Census
Microcopy 704 Roll 524

Page 182   John L. Spence   20111-1001

1840 Lincoln County Census
Microcopy 704 Roll 531

Page 91   Hugh Spence   00010001-00010001
Page 96   M. G. Spence   000001-222001

1840 Marshall County Census
Same as Lincoln above

Page 173   Jane Spence   00111-0011001

1840 Weakley County Census
Microcopy 704 Roll 530

Page 280   Elizabeth Spence   001-10010001
Page 281   James Spence   2200001-110001
Page 281   Wm. Spence   100001-1100001
Page 288   Levy Spence   121101-100001

1840 Williamson County Census
Microcopy 704 Roll 537

Nineteenth Civil District
Page 150   Bartholomew Spence 00001-0001

25th District
Page 205   Joseph Spence   20001-01001

Most of the **Spence** families in the 1840 census schedules above were in Western counties in Tennessee. In Lincoln County were living the **Brim** descendants of **Henry Rice**. Also a **John Brim** was head of the household in Williamson in 1840, with **Peter H. Brim** and **Thos. Brim** heads of households in Weakley in 1840. These **Brim** census records will be given in the next chapter, **Lavina Rice - Lewis Brim**.

B. **Spences in 1850 IN TENNESSEE COUNTIES**

1. East Tennessee Counties

1850 Blount County Census (36)

Page 127, "**SPENCE, James 50, Will S. 12, Robt. V. 10,** NC
T, Bo--1734--238."

On the 10th day of December 1850, **James Spence** was recorded
on page 119, line 12, at dwelling number 1734, and family 1734.
It was the 15th Civil District. **James Spence** was a farmer and
born in North Carolina, while his sons **Will S.** and **Robert V.**
went to school and were born in Tennessee. (Blount, Microcopy
432, roll 871)

1850 Hawkins County Census (36)

Page 127, "**SPENCE, Isabella 40, Ellison 14, Sarah 10,** NC
NC, Hw--72--784."

1850 Hawkins County Census
Microcopy 432 Roll 882

Dist. No. 11, 10th day of Dec. 1850, Page 392, Line 36,
Household and Family 72:

Isabella Spence	40 F	N.C.
Ellison	14 M	N.C.
Sarah	10 F	N.C.

1850 Knox County Census (65)
H - Z of the Cross Index

Page 186 **SPENCE, Calvin, 36, Gainum C. McBee,** K--892--213."

The actual census for **Calvin Spence** is as follows:

1850 Knox County Census
Microcopy 432, Roll 886
Page 313 handwritten in (60), Page 157 (printed on microfilm),
line 9, Household 883, Family 892.

Gainum C. McBee	51 M	Farmer	20,000	Tenn.
Sarah	48 F			"
William	24 M	Merchant		"
Robert	21 M	Merchant		"
Albert	15 M	Student school		"
Louisa	12 F	school		"
Gainum	8 M	school		"
Susanna	7 F	school		"
Calvin Spence	36 M	Farmer		"
Brad Huddleston	20 M	Student school		"

1850 Roane County Census(36)

Page 127 "SPENCE, Robt. 64, Margaret 57, John E. 22, James C. 19, Mary 16, Margaret 14, SC SC, Ro--863--761."

2. West Tennessee Counties

The Spences in 1840 census schedules were numerous, but now in 1850 there are even more. A Spence in Bedford County is given next.

1850 Bedford County Census (36)

Page 127, "SPENCE, J. M. 28, Rhoda H. 30, Edward M. 6, John W. 5, Nancy T. 2, Rhoda Tennessee 1, Ledea DAMERIN 60, T T, B--68--250."

1850 Davidson County Census (36)

Page 127 "SPENCE, Brent 54, Nannie 20, Martha 17, Philip 13, Joseph 16, George LEISSEN 29, Mary 24, Ireland   T, D--970--672."

Page 127, "SPENCE, CHARLOTTE B. C. 30, Ky, D--1382--341."

1850 Dyer County Census (36)

Page 127, "SPENCE, Geo. E. 29, A. E. 21, A. R. 1, Andrew HART 25, E. WILKINS 15, NC NC, DY--574--421."

Page 127, "SPENCE, Mark 53, Margaret 42, M. J. 22, E. S. 18, H. E. 16, J. E. 14, NC NC, DY--569--421."

Page 127, "SPENCE, W. W. 45, A. M. F. 34, Mary 18, Jno. 10, Elizabeth 8, R. K. 7, Henry 5, W. MICHAEL 30, Va Va, Dy--184--361."

1850 Decatur County Census (36)

Page 127, "SPENCE, C. P. 41, Elizabeth 39, Jas. M. 18, John F. 14, Wm. P. 12, Joseph A. 10, Geo W. 8, Calvin T. 6, Mary P. 3, Louis C. 1, Jeremiah ODLE 74, NC NC, De--2--111."

1850 Fayette County Census (36)

Page 127, "SPENCE, William W. 33, Mary E. 24, Margaret C. 2, Va T, F--1520--686."

1850 Hickman County Census (36)

Page 127, "SPENCE, John L. 40, Tennessee 33, Josephine 14, Jerome 12, David 10, Kathleen 8, Geraldine 7, Ellen 4, Mary 2, T T, Hi--751-106."

Page 127, "SPENCE, William 55, Pheoba 47, Mark A. 16, Nancy E. 13, Tennessee 8, John D. 5, NC NC, Hi--63--9."

1850 Lauderdale County Census (36)

Page 127, "SPENCE, Wm. G. 25, Rebecca BARNES 55, Jane FORBES 30, Madeline SPENCE 26, Nancy 26, Sarah BARNES 20, Amanda 17, Eliza 14, Mary A. FORBES 13, Martha 12, William 10, John 7, Alfred COOP 29, Caroline 21, Wm. R. 2, Virginia C. 1, T T, L--386--550."

1850 Lincoln County Census (36)

Page 127, "SPENCE, James 35, Mary 35, Elizabeth McCARMACK 15, Thomas TAYLOR 3/12, SC SC Li--615--300."

Page 127, "SPENCE, W. G. 47, Tiny 43, Mary 23, Martha 20, Nancy 17, Eliza 15, Tanil 14, Aramantha 12, SC SC, Li--1404--416."

1850 Rhea County Census (36)

Page 127, "SPENCE, John 30, Mahala 37, Myea A. 1, NC T, R--511--616."

Page 127, "SPENCE, John 27, Tennessee 19, T T, R--533 --618."

Page 127, "SPENCE, Stephen 49, Martha 49, Jane 21, Stephen 18, Mary 14, Franklin 12, Sarah 8, George M. D. 6, NC NC, R--509--616."

1850 Rutherford County Census (36)

Page 127, "SPENCE, Alson 27, Mary A. 28, Francis 8, Sarah J. 6, Kinchen 4, T T, Ru--946--429."

Page 127, "SPENCE, John C. 41, Elizabeth 37, Sarah 14, Wm. 12, Mary 10, T Ireland, Ru--1364--692."

Page 127, "SPENCE, Joseph 34, Mary A. 33, Nancy 16, Britton 14, Wm. 11, Elisha 9, Jas. 4, Fanny 1, T T, Ru--1017--438."

Page 127, "SPENCE, Renshaw 52, Nancy 57, Abner 22, Britton 22, Nancy C. 20, Bev. B. 18, Jas. D. 15, Alsa 14, Martin V. 10, Mary W. C. 7, NC NC, Ru--28--463."

Page 127, "SPENCE, Richard 64, Sarah 65, Charlott 27, Sarah 19, William HAMILTON 12, Hance, 10, Ireland Ireland, Ru--17--461."

Page 127, "SPENCE, Sarah 55, David H. 24, Margaret 19, Sarah 18, David R. BRINDENTTOLL 27, Catherine L. L. 23, Ireland T, Ru--1466--710."

Page 127, "SPENCE, William 34, Matilda 23, William 5, Emma 2, Jacob SLACK 24, Henry C. WRIGHT 19, John N. SPERRY 20, Ireland Va, Ru--1395--698."

Page 127, "SPENCE, William J. 27, Ana 24, Thos 3, Sarah 2, T, T, Ru--239--494."

1850 Weakley County Census (36)

Page 127, "SPENCE, J. 58, Delila 55, Parthena 33, Margaret 29, Abner 19, Wilson 17, Ira 13, NC VT, We--33--791."

Page 127, "SPENCE, Mary 45, John 20, William 18, Nancy 16, Levi 14, Henry 12, Mark 10, Elisha 7, T T We--24--789."

Page 127, "SPENCE, S. 23, Sarah 22, Tennessee 4, Elizabeth 55, NC NC, We--112--802."

Page 127, "SPENCE, W. 42, Nancy 46, Sarah 16, Thornton 14, Rebecca 11, Joseph 9, Mark 7, Daniel 5, John 2, NC, NC, We--10-806."

Most of the above **Spence** families are not related to **Rosa**, and even some of them came from Ireland. It is hoped that descendants trying to connect back to **James** and **Rosa Spence** will find this information useful.

B. ALEXANDER MORROW

There is an extensive history of **Morrows** in a book by **Worth Stickley Ray** (Tennessee Cousins, A History of Tennessee People, published by the author at Austin, Texas, 1950, 1966 (61). More information on **Morrows** will be found in that book than here.

On page 235 of **Ray's** book are "The Knox County Marriages of the **Morrow** Family." The first is **Alexander Morrow** and **Rosanna Spence**. "The following marriage records on file in KNOX COUNTY pertain to members of the **MORROW FAMILY**: "**Alexander Morrow** to **Rosanna Spence**, Dec. 2, 1809. **John Wear**, Security."

On page 264 is a list of the children of **Alexander Morrow** and **Elizabeth Armstrong**, the parents of **Rosa's** husband. "After many years of research among the records it is possible to say that **ALEXANDER MORROW** and his wife **ELIZABETH ARMSTRONG** had the following children:

1. **ALEXANDER MORROW** m. **ROSANA SPENCE** (Married in 1809)
2. **DANIEL MORROW** m. **ELIZABETH COONS** (Dau. of **Michael Coons**)
3. **ROBERT MORROW** m. **NANCY DOBSON**....1799
4. **AMELIA MORROW** m. (her cousin)....**ARMSTRONG**
5. **RICHARD MORROW** m. (1____? 1790, (2) **PRUDENCE WALKER** ca. 1800
6. **WILLIAM MORROW** m. (1) **NANCY MEBANE** (2) **ISABELLA MEBANE**
7. **DAVID MORROW** M. **PRISCILLA DOUGHERTY** ca. 1800, in JEFFERSON COUNTY
8. **JOHN MORROW**
9. **SAMUEL MORROW**
10. **HANNAH MORROW** m. **THOMAS OLIPHANT** April 7, 1802

"**ALEXANDER MORROW** who married **Rosanna Spence** sold 250 acres of his land on Doak's Creek to **Moses Lisby** in 1823. This shows he was still living there at that time. No later or other record of him after that time." [This quotation is right after the list of children.]

The **Morrows** in **Ray's** book go back to **Daniel Morrow** in 1636 or 1651. This will be covered under "Origin of the **Morrows**." Also there are more Knox County records to look up on the father-in-law of **Rosanna Rice Spence**.

C. MORROWS IN EAST TENNESSEE CENSUS SCHEDULES 1830-1850

When this chapter was first written but unpublished, the author thought that **Alexander** and **Rosanna Morrow** had moved to Maury County, Tennessee, and were included in the 1820 census for that county. Then later **Alexander** sold the above Knox County land.   The deed has not been seen to know for sure.   The Alexander Morrow who was in the 1820 Maury County census could be the father (the husband of Elizabeth Armstrong.)   There will be a subchapter on Maury and Related County Morrows.   Many more records may be seen after publication of this book.

The Alexander Morrow, husband of Rosa or Rosanna, was not found in census schedules for East Tennessee from 1830 and later on, but a Rosanna Morrow, 70 to 80 years of age, was found in Knox County in 1840.   The Morrow families with Rosanna in Knox County in 1840 are George, John, Samuel, Charles and Esther. Rosanna did have two sons William and James, and James had sons William, John, Charles, James, Daniel and Levi.   The John and Charles Morrow in 1840 could be grandsons of Rosanna.

1830 East Tennessee Census (35)
Anderson County Page 181

Morrow, Ann	0-012001

Grainger County Page 389

Morrow, John	1111001-001001

Greene County Page 229

Morrow, Elizabeth	0-0000000001
Morrow, John	12100001-110001
Morrow, Jas.	00000001-0110001

Blount County Page 277

Morrow, James	1110001-12001

Jefferson County Page 335

Morrow, Priscilla	0010110001-1222301

Knox County Page 340

Morrow, George	110001-01101
Morrow, Isabella	00211-00000010001

Knox County Page 330

Morrow, John	02100001-1011001

The age categories for the above census are: under 5; 5 to 10; 10 to 15; 15 to 20; 20 to 30; 30 to 40; 40 to 50; 50 to 60; 60 to 70; 70 to 80; 80 to 90; 90 to 100; 100 and over. There is no woman in the 60 to 70 group.   Rosanna was ten years older in 1840, below.   Charles, who was 30 to 40 in 1840, was not listed in 1830.

1840 East Tennessee Census

Campbell County
Microcopy 704, Roll 518

Page 301 **Robert Morrow**   10001-000011

Greene COUNTY
Microcopy 704, Roll 525

Page 14   **John Morrow**   101120001-2211001
(The oldest male was 60-70, the oldest female
was 40-50)
Page 15   **James Morrow**   000000001-000010001

Knox County
Microcopy 704, Roll 527

Page 11   **Rosanna Morrow**   00011-0010000001
(The oldest female is 70-80)
Page 13   **George Morrow**   1210001-000101
Page 51   **John Morrow**   00001-10001
Page 52   **Samuel Morrow**   01001-01001
Page 53   **Charles Morrow***   100001-2011
Page 75   **Esther Morrow**   00021-00101001

*A **Charles Morrow** was the Register of Deeds in Knox County
in December 1870, for a deed from **Josiah Roady** to his offspring. This land was the same place on Bull Run Creek
in Knox County, where my grandparents **Marcellus Moss Rice**
and **Ibby Jane Weaver Rice** lived and where my mother **Ruby**
and her sister **Ruth** were born.

All these **Morrow** families were in the County, not in the
city of Knoxville. The index book gave "no township listed"
in each case.

1850 East Tennessee Census

In the year 1850, there are census Indices for Tennessee.
Most of the Tennessee **Morrows** are in **Sistler** 62) but a **Robert
Morrow** in Campbell County was mentioned only in **(38)**. **Robert**
was looked up in the census, after seeing the Index. Some of
the **Morrows** in **Sistler** are in **(60)**, which is a cross index,
having **Morrows** under heads of families with different last
names.

1850 Blount County Census

Page 107   Ann Morrow 23, Reuben Brooks, Bo-301-42 (65)
              E. J. Morrow 3, Reuben Brooks, Bo-301-42 (65)
              Hester Morrow 1/12, Reuben Brooks, Bo-301-42 (65)
              James Morrow 12, James Allen, Bo-340-50 (65)
              Jane Morrow 18, Matthew Blackburn, Bo-249-35 (65)
              Margt. Morrow 8, John Tucker, Bo-402-59 (65)
              Mary Morrow 25, John Tucker, Bo-402-59 (65)
              Rufus Morrow 16, Wm. McTeer, Bo-986-137 (65)
              Sarah A. Morrow 14, John Taylor, Bo-116-17 (65)
              Will Morrow 15, Robt H. Catton, Bo-1795-245 (65)

Page 312   MORROW, Thomas 37, Lavinia 30, Sarah 15, Hezekiah 13,
              Mary 11, Robt. 10, Martha 7, Dialtha 4, Thomas 2,
              Myra 5/12, NC SC Bo-434-64 (62)

1850 Campbell County Census
(Ref 38, page 290)

Morrow, Robert   Camp 281   17th Sub

Microcopy 432, Roll 872
24th day of Aug. 1850
17th Subdivision, Page 281, Line 31
Household 58, Family 58

Robert Morrow	39 M Merchant	5000	Tenn.
Mary E. Morrow	34 F		Tenn.
William Morrow	11 M School		Tenn.
Sarah Smith	35 F		N.C.
James A. Wayman	25 M Saddler		Va.

The **Robert Morrow** above was 20-30 in 1840. **William**, 11, above could be the male under 5 in 1840. **Mary E. Morrow**, 34, could be the female 20-30 in 1840, but the female who was 30 to 40 under **Robert** in 1840 is not known to me, and is not here in 1850.

1850 Greene County Census

Page 312   MORROW, Elizabeth 15, Irwin TAYLOR 33, Mary 26,
              Major T. 8, Elizabeth 5, Nancy 2, John LANEY 24,
              T Va, Ge-2122-560 (62)

              MORROW, Adam 29, Margaret 26, John 5, Thomas 4,
              James 2, T T, Ge-265-310 (62)

              MORROW, John 72, William 28, David 24, Ebenazor
              21, Mary 22, Margaret 18, Elizabeth 15, Hannah 13,
              Isabella 13, Samuel 8, Va T, Ge-751-374 (62)

1850 Greene County Census
(Continued)

Page 107   **MORROW, Malinda** 32, **John HALE**, Ge-749-374 (62)
(Ref. 38 has microfilm page 188, 9th Division.)
Malinda, at household 749, was living next door
to **John**, 72, who was at household 751.

1850 Jefferson County Census

Page 107   **MORROW, Priscilla** 68, **Andrew BLACKBURN**, Je-518-
728 (62)

1850 Knox County Census

Page 312   **MORROW, Charles** 45, **Sally** 40, **Angeline** 16,
John W. 11, **William W.** 7, **Elizabeth** 6, **Prudence**
3, T T, K-957-322 (64) (Ref. 38 has page 161,
15th Sub)

           MORROW, Esther 66, **William** 27, **Joseph** 22,
Nancy E. 18, Ireland T, K-389-243 (Ref. 38 has
page 122, 15th Sub)

Page 107   **MORROW, George** 23, **Jessee JONES**, K-549-265 (Ref
38 has page 133, 15th Sub). **George** was a lodger,
could not read nor write, and was born in Tenn.)

1850 Washington County Census

Page 312   **MORROW, MARY A.** 35, **John** 7, T T, Wa-233-235 (62)

In all of the above census data from **Sistler's** Index to
1850 Tennessee, the first name is head of the family with age,
followed by names and ages of all others, with last names of
different surnames in all capitals (except in the cross index),
place of birth of the first two people (abbreviated), County
abbreviation, household number, and handwritten page number
(ref. 38 has the printed page number). There were numerous
Morrow families in Tennessee. **Charles Morrow** will be given in
the 1860 and 1870 Knox County census schedules.

Page 312   **MORROW, Samuel** 34, **Malinda** 33, **Isabella** 70,
Amelia J., 8, **Mary E.** 6, **Robert** 4, **Anna H.** 2,
Ann E. WAMACK 18, Va Va, K-164-209 (64). The
census on microfilm gives **Samuel's** occupation
as clerk; **Isabella** was born in N.C. **Samuel** had
$400 and **Isabella** $1000 in real estate. All
the children, including the last, were born in
Tenn. **Amelia** and **Mary** went to school. **Samuel**
lived in Knoxville.

D. Charles Morrow in the 1850 through 1860 Knox County Census

The **Charles Morrow**, son of **James** and grandson of **Rosanna Morrow**, was in the 1850 Knox County census above, but more data is given on the census pages than in the Index.

1850 Knox County Census
Microcopy 432, Roll 886
15th Subdivision, Page 161, Line 40
Household 948, Family 957
15th day of October 1850

Charles Morrow	45	M	Brick Mason	400	Tenn.
Sally "	40	F			"
Angeline "	16	F			"
John W. "	11	M	[Page 162, line 1]		"
William W."	7	M			"
Elizabeth "	6	F			"
Prudence "	3	F			"

1860 Knox County Census
Microcopy 653 Roll 1259
1st District, Post Office Knoxville, 24 July 1860
Page 100, Line 24, Household 790, Family 621

R. Morrow	51	M	Broker	60,000	25,000	Tenn.
Malinda E.	42	F				"
William M.	21	M				"
Sarah SMITH	42	F				"

Same District and Post Office, 18th day of July 1860
Page 96, Line 17, Household 781, Family 609

Sam Morrow	44	M	Banker	13,000	7,000	Tenn.
Melinda	43	F				"
Amelia	18	F				"
Mary E.	16	F				"
Robert	14	M				"
Anna H.	12	F				"
Saml J.	7	M				"

Same District and Post Office
Page 63, Line 40, and Page 64
Household 521, Family 392

Chls Morrow	50	M	Policeman	Tenn.
Mary Morrow	45	F	(Page 64, line 1)	"
Prudence Morrow	13	F		"
Randall SHIPE	29	M		"

The **R. Morrow** was a broker with $60,000 value in personal estate and $25,000 value in real estate. There is a **Robert**, 39, with wife **Mary E.**, 34, son **William**, 11, and **Sarah Smith**, 35 and **James A. Wayman**, 25, in Campbell County in 1850. Here most of the names and ages are close to what they should be. This **Robert**, then, must have moved to Knoxville between 1850 and 1860.

The **Samuel Morrow** in Knox County in 1850 is now a banker with personal estate of $13,000 and real estate of $7,000. The **Isabella**, 70, in Knox County in 1850, is not here in 1860, but there is a son **Saml J.**, 7.

The **Charles Morrow** in 1850 was a brick mason; now he is a policeman. His wife was named **Sally**, now the same lady is named **Mary**. Both of their ages are greater by five years. **Prudence**, 3 in 1850, is now 13. **Angeline, John W., William W.**, and **Elizabeth** are now probably with spouses and starting their own families. Above there is also a **Randall Shipe**, 29.

E. EAST TENNESSEE MORROWS IN TAX LISTS

There were **Morrows** in the tax lists of Greene, Grainger, Campbell and Anderson Counties:

    a. 1805 Greene County list of free taxable inhabitants
        James Morrow
        John Morrow

    b. 1805 Grainger County Taxable Inhabitants
        Robert Morrow

    c. Campbell County Tax Lists - 4th District
        Robert Morrow

    d. 1839 Anderson County Tax List

District	Name	Acres	Value	Tax	Total
4	**Morrow** Heirs	180	$200	$.10	$.10

F. TENNESSEE RECORDS IN MAURY AND OTHER COUNTIES ON ALEXANDER MORROW AND ELIZABETH ARMSTRONG

Some of the **Morrows** must have moved from East Tennessee before 1820 (see page 197) for **Alexander** and the following **Morrows** were in counties immediately around Maury: **Benjamin**, Lawrence Co.; **John**, Hickman Co.; **Thomas**, Hickman Co.; and **William**, Wayne Co. There were also **Morrows** in middle to western counties other than those above.

There were **Morrows** in Maury County in 1840, and by 1850 they had spread to the south (Giles County, with Pulaski as the County Seat. Columbia is the County Seat of Maury County. Also Lawrence, Lewis, and Wayne Counties, just west and southwest of Maury County, had **Morrows** in the census schedules of 1820 through 1850. These are just some of the counties that apply to **Henry Rice's** line through **Morrows**. It is assumed that all **Morrows** in Tennessee go back to one source eventually.

Tennessee 1820 Census Index (16)
Edited by **Ronald Vern Jackson** and **Gary Ronald Teeples**, 1974, Accelerated Indexing Systems, Inc.
Computer Index to Tennessee 1820 Census, page 376

Name		County	Page	Birthplace	Census Data
Morrow,	**Alexander**	Maury	-	Tenn.	221301-00001
"	**Benjamin**	Lawrence	1	Tenn.	211101-21010
"	**John**	Hickman	3	Tenn.	300010-13010-00
"	**Leonard**	Wayne	325	Tenn.	2220001-01001
"	**Polley**	Giles	16	Tenn.	110100-22010
"	**Thomas**	Hickman	3	Tenn.	000001-31011-00
"	**William**	Wayne	333	Tenn.	130101-10001

The age categories for 1820 are as follows:
Males "un. 10; 10 to 16; 16 to 18; 18 to 26; 26 to 45; and 45+."
Females "un. 10; 10 to 16; 16 to 26; 26 to 45; and 45+."
"Other free."
"Slaves."

1830 Maury and Lawrence County Census
FM 19, Roll 177

Maury County

Page 373,	**Alex Morrow**	001201001-000000001
	George Morrow	10001-10101
Page 419,	**Alex Morrow**	021101-30001
Page 339,	**Leonard Morrow**	020001-310001

Lawrence County

Page 308,	**John Morrow**	31001-00001

1830 Giles County Census
FM 19, Roll 176

Page 155,	**Thos. Morrow**	00001-1001
Page 183,	**Jno. W. Morrow**	20001-00001
Page 187,	**Thos. Morrow, Jr.**	0001-010001
	A. Morrow	10001-00101
	Paul Morrow	100001-10001
Page 188,	**Polley Morrow**	00002-00011001

1830 Wayne County Census
Microcopy FM 19 Roll 182

Page 300,	**William Morrow**	100010001-00001001
	William Morrow Jr.	30010001-20001
Page 301,	**John Morrow**	30100001-10001

The age categories for both sexes for 1830 and 1840 are:

"un. 5; 5-10; 10-15; 15-20; 20-30; 30-40; 40-50; 50-60; 60-70; 70-80; 80-90; 90-100; 100+."

John Morrow was 50-60, while the two **Williams** were 60-70 and 50-60 respectively.

Alexander Morrow (Maury County Census 1820), maybe the father-in-law of **Rosanna**, was over 45 years of age in 1820 and his wife **Elizabeth** was the same age. They were 60-70 in 1830, which means they were 50-60 in 1820. There were eight sons in 1820 with four left in 1830. The **George** could be 10-16 in 1820, while the younger **Alex** and **Leonard**, both 30-40 in 1830, would be 20-26 in 1820. Two **Alexanders** are in Fayette and Lowndes Counties, Alabama. There is a **James M. Morrow** in Fayette County, too.

G. 1840 ALABAMA CENSUS, FAYETTE AND LOWNDES COUNTIES

After realizing that, since there were no **Alexander Morrow** wills in Maury County, and that the second **Alexander Morrow** in 1840 was younger than the second **Alexander** in 1830, it occurred to me to search the census indexes for 1840 in other states. Two **Alexanders** were found, one in Fayette County and one in Lowndes County. **James M. Morrow** also was found in Fayette County. The oldest **Alexander Morrow** remained in Maury County with his wife **Elizabeth Armstrong** in 1840, but neither was there in 1850.

There were many **Morrows** in Alabama in 1940. Only the two **Alexanders** and the **James M. Morrow** are given here.

1840 Fayette County Alabama Census
Microcopy 704, Roll 4

Page 217, **Jas M. Morrow**, 1 m 60-70; 2 f un. 5; 1 f 15-20;
                                1 f 30-40; 1 f 60-70.

Page 219, **Alex^r Morrow**, 1 m un. 5; 1 m 30-40; 1 f un. 5;
                                1 f 5-10; 1 f 15-20; 1 f 30-40

The town of Fayette is the county seat of Fayette County.

1840 Lowndes County Alabama Census
Microcopy 704, Roll 6

Page 238, **Alex^r Morrow**, 1 m un. 5; 2 m 5-10; 1 m 10-15;
                                1 m 30-40; 1 m 40-50; 1 f un. 5;
                                1 f 15-20; 1 f 30-40.

H. MAURY AND NEIGHBORING COUNTIES IN 1840

1840 Maury County Census
Microcopy 704, Roll 532

Page 336,	**Alexander Morrow**	000000001-000000001*
Page 352,	**Alexander Morrow**	00001-00001**
Page 366,	**John Morrow**	203001-010001
Page 328,	**Leonard Morrow**	2002001-0231001

* **Alexander Morrow** and his wife, **Elizabeth Armstrong** in 1830 are both 60-70, but in 1840 they are listed as 60-70 and 70-80, respectively. There are errors every now and then in the census records. This **Alexander Morrow** was the father-in-law of **Rosanna**.

** The second **Alexander** was 30-40 in 1830, while this **Alexander** and his wife were 20-30; one **Alexander Morrow** was 44 in 1850, in Choctaw County, Mississippi.

The **George Morrow** who was 20-30 in 1830, is not here in 1840, while the **John Morrow** 20-30 in 1830, is 30-40 in 1840. Also, the same is true for **Leonard**.

<u>1840 Giles County Census</u>
Microcopy 704 Roll 523

Page 151, **John Morrow**   00001-10001
   Mary Morrow   (no males)-10010001
   Samuel Morrow 020001-10001
   Thos. Morrow* 120001-21001
   Alex^r Morrow* 1011010002-120012
          (2 males 70-80)

* This name was hard to read and the editors of the Census Index recorded the name as **"Marrow."** It was grouped together with the **Morrows**.

<u>1840 Wayne County Census</u>
Microcopy 704 Roll 536

Page 079, **James Morrow**   220001-10001
   John Morrow   020001-211001
   William Morrow 1 m 70-80; 1 f 60-70
Page 080, **Thomas Morrow** 21001-10002

The **William Morrow, Jr.** family is gone, and the son and daughter, both 20-30 in 1830 under **William Morrow, Sr.**, are not under him here.

<u>1850 Maury County Census</u> (64)
From <u>1850 Tennessee Census Index</u>
Vol. 4, **Jones** through **Murley**, by
Byron and **Barbara Sistler**, 1975, Evanston, Ill., page 312

No **Alexander Morrow** was found in Maury County, but in Giles County there was an **Allascander K.** or **Allaxander** in the other Census Index (**Tenn. 1850 Census Index, etc.**). He is 44, and there is an **A. Morrow** in Giles in 1830, in the age range of 20 to 30 (38).

It occurred to me, while writing this record, that since no **Alexander Morrow** was in Maury County in 1850, the Census Indexes for 1850 for other states should be checked. The best information came from Mississippi, although Alabama was seen also.

Mississippi

1850 Choctaw County Census
MC 432, roll 370
The Western Division, 6 November 1850
Page 12, line 37, household 168, family 168

Alexander Morrow	44	M	Farmer	1200	S.C.	
Adeline Morrow	23	F			Ala.	
Mary Morrow	13	F			Ala.	School
Thomas Morrow	11	M			Ala.	School
Ann Morrow	9	F			Ala.	
William Morrow	1	M			Miss.	

This could be the **Alexander Morrow** who was 20-30 in 1840 in Maury County; but note that he was born in S.C., probably married in Ala., and moved to Mississippi (presumably from Ala.) after the 1840 census.

Next are the **Morrows** in the 1850 census for Maury, Giles, and other nearby Tennessee counties.

(1) **Maury County Morrows.** (62)

"**Morrow,** James 65, Elizabeth 51, Anne WARY, 34, Edward SORRELL, 9, SC SC, MU-129-325."

"**Morrow,** John 47, Susanna 47, Rachael A. 18, John J. 16, Robert 12 Andrew 10, Martha J. 7, Susan W. 6, SC T, MU-1101-455."

"**Morrow,** Joseph W. 23, Nancy C.18, Mary Jane 4/12, T T, MU-1102-456."

"**Morrow,** Leonard 53, Jane 55, Thos. F. 26, Mary A. 22, Minerva J. 20, Esther E. 18, Susan P. 16, Andrew 15, James L. 12, SC SC, MU-1488-694."

"**Morrow,** Noah 26, Cintha C. 22, T T, MU-758-412."

"**Morrow,** Wm. 25, T, MU-1475-692."

"MU" is the symbol for the county Maury. The first number following "MU" is the household number, while the second is the microfilm page. **James** and **Elizabeth** were both born in South Carolina. There was a **James Morrow** in Wayne County in 1840.

Also, **William** and **Joseph W. Morrow** could be the sons of the **John** age 47, for **John** had 3 sons, 10 to 15, in 1840. And **Noah** could be the son of **Leonard,** for he had two sons 15 to 20 in 1840.

208

(2) Giles County Morrows.

"Morrow, Allascander K. 44, Catherine 43, Elizabeth 18, Nancey C. 16, Mary S. 14, Mashie B. 12, Thomas A. 9, Louisa E. 4, William D. 1, T T, Gi-76-692."

"Morrow, Asubry 23, Usley 19, Malissa P. 2, Isaac D. 4/12, T T, Gi-131-699."

"Morrow, Daniel 50, Ellender U. 46, Mary Jane 20, Elizabeth 18, Ruth Ann 16, William A. 13, Nancey D. 9, Samuel L. 07, John T. 5, Martha E. 2, SC SC, Gi-134-700."

"Morrow, Eliza Ann 35, Narcissa Jane 21, William F. 19, John D. 18, Manerva 16, Thomas J. 13, Martha E. 10, Masry M. 7, T T, Gi-135-700."

"Morrow, John D. 28, Mary Neomi 24, Sarah E. 5, Martha Jane 4, Sabrina E. 2, T T, Gi-116-697."

"Morrow, John F. 36, Easther 33, Elizabeth 11, James A. 9, Thomas L. 5, Daniel A. 3, Wade B. C. 1/12, T T, Gi-80-692."

"Morrow, John L. 20, Mary C. C. 27, T T, Gi-77-692.

"Morrow, Samuel 42, Anna 39, Mathew 14, Mary 12, William K. 11, Nancey L. 9, James K. 5, Mary 70, T NC, Gi-46-687."

The oldest of the Giles County **Morrows** was Daniel. He and his wife **Ellender U.** were both born in South Carolina. Eliza Ann was living right next to **Daniel**, with **Asubry** close by. **Allascander K.** could be the father of **John L.** and the brother of John F. **Morrow**, for both **Johns** are living very near to **Allascander.**

(3) Morrows in Lawrence County

"Morrow, Benjamin 74, Nancy 72, Wm. 20, Martha A. 16, SC NC, La-550-657."
"Morrow, Martha 48, Sarah 16, Jas. F. 14, Aretha 13, Martha 10, George W. 9, Unk T, La-113-731."

"Morrow, John 26, Elizabeth 27, Mary F. 7, Lycurgus 6, Martha O. 3, R.E. 1, T NC, La-576-661.

(4)   Morrows in **Lewis County**

"**Morrow**, **Elijah** 35, **Elizabeth** 32, **William** 17, **Lumiza J.** 12,
        Anderson 9, **Sarah E.** 5, **Elijah G.** 2, **George D. L.** 1/12,
        T T, Le-489-849."

(5)   Morrows in **Wayne County**

"**Morrow**, **John** 49, **Elizabeth** 44, **Jamima** 19, **William** 17, **Jesse C.**
        16, **Nancy** 13, **Sarah** 11, **Mary R.** 10, **Elizabeth** 8, **Emily** 7,
        Martha 1, T T, Wy-771-642."

(4) **Other South Carolina Born Morrows**

There were **Morrows** born in South Carolina, in Coffee,
Franklin, and Tipton Counties.

Franklin County, Tennessee

"**Morrow**, **James A.** 36, **Ilione** 28, **James M.** 6, **David M.** 4, **C. F. R.**
        1, SC NC, F-102-478."

"**Morrow**, **Robert** 31, **Wm. B.** 22, **George W.** 27, SC SC, F-1894-742."

"**Morrow**, **Saml. R.** 39, **Alenda C.** 33, **Wm. A.** GELLASPIE 17, SC T,
        F-1895-742.

"**Morrow**, **William** 73, **Jane** 63, **Frances** 31, **Ellinor** 27, **Malissa** 25,
        John T. 21, SC SC, F-1917-745."

Coffee County, Tennessee

"**Morrow**, **John** 76, **Mary** 57, **Francis** 20, **Robert Carder** 22, SC SC,
        Cf-831-118."

"**Morrow**, **John M.** 44, **Tabitha** 38, **Margaret** 13, **Sarah** 11, **Susan** 9,
        William 6, **Louisa** 4, **Anderson** 2, **Drury Webb** 18, NC T,
        Cf-819-116."

"**Morrow**, **Samuel** 30, **Catherine** 26, **James** 6, T T, Cf-601-87."

Tipton County, Tennessee

"**Morrow**, **Josiah** 38, **Mildred N.** 33, **Martha Champion** 12, **Robert H.**
        Winn 6, SC T, T-274-656."

I. THE 1790 SOUTH CAROLINA CENSUS FOR MORROWS

There are a lot of **Morrows** in the 1790 South Carolina Census, and some along with **Charles** and other **Rices**. (**Heads of Families at the First Census of the United States Taken in the Year 1790, South Carolina**, Baltimore, Genealogical Publishing Co., 1966, Originally Published, Washington, Government Printing Office, 1908.) (20) The age categories are:

1st column, free white males over 16, including heads of families.
2nd column, free white males under 16.
3rd column, free white females including heads of families.
4th column, all other free persons.
5th column, slaves.

Page 13, Camden District, Chester County
    Morrow, Joseph   133--
          David   132--
          Mary   -23--

Page 14, Camden District, Chester County
    George Morrow   1-324
    David Morrow   232--

Page 29 Camden District, York County
    James Morrow   114--
    David Morrow   215-3

Page 55, Georgetown District, Prince Georges Parish
    Ezekiel Morrow   113--

Page 57, 96 District, Abbeville County
    Jn⁰ Morrow   123-1
    Hugh Morrow   1-1--
    Morrow, Arthur   235--
    Morrow, Eliz^th   --3--
    Spence, Alex^r   144--

Page 58, 96 District, Abbeville County
    Morrow, Hugh   1-2--
    Morrow, Thomas   231--

Page 70, 96 District, Greenville County
    Rice, Thomas   325--
    Morrow, Robert   143--

```
Page 80, 96 District, Newberry County
        Morrow, William          122--
        Morrow, Chrisr           1-1--

Page 81, 96 District, Pendleton County
        Morrow, John             143--
        Rice, Charles            123--

Page 83,  Rice, James            212--

          Rice, Ezekiel          1-2-2
          Morrow, Richard        255--

Page 95, Orangeburgh District (North Part)
        Morrow, Mathew           312--
               John              134--
               Thomas            215-5

Page 99, Orangeburgh District (South Part)
        Rice, John               1-2--
        Rice, Micajah            212--
        Morrow, Robert           122-1
```

Two comments are made here. First, the **Rices** here, including **Henry's** son **Charles**, were on the pages with the **Morrows**. **James Rice**, your compiler's link to **Henry**, was on page 83.

Second, these **Morrows** might have been from the English origin, but could have come separately to South Carolina (not checked), as could Pioneer **Henry Rice**. But the Virginia **Morrows** came to Tennessee through North Carolina, and are the ancestry of **Alexander Morrow**.

J. MORROW ORIGINS

This will be a summary of the big section by **Worth S. Ray** on **Morrows** in his book, Tennessee Cousins. **Ray** cites Nugent's Cavaliers and Pioneers, Abstracts of Virginia Land Patents and Grants. He made a chart (his page 256) based on the patent records in the above work (see page 213). [The Colonial Abstracts have also been seen for other ancestors, such as Jordans, Mosses, Claybournes, Brantleys.]

Ray wrote, The early VIRGINIA LAND records (**Nugent**, pp. 493-494) show that DANIEL MORROW was the owner of a tract of land in LOWER NORFOLK CO. in LYNHAVEN PARISH adjoining land patented by RICHARD KING in 1662." (Page 257.) (ref. 61)

THE ANCESTRY OF OUR MORROW FAMILY COUSINS

CHARTED FROM THE OLD RECORDS

Inserted here PARENTHETICALLY

— — —

D A N I E L   M O R R O W

Ch: :   NO. 1

DANIEL MORROW (2)	DAVID MORROW (3)	JONATHAN MORROW (4)	OWEN MORROW (5)	HENRY MORRW (6)
Nugent p.493-4	Nugent p.222	Nugent pp 351-438	Md.Cal 2-64	Nugent p.
		THOMAS MORROW (7)	WILLIAM MORROW (8)	
18. DOROTHY MORROW		Nugent p. 125	Va.Col.Abs 27-6	HENRY MORR
19. DANIEL MORROW				31. CHRISTOPHER MORROW
20. JOHN MORROW				32. RICHARDSON MORRW.
	21. DAVID MORROW	25. WILLIAM MORROW		
	22. ALEXANDER MORROW	26. DOROTHY MORROW		
		27. JOHN MORROW		
	23. JOHN MORROW	28. WALTER MORROW		
	24. ANN MORROW	29. AUGUST MORROW	40. OWEN MORROW	
		30. ADAM MORROW	41. WILLIAM MORROW	
		33. DANIEL MORROW	42. JOHN MORROW	
		34. KATH. MORROW.	43. RICHARD MORROW	
(1st to 3rd generations)			44. DAVID MORROW	
		THOMAS MORROW	WILLIAM MORROW	45. MARY MORROW
		ELIZABETH MORROW	JOHN MORROW	

ALEXANDER MORROW (22)	WILLIAM MORROW (25)	WALTER MORROW (28)	AUGUST MORR (29)
50. DAVID MORROW	60. DAVID MORROW	70. SAMUEL MORROW	75. JOHN MORR
51. JEREMIAH MORROW	61. SAMUEL MORROW	71. JOHN MORROW	76. ELIZA MOR
52. ALEXANDER MORROW	62. WILLIAM MORROW	72. MARY MORROW	77. MARGARET
53. JOHN MORROW	63. ROBERT MORROW	m. RICHARDSON.	
54. CALEB MORROW	64. CATHERINE MORROW		
55. DANIEL MORROW	65. DOROTHY MORROW		(3rd and 4th generations)
56. THOMAS MORROW			

DAVID MORROW (50)	DAVID MORROW (60)	SAMUEL MORROW (70)
100. REV. DAVID MORROW	110. DAVID MORROW	120. SAMUEL MORROW
101. ALEXANDER MORROW	111. SAMUEL MORROW	121. DAVID MORROW
102. SAMUEL MORROW		122. ROBERT MORROW
103. ADAM MORROW		124. MARGARET MORROW
104. JOHN MORROW		125. DOROTHY MORROW
106. JAMES MORROW		
107. SARAH MORROW		
. WILLIAM MORROW		(4th and 5th generations).

See Nugent p. 40
No claim is made that DANIEL MORROW (1636 CHAS CITY CO. VA.) was the ANCESTOR.

On **page 256 Ray** wrote, "See **Nugent** p. 40 - No claim is made **DANIEL MORROW** (1636 CHAS [Charles] CITY CO. VA.) was the ancestor."

The name is **Marrow** in the Virginia passenger lists of **Hotten** and **Greer**. Maybe the name had a different spelling. **Ray** wrote on page 257 the following:

"The ELIZABETH CITY COUNTY records show constant associations between the **KINGS** of that county and the `MARROWS.` This relationship started in Lower Norfolk County, when **RICHARD KING** owned land there:

> **RICHARD KING** (granted) 200 acres in LOWER NORFOLK CO. Dec. 5, 1662....running southly to **WILLIAM WILSON`S** stakes to W. along **DANIEL MORROW`S** Trees.--**Nug.** 493-4."

Ray also mentioned that **Henry Morrow** and **David** each had land patents, respectively.

Ray also wrote about the name **MARROW**, as follows:

"There was a **JOHN MORROW** (20) a carpenter, who lived in Northampton & ACCOMAC Counties, prior to 1700, and **Daniel Morrow** (2) and also (20) father and son, were the ancestors of the **MORROW** FAMILY of Elizabeth City County that spell the name `MARROW` and claim that it is of English origin." (p. 257.)

Then on page 258, **Ray** wrote "There is a lot of evidence tending to establish a close relationship of **JONATHAN MORROW** of LANCASTER & NORTHUMBERLAND COUNTIES in Virginia with the **DANIEL (2)** and **DAVID (3) MORROW** of the family chart.

"**JONATHAN MORROW** came to the colony of VIRGINIA as a headright of **Mr. HUGH LEE**, who, in 1657 patented a tract of 1100 acres of land in the `freshes` of the POTOMAC RIVER above Piscatawah, adjoining 'Mr. Clay's land.' In his coming (which was in all probability several years before 1657) he has as company, **MARY MORROW** and **DOROTHY MORROW, GEORGE WILSON**, whom we associate with **WILLIAM WILSON**, of Lower Norfolk, on Wilson`s Creek, where **DANIEL MORROW** owned lands ....." (p. 258.)

Then on page 259, **Ray** wrote about **Rev. David Morrow** and **Alexander Morrow**, the father-in-law of **Rosa Rice Spence**.

"**Rev. DAVID MORROW**, of Caroline Co., VIRGINIA, No. 100 on Charts, was a brother of **ALEXANDER MORROW**, KNOX COUNTY, Tennessee....[and] **REV. DAVID MORROW'S** wife was a **CATLETT**. We know her name was **ELIZABETH**. They had the following children:

"1. **ROBERT MORROW** m. **ELIZABETH SHAW** ....

ROBERT MORROW who married **ELIZABETH SHAW** in ORANGE COUNTY,

"This **ROBERT MORROW'S** marriage bond to **ELIZABETH SHAW** is on file in the department of archives and history at Raleigh. They were married in GUILFORD COUNTY, May 20, 1773, with **WILLIAM DENT** and **WILLIAM DICK** as securities. It may have been in that part that had been taken from ORANGE COUNTY." (p. 259.)

Robert Morrow's children are on this same page (259), which also tells that he went to Wilkes Co., Georgia, and then to Warren County, Tenn. It gives much more on relationships, too.

2. **On page 260 (KNOX COUNTY, TENNESSEE) Ray** wrote about **David Morrow** and the first **Alexander Morrow, David's** son:

"The will of the first **DAVID MORROW**, the emigrant ancestor of **ALEXANDER MORROW**, of KNOX COUNTY, and in the will called **DAVID MORROW** 'of Elizabeth River in ye County of Norfolk' was executed (written) November 5, 1692 and probated May 16, 1693. In substance the will provides legacies and legatees as follows:

1. **DAVID MORROW** (son) deceased...
2. **ALEXANDER MORROW** 260 by 2 acres of land lying to the westward side of (the land of) my son **DAVID MORROW**. If **ALEXANDER** dies without heirs of his body the land is to revert to the next of blood, viz: to my son **JOHN, DAVID'**s two sons, and to my **SON, JOHN'S SON**, they three.
3. **JOHN MORROW**....
4. **ANN MORROW**, daughter, the wife of **JEREMIAH BECK**. Son **JOHN MORROW**, sole executor.
                    (Signed) **DAVID MORROW**
    Witnesses: **JOHN EDWARDS** and **MARY MORROW** (by mark)."

Also, **Ray** on page 261 made another chart, given here:

"**DANIEL MORROW** (1636) CHARLES CITY COUNTY VIRGINIA - CHART
: :

     DAVID MORROW   **DANIEL MORROW**
       1651 (3)   1650

Had
        :
        :
    ALEXANDER MORROW
     1669   (22)
        :
Had
        :

DAVID MORROW (50)
JEREMIAH MORROW
ALEXANDER MORROW
JOHN MORROW   )
CALEB MORROW   )   Mentioned in the will
DANIEL MORROW)
THOMAS MORROW)

        DAVID MORROW (50)
            :
      Had   :
.......................:..................
100. **REV. DAVID MORROW** (Caroline Co. Va.)
101. **ALEXANDER MORROW** m. **ELIZ. ARMSTRONG.**"

Worth Stickley Ray's compilation on the **Morrows** continues on page 262, as follows:

"**ALEXANDER MORROW** (22) son of **DAVID** (possibly an imaginary) son of **DANIEL MORROW** (1) of the chart, was left a legacy by his father's will if he had heirs at the time of his father's death. **ALEXANDER** was probably married and a father at that time, but the testator wanted him to raise them and to be sure he had <u>living</u> <u>heirs</u> at his death. We have concluded that his children, excluding daughters, were:

50. **DAVID MORROW**
51. **JEREMIAH MORROW** (named for **JEREMIAH BECK** husband of
      his aunt, **ANN MORROW.**
52. **ALEXANDER MORROW**
53. **JOHN MORROW** (died 1744)
54. **CALEB MORROW**
55. **DANIEL MORROW**
56. **THOMAS MORROW.**"

Then **Ray** gives the children of **David Morrow** (50) with the
second child, being **Alexander**, the <u>father-in-law</u> of **Henry Rice's**
daughter, **Rosa Rice Spence**.

"CHILDREN OF **DAVID MORROW**, SON OF **ALEXANDER MORROW**

"The children of **DAVID MORROW**, son of the first **ALEXANDER
MORROW** were as follows:

1. **REV. DAVID MORROW** of KING GEORGE and CAROLINE COUNTIES.

2. **ALEXANDER MORROW** who finally located in EAST TENNESSEE.

3. **SAMUEL MORROW**, born Md. lived in Virginia, served in
   the revolution in Maryland, and finally located in
   SOUTH CAROLINA where he died in 1796.

4. **ADAM MORROW** who married **ISOBEL ALLEN** (?) and died in
   GREENE COUNTY, TENNESSEE.

5. **JOHN MORROW**, of PRINCE EDWARD & later MECKLENBURG CO. N.C.

6. **JAMES MORROW** who married **ELIZABETH FRAME**; died in
   Kentucky.

7. **SARAH MORROW** who married **ALEXANDER WALKER** in VIRGINIA.

8. **WILLIAM MORROW** who settled in ORANGE COUNTY, N.C. on
   HAW RIVER.

THE ABOVE list of children of **DAVID MORROW** may not be
absolutely correct, but it has taken me [**Ray**] over twenty
years to acquire the information included in it." (page
262.)

Then on page 263 **Ray** wrote, "**RODHAM KENNER** and **ALEXANDER
MORROW** came to East Tennessee together. **ALEXANDER MORROW**
obtained his lands on BIG LIMESTONE in Washington County in
1782, and **RODHAM KENNER** located in 1783 in HAWKINS COUNTY
about one mile above **SPEAR'S** MILL....It is interesting to
note, as the genealogists always say, that **MRS. JOHN C.
KENNER**, whose last address was 3101 Woodbine Avenue, in
KNOXVILLE, TENNESSEE, is a grand-daughter of **CHARLES MORROW**
and the great great grand-daughter of **ALEXANDER MORROW** and
his wife **ELIZABETH ARMSTRONG**."

217

Then **Ray** wrote about the relation of **Morrows**, **Armstrongs** and **Gaines** families, that they came from the "Old Rappahannock section of Virginia," which, in the early 1700's, became Essex County, Virginia (Page 263).

The land that **Alexander Morrow** had on Big Limestone Creek is as follows:

> N.C. Grant #283, 300 Acres
> Oct. 24, 1782, Washington County
> Watauga Book p. 228
> head of Big Limestone Creek.

3. ANN MORROW - CHARLES A. LINDBERGH

The **Ann Morrow** who was wife of the famous aviator is descended from **Daniel Morrow**, the brother of **Alexander**, the husband of **Rosa Rice Spence**.

On pages 264-265 is given the descent from **Daniel** and **Elizabeth Coons Morrow** through their fourth child **Alexander Morrow**, then **Alexander**'s son **James Elmore Morrow**, then **James**' son was the Honorable **Dwight Whitney Morrow**, the father-in-law of **Charles A. Lindbergh**.

Ray wrote that the "Hon. **DWIGHT MORROW**...had a distinguished career as an ambassador to MEXICO, was a great great grandson of **ALEXANDER MORROW**, who settled on DOAK'S CREEK in Knox County, Tennessee, in an early day."

"**DANIEL MORROW**, one of the sons of **ALEXANDER MORROW**, married **ELIZABETH COONS**....[they] had the following children:

1. JOSEPH MORROW
2. MICHAEL MORROW
3. ELIZABETH MORROW
4. ALEXANDER MORROW"

Then **Ray** goes on to say that "**ALEXANDER MORROW**, after he was of age, moved to HANCOCK COUNTY, in the extreme Northern part of (then) VIRGINIA, now West Virginia, where he married **MISS ELMORE**. They were the parents of **JAMES ELMORE MORROW**, among others, who was born March 28, 1837. [Then] **JAMES ELMORE MORROW** married **CLARA JOHNSON**, the daughter of **JOHN J. JOHNSON** and his wife **REBECCA JEFFERS**, by whom he had the following children:

218

1. JAMES WILLIAM MORROW
2. LEWIS MORROW
3. HUGH MORROW
4. ELIZABETH MORROW
5. JAY MORROW
6. DWIGHT WHITNEY MORROW

Then **Ray** wrote about **Ann Morrow's** parents and brothers and
sisters: "Hon. **DWIGHT WHITNEY MORROW** married **ELIZABETH REEVE
CUTTER**, of Cleveland, Ohio, June 16, 1903, and they had the
following children:

1. ELIZABETH R. MORROW
2. ANN S. MORROW married CHARLES A. LINDBERGH
3. DWIGHT MORROW, JR.
4. CONSTANCE O. MORROW."

Lastly, there are **Elmores** on the father's side of MWL.

K. MORROW PASSENGER LISTS

The name was at first **Marrow**, as previously cited from Ray's
book **Tennessee Counsins** (page 257). (61)

a. In **John Camden Hotten's** book (**The Original Lists of
Persons of Quality 1600-1700**, 1874, pages 41 and 389) there were
four **Marrow** names, three of which I have found. (44)

Page 39 - 17 February, 1634,
Page 41 - (name) **William Marrow** (years) 25."
Page 389 - "Tickets Granted
          May the 23^d 1679,
          Marrow, Cornelius C KATHERINE in the Ship
          Society for Bristoll.
          Edmond Ditty Comander....time out."

b. There are two names in **George Cabell Greer's** book
(**Early Virginia Immigrants 1623-1666**, page 217) with one name
spelled with an "e" on the end. (45)

Page 217 - "**Marrow, Geo.**, 1647, by **Richard Bland**, _____ Co.
          Marrowe, Alen, 1650, by **John Hallawes**, Gent.,
          Northumberland."

L. BIBLE AND CEMETERY RECORDS FOR **MORROWS** IN MAURY COUNTY, TN.

Recently in the Library of Congress two books were found on **Morrows** in a card catalogue of birth records and wills. This set of cards is not recommended, for there is a better approach through state and county books and histories. But this set of cards has opened the tracing of some families back to England, such as **Gibbs, Millers** and **Sharps**. This catalogue was by first names of cities, counties and/or place names here and abroad.

a. A **Morrow** Bible

The Maury County Tennessee Historical Society in 1967 wrote a book <u>Maury County Cousins</u> with <u>Bible</u> and <u>Family Records</u>, page 413. (63)

"The Holy Bible with Revised New Testament by Southwestern Publishing House, Nashville, Tenn., 1885. Originally belonged to **Andrew A. Morrow**, now owned by Mrs. **James M. Morrow** and copied by **Mrs. Clyde A. Morrow**, Aug. 14, 1967 for Maury County Historical Society.

Births:
Andrew A. Morrow, Feb. 6, 1836 died June 18, 1898
Sarah C. E. Morrow (wife) Jan. 18, 1843, died Nov. 8, 1878

Children:
Miles Leonard, May 24, 1862, died Jan. 1, 1863
Eleanor Jane, Oct. 29, 1863, died Feb. 22, 1928
Wm Theodore Lee, Nov. 20, 1865, died Sept. 20, 1918
Robert Andrew, Sept. 22, 1868, died May 5, 1911
Nancy Roberta, Jan. 20, 1871, died Apr. 30, 1934
James Murphy, July 13, 1873, died June 29, 1964
John Pinkney, Apr. 3, 1876
Joseph Franklin, Sept. 25, 1878, died 1947
Garfield, Aug. 16, 1881, died Aug. 29, 1943

Marriages:
Andrew A. Morrow - **Sarah C. E. Murphy**, July 28, 1861
Eleanor Jane Morrow - **James G. West**, Sept. 19, 1886
Wm. L. Morrow - **Linda Lee Tarpley**, Jan. 24, 1889
John P. Morrow - **Mary Catherine Farris**, Nov. 28, 1897
Robert A. Morrow - **Margaret Patton**, Feb. 1, 1901
Jas. M. Morrow - **Minnie Lula Tarpley**, Dec. 11, 1895
Joseph F. Morrow - **Elizabeth P. Redding**, Sept. 28, 1900
Garfield Morrow - **Lena Richardson**, Sept. 10, 1925
James M. Morrow, 2nd marriage - **Nettie A. Walker**, May 12, 1918"

The Bible record continues on the next page in this book.

"Children of **James M. Morrow & Minnie Lula Tarpley**:

   Thomas Reed Morrow, Dec. 1, 1896
   Clyde A. Morrow, July 16, 1898
   Joe Mack Morrow, Apr. 26, 1900
   Paul N. Morrow, Apr. 20, 1904
   James T. Morrow, Jan. 29, 1906
   William A. Morrow, Dec. 1, 1908 - died Aug. 15, 1909
   Sarah Lucy Morrow, Dec. 16, 1921 - of 2nd marriage

Children of **Joseph Franklin Morrow & Elizabeth P. Redding**:

   Hazle Paxton Morrow - Sept. 15, 1901
   Edwin Harlan Morrow - Sept. 11, 1903
   Edith Clementine Morrow - June 4, 1906
        2nd marriage to **Clara Craig**, children:
   Joseph Franklin Morrow, Jr. - Jan. 4, 1919
   Sarah Elizabeth Morrow - Jan. 24, 1921
   Charles Craig Morrow - June 30, 1923
   William Mack Morrow - Aug. 21, 1924

Children of **Garfield Morrow & Lena Richardson**

   Martha Jean Morrow, Oct. 20, 1932"

   b. <u>Cemetery Records on Morrows</u>

   The second book is entitled **They Passed This Way** (64).
The pages are A-177 and A-145.

MORROW CEMETERY, on old **John Morrow** place, now **Ocie Blocker**
place, **Love's** Branch (**Cathey's** Creek vicinity). This cemetery is
partially listed on page A-145."

I give the tombstone names for **Love** and **Morrow** from all of the
surnames:

   One stone: **LOVE, William T.**, 1880-1954
               "   **Susie B.**, 1900-

   One stone: **MORROW, John E.**, 1872-1939
               "   **Annie E.**, 1874-19__

               MORROW, William M., 29 Sept. 1877 - 21 Sept.
                              1942
               "   **Matilda E.**, 21 Apr. 1879 - 5 Dec. 1952
               "   **Jimmie H.**, son **J. W. & Alice R.**, 20
                              Sept. 1880 - 2 Oct. 1881
               "   **W. O.**, 1868-1941
               "   **Leffie B.**, 1897-1927
(List continued on the next page.)

```
One stone:   MORROW, Manley W., 25 Sept. 1893 -
               "       Lettie A., 5 June, 1897 - 10 Feb. 1951

One stone:   MORROW, Connie U., 12 Jan. 1895 - 23 Jan. 1957
               "       Edna A., 14 Oct. 1894 -

             MORROW, Carnice H., 1898 - 1943
               "       Inf. Mr. & Mrs. M. W., 10 Apr - 12 Apr
                          1923

One stone:   MORROW, Alvin, Father, 4 Apr. 1909 - 18 Sept.
                          1951
               "       Mary, 16 Nov. 1909 -
             MORROW, Eva Gray, 24 July, 1924 - 10 May, 1926
               "       Dorothy May, 26 Aug. 1927
               "       James Benton, died 10 March, 195_,
                          8 days, Undertaker's Mkr
```

```
     SCOTT, Willie S. Morrow, 1899 - 1925
```

Listed August 17, 1964, **Marise P. Lightfoot & J. C. Parish**"
Page A-177.

"OLD LOVE CEMETERY, on **Robert Morrow** place, **Love's** Branch.
There are no marked graves in this cemetery. List from family
records. Information given by **Mrs. C. U. Morrow**, 11 July, 1964."
......

MORROW CEMETERY, on old **John Morrow Place**, now **Ocie Blocker**
place, **Love's** Branch.

LOVE, J. A., 27 July, 1842 - 1 Feb. 1914.
MORROW, John W., 15 June, 1836 - 5 Apr. 1881 (Federal Soldier).
   "   Alice R., 25 Jan. 1842 - 1 Feb. 1917.
EARP, Dora Voss, wife of **C. F. Earp,** 13 Sept. 1878 - 1 Oct.
                    1906.
VOSS, F. J., 13 Nov. 1847 - 9 Dec. 1913.
   "   W. J., June, 1849 - 8 Sept. 1906." Page A-145.

Lastly, there were many **Morrows** who served in Indian Wars.
These wars lasted from 1815 until the Mexican War which began
in 1846.

LAVINA RICE - LEWIS BRIM

Chapter summary on page viii

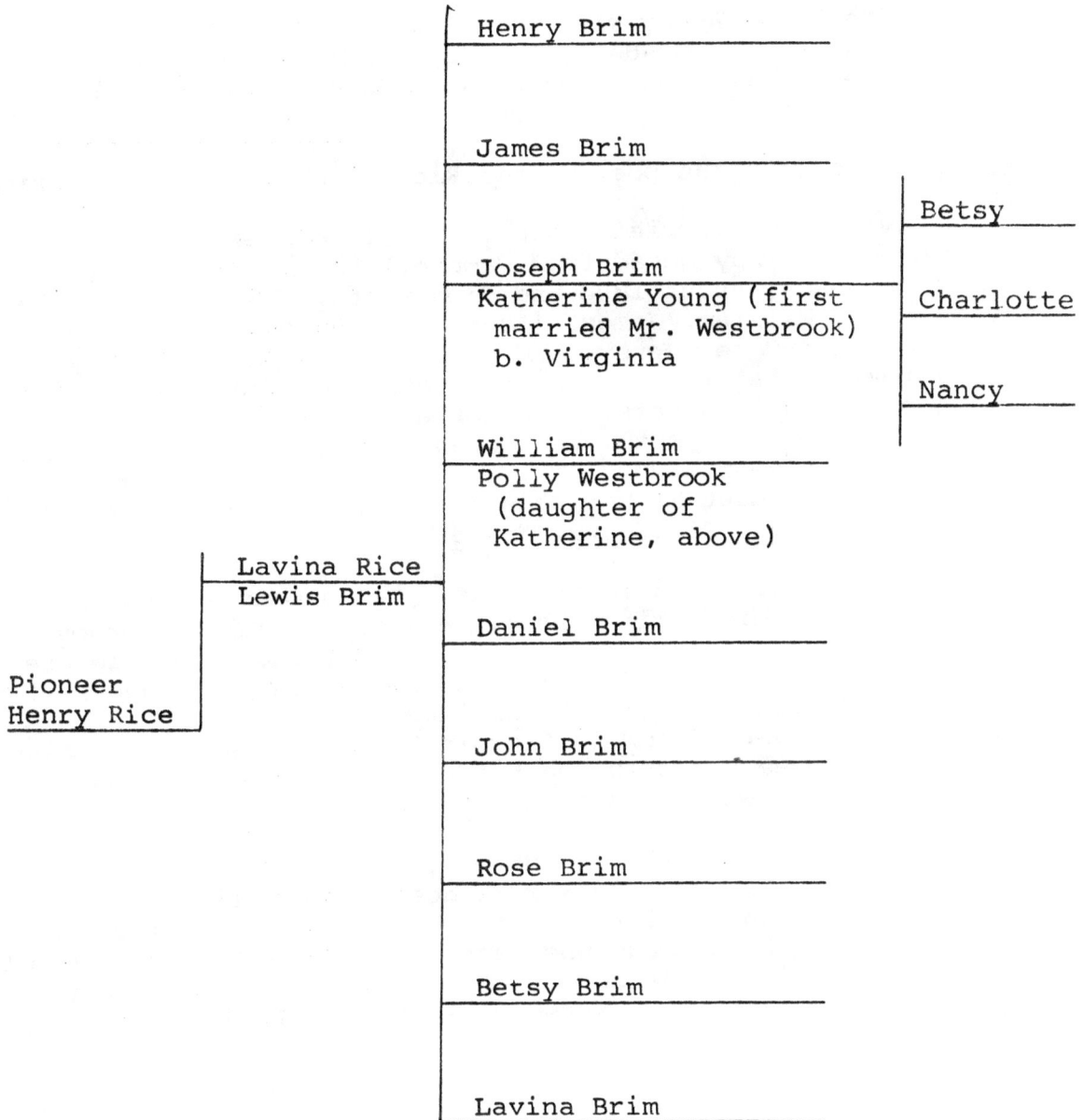

```
                              ┌ Henry Brim ──────────────────
                              │
                              │
                              │ James Brim ──────────────────
                              │                               ┌ Betsy ──────────
                              │                               │
                              │ Joseph Brim                   │
                              │ Katherine Young (first        ┤ Charlotte ──────
                              │   married Mr. Westbrook)       │
                              │   b. Virginia                  │ Nancy ──────────
                              │                               └
                              │ William Brim ────────────────
                              │ Polly Westbrook
              ┌ Lavina Rice   │  (daughter of
              │ Lewis Brim ───┤   Katherine, above)
              │               │
              │               │ Daniel Brim ─────────────────
Pioneer       │               │
Henry Rice ───┘               │
                              │ John Brim ───────────────────
                              │
                              │
                              │ Rose Brim ───────────────────
                              │
                              │
                              │ Betsy Brim ──────────────────
                              │
                              │
                              └ Lavina Brim ─────────────────
```

CHAPTER XII. LAVINA RICE - LEWIS BRIM
Chapter summary on page viii

A. LAVINA RICE

Lavina Rice, **Henry Rice's** daughter, was a bride to **Lewis Brim**. As with most of **Henry Rice's** children, there is no known marriage record (the marriage of **Rosanna** or **Rosa Rice Spence** to **Alexander Morrow** is the exception.)

Here is what the poet **Martin Rice** recalled about the **Brims**:

"**Lavina Rice** married **Lewis Brim**. I remember them in my boyhood. They moved from Campbell to Lincoln County (Tennessee) about 1828 and died there. They had sons **Henry, Joseph, William, James, (John)**, and **Daniel**, and three daughters **Rose, Betsy**, and **Lavina**. **Joseph** married my mother's sister **Katherine** (or **Catherine Young Westbrook**) and their daughters **Betsy, Charlotte** and **Nancy** were my playmates and cousins in youth, but moved to Lincoln County (Tennessee) about the year 1825. **William Brim** married my cousin **Polly Westbrook**, Aunt **Katherine's** daughter by a first marriage." (From <u>Charles Rice, etc</u>., page 9). (2)

Some additions are that it was Lincoln County, Tennessee, not Lincoln County, Missouri; **Joseph, Levina,** and **William Brims** are in the 1830 Lincoln County, TN, census. **Henry** and **John Brim** are with their families in the 1830 Campbell County census. Then in 1840 there is a **Thomas Brimm** in the Grainger County census, with **George W., John** and **Joseph Brimm** in Lincoln County. However, no census in East Tennessee has survived before 1830, except for the 1810 Grainger County, which has no **Brims.**

A **Catherine** or **Katherine Brim** witnessed, with **Henry Brim, Joseph Brim** and **Nicholas Mozier**, a deed between **Lewis Brim** and **Jeremiah Oaks**. This **Katherine** must have been the poet's Aunt **Katherine Young Westbrook**, who married **Joseph Brim**. A **Joseph Oaks** later was one of two deacons of the Old United Baptist Church at Lost Creek who received 5 acres of land from **George Rice** on Nov. 8, 1859, for the Lost Creek Cemetery.

Lavina Brim is in the 1830 Lincoln County Census, with three children:

<u>1830</u> **Lincoln** <u>County</u> **Census**
FM 19, roll 177, page 212

Brims, Levina. 2 males 15-20; 1 female 20-30; 1 female 50-60.

Lavina Rice Brim was not in the 1840 census schedule as head of a family, but John and Joseph each had a woman 50 to 60. There could have been an error in the counting of the years; maybe one is Catherine Westbrook Brim.

B. LEWIS BRIM

The "old" Henry Rice's son-in-law Lewis Brim was a witness on a land plat for Nathan Watson and/or Henry Rice on July 12, 1794, for 200 acres. Nathan's name was on the drawing of the plat, but in the description Nathan's name was crossed out with Henry Rice's name put in on the grant. But later Henry Rice sold the 200 acres to Molly Rice's husband. The Tennessee Grant No. is 599. (See page 15 for the Hawkins County deed to Nathan Watson.)

Since Lewis Brim witnessed this deed in 1794, he must have married Lavina before this, maybe in the 1780's or early 1790's. The son Henry Brim was 40 to 50 in the 1830 Campbell County census; this would mean that he was born between 1780 and 1790. Joseph Brim was 30 to 40 in 1830 Lincoln County census; this would mean he was born between 1790 and 1800.

Lewis Brim had deeds in Campbell and Knox Counties.

(a) Campbell County Deeds Index

Grantee	Grantor	Book	Page	Date		Acres
Lewis Brim	Sugar Jones	A	1641-2	Feb. 5, 1813	$50	100$\frac{1}{}$/
Jeremiah Oaks	Lewis Brim	B	199-200	Feb. 23, 1814	$10	100$\frac{2}{}$/
William Mitterbarger	Lewis Brim	C	26	May 18, 1815	$50	100$\frac{3}{}$/
Matthew Hill	Lewis Brim	G	150	Sep. 27, 1825		*

1/, 2/, 3/, Deeds described below.
* Located at Clinch River.

1/ Book A, pages 1641-42.
   Brim, Lewis. Deed from Sugar Jones
   5 Feb. 1813
   $50 - 100 acres.
   Lewis Brim's line
   Survey in name of Stokely Donaldson

(Continued next page)

```
In presence of us     :
Jeremiah Oaks         :
Joseph Brim**         :
Henry Brim**          :
        his           :
Henry  X   Sharp      :
        mark          :
```

** **Henry** and **Joseph Brim** must have been 21 years of age to witness this deed, so they were born before 1792.

2/ Book B, pages 199-200.
Brim, Lewis. Deed to **Jeremiah Oaks**
23rd Feb. 1814
$10 - 100 acres.
Brim's spring branch
Henderson's line

```
in presence of us     :
Catherine Brim        :
Henry Brim            :
Joseph Brim           :
Nicholas Mozier       :
```

3/ Book C, page 26, 18 May 1815.
Brim, Lewis. Deed to **William Mitterbarger**
$50 - 100 acres the same more or less.

```
In the presence of us:
Henry Brim            :
James Brim***         :
George Rice           :
```

*** This is the only mention that I have of **James Brim**, other than his being listed as a son by the Bard of Lone Jack.

(b) Knox County Deeds (Reverse Index)
Knox County Court House; page 125

Grantee	Grantor	Book	Page	Date	Acres	Location
Rice, John	Brim, Lewis	E,v.1	401	Oct.12,1798	102	Tenn. R.

The above is the deed mentioned earlier (page 28) which was bought by **John Rice**, the preacher son of **Henry Rice**.

Lewis Brim is included in several tax lists (**Early Tennessee Tax Lists**, by Byron and Barbara Sistler, Evanston, Illinois, 1977, page 22). The list shows just an abbreviation for county and the year:

"Gr-1804, A-1805, C-1818, C-1823."

The counties are Grainger, Anderson, and Campbell. The actual tax information is in the register books of the respective courthouses.

Lewis Brim must have died between 1825 and 1830, for **Lavina** is the head of the family in the Lincoln County 1830 census.

C. HENRY BRIM

Henry was the first son mentioned by **Martin Rice** in 1891. He was 40 to 50 in the 1830 Campbell County census.

1830 Campbell County, Tennessee Census
FM 19, roll 178
Henry Brim: 1 male under 5; 1 male 10-15; 1 male 40-50. 1 female 5-10; 1 f. 10-15; 2 f. 15-20; 1 f. 40-50.

Henry Brim is not in Campbell or Lincoln County in the 1840 census; however, he did witness three of his father's deeds (see **Lewis Brim**). This son of **Lewis** and **Lavina Brim** was in the tax lists for Campbell County in 1818 and 1823. **Henry Brim** was also in the 1837 Campbell County tax list, but your researcher did not look up the data when in Jacksboro.

There is a **Thomas Brimm** in the Grainger County census for 1840. He could have been the son of **Henry**, for he was 20 to 30 in 1840, and **Henry Brim** had a son, above, 10 to 15 in 1830.

1840 Grainger County Census
MC 704, roll 525
Brimm, Thomas: 2 m. un. 5; 1 m. 5-10; 1 m. 20-30. 2 f. un. 5; 1 f. 10-15; 1 f. 30-40.

There is a **Thomas Brim** age 46 in the **Tennessee 1850 Census** (38)
Index, but in Dickson County. This is two counties west of
Nashville, and this **Thomas** belongs to another set of **Brims** in the
north to northwestern part of the State, from the Cumberland
Plateau through Smith, Wilson, Sumner, Davidson, Williamson and
Weakley Couties. These **Brims** are probably related to **Henry Rice's**
son-in-law **Lewis Brim**, but your researcher has not yet connected

them.

D. JOSEPH BRIM

This second son of **Lavina Rice** and **Lewis Brim** was mentioned
earlier as witness to two of his father's deeds. His wife,
Catherine or **Katherine Westbrook**, witnessed one of the two deeds.

Joseph was listed in the 1818 and 1823 tax lists for Campbell
(42) County (**Early Tennessee Tax Lists**, page 224). He is also in the
1830, 1840, and 1850 census schedules for Lincoln County,
Tennessee (**Tenn. 1830 Census Index; Tenn. 1840 Census Index; 1850
Tenn. Census Index**).

Tennessee 1830 Census Index
(65, page 22)

Brim**s**, Joseph, Linc.212, No TWP L (No township listed).

Microfilm, Lincoln County, Tennessee
FM 19, roll 177, page 176

Brim**s**, Joseph: 1 male 30-40; 1 female 10-15; 2 females 15-20

Tennessee 1840 Census Index
(18) page 27

Brim**m**, Joseph, Linc 010.

Microfilm, Lincoln County, Tennessee
Microcopy 704, roll 531

Brim**m**, Joseph: 1 male 10-15; 1 male 40-50.
1 female 20-30; 1 female 50-60.

Brim, Joseph, 47; Catherine, 66; Jasper N., 18; T, VA, Li-
-568-78. (T = father born in Tennessee; VA = mother
born in Virginia.)

The **Catherine,** wife of **Joseph** in the 1850 census, is
Katherine Young Westbrook, aunt of the "Bard of Lone Jack."
According to the above census record, **Joseph** married her between
1830 and 1840; but **William Brim,** who married **Katherine's** daughter
Polly Westbrook, is in the 1830 census with a wife between 20 and
30 and a son under 5. The poet gave the names of **Joseph's**
daughters as **Betsy, Charlotte** and **Nancy.**

     1. The Youngs. The name **Young** is found in Virginia
(**First Census of the United States, 1790, (Records of the State
Enumerations: 1782 to 1785, Virginia,** U.S. Gov't Printing Office,
1908) for those interested in tracing them. There were many
Youngs, and not so many **Westbrooks.** (See Reference 66)

     2. The Westbrooks. Katherine Young married a **Mr.
Westbrook.** The name is found in "**Heads of Families--Virginia,
1782--Amelia County,** in "**Heads of Families--Virginia, 1785--Amelia
County**" and is found with the **Brims** in "**Heads of Families--
Virginia 1785--Pittsylvania County.**" **Westbrooks** are also in the
Lincoln County Census along with the **Brims** in 1830.

Heads of Families--Virginia, 1782--Amelia County
List of **Sam'l Sherwin,** pages 11-12

Name	White	Black
Westbrook, Phebe	6	3
Westbrook, Lucy	3	1
Westbrook, Henry	6	–

List of **Stephen Cocke,** page 13

Westbrook, Amos	2	–

Heads of Families--Virginia, 1785--Amelia County
pages 81-82

Westbrook, Phebe	White souls 5;	Dwellings 1;	other bldg. 2			
Westbrook, James	" " 10	" 2	" " 1			

Heads of Families--Virginia, 1785--Pittsylvania County
Pages 98-99

Westbrook, Henry   White Souls 6; dwellings none;
other bldg. 1.

There were **Brims** in Pittsylvania County, Virginia, in 1782 and 1785, in Essex County in 1783, and in Hanover County in 1782. However, your compiler did not find **John Brim** in Hanover County. (See page 17.)

Johnson Westbrooks is in the 1830 Lincoln County, Tennessee, Census on page 214 (**Tennessee 1830 Census Index,** edited by **Ronald Vern Johnson** and **Gary Ronald Teeples,** Accelerated Indexing Systems, 1976). (6 5)

E. WILLIAM BRIM

William was the third son listed by **Martin Rice**. He is in the Lincoln County census for 1830, on page 214 with **Johnson Westbrooks**. Also there is a **William Brim** in the 1840 Hardin County census in West Tennessee. Hardin County is two counties east of Memphis, with the county seat at Savannah.

Lincoln County Census for 1830
FM 19, roll 177, p. 214

Brims, William: 1 male under 5; 1 m. 20-30; 1 female 20-30.

Most of the **Brims** were in Lincoln County in the 1850 census, but court records have not been seen to trace Brims past Lincoln County.

1840 Hardin County Census
Microcopy 704, roll 522, page 243
South Civil District

William Brim: 2 males under 5; 1 male 30-40; 1 female 20-30.

This **William** is 10 years older than the above **William**, but there is no son 10-15. The female was listed as the same age 10 years earlier. No other state indices have been seen for **Brims**.

A **William M. Brimm** was listed in Haywood County in 1850, but the census data was not seen. See also Section "**J. George W. Brim**" for a **William D. Brim**, 42, listed under **George Brim**.

230

F. JAMES BRIM

This son, of **Lewis** and **Lavina Rice Brim**, and grandson of **Henry Rice**, witnessed, along with **Henry Brim** and **George Rice**, a **Lewis Brim** land indenture to **William Mitterbarger**. See **Lewis Brim** for Campbell County deeds (page 4).

James Brim must have been at least 21 years old in 1815, when he witnessed the above. That would make his year of birth 1794.

James is not in the 1830 census, but he could be one of the two sons under **Lavina** in Lincoln County as 15 to 20. The other could be the next son, **Daniel**.

There is a **Jas. A. Brim** in Haywood County census in 1840, but no **James** in Tennessee in 1850.

1840 Haywood County Census
Microcopy 704, roll 522, p. 402

Jas. A. Brim. 1 male under 5; 2 males 5 to 10; 1 male 15 to
                    20; 1 male 30 to 40.
                   1 female 5 to 10; 1 female 30 to 40.

G. DANIEL BRIM

Your compiler has found no reference on **Daniel Brim**, except that he was mentioned by **Enoch Rice's** son, **Martin Rice**, the poet. The compiler failed to look up the Lincoln County court records on **Brims** in the Tennessee State Library and Archives in the summers of 1972 and 1978.

H. JOHN BRIM

John Brim was not mentioned by **Martin Rice**. However, he was in the 1830 Campbell County census with **Henry Brim**, as also having a family. He is in the Lincoln County census schedules for both 1840 and 1850, being 41 years old in 1850. **Joseph** was 47. There was a **George W. Brim**, 29, in the 1850 census, and he was probably a grandson of **Lavina** and **Lewis Brim**.

1830 Campbell County Census Schedule
FM 19, roll 178

John Brim.   1 male under 5; 1 male 20-30.
1 female under 5; 1 female 20-30.

1840 Lincoln County Schedule
Microcopy 704, roll 531, page 9

John Brimm. 2 males under 5; 1 male 5-10; 1 male 10-15;
1 male 20-30; 1 male 30-40.
1 female under 5; 2 females 5-10; 1 female 10-15;
1 female 15-20; 3 females 20-30; 1 female
30-40; 1 female 50-60.

Levina was 50 to 60 in 1830, so this female 50-60 could not
be her. This John Brimm had five sons and eight daughters, with a
total of ten women. The family totals sixteen.

1850 Lincoln County Census
MC 432, roll 887, page 42,
Subdivision No. 2, household 601, family 601

John Brim	41 m.	Wagon maker	(born) Tenn.
Lyddia	42 f.		"*
Cynthia	16 f.		"
Daniel L.	12 m.		"
Henry R.	10 f.**		"
Louisa	8 m.**		"
John G.	6 f.**		"
Lucinda S.	3 f.		"
Margaret C.	21 m.**		"

* Ditto marks added by the compiler.
** Sex was given wrong in the census books.

The same census record is on page 194 of the 1850 **Tennessee
Census Index** (see Byron & Barbara Sistler, vol. 1, p. 194, 1974).
The **Margaret** could be the oldest child, or a younger sister. (39)

Brim, John, 41; Lyddia 42; Cynthia 16; Daniel L. 12;
Henry R. 10; Louisa 8; John G. 6; Lucinda S. 3;
Margaret C. 21. 'T T Li-601-84. [TT = Both
parents were born in Tennessee, and 601 was the
family number. The number 84 for the page was
hand written instead of being typed.]

232

I. ROSE, BETSY, and LAVINA BRIM

These are the names that **Martin Rice** gave for the daughters of **Lavina** and **Lewis Brim**. Since the court records, especially the Lincoln County Marriage Register, have not been seen, it is not known what happened to them.

J. GEORGE W. BRIM

In the same **Sistler** census book for 1850, there is a George W. Brim. He is assumed to be a relative, either a son of **Lavina** or a grandson. His census data are as follows:

"Brim, George W., 29; Rebecca 1; William D. 42;
      T T, Li-608-84." (39, Vol. I)
["T T" is the birthplace of the first two people.
William D. Brim's relationship to **George** has not been
determined. "Li" is the abbreviation for Lincoln
County. "608" is the household number, 84 the page.
William does not show up by himself in Lincoln County
in 1840. See section on **William Brim.**]

K. ROBERT BRIM; ROSANNA BRIM

1. There was a **Robert Brim**, age 4, in Knox County in 1850 under **Jacob** and **Elizabeth Helbert.** (1850 **Knox County, Tenn.,** MC 432 roll 886, page 225, household 1870, family 1879.) Jacob **Helbert** was 63, farming, with $50 real estate, and born in Virginia, while his wife was 54, born in Pennsylvania. Neither could read or write. But **Robert B. Brim** does not show up ten years later in the 15th subdivision; nor do the **Helberts.**

2. **Rosanna Brim** was in Lincoln County in 1850 (**Tennessee 1850 Census Index,** page 46): "**Rosanna Brim** LINC 106 1st Subdivision." (38)

<u>1850 Lincoln County, Tennessee Census</u>
MC 432, roll 887, page 106, line 35
Household 53, family 53

Joseph Scott	40 M	Cabinet workman	800 r.e.	VA	*
Rebecca	28 F			TN	
Harvey	18 M	Laborer		"	School
Samuel	16 M	"		"	"
James Jones	24 M			"	
Rosanna Brim	20 F			"	

* Married within the year.

L. BRIMS IN SOUNDEX CODE SYSTEM AND CENSUS

Of the **Brim** families in Texas in 1880, three of them had the birthplace of the head and the head's parents as the glorious State of Tennessee; one was born in Alabama and one in Georgia. The Code for **Brim** is B-650; however this code number includes hundreds of **Browns**. Since Lincoln County is on the border of Alabama, other States were checked for the names **Joseph, John,** and **George.**

<u>1880 Soundex</u>
MC T 773 rolls 9 and 10
(National Archives)

1. Texas Vol. 2, E.D. 1, sheet 75, line 46:

Brim, J. K. P.
     W. M. 31 Birthplace Tennessee
     Bell County — Just. Prec. #1.

Other members of the (**J.K.P. Brim**) family:

	Relationship	Age	Birthplace
Brim, N. A.	W	29	GA
Brim, N. E.	D	12	TN
Brim, Tom	S	10	"
Brim, M. V.	D	8	"
Brim, J. B.	S	4	"
(the following names on second card)			
Brim, E. V.	D	2	TX
Brim, M. E.	D	5/12	"

2. Texas Vol. 17 E.D. 73, sheet 29, line 31:

Brim, John
    W   M   32   Birthplace Tennessee
    Hill County - Just Prec. #3

Other members of the family:

Brim, Susan V.	W	29	TN
____, S. F.	D	6	TX
____, Alice V.	D	2	"
____, Mary B.	D	4/12	"

3. Texas Vol. 25 E.D. 136, sheet 40, line 40.

Brim, Linza R.
    W   M   51   (Birthplace) Tennessee
    Navarro County - Comm. Prec. #5
    Dresden City, no house number, no street number

Other members of the family:

Brim, Sallie	W	32	Miss.
Brim, Mary A.	D	31	"
Brim, William T.	S	27	"
Brim, Willie	S	7	TX
Brim, Minnie	D	4	"
(Name on second card:)			
Brim, Callie	D	1/12	"

The regular census records are given next; only the heads of families are listed, for brevity.

1880 Bell County, Texas, Census
MC T-9, roll 1290

Justice's Precinct No. 1, 22nd day of June 1880, page 75, Supervisor's Dist.4, E.D. 1, line 46, household 641, family 691.

Brim, J. K. P.
    W   M   31   Married   Farmer   TN   TN   TN

1880 Hill County, Texas, Census
MC T-9, roll 1311

Justice's Precinct No. 3, page 29, Sup. Dist. 3, E.D. 73, line 31, household 244, family 264.

Brim, John
W	M	32	Married		Farmer	TN	TN	TN

Susan
W	F	29	Wife, Married		Keeping house*	TN	TN	TN

---

* Maimed, crippled, bedridden, or otherwise disabled.

1880 Navarro County, Texas, Census
MC T-9, roll 1321

Comm. Prec. No. 5, page 40, Sup. Dist. 4, E.D. 136, line 40, household 351, family 357.

Brim, Linza R.
W	M	51	Married	Carpenter	TN	TN	TN

M. THOMAS O. BRIM

Mrs. Charles A. Rice (Ila Rice) has been helped on her Rice line by your compiler. Her Rice line has not yet been connected to Henry Rice, but research continues. Ila contributed to The Epistle information on the 1860 Dallas County, Missouri, census on Rhoadman Hickory Rice, a grandson of Levi Rice (page 34).

In a letter dated February 4, 1981, Ila gave me information on Mitchell and Thomas O. Brim. Ila's husband Charles Rice and his Aunt Ora claimed kin with Mitchell Brim. Mitchell Brim resided in Pittsburg, Kansas, selling cattle for the packing company. [**Charles** and **Ila Rice** live at 8 Quincy Court, Pittsburg, KS, 66762.] The **Rice** line and **Brim** line were in Missouri, and earlier from North Carolina and Tennessee. I quote from **Ila Rice's** letter:

"Aunt **Ora's** mother was **Dora Emily Robertson**, d/o **Thomas Asbury Robertson** and **Rhoda Emily Mitchell**. In the **Mitchell** Campground cemetery in Polk Co., Missouri is a tombstone as follows: **Thomas O. Brim**, 2-13-1835--5-28-1914 (/) wife **Mary F.** 5-12-1850--2-4-1929. There was also a **Mackey** grave there; **Sarah** I believe her name was. These families all came to Missouri from Tennessee I believe together but it was around the period 1838-1841. There were **Mackeys, Mitchells, Bonds, Robertsons, Ewings**; **Morris Mitchell** the father of all the **Mitchell** clan died in 1848. One girl married a **Sullens** who was a well known Methodist minister and two married (men) by the name of **Winton**. This was in early Tenn. and in the area of Roan Co., Knox Co. and earlier. **Morris Mitchell** came from Maryland and Pa. and his first child was born in Tenn. in 1782. I think he had a brother **Mordeci**...."

Mackey or **Mackie** is one of three names in the book **Cantrell-Rice-Mackie**, 1960, by **Lucylle Davis Rice**, P.O. Box 114, Waynesville, Mo., 65583 (30).

On page 65 of the chapter on **Henry Rice** the Pioneer Gristmiller, there is a citation that "**Henry Rice** married **Mary C. Mitchell**, daughter of **Isaac** and **Mary Williams Mitchell**...." This comes from **Lucylle's** book. **Isaac** and **Mary Mitchell** lived in Newberry and Abbeyville Districts of South Carolina. **Levi Rice's** brother, **James Rice**, was married to **Rebecca Miller** in Newberry District, but the record was destroyed in a courthouse fire. **Isaac Mitchell** had children **Ursula, Mary Catherine, Sarah** and **Isaac, Jr.**

Whether this **Isaac Mitchell** and the above **Morris Mitchell** are related is not known by your compiler. The book **Tennessee Cousins** by **Worth Stickley Ray** contains references to the above families.

N. THE VIRGINIA BRIMS AND THEIR ORIGIN

Two **Brim** names are in the early patent books (**Cavaliers and Pioneers Abstracts of Virginia Land Patents and Grants**, Abstracted by **Nell Marion Nugent**, indexed by **Claudia B. Grundman**. Vol. II, 1666-1695, 1977, pp. 149 and 350. Virginia State Library, Richmond.) (67)

1. **Passenger Data:**

"Patent Book No. 6.
**Lt. Col. Jno Smith, Mr. John Buckner, Mr. Phill Lightfoot,
Mr. Tho. Royston & Mr. John Lewis**, 10,050 acs., New Kent
Co.; on Mattapony Riv. adj. **Mr. Tho. Hall & John Pigg, &
Henderson & Bagby**, 25 Feb. 1673/4, p. 518. Trans of 201
pers: **Ja. Brims**."

"Patent Book No. 8.
John Brim, 200 acs., Middlesex Co., 23 Oct. 1690, p. 81.
105 acs beg. at **Hooper's** Neck Land, now **Mr. Morris Cocks**,
to land of **Dodes Minor** (?), 95 acs. beg. at sd. Neck; to
Jamaco Land; to **Nich. Pain**, on E. side of the **Reedy** Br.;
to **Thackwell's** Neck, &c Imp. of 4 pers: **Robt. Glenn,
Jno. Streate, Tho. Falmar, Geo. Turner**."

2. **Brim Christenings in Middlesex County**

(Reference: **The Parish Register of Christ Church,
Middlesex County, Virginia, from 1653 to 1812**, published
by the National Society of the Colonial Dames of America
in the State of Virginia, Richmond, **Wm. Ellis Jones**, Steam
Book and Job Printer, 1897.) (68)

Page 19. "Christenings, &c. An accompt of Christenings
ffor the yeare 1682. **Mary Brim** daughter of **Jno. & Mary
Brim** was borne 7th of Jan^{ry} last and baptized the 16th
of Aprill."

"**Elizabeth Brim** Daughter of **Jno. & Mary Brim** was borne 7th
of Jan^{ry} and baptized 16th of Aprill."

Page 27. "Christenings—1685 &c."
Page 28. "**John Brim** ye sone of **John & Mary Brim** was
bap^{tz} 14th of ffebruary 1685/6."

Page 38. "Christenings—1688 &c.
Alice ye Daughter of **Jno & Mary Brim** borne 10th ffeb^y bat^z
16th June 1688."

Page 40. "Christenings—1689 & 1690.
Richans ye Sone of **John & Mary Brim** bap^{tz} 23th ffeb^y
168-9/10 (a fraction)."

238

Page 54. "Christenings"

Page 55. "**Peter Brim** the Sone of Jn⁰ **& Mary Brim** was borne 6th of Aprill and Baptized the 12th of May 1702."

3. The First Census of Virginia

The following **Brims** are in the first census schedule of Virginia as State enumerations (**First Census of the United States, 1790, Records of the State Enumerations: 1782 to 1785, Virginia.** Washington, Government Printing Office, 1908). (67) They have not been connected up with **Lewis Brim**.

Page 42. "Heads of Families--Virginia, 1782. Pittsylvania County."

Name of head of family	whites	blacks
Brim, Joseph	16	-
Brim, Richard	5	-

Page 52, "Heads of Families--Virginia, 1783. Essex County. List of **Colo. Beal**."

Brim, Jno.	8	1

Page 98. "Heads of Families--Virginia, 1785. Pittsylvania County."

Name	White souls	Dwellings	Other Buildings
Brim, Elijah	3	-	1
Ingrum, Wm.	7	-	2
Brimm, Rich^d	6	-	-

This concludes the section on **Brims**. Hopefully this will help **Henry Rice's Brim** descendants to trace their **Brim** ancestors. Revolutionary and other military records have not been checked.

O. BRIMS IN FURTHER CENSUS SCHEDULES

The name of **Brim** has been found in Missouri, Utah, Nevada and Washington, and all western states checked. The **Brims** in Colorado were of foreign birth.

1840 Scott County Missouri
Microcopy 704 Roll 232

Page 65, **John Brim**   1 male 20-30; 1 female 20-30
Wolf Island Township

1850 Cedar County Missouri
Microcopy 432 Roll 395
District No. 17, 15th day of Sept. 1850
Page 147, Line 20, Household 300, Family 300

John A. R. Brim	30 M	Farmer	Tenn.
Elizabeth	29 F		Ky
Wm	9 M		Mo
Melissa	7 F		Mo
James	5 M		Mo
Margaret	3 F		Mo
Sarah	1 F		Mo

This **John A. R. Brim**, with three more children, is in the next census for Cedar County, but he said he was born in Virginia and his wife in North Carolina. This census will be shown after the remaining 1850 Missouri censuses.

1850 Greene County Missouri
Microcopy 432 Roll 400
Boone Township 26th October 1850
Page 329, Line 4, Household 1271, Family 1271

Paul Brimm	39 M	Farmer		Va
Margaritte	36 F			Ky
Martha J.	16 F			Ky
Melinda	14 F			Mo
Elizabeth	18 F			Ky
Joseph	12 F	[?]		Mo
David S.	10 M			Mo
John H.	8 M			Mo
James H.?	7 M			Mo
Celia H.	5 F			Mo
Huiza	3 F			Mo

On the next page of this compilation will be the family of **James Brimm** in Greene County.

1850 Greene County (Continued)
Boone Township
Page 331, Line 36, Household 1297, Family 1297
28th October 1850

James Brimm	44	M	Farmer		Va
Mary	36	F			Ky
Sarah	14	F			Mo
Barbara	13	F			Mo
Elizabeth	10	F			Mo
Jane	6	F			Mo
James	4	M			Mo
John P.	3	M			Mo
Martha	5/12	F			Mo
James	7	M	[Parentage?]		Mo
Ann C.	6	F	"		Mo

1850 Osage County Missouri
Microcopy 432, Roll 408
Crawford Township
Page 448, Line 37, Household 468, Family 468

John C. Brim	41	M	Farmer	600	Ten
Louisa	38	F	Cannot read or write		Va
Sarah	17	F			Ten
Thomas	13	M	School		Ten
Lucy	11	F	School		Mo

(Page 449, Line 1)

John	8	M			Mo
Joseph	6	M			Mo
Melinda	3	F			Mo
Nisa	1	F			Mo
Nancy Holloway	80	F			Va

There is a **John Brim** in the 1860 Osage County census with a son **Joseph** 16 and a daughter **Malindy** 14. The family has some new additions as follows:

1860 Osage County Missouri
Microcopy 653, Roll
Crawford Township, Post Office Linn
14th day of July 1860
Page 99, Line 27, Household 745, Family 707

John Brimm		51	M	Farmer	2000	1500	Tenn
Mary	"	40	F	[new wife?]			Ark
Wm. R.	"	17	M				Ark
Joseph	"	16	M				Mo
Malindy	"	14	F				Mo
William	"	10	M				Mo
Frank A.	"	5	M				Mo
Adelia	"	2	F				Mo

Microcopy 653, Roll
Benton Township, Post Office Mule Creek
7 Sep 1860, Page 108, Line 1, Household 757, Family 757

John A. R. Brim	40	M	Farmer	Tenn
Elizabeth	39	F		Ky
Wm	19	M		Mo
Melissa	17	F		Mo
James	15			Mo
Margaret	13	F		Mo
Sarah	11	F		Mo
Eliza	6	F		Mo
Mary	4	F		Mo
Lima F.	2/12	F		Mo

There are seventeen families in Salt Lake County and Salt Lake City and 1st W. Salt Lake City. Two of these families are from the State of New York. This data is from **Utah 1860 Territorial Census Index**, edited by **Ronald Vern Jackson**, 1979, Accelerated Indexing Systems. The rest of these **Brims** are from other states than Tennessee.

A **Daniel Brim**, 34 and born in Tennessee, had parents of foreign birth. This **Daniel** could not read nor write, had a wife and three children, and was a laborer. This was in Washoe County in the 1870 Nevada Territorial Census (Microcopy 593, Roll 835). He was born in 1836, so could not be the same **Brim** line. His wife was **Florence** and children were **John, Julia** and **Sarah**. Before seeing the census, I researched the **Nevada 1870 Territorial Census Index** (ed. **Ronald Vern Jackson**, 1979, from Accelerated Indexing Systems, Inc., Bountiful, Utah; ref 69).

A **J. P. Brim** family was found in **Washington 1880 Census Index** (70), 1980 (same as above Nevada Index). Afterwards the 1880 Soundex Code System and the regular 1880 census were seen.

Washington 1880 Census Index

Page 19,	Brim,	Elizabeth C.	Lewis	338	No	TWP	L
"		J. P.	"	"	"	"	"
"		James C.	"	"	"	"	"
"		Louis	"	"	"	"	"
"		Minnie E.	"	"	"	"	"

These **Brim** names are listed alphabetically, but **J. P.** is the head of the family.

The family of **J. P. Brim** is next found in the 1880 Soundex
Code for the purpose of locating him in the 1880 census. The
information in the Code is as follows:

<u>**1880 Soundex Code System**</u>
Microcopy T-777, Roll 1
Codes from A-000 to G-466 (Code for **Brim** B-650)

B-650	Washington Territory
Brim, J. P.	Vol 1 Enumeration District 18
W M 37	Sheet 17 Line 14
Lewis Missouri	(Township) Not reported

Other members of the family:

Brim, Elizabeth C.	W(ife)	32		Missouri
" Louis	S	14		"
" James C.	S	11		"
" John	S	5	Washington Territory	
" **Minnie E.**	D	4	"	"

<u>**Washington Territory 1880 Census**</u>
Microcopy T-9, Roll 1397
Lewis County, Territory of Washington
15 & 16 day June 1880
E.D. 18 Sheet 17 Line 14 Household 176 Family 175

Brim, J. P.	W M	37		md.	Farmer		Mo Va Tenn
" **Elizabeth C.**	W F	32	wife	md.	Keeping house		Mo Tn Tenn
" **Louis**	W M	14	son	sg.	Attending school		Mo Mo Mo
" **James C.**	W M	11	son	sg.	"	"	Mo Mo Mo
" **John**	W M	5	son	sg.		Wash Terr Mo Mo	
" **Minnie E.**	W F	4	dau	sg.		Wash Terr Mo Mo	

This **J. P. Brim** could not be a son of **Lavina** and **Lewis**
Brim, for his father was born in Virginia while his mother was
born in Tennessee. **Elizabeth's** parents were from the state of
Tennessee. **Louis Brim** attended school during the census year.
However, even though there is only one roll of microfilm for
Washington Territory, no other county besides Lewis County was
seen for 1870. And since there is no Census Index for Missouri
in 1870, I do not know what county **J. P. Brim** was from.

The above Soundex Code listed **Brims** in Arapahoe and Gun-
nison Counties, Colorado. These **Brims** were not from the right
states to be related to **Lavina** and **Lewis Brim.**

CHAPTER XIII. ELIZABETH RICE - DAVID SMITH
Chapter summary on page viii

A. ELIZABETH RICE

Elizabeth Rice was the youngest daughter of the pioneer ancestor, Henry Rice. The poet Martin Rice wrote, "Elizabeth Rice married David Smith. They were early settlers on Lost Creek, in Campbell, now Union County. The Lost Creek post office is now on the site of their early home, and occupies the spot where Henry Rice, my great-grandfather, died. It is also the spot where my father [Enoch] and mother [Mary Young] were married in 1813, and is the home of one of my cousins, [Henry] Rice Snodderly." (Quoted in Charles Rice, etc., page 9.) (2)

Elizabeth and David were married on December 23, 1801, with just a bond, and Henry Rice as bondsman. (Grainger County Marriages, Roll 20, vol. 1, 1796-1837, page 143. See also page 17 of this book. Microfilm roll 20 is at the Tennessee State Archives.) (12)

Elizabeth is in "McWilliam's Company, 1809" with 160 acres, no "white poll" but with "3 black polls." (Grainger County Tax Lists, 1809-1812; 1810 Grainger County Census. (13) Where was David Smith in 1809?

Earlier, under Pioneer Henry, David Smith was a private in an expedition under Col. Christian with Henry Rice, William Rice and Benjamin Rice. (Cantrell-Rice-Mackie, circa 1960, page 67. See also page 17 of "Henry Rice" chapter.) (30)

B. DAVID SMITH

There were three David Smiths in the 1790 South Carolina, 96th District, census. (1790 South Carolina Census.) (20)

1790 S.C. Census, 96 Dist. Pendleton County

Page 82	David Smith	1	2	3	-	-
Page 84	David Smith	2	1	2	-	-

1790 S.C. Census, 96 Dist. Union County

Page 90	David Smith	3	2	4	-	-

The first column in the 1790 S.C. Census above represents free white males 16 and over, including heads of families. The second is free white males under 16. The third is free white females including heads of families. The fourth is all other free persons, and the fifth represents slaves.

Two of the three **David Smiths**, at least, are not **Henry Rice's** son-in-law; but since the old gristmiller did have land with his sons **James** and **Charles Rice** in Pendleton (now Pickens) County near the present town of Pickens, maybe **Elizabeth's** future husband had land there too. **David Smith** bought three plots of land and sold one. (The above records indicate that **Elizabeth** could have been **David Smith's** second wife.)

Spartanburg Court House Register of Mesne Conveyance

Grantor	Grantee	Book	Page	Year of Inst.	Year of Record	Acres	Location
Smith, David	Nehemiah Norton	C	122	1791	1793	120	No. Pacolet River

Spartanburg Court House Register of Mesne Conveyance
(Cross Index)

Grantee	Grantor						
Smith, David	Adam Potter	C	119	1785	1793	100	Pacolet R.
Smith, David	Adam Potter	C	120	1785	1793	100	Pacolet R.
Smith, David	Zachs Bullock	C	121	1790	1793	160	Pacolet R.

All of these deed instruments were recorded in the court records in the year 1793, but all the transactions were earlier. The same thing happened with **Henry Rice**; the land was bought from the state as land grants and then sold to others. The Pacolet River runs through the northeastern part of present Spartanburg County.

David Smith had a Tennessee State grant in Grainger County:

Tennessee State Grants

Number	Acres	Date	County	Location	Book	Vol	Page
3730	50	2/4/1816	Grainger	East Tenn. District	4	2	531

This son-in-law of **Henry Rice** attested to many of his father-in-law's records and also bought one deed and helped to sell another. On page 16 under Claiborne County Deeds, **James Rice** bought 400 acres from **Henry**, and **David Smith** bought the rest of the 640 acres.

Claiborne County Index to Deeds

Grantor	Grantee	Inst.	Date	Book	Page	Amount
Rice, Henry	Smith, David	D	1806	A	253½	400.00

This deed, summarized below, is the 240 acres of **Henry Rice's** Lost Creek state grant which **James Rice** did not buy.

Claiborne County Deeds

Grantor	Grantee	Summary
Rice, Henry	**David Smith**	Deed Book A-1, p. 253½-254. Copied from Book A, p. 301, 23rd day January 1806. 400 dollars - 240 acres in the big valley on lost creek in Claiborne County, (p. 254) part of a tract granted to the said **Henry Rice** north side of lost creek running thence south....

in the presents of :
James Rice : March Term 1806
Josiah Grimmel :

Claiborne County March term 1806
oath of **James Rice**
Attest **Walter Evans** Clerk.

246

Campbell County Deed Direct Index
Campbell County, Roll 27 EX17485 Register's
Deed Index, vol. 1, Direct and Reverse
1804-1890

Grantor	Grantee	Book	Page	Instrument	Date
Smith, David	George Snodderly*	C	154	Warranty	May 29, 1819
Smith, David	Isaac Wilson*	C	157	W	June 1, 1819
Smith, Robert	Elijah Longmire*	C	161	W	May 26, 1819
Smith, Robert	William McNew	C	176	W	May 27, 1819
Smith, David	Thos. Barnes	C	41	W	Oct.17, 1814

Campbell County Deed Reverse Index
(Cited above)

Grantee	Grantor	Book	Page	Instrument	Date, Place
Smith, David	E. C. Harden	D	56	W	June 4, 1819
Smith, David	Mary Hancock	D	218	W	Jan. 30, 1823 Loss Creek
Smith, David	Levinah Hancock	D	219	W	May 30, 1823
Smith, David	George Rice*	D	337	W	JanY 23, 1824 Loss Creek
Smith, David	Nicholas Long				
Smith, David	George Snodderly*	E	161	W	Sept.26, 1828 Loss Creek

* = **Rice** lines down to today.

David Smith was with **Levi Rice** in a Grainger County list of taxable inhabitants for 1805, and also for the year 1826.

(13) 1810 Grainger County Tennessee Census

Page 11. **David Smith**, 1 male 10-16; 1 male 45 and over;
1 female 45 and over.
Page 11, **Evan Smith** 1 male 10-16; 1 male 16-26;
1 female under 10; 2 females 26-45.

David Smith was with **Evan Smith** and his father-in-law **Henry Rice** in the 1810 Grainger County, Tennessee, census. His name was between **Levi Rice** and **Henry Rice**. In the same census there were also other **Smiths**, included here by first names: **Mary, John, Thomas, Elijah, and Edward.**

David Smith did not leave a will, but he witnessed the will of another ancestor of your compiler, Conrad "Coonrod" Sharp. Also, he was one of three commissioners who appraised the estate of David Wilson, as mentioned in the Wilson chapter.

The last part of the Conrad Sharp will is cited now:

"In witness whereunto I have hereunto set my hand and affixed my seal this 20 day of October 1826.

signed sealed and acknowledged in presence of us	:	
	:	
Jo Hart	:	his
his	:	/s/ Conrad X Sharp
Daniel X Heath	:	mark
mark	:	
David Smith		

(Quoted from Know Your Relatives, page 25.) (27)

Lastly, David Smith must have died after September 26, 1828, when he sold the Henry Rice estate to George Snodderly, which later came under the ownership of George Snodderly's son Henry Rice Snodderly. The year of Elizabeth Rice Smith's death is not known. They did not receive any part of the estate of Elizabeth's brother James Rice in 1830.

C. OTHER SMITH RECORDS

There is a David H. Smith in the 1836 and 1837 Hawkins County tax lists, with the same total tax for both years.

1836 Hawkins County Tax List, District #7

"Smith, David H. 160 A old granted land, 1 white poll, tax 56-1/4, state tax .12-1/2, total tax .56-1/4."

There is also a Jane Smith in the 1837 Hawkins County tax list.

"Smith, Jane. 14 acres 500, tax .25, state tax .25, total $1.25."

A Betsy Smith was the bride of John Simmons on June 2, 1832, with bond by David Crain. Then the marriage was solemnized on June 3, 1832, by Justice of the Peace Robert Gaines. (Grainger County Marriages, Roll. No. 20, vol. 1, 1796-1837 EX20081.)

A **David Smith** from North Carolina served in the American Revolution, according to "New Ancestor Records," Daughters of the American Revolution Magazine vol. 116, page 371, May 1982. The citation is as follows: "**Smith, David**: b c 1760 d a 5-17-1784 m **Ann Coker** Pvt NC." Whether or not there is a connection between this **David Smith** and the **Smiths** of South Carolina has not been determined.

D. RACHEL SMITH, DAUGHTER OF ELIZABETH AND DAVID

Mrs. Lucylle Rice Davis, in her book <u>Cantrell-Rice-Mackie</u> (30) has written about a link between descendants of **Levi Rice** and those of his sister **Elizabeth**. **Mrs. Davis** and her husband are both descended from **Levi Rice**.

Pages 66-67:

"35-1. (Henry) **ELIZABETH** married **David Smith**....
36-1. (Elizabeth) **RACHEL** married **Edmund Chissler**, after his first wife's death, **Mary Rice**, a cousin of **Rachel**."

Page 76:

"35-11 (Henry) **LEVI**, youngest son of the pioneer **Henry**, married **Mary C. Mitchell**....
36-2. (Levi) **MARY** married **Edmond Chisslers**. She died at the birth of her daughter, **Polly Ann**. He married **Rachel Smith**, daughter of **David Smith**, **Mary's** first cousin. **Rachel** believed to have removed to Cedar County, Missouri."

Pages 79-80:

"**Harper** my sister **Mary** that married **Edmond Chisslers** .... His second wife **Rachel Smith** was my cousin and was of Granger County, Tenn. **Harper** if you can learn anything of that family I would like to hear, Sister **Mary's** two sons **John Baptist** and **James Pryor Chissler**. **Harper**, **Polly Ann's** stepmother if she's living is of Cedar County, Missouri. **Edmond Chissler's** widow, his last wife, **David Smith's** daughter, his first wife was **Mary**...."

The family of **Edmond** and **Rachel Chisslers** was sought in the census schedules for Cedar County, Missouri, with no success. This was for the years through 1850. The writer of the letter quoted above was **James Samuel Rice**, who could not find out about the **Chisslers** either.

See pages 65-70 in this book, CHAPTER VII. LEVI RICE.

Lastly there are **Smith** wills in Hawkins and Grainger Counties. In Hawkins County **Samuel Smith** left a will dated September 6, 1798, that mentions wife **Ann** and son of the same name, **Samuel**. **Peter Smith** left a will on October 8, 1808, with son **Able**, and mentioning **Joshua** and **Samuel Smith**. (<u>Hawkins County Wills</u> Roll 31 EX13758, vol. 1, Nov. 1797-Aug. 1826, pp. 432, 433-34.)

There might even be records to try to learn the parentage of **David Smith**, although your compiler has not sought to do so.

SOURCES AND BIBLIOGRAPHY

The following references are listed in the order of their first mention in the book. There were many other sources such as county court records, National Archives records, State Archives and Libraries, that are not listed here, but which are cited at appropriate places throughout the book.

1. Rice Trails 1717-1977, by Mrs. Nan (Frances) Rice Shute, Bethesda, MD. Mimeo, 1977.

2. Charles Rice, His Ancestors and Descendants, by Alva Silas Turnbow and Maude Ina Turnbow, Eugene, OR. Privately printed, 1957.

3. Nicholas Gibbs and His Descendants, 1733-1977, by the Nicholas Gibbs Historical Society, Knoxville, TN. Southeastern Composition Service, Knoxville, and Davis Printing Co., Maryville. 1977.

4. An Outline of the History of the Church in the State of Kentucky, Reverend David Rice's Memories during a period of forty years, containing the memoirs of Rev. David Rice, by Robert Hamilton, Bishop. Lexington, T. T. Skillman, 1824.

5. South Carolina: A Bicentennial History, by Louis B. Wright. American Association for State and Local History, Nashville. New York, W. W. Norton & Co., 1976.

6. Annals of Southwest Virginia 1769-1800, by Lewis Preston Summers. Abingdon, VA, 1929.

7. History of Southwest Virginia 1746-1786, Washington County 1777-1870, by Lewis Preston Summers, 1903. Richmond, VA, J.L. Hill Printing Company.

8. History of Corn Milling, Vol. II, Watermills and Windmills, by Richard Bennett and John Elton, 1899. London (Simpkyn, Marshall & Co.), New York (B. Franklin), 1964.

9. South Carolina Department of Archives and History, Columbia.

10. North Carolina Land Grants in Tennessee 1778-1791, by Betty Goff Cook Cartwright and Lillian Johnson Gardiner. Memphis, 1958.

11. North Carolina State Archives, Raleigh, NC. (Department of Cultural Resources, Division of Archives and History, Archives and Records Section.)

12. Tennessee State Archives and Library, Nashville, TN.

13. <u>1810 Grainger County Census</u>, by Pollyanna Creekmore, 1956. (Grainger County, Tennessee, Federal Census of 1810.... County Tax Lists for 1810, edited by Pollyanna Creekmore) McClung Historical Collection, Lawson McGee Library, Knoxville, TN.

14. <u>Notes</u> by John Rice Irwin. Unpublished.

15. <u>Early Travels in Tennessee 1540-1800</u>, "Account of the Journey...." by John Lipscomb. McClung Historical Collection, Lawson McGee Library, Knoxville, TN.

16. <u>Tennessee 1820 Census Index</u>, Accelerated Indexing Systems, (Computer Index to Tennessee 1820 Census, edited by Ronald Vern Jackson and Gary Ronald Teeples 2nd ed. 1974.) Dana Press, 3346 South Orchard Dr., Provo, UT, 84010.

17. <u>1830 Census Middle Tennessee</u>, transcribed and indexed by Byron Sistler, 1971, Evanston, IL.

18. <u>Tennessee 1840 Census Index</u>, Accelerated Indexing Systems, Inc. edited by Ronald Vern Jackson and Gary Ronald Teeples 1976. Dana Press, Provo, UT, 84010.

19. <u>1800 Census of Pendleton District South Carolina</u>, by William C. Stewart, Washington National Genealogical Society No. 26, 1963.

20. <u>Heads of Families at the First Census of the United States Taken in the Year 1790, South Carolina, 96 District</u>. Genealogical Publishing Co., Baltimore, Md., 1966. (Originally published by the Government Printing Office, Washington, DC, 1908.)

21. <u>South Carolina 1800 Census</u>, Acceleraged Indexing Systems, Inc. Edited by Ronald Vern Jackson and Gary Ronald Teeples, 1973 (2nd ed. 1975). Provo, UT.

22. <u>Index to the 1800 Census of South Carolina</u>, by Brent Holcomb. Genealogical Publishing Co., Baltimore, MD. 1980.

23. The Story of Marcellus Moss Rice and His Big Valley Kinsmen, by John Rice Irwin. Times Printing Co., Montevallo, AL, 1963.

24. Land of the Lake, a History of Campbell County, Tennessee, by George L. Ridenour. LaFollette Publishing Co., Inc., LaFollette, TN, 1941.

25. 18th Century Gristmill, by John Rice Irwin, 1949, 1958, 1963, 1975.

26. "Rice's Mill--A Symbol of Cooperation," Cooperative Farmer, 1952, pp. 46-47.

27. Know Your Relatives, the Sharps, Gibbs, Graves, Eflands, Albrights, Loys, Millers, Snoderlys, Tillmans and Other Related Families, by Mrs. Genevieve E. Peters (Elizabeth Cummings), Arlington, VA. 1953, 1957 and 1972.

28. Civil and Political History of Tennessee from its earliest settlement up to the year 1796, including the boundaries of the State, by W. H. Haywood. Publishing House of the Methodist Episcopal Church, South, 1823 and 1971.

29. Big Valley, Tennessee, and Lost Creek Memories, by Professor William Henderson Thomas, 1968. Unpublished Ms.

30. Cantrell-Rice-Mackie, by Lucylle Rice Davis, ca. 1960.

31. Roster of Soldiers and Patriots of the American Revolution Buried in Tennessee, compiled by Lucy Womack Bates, 1974; revised by Helen Crawford Marsh, 1979. Published by the Tennessee Society, NSDAR. Brentwood, TN 37027.

32. Tennessee Records, vol. 2., by Mrs. Jeannette Tillotson Acklen. Cullom & Ghertner, Nashville, TN. 1933.

33. The Outlaw Years, History of the Land Pirates of the Natchez Trace, by Robert Myron Coates, 1930 and 1974. Detroit, Gale Research Co., 1974. New York, The Macaulay Co., 1930.

34. The Outlaws of Cave-In-Rock, by Otto Arthur Rothert, 1924 and 1970. Cleveland, The Arthur H. Clark Company. Reprinted 1970, Freeport, NY, Books for Libraries Press.

35. 1830 Census East Tennessee, transcribed and indexed by Byron and Barbara Sistler, 1969. Evanston, IL.

36. <u>1850 Tennessee Census Index</u>, Vol. VI, transcribed and indexed by Byron and Barbara Sistler. (RUDDEL through WALLACE.) Evanston, IL., 1974 and 1976.

37. <u>The Epistle</u>, a Bi-Monthly Magazine for the Bachellor, Carpenter and Rice Families, by Rosemary A. Bachelder, Machias, Me. Vol. IV No. 2, Aug. 1977 (page 45); Vol. III, No. 3, Sept. 1976 (page 49, #616).

38. <u>Tennessee 1850 Census Index</u>, Accelerated Indexing Systems, Inc., Bountiful, UT, 1977. Editors Ronald Vern Jackson and Gary Ronald Teeples. Ambassador Press, Salt Lake City.

39. <u>1850 Tennessee Census Index</u>, Vol. I (AARON through CHILD-RESS), transcribed and indexed by Byron and Barbara Sistler, Evanston, IL. 1974.

40. <u>Missouri 1850 Census Index</u>, Accelerated Indexing Systems, Inc., editors Ronald Vern Jackson and Gary Ronald Teeples. Ambassador Press, Salt Lake City, UT. 1976.

41. <u>The History of Cass and Bates Counties, Missouri</u>, by the National Historical Company, St. Joseph, MO, 1883.

42. <u>Vital Historical Records of Jackson County, Missouri, 1826-1876</u>. Collected, compiled, and published by Daughters of the American Revolution, Missouri, Kansas City Chapter, 1933-34.

43. <u>Index to Early Tennessee Tax Lists</u>, transcribed and indexed by Byron and Barbara Sistler, Evanston, IL, 1977.

44. <u>The Original Lists of Persons of Quality</u>, ed. by John Camden Hotten. Originally published London, 1874, with the title: <u>The Original Lists of Persons of Quality</u>; Emigrants; Religious Exiles; Political Rebels; Serving Men Sold for a Term of Years; Apprentices; Children Stolen; Maidens Pressed; and Others Who Went From Great Britain to the American Plantations 1600-1700. Reprinted Baltimore, Genealogical Publishing Co., Inc., 1974, 1976, 1978.

45. <u>1623-1666 Early Virginia Immigrants</u>, by George Cabell Greer, Clerk, Virginia State Land Office. Genealogical Publishing Co., Baltimore, MD., 1960.

46. <u>Rice Trails, 1717-1975</u>, by Nan (Frances) Rice Shute, Bethesda, MD, 1975. Mimeo.

47. *1850 Tennessee Census Index*, Vol. VII, WALLAND through ZUMBRO and "A-E" of the Cross Index, transcribed and indexed by Byron and Barbara Sistler. Evanston, IL, 1976.

48. *The Wilson Generation*, by D. Maynard Wilson. Unpublished manuscript.

49. *Goodspeed's History of Tennessee*, by Goodspeed Brothers, Nashville, 1887. Reprinted 1980.

50. *The Descendants of Henry Rice Pioneer to Tennessee*, compiled by Martin Rice, added to by (Professor) Willie H. Thomas. Unpublished ms.

51. *The State Records of North Carolina*, Vol. XVII, 1781-'85, collected and edited by Walter Clark, one of the Justices of the Supreme Court of N.C., 1899. Nash Brothers, Book and Job Printers, Goldsboro, NC.

52. *The State Records of North Carolina*, Vol. XVI, 1782-'73, by Walter Clark, ed. Nash Brothers, Book and Job Printers, Goldsboro, NC, 1899.

53. *The State Records of North Carolina*, Vol. XVIII, 1779, with Supplement, by Walter Clark, ed., Nash Brothers, Book and Job Printers, Goldsboro, NC, 1900.

54. *The State Records of North Carolina*, Vol. XXII, Miscellaneous, by Walter Clark, ed. Nash Brothers, Book and Job Printers, Goldsboro, NC. 1907.

55. *The Colonial Records of North Carolina*, Vol. I, 1662 to 1712, collected and edited by William L. Saunders, Secretary of State. P.M. Hale, Printer to the State 1886, AMS Press, Inc., New York, 1968.

56. *Colonial Records of North Carolina*, Vol. II, 1713 to 1728, collected and edited by William L. Saunders, Secretary of State. P.M. Hale, Printer to the State, Raleigh, NC, 1886. AMS Press, Inc., New York.

57. *The State Records of North Carolina*, Vol. XXV, Laws 1789-1790 and Supplement Omitted Laws 1699-1783, with index to Vols. XXIII, XXIV, XXV, by Walter Clark, Chief Justice of the Supreme Court of North Carolina. Nash Brothers, Book and Job Printers, Goldsboro, NC, 1906.

58. The State Records of North Carolina, Vol. XXIII, Laws 1715-1776, collected and edited by Walter Clark, Chief Justice of the Supreme Court of North Carolina, Nash Brothers, Book and Job Printers, Goldsboro, NC, 1904.

59. The State Records of North Carolina, Vol. XXII, Miscellaneous, collected and edited by Iter Clark, Chief Justice of the Supreme Court of North Carolina, Nash Brothers, Book and Job Printers, Goldsboro, NC, 1907.

60. 1850 Tennessee Census, Vol. 8, "H-Z" of the Cross Index, transcribed and indexed by Byron and Barbara Sistler, Evanston, IL, 1976.

61. Tennessee Cousins, A History of Tennessee People, by Worth Stickley Ray, Austin, TX, 1950. Baltimore, Genealogical Publishing Co., 1966.

62. 1850 Tennessee Census Index, Vol. IV, JONES through MURLEY, transcribed and indexed by Byron and Barbara Sistler, Evanston, IL. 1975.

63. Maury County Cousins; Bible and Family Records. Maury County, Tennessee, Historical Society, Columbia, TN., 1967.

64. They Passed This Way, by Marise P. Lightfoot and Evlyn B. Shackelford, 1964.

65. Tennessee 1830 Census Index, Accelerated Indexing Systems, Inc., editors Ronald Vern Jackson and Gary Ronald Teeples, Bountiful, UT, 1976.

66. Heads of Families at the First Census of the United States taken in the Year 1790 (Records of the State Enumerations: 1782 to 1785) Virginia, U.S. Gov't Printing Office, Washington, DC, 1908.

67. Cavaliers and Pioneers Abstracts of Virginia Land Patents and Grants, abstracted by Nell Marion Nugent, Vol. III: 1695-1732; Vol. I, 1623-1666; Vol. II, 1666-1695. 1979, 1974, and 1977 resp. Richmond, VA, and Baltimore, MD.

68. The Parish Register of Christ Church, Middlesex County, Va., from 1653 to 1812, published by the National Society of the Colonial Dames of America in the State of Virginia. Genealogical Publishing Company, Baltimore, Md., 1964. "Originally published Richmond, 1897."

69. Nevada 1870 Territorial Census Index, Accelerated Indexing
     Systems, Inc., edited by Ronald Vern Jackson, Dana Press,
     Provo, Utah. 1979.

70. Washington 1880 Census Index, ed. by Dr. Ronald Vern
     Jackson, Senior Archivist, Bountiful, UT. Ambassador
     Press, Salt Lake City, UT. 1980.

71. Mortality Schedule Tennessee 1850, Dr. Ronald Vern Jackson,
     Editor, and Publisher, Accelerated Indexing Systems, Inc.,
     3346 South Orchard Drive, Bountiful, Utah, 84010, Copyright
     and First Printing, 1979.

LIST OF ITEMS IN THE APPENDIX

I.   State of South Carolina Grant to Henry Rice, 1787.

II.   State of South Carolina Grant to Charles Rice, 1787.

III.   State of South Carolina Grant to Charles Rice, 1787.

IV.   State of South Carolina Plats to Charles Rice: (a)
        Mill Creek, 1785, and (b) Goolding's Creek of Twelve
        Mile River (no date).

V.   South Carolina State Plats, Descriptions, two for
        Charles Rice and one for Ferdinand Hopkins et al,
        for land adjoining Charles Rice's land.

VI.   U.S. Geological Survey Topographical Map 1957, showing
        Rice's Creek and other waterways mentioned in Grants
        to Henry, Charles, and James Rice.

VII.   U.S. Geological Survey Topographical Map of the TVA
        area, 1959, showing Henry Rice's Mill, Patterson's
        Mill, and Hord Cemetery, in the Church Hill, Tennessee,
        Area.

VIII.   Map of Tennessee, 1795-1796, showing the Kingsport-
        Rogersville area, also Knoxville.

IX.   Map of the Holston River Headwaters Area, showing
        location of Kingsport and the approximate location
        of Henry Rice's Mill. (This map shows some railroads,
        so would have been drawn in the post-Civil War era.)

X.   Map of Tennessee, 1832. Shows Rice Creek, Kingsport,
        and other landmarks.

XI.   Map of Tennessee 1839-1841. Present-day Church Hill
        was known at that time as New Canton. Lost Creek
        was in Anderson County. Note the existence of Powell
        County.

XII.   Map of East Tennessee, showing New Canton, Rogers-
        ville, Knoxville, Clinton.

XIII.   1914 Postoffice Department map of Rural Delivery
        Routes, showing a portion of Hawkins County. Rice's
        Mill is indicated by an arrow.

258

LIST OF ITEMS IN THE APPENDIX (Continued)

XIV.   A Topographic Map of 1900, from the U. S. Geological Survey. Fountain City, a suburb just north of Knoxville, is at the lower edge, and Lost Creek at the upper edge of this map.

XV.   1812 Military Service Record of George Rice.

XVI.   Pages from Henry Rice's Bible (maternal great-grandfather--<u>not</u> pioneer Henry Rice). The publication date of the Bible was probably in the mid-1850's. In addition to births, deaths and marriages, other memorable events were scribbled on these pages. Present owner of the Bible is Mrs. Stella Clapp of Corryton, Tenn.

XVII.   The House that James Rice Built

I. State of South Carolina Grant to Henry Rice, 1787

Description

Henry Rice
Mar. 23, 1787

(*186*)

Reference - S. C. Archives
State Grants
Vol. 22, p. 186

STATE of SOUTH-CAROLINA.

To all to whom these Presents shall come, GREETING:

KNOW YE, That for and in consideration of *Ten pounds 18/4ᵈ* Sterling Money, paid by *Henry Rice* into the Treasury for the use of this State, we have granted, and by these Presents do grant unto the said *Henry Rice his* Heirs and Assigns, a Plantation or Tract of Land containing *four hundred and sixty eight* ----- Acres *Situate in the District of Ninety Six, on the branches of Wbolf and Rices Creeks of Twelve Mile River bounding all sides on Vacant Land*

Having such Shape, Form and Marks as are represented by a Plat hereunto annexed; together with all Woods, Trees, Waters, Water-Courses, Profits, Commodities, Appurtenances and Hereditaments whatsoever thereunto belonging, TO HAVE AND TO HOLD, the said Tract of *Four hundred and Sixty Eight* Acres of Land, and all and singular other the Premises hereby granted unto the said *Henry Rice his* Heirs and Assigns, for ever, in free and common soccage.

GIVEN UNDER THE GREAT SEAL OF THE STATE. WITNESS, his Excellency *Thomas Pinckney,* Esquire, Governor and Commander in Chief in and over the said State, at Charleston, this *Fifth* Day of *November* ---- Anno Domini, One Thousand Seven Hundred and *Eighty Seven* and in the *Twelfth* Year of the Independence of the United States of America.

Thomas L. M. S. *Pinckney,*

And hath thereunto a Plat thereof annexed, representing the same, certified by

F Bremar for SURVEYOR-GENERAL.

23ᵈ March 178

II.   State of South Carolina Grant to Charles Rice, 1787

Reference – S. C. Archives State Grants Vol. 16, p. 605	(605)	Description Charles Rice Jan. 1, 1787

STATE of SOUTH-CAROLINA.

To all to whom these Presents shall come, Greeting:

KNOW YE, That for and in Consideration of *four pounds 13/4* ———— Sterling Money paid by *Charles Rice* into the Treasury for the use of this State, We have granted, and by these Presents do grant unto the said *Charles Rice his* Heirs and Assigns, a Plantation or Tract of Land, containing *Two hundred* — — Acres *Situate in the district of Ninety Six West of the Ancient Boundary Line of Mile Creek of Twelve Mile River* — having such Shape, Form and Marks, as are represented by a Plat hereunto annexed, together with all Woods, Trees, Waters, Watercourses, Profits, Commodities, Appurtenances, and Heriditaments whatsoever thereunto belonging, *To have and to hold* the said Tract of *Two hundred* Acres of Land, and all and singular other the Premises hereby granted unto the said *Charles Rice his* Heirs and Assigns, for ever, in free and common Soccage.

Given under the Great Seal of the State.

WITNESS, *his Excellency William Moultrie Esquire, Governer and Commander in Chief in and over the said State, at Charleston,* this *first* Day of *January* Anno Domini, One Thousand Seven Hundred and *eighty Seven*, and in the *Eleventh* Year of the Independence of the United States of America.

W^m. M. S. *Moultrie*

And hath thereunto a Plat thereof annexed, representing the same, certified by *Bremar D^o. Surveyor-General.*

6th April 1785

III. State of South Carolina Grant to Charles Rice, 1787

Description		Reference - S. C. Archives
Charles Rice Apr. 7, 1785	(*548*)	State Grants Vol. 16, p. 548

STATE OF SOUTH-CAROLINA.

To all to whom these Presents shall come, Greeting:

KNOW YE, That for and in Confideration of *four pounds 13/4¼* Sterling Money paid by *Charles Rice* into the Treafury for the ufe of this State, We have granted, and by thefe Prefents do grant unto the faid *Charles Rice his* Heirs and Affigns, a Plantation or Tract of Land, containing *Two hundred* Acres, *Situate in the district of Ninety Six West of the Ancient Boundary on the Branches of Goldings Creek of twelve Mile River* having fuch Shape, Form and Marks as are reprefented by a Plat hereunto annexed, together with all Woods, Trees, Waters, Water-Courfes, Profits, Commodities, Appurtenances and Hereditaments whatfoever thereunto belonging, *To Have and to Hold* the faid Tract of *Two hundred* Acres of Land, and all and fingular other the Premifes hereby granted unto the faid *Charles Rice his* Heirs and Affigns, for ever, in free and common foccage.

Given under the Great Seal of the State. WITNESS his Excellency *William Moultrie* Efquire, Governor and Commander in Chief in and over the faid State, at Charlefton, this *first* Day of *January* Anno Domini, One Thoufand Seven Hundred and *eighty Seven* and in the *Eleventh* Year of the Independence of the United States of America.

L. M. S. *Moultrie*

And hath thereunto a Plat thereof annexed, reprefenting the fame, certified by *Bremar* *Surveyor-General.*

(7 April 1785)

APPENDIX

IV. State of South Carolina Plats to Charles Rice
(a) Mill Creek, 1785
(b) Goolding's Creek of Twelve Mile River (no date)

APPENDIX

V. South Carolina State Plats, Descriptions
Two for Charles Rice, and
One for Ferdinand Hopkins et al, for land adjoining Charles Rice

S. C. State Plats

Vol. 15 q - 106. To Charles Rice for 200 acres in 96 District
and is West of the Ancient Boundary line and on branches of
Golding Creek of 12 Mile River and is adjacent to vacant land.
No Date. William Benson, D.S.

Vol. 15 q - 106. To Charles Rice for 200 acres in 96 District
and is West of the Ancient Boundary line and is on Mill Creek
of 12 Mile River and is adjacent to vacant land. Cert. 6 April·
1785. William Benson D. S.

Volume AA - 73. Cert. for Ferdinand Hopkins for 2, 782 acres
surveyed for Newton Hopkins, Jeremiah Kingsley, James Glenn,
John Wallace, and Robert Glenn on the 10 March 1787 and is in
96 District on waters of 12 Mile River and is on the south side
of Wolf Creek where it joins 12 Mile River and is bounded by
land unknown, vacant land, Charles Rice and land unknown.
Sg. 19 December 1791. Dd. Hopkins D. S.

VI. U.S. Geological Survey Topographical Map, 1957
Showing Rice's Creek and other waterways mentioned in grants to Henry, Charles and James Rice

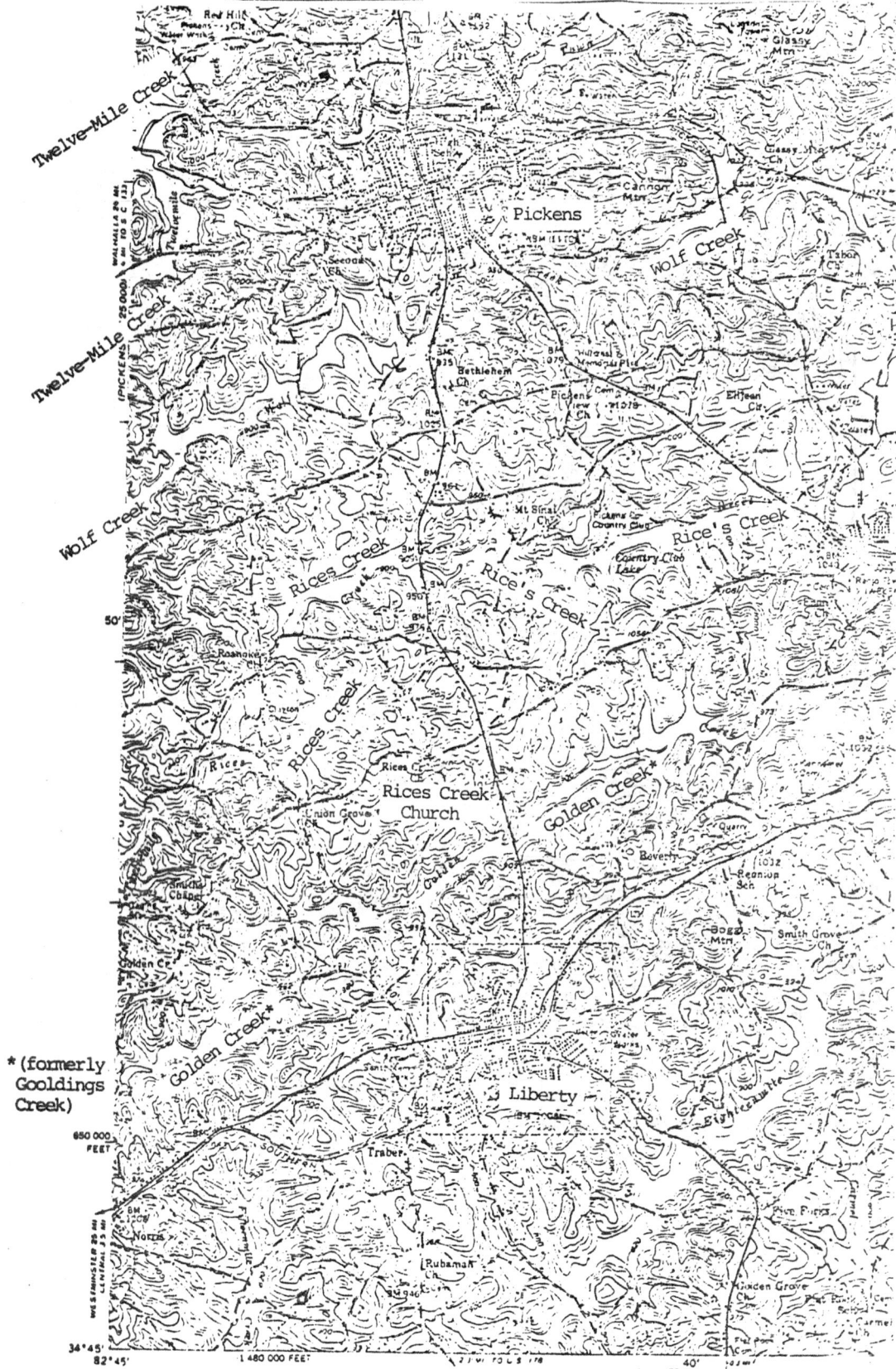

* (formerly Gooldings Creek)

Mapped, edited, and published by the Geological Survey
Control by USGS, USC&GS, and South Carolina Geodetic Survey
Topography from aerial photographs by Kelsh plotter
Aerial photographs taken 1955   Field check 1957
Polyconic projection   1927 North American datum

APPENDIX

VII. U.S. Geological Survey Topographical Map of the TVA Area, 1959
Showing Henry Rice's Mill, Patterson's Mill, and Hord Cemetery in the Church Hill, Tennessee, Area

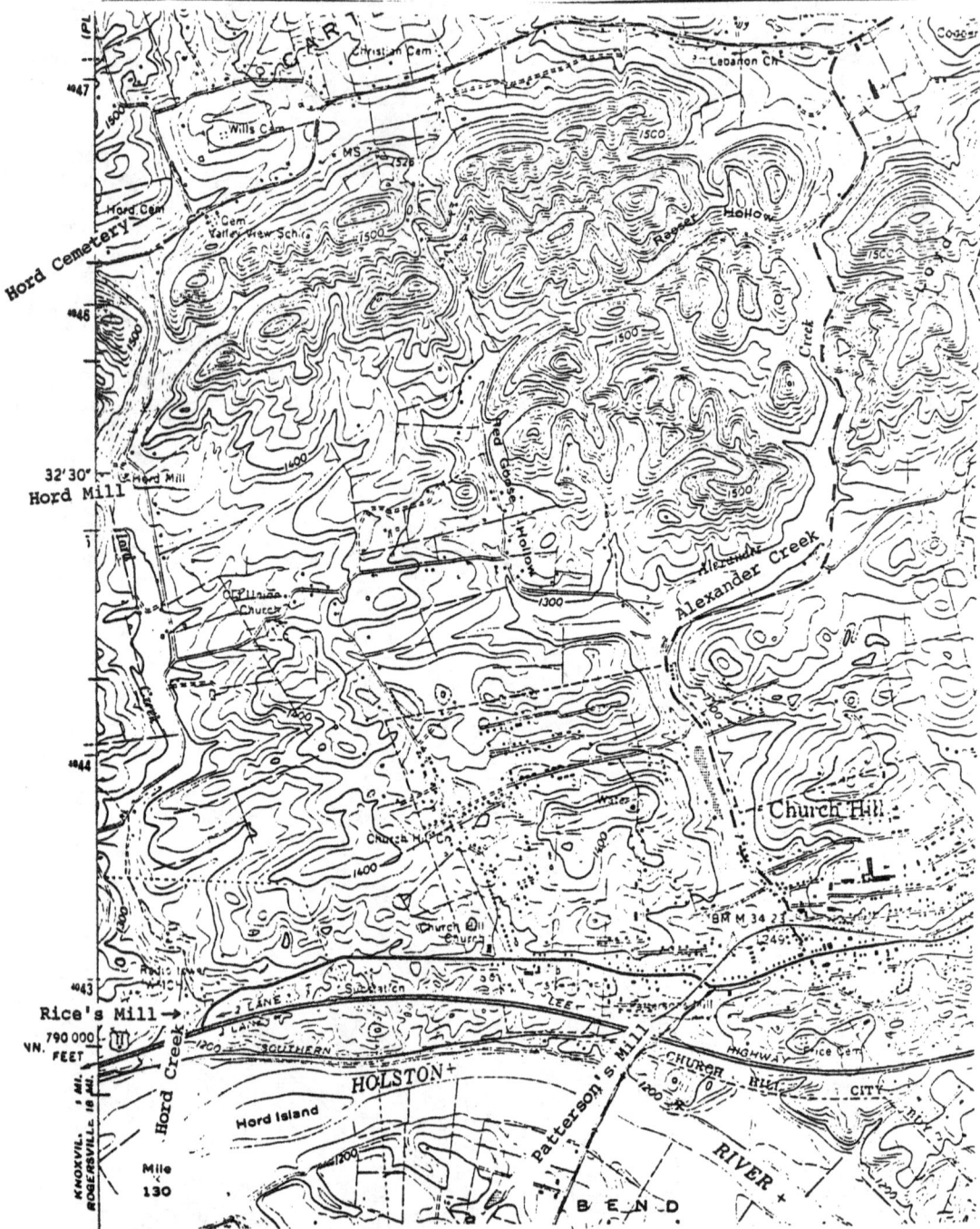

Mapped and edited by Tennessee Valley Authority
Published by the Geological Survey

Control by USC&GS, USGS, and TVA

Revised by TVA in 1959 by photogrammetric methods using
aerial photographs taken 1953 and by reference to TVA-USGS
quadrangle dated 1939. Map field checked by TVA, 1959

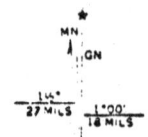

Polyconic projection, 1927 North American datum

VIII. Map of Tennessee, 1795-1796
showing the Kingsport (Rosville)-Rogersville-
Knoxville-Kingston area

Tennessee (1795-1796) 1:1,715,000, from
Carey's General Atlas, 1818.

Shows Great Island and Rossville (Rosville
(Kingsport); the Powell, Clinch, and Tennessee Rivers; Cherokee Indian Territory
(Cross-hatching added). General vicinity
of Rice's Mill is near Rossville; general
vicinity of Lost Creek is near confluence
of Powell and Clinch Rivers.

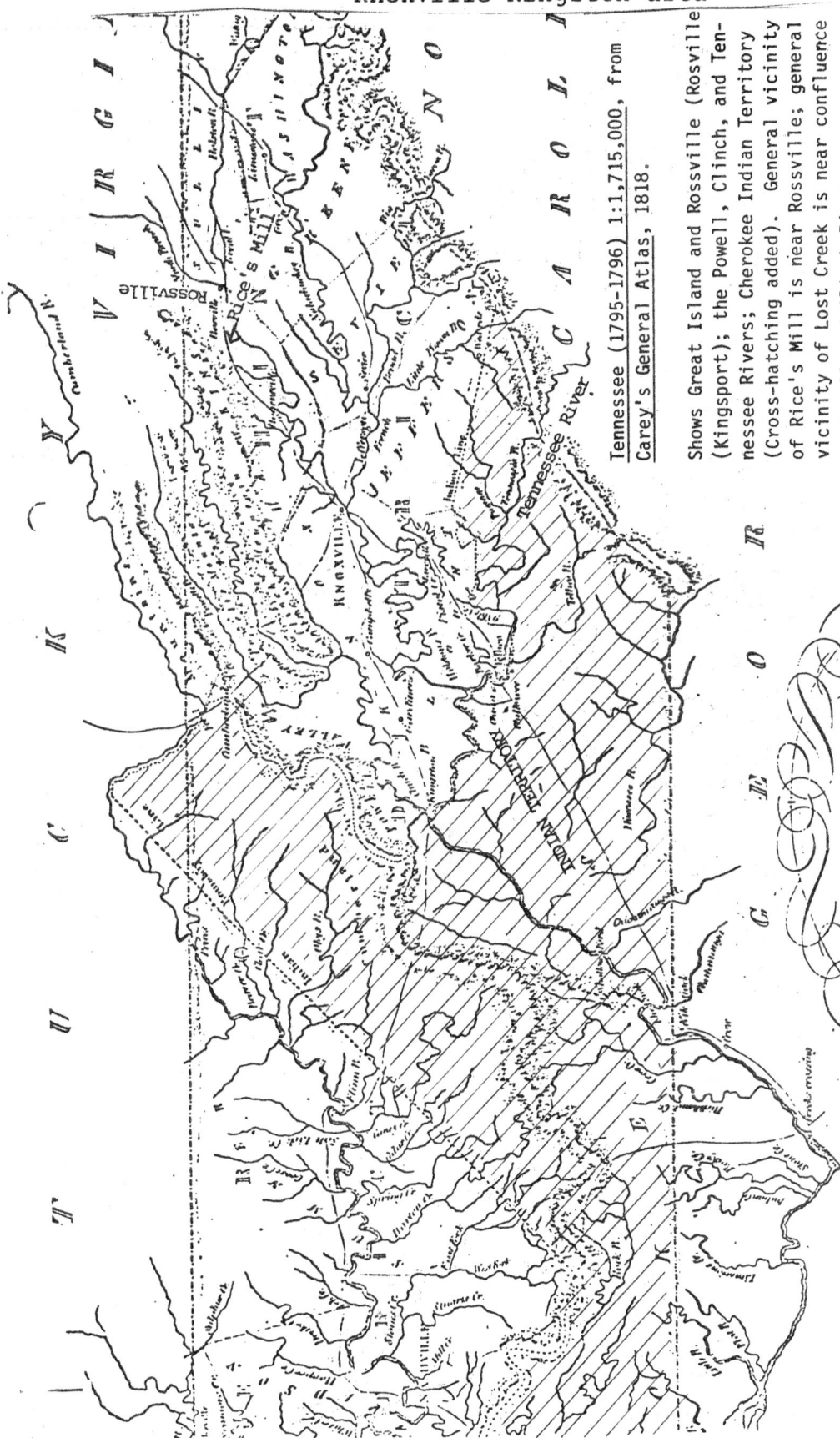

APPENDIX
IX. Map of the Holston River Headwaters Area
(Date between 1830 and 1840?)
Showing Location of Kingsport and Approximate Location of
Henry Rice's Mill

Rice's Mill around here

Tennessee (Holston River Headwaters Area 18--? Draper ms. 6C65 (Z6621.W79) (From Library of Congress collection).

268

X. Map of Tennessee, 1832
Shows Rice's Creek, Kingsport, and Other Landmarks

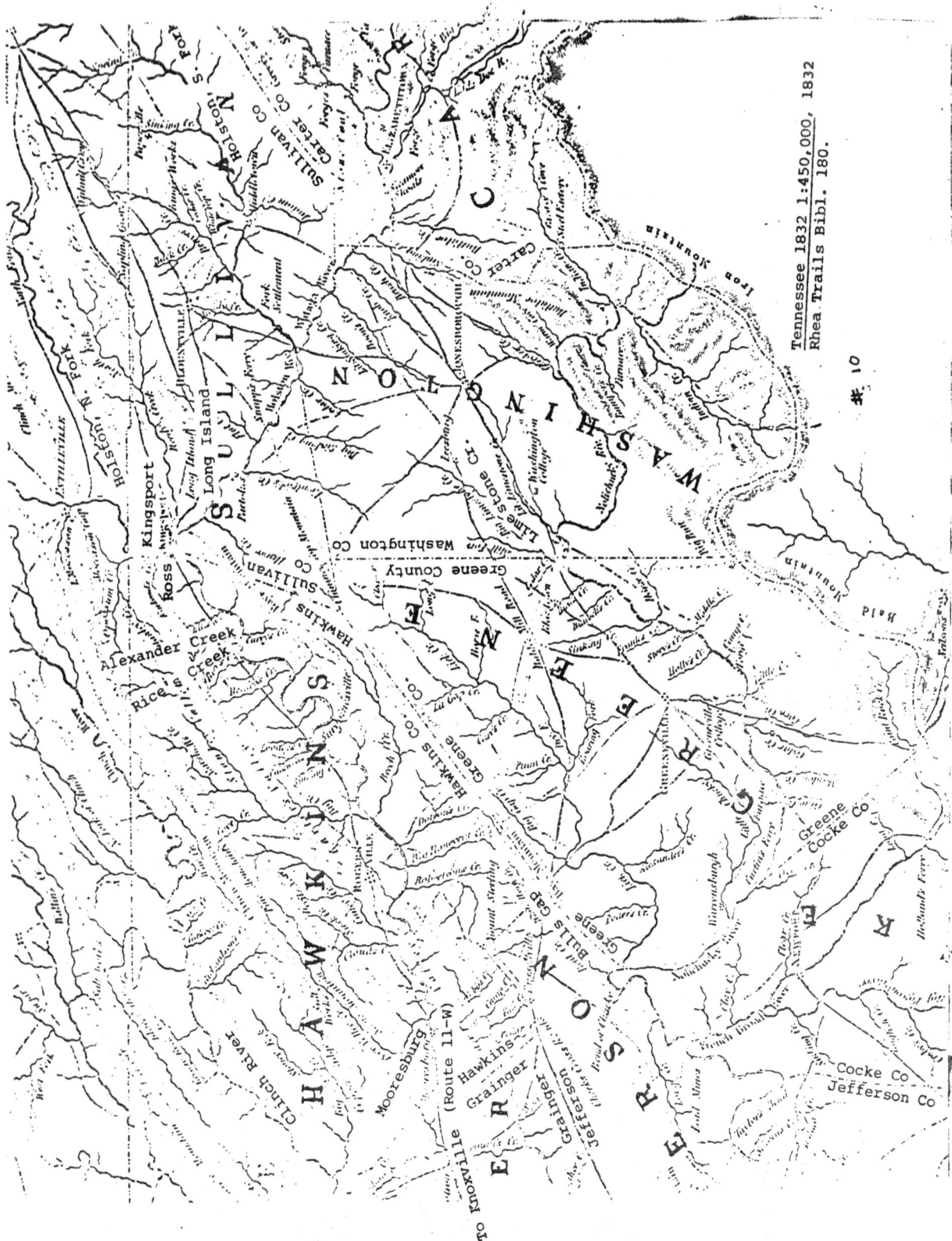

XI. Map of Tennessee 1839-1841.
Church Hill was known at that time as New Canton

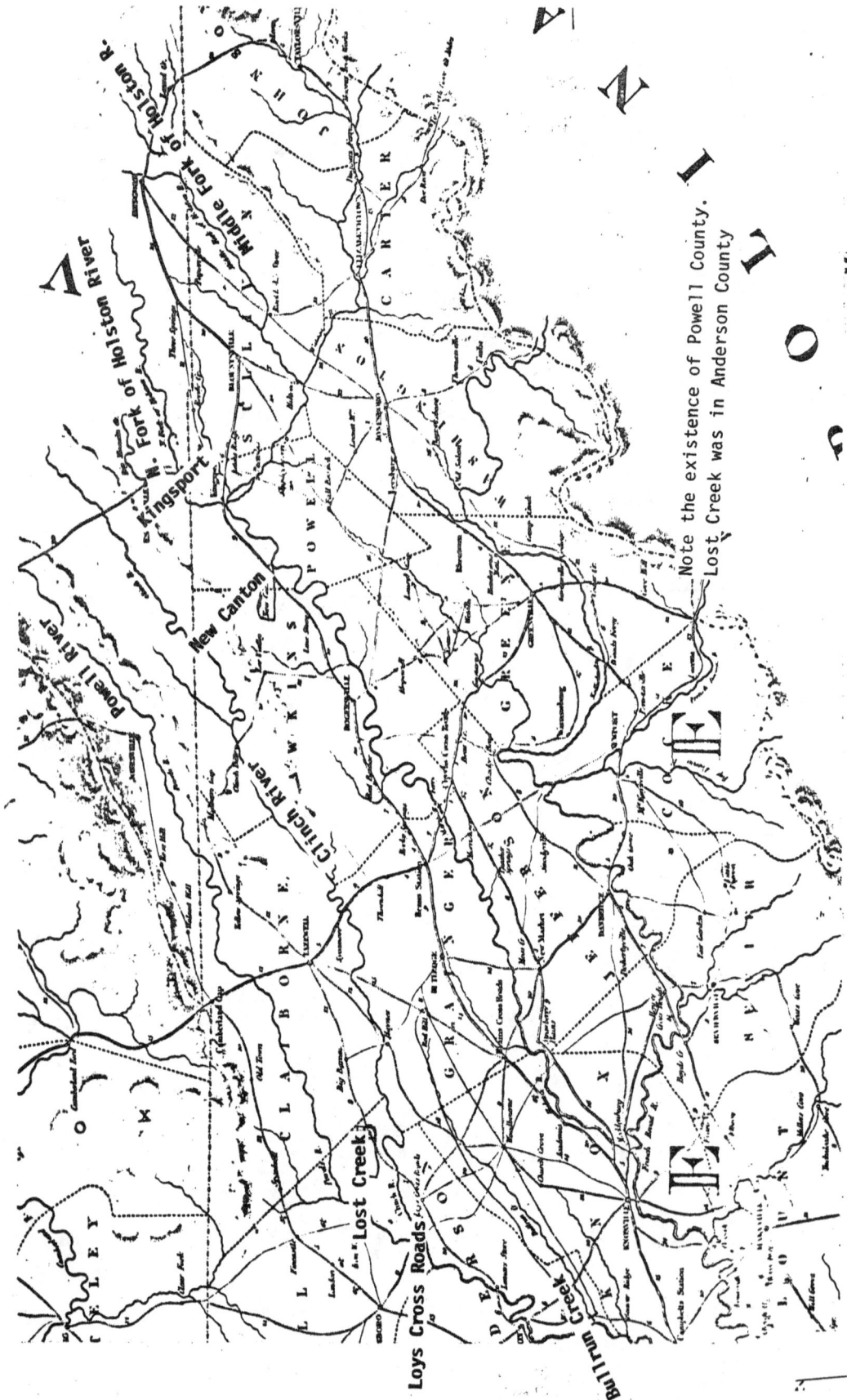

XII. Map of East Tennessee (Date unknown)
Showing New Canton, Rogersville, Knoxville, Clinton

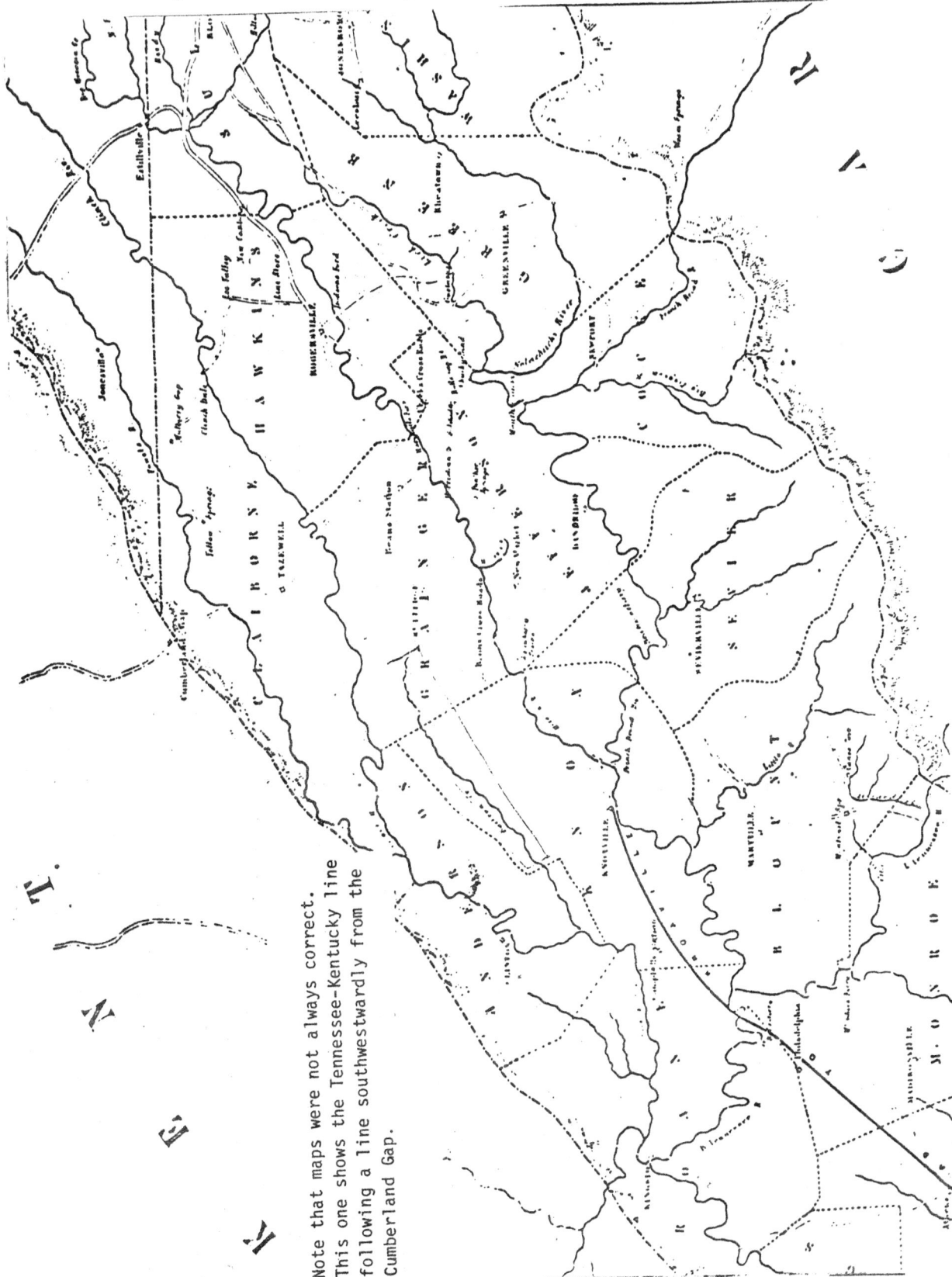

Note that maps were not always correct. This one shows the Tennessee-Kentucky line following a line southwestwardly from the Cumberland Gap.

271

XIII. Post Office Department Map of Rural Delivery Routes, 1914
Shows a Portion of Hawkins County
Rice's Mill is Indicated by an Arrow
(at "L. Hoard")

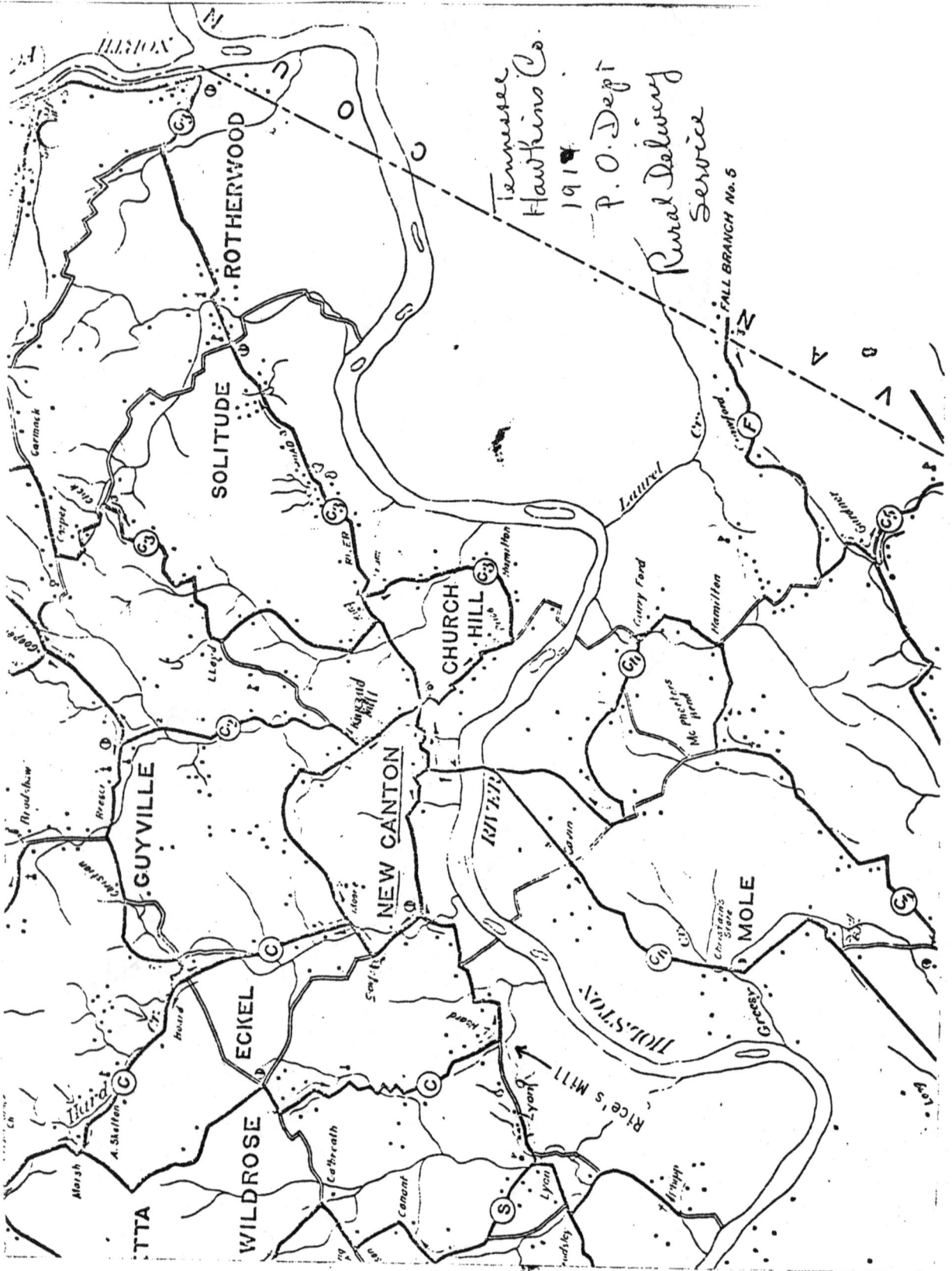

APPENDIX

XIV. U.S. Geological Survey Topographic Map, 1900
Landmarks include Fountain City (North of Knoxville), Lost Creek (upper edge of map segment), and Marcellus Moss Rice's Farm

THE

NEW TESTAMENT

OF OUR

LORD AND SAVIOUR

JESUS CHRIST,

TRANSLATED OUT OF

THE ORIGINAL GREEK;

AND WITH

THE FORMER TRANSLATIONS DILIGENTLY COMPARED AND REVISED.

STEREOTYPED BY E. WHITE, NEW-YORK.

Associations at Lost Creek

August 1880. Tenn

August 1894 Snowed one foot Deep

October 1906 May 20 # 1869

August 1918

Sick green Beans

2 mess Oct 2 1906

ACCOUNT

OF THE

DATES OR TIME OF WRITING THE BOOKS

OF THE

NEW TESTAMENT.

	Years from the death of Christ.	Years from the birth of Christ.		Years from the death of Christ.	Years from the birth of Christ
MATTHEW's Gospel,	6	39	Acts of the Apostles by Luke,	30	63
Mark's Gospel,	10	43	Paul's two Epistles to Timothy,		
First Epistle of Peter,	19	52	the one to Titus, and the 2nd		
Paul's 1st und 2d Epistles to			Epistle general of Peter,	30	63
the Thessalonians,	19	52	John in the Isle of Patmos wrote		
Luke's Gospel,	23	56	the Revelation,	81	94
Paul's Epistle to the Galatians,	23	56	—— Gospel,	63	96
—— two Epistles to the Corinthians, and that to the Romans,	24	57	—— three Epistles near the end of his life,	65	98
—— to the Philippians, to Philemon, Colossians, Ephesians, and Hebrews,	29	62	N. B. The times of writing the Epistle of James and that of Jude not so certainly known, but supposed,	33	66

FAMILY RECORD.

BIRTHS.

James Rice birth unknown

George Rice was Born in
March the 27th 1794

Sarah Rice was Born
March the 5th 1794

Luie Bell Rice Rodgers
Died DEC.
22 1949

R. Rice Born
April 1881

Bart Hill was
Died may 25
Oct 15 1951 1873

BIRTHS.

Henry Rice was Born
May the 23rd 1822

Rebekah Rice was Born
November the 2 1823

Irving Rice october
the 7th 1825

John Rice was Born
December the 5th 1826

Susanna Rice was Born
october 21st 1829

Nancy Rice was
born November the
10th 1834

Elizabeth Rice was
Born November the
10th 1836

XV. Pages from the Bible of Henry Rice (1822-1896) (Continued)

FAMILY RECORD.

Died monday
april 2 1946

BIRTHS.

BIRTHS.

James R. Rice was
Borned July the
27th day 1859

Rebecah F. Rice
Borned Jan. 12
day 1861

Matilda C Rice was
Borned Nov. the
10th day 1862

Manervy C. Rice
was Borned March
the 14th day 1865

Sarah A Rice
was Borned

Nervy J. Rice
was Borned Ja-
the 14 day 1867

Sarah A Rice
was Borned March
the 2 day 1869
Died Jan 8
8. 1954

Alvy H. Rice
was Borned June
the 29 day 1871

Wallis M. Rice was
Borned Sept the 3. 1873

Necy C Rice was
Borned Feb 1875

Martin Iday Rice was bo
September the 19th day 1878

Lissie B Rice was
born 1881

Died Tuesday
Dec. 22. 1949

FAMILY RECORD.

Union to

MARRIAGES.

Ida & Bart Hill
married Dec
15, 1898

Stella Pearl Hill
Borned Dec
22, 1899

Roy Esten Hill
Borned June
16, 1900
Died November
27, 1903

Esther Hill
Borned January
26, 1906

Mary Ellen Hill
Borned June 16
Lost Will ? 1911

MARRIAGES.

Stella P Hill married
Feb 16, 1923

Fay Hill married
July 15, 1924
Ellen Hill married
July 28, 1940

Stella Pearl Hill
was Borned
Dec 22, 1899

Tenn

FAMILY RECORD.

age unknown
Henry Rice Died 1818

DEATHS. 1829

James Rice Died 1848

Sarah Rice died
October the 21st 1855

George Rice
Died
November 30
1869

Anna Wood Died
April the 21 day 1873

Rebecah Gentry
Died August 23 1877

John Rice Died
June 4 1889

Henry Rice Died
November 8 1896
Age 74 years 1 month
& 16 days

DEATHS.

Matilda Catherine Rice
died March 3 1882

Necey Carr Rice
"   March 2 1883

Minerva Caroline Rice
"   September 12 1888

Alva Hazeltine Rice
"   October 20 1889

Mrs Curtis Hawkins
Born Oct 24 1400

Curtis Hawkins
Born Feb 24 1900

Susan Rice
Died Oct 13 1911

[handwritten Bible pages, partially legible]

was born July the 27 day in 1859

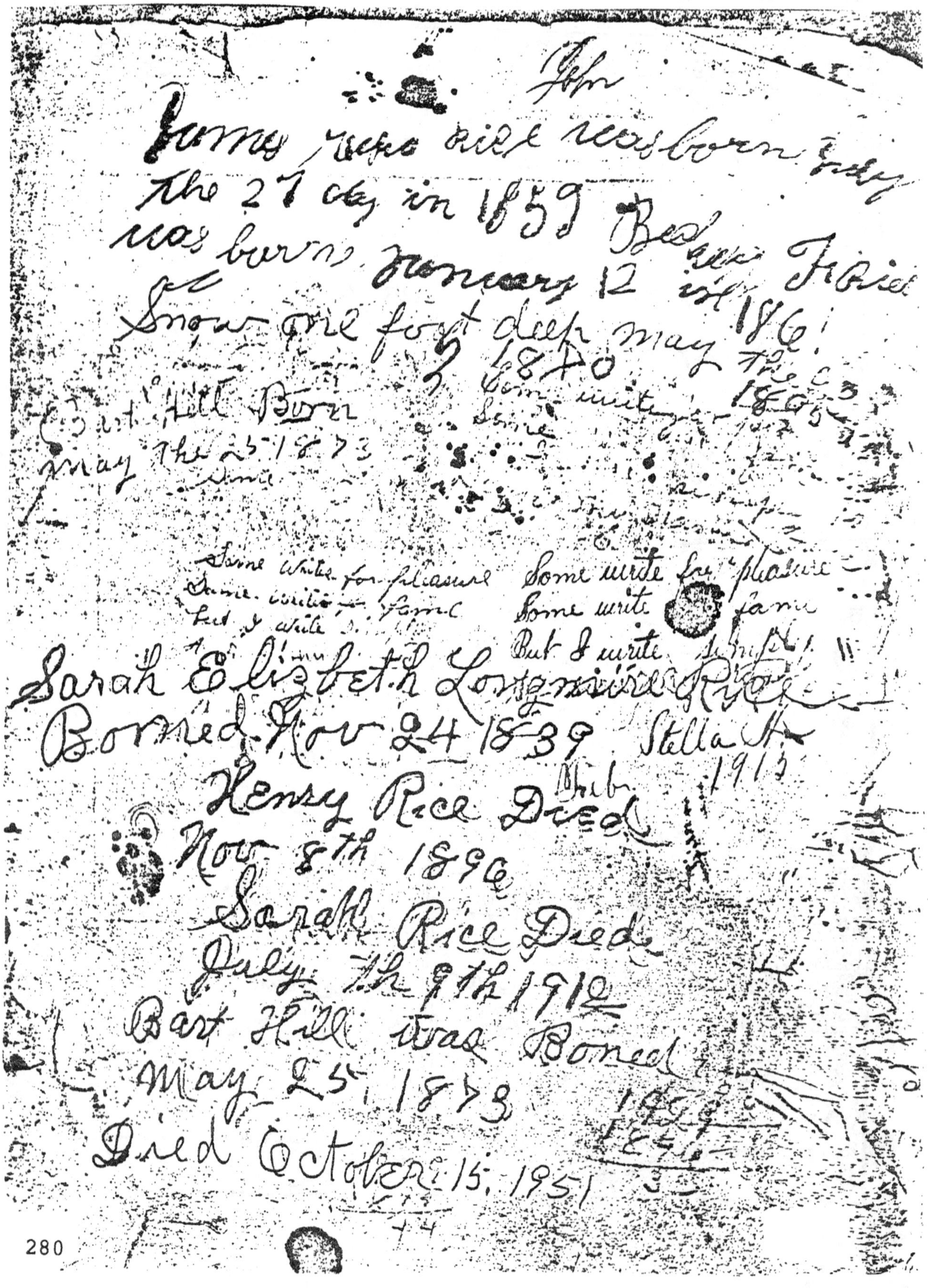

was born January 12 ... 186_

Snow one foot deep may the ... 1840

Bart Hill Born may the 25 1873

Some write for pleasure   Some write for pleasure
Some write for fame   Some write for fame
But I write ...   But I write ...

Sarah Elizbeth Longmire Rice
Borned Nov 24 1839   Stella A
                          1915
Henry Rice Died
Nov 8th 1896
Sarah Rice Died
July the 9th 1912
Bart Hill was Borned
May 25 1873
Died October 15 1951

280

THE HOUSE THAT JAMES BUILT

(Note: The sketch does not represent the true proportions of the house; Stella describes it as much longer than shown.) (Also were there windows first floor, was there a back porch & doors?)

When James Rice built his mill about 1798, he also built the log cabin which, with its modifications, served the family until about 1913. Tradition has it that James' son George (born 1794) remembered climbing up on the logs when they were being laid, when about four years old. The sketch and description here are based largely on conversations with Stella Hill Clapp, (Esther) Faye Hill Anderson, and Tina Baker. Stella and Faye, daughters of Ida Rice and Bart Hill, lived in the house until fourteen and seven years old respectively; and Tina Baker visited it many times. My mother also barely remembers seeing the house before her grandmother died here in 1912. Wayne Longmire's memory of his boyhood home was one of similar design.

Stella described the house and its history as she knew it. Originally it was two separate cabins, each with a loft and a large fireplace with hewn stone chimneys, and neither with a floor. Eventually the passage between the two cabins was made into a third room with a stairway to the loft(s). There were no connecting doors between the three rooms; going from one room to another meant going outside along the porch. While many of the Rices lived long lives, "consumption" was a common cause of early death, and no wonder.

The kitchen was at the right end of the finished house. Faye Hill liked to clamber up the outside to play in the kitchen loft, as there was no glass in the window. My grandfather, Marcellus Moss Rice, told of going with his father by wagon to Knoxville, a 30-mile trip taking two or three days, to bring back for his mother the first cookstove known in the area. Previously, of course, she cooked in the open fireplace.

The living-bedroom (left in the sketch) held two beds, one at each side of the fireplace. One was occupied by Sarah Longmire Rice, an invalid unable to turn herself, for three years before she died; and the other by Susan Rice, also an invalid. Both were cared for by Ida Rice Hill, who must have been in a constant state of exhaustion and frustration, having to run back and forth between kitchen and sickroom always via the porch, no matter how raw the weather. Besides all kinds of other indoor and outdoor chores. The loft above the living room had glass windows and was, in the words of Stella, "full of beds." Besides the many children who grew up in the house during its 116 years, weary travelers also were welcomed here; one such group was a dozen exhausted black raftsmen trudging homeward to Virginia after having rafted logs down the flooded Clinch and Tennessee Rivers to market in Chattanooga.

My grandfather liked to recall a scene that took place on the long porch. Being too young to work or go to school, he was alone with his mother playing around her knees and perhaps being somewhat mischievous. (It's hard to imagine one's grandfather being mischievous!) When his mother scolded him, he threatened to go "lay down and die" in retaliation. His mother agreed he should do that, whereupon he disappeared out back for a brief period of sulking. However, he soon gave up the idea, citing the excuse that he "couldn't die in this old linsey-woolsey dress." Linsey-woolsey was a very harsh home-crafted fabric made of flax and wool.

281

BAILEY, Annie D., 86
" Anthony, 107
" Arminda, 91, 93
" B. A., 100
" Belle, 85
" Betsey, 100, 105
" Birtha A., 91, 94
" C. C., 85
" C. M., 86-88
" Caroline, 81-82, 99
" Carr, 102, 104-05
" Chahaley, 102
" Charles, 102
" Charles S., 84
" Chas., 90, 92
" Chas. W., 92
" Christian, 105
" Christopher, 104
" Clara, 86, 88-89
" Clementine, 81-82,
  86, 88
" Claudius, 104
" Colman, 85
" Corrie, 95
" D. C., 95
" Daniel, 73-76, 109-10
" Darious, 89-90
" David, 1-2, 73-74,
  76-77, 80, 83, 87-88,
  95, 97, 101, 103,
  106, 109-110
" David H., 95
" Dora B., 89-90
" Mrs. E. D., 99
" Eddie, 100
" Edward, 86, 88
" Edwin, 91, 93
" Elisha, 102, 105
" Eliza, 84, 86, 88,
  94, 106
" Elizabeth, 79, 99
" Mrs. Elizabeth, 78-79,
  83, 97
" Elizabeth A., 79, 82,
  99
" Elizabeth C., 79, 82

BAILEY, Elizabeth J., 79, 106
" Elizabeth Storey, 87, 92
" Ella, 86
" Ella G., 96
" Ella Grace, 91, 93
" Ellie, 84
" Emma, 85, 100
" Ernest, 90, 92
" Ethel May
" Ewing M., 91, 93
" Ezekiel, 104
" Fannie, 100
" Fields, 105
" Florence J., 85
" Francis M., 106
" Frank, 86, 88
" Geo. M., 80
" George M., 97
" George T., 86, 97
" George W., 99
" Gertrude, 87-88
" Hattie, 86, 91, 93
" Hattie E., 96
" Bro. Hiram, 98
" J. A., 86
" J. C. A., 88
" J. W., 101
" James, 73-74, 76-80,
  82, 85, 88, 91, 95,
  101, 104-105, 110-113
" James B., 76, 78-83,
  85, 89-90, 95, 99,
  106, 112
" Jane, 85
" Janetty, 78
" Jeanette, 82, 98
" Jeannette, 98
" Jeremiah
" Jesse, 104
" Jesse W., 99
" Jesse W., Jr., 99
" Jesse W., Sr., 101
" Jno., 76, 102, 104-05
" John, 74, 76, 104-05
" John B., 106
" John Mark, 99, 101

BAILEY, Joseph, 100, 106
"   Julia, 86, 88, 91, 94
"   Julia Ann, 106
"   Laura, 89-90, 95
"   Laura B., 87-88
"   Lawson, 104
"   Lee, 85
"   Libby, 85
"   Lillia, 86
"   Lillian, 95
"   Lillie, 86, 88
"   Lizzie, 90, 92, 95
"   Luella, 85
"   M., 100
"   Madera, 88
"   Madona, 87
"   Mahala, 79, 100
"   Margaret, 88
"   Margaret C., 78
"   Martha (Patsy) Rice,
      1-2, 73, 77, 80, 83,
      87-88, 97, 101, 103
"   Mary, 79, 82, 85, 99,
      102, 108
"   Mary A., 85
"   Mary C., 85, 89-90,
      99
"   Mary E., 79, 99
"   Mary F., 101
"   Mary H., 81-82
"   Mary J., 84, 91, 93,
      97, 101
"   Mary Jan, 78
"   Mary Jane, 99
"   Mary M., 89
"   Matilda, 97
"   Mehala, 79
"   Melissa, 99
"   Moses, 78-80, 82, 98,
      100
"   Moses E., 100
"   Nancy, 79, 102, 106
"   Nancy M., 79
"   Nannie, 90, 92
"   Owen, 79
"   Owen M., 78

BAILEY, Oscar, 100
"   Pearl, 95
"   Pleasant, 79, 98
"   Pleasant F., 77-80, 82
"   Polly, 105
"   Robert, 77, 80, 102,
      104
"   Rosaicah, 106
"   S., 105
"   Sadie, 96
"   Samuel, 104-05
"   Sarah, 75, 102
"   Sarah Matilda, 79
"   Sib., 104
"   Stacy, 105
"   Stephen, 104
"   Susan, 96
"   Temperance, 109
"   Thomas, 75-76, 84, 91,
      93, 104-05, 109
"   Thos., 104-05
"   Una, 84-85
"   Varotee?, 88
"   Vewter?, 86
"   Wiley, 78-80, 85, 91,
      93
"   Wiley F., 91, 94
"   Willie, 85, 95
"   William, 73-74, 76-80,
      82-83, 85-91, 94-95,
      97, 100-102, 105, 108
"   William, Jr., 88, 105,
      112
"   William, Sr., 76, 101,
      105
"   William J., 112
"   William J. R., 78, 88
"   William K., 106
"   William P., 79-80, 83,
      87-88, 97
"   Wily, 84-85, 91
"   W. J. R., 79, 83, 97
"   Wm., 86, 88, 99, 102
"   Wm. Henry, 84
"   Wm. J. R., 79, 87, 92,
      97, 111

BAILEY, Wm. P., 87-88
BAILIE, Margaret, 107
"   Wm., 107
BAILY, Anna, 84
"   Columbus, 84
"   Edward, 84
"   Eliza, 84
"   Elizabeth, 79-80
"   Florence J., 80, 85
"   Geo. M., 80, 87, 89
"   James A., 83
"   Jane, 84
"   Jeremiah, 81
"   John, 106-07
"   Margaret, 80-81, 84
"   Mary, 80-81, 84, 106
"   Mary A., 80, 85
"   Mary E., 79, 99
"   Mary J., 80
"   Matilda, 80
"   Mehaly, 81
"   Moses, 81
"   S. C., 80
"   Sarah, 80, 83
"   Sarah M., 79
"   Temperance, 106, 108
"   Thomas M., 83
"   William, 80, 82-84,
       106
"   William H., 83
"   Wm. P., 79-80
BAKER, Charlotte, 52
"   George, 176
"   George, Sr., 45
"   John, 56, 146-47
"   Sarah, 52
"   Thomas, 14
"   Thomas Winfield, 154
"   T. W., 153-54
BALEY, Ann, 106-06
"   David, 109
"   James, 111
"   Lewis, 106, 108
"   Mary, 106, 108
"   Nicholas, 106-07
"   Temperance, 106

BALEY, Thomas, 106
"   William, 106
"   Wm., 107
BALL, John, 102
"   Wesley, 102
BALY, Ann, 108
"   Nicholas, 108
"   Richard, 107
"   William, 108
"   Wm., 107
BARNARD, Jona, 102
"   Ruben, 105
BARNES, Amanda, 195
"   Eliza, 195
"   Levi, 60
"   Rebecca, 195
"   Sarah, 195
"   Thos., 247
BARNETT, Alexander, 6
BARTON, Bailey, 38
BARTTEL, Jos., 64
BASS, Capt. Ezekiel, 24
BAULDRY, Robt., 130
BAYLEY, Ann, 106
"   Charles, 106
"   Chas. C., 81, 92
"   E. Jane, 81
"   Eliza E., 81
"   George, 106, 108
"   Geo. T., 81, 86
"   Henry, 106
"   James, 81-82
"   James B., 99
"   John, 106, 108
"   Margaret, 106
"   Mary, 81-82, 108
"   Mary A., 81
"   Mary J., 81-82
"   N., 81-82, 86, 92
"   Richard, 106
"   Thomas, 108
"   Wm., 106
"   Wm. H., 81
"   William, 108
BAYLIE, Henry, 107

BAYLIE, Jo., 107
    "   Richard, 107
BAYLIFE, Temperance, 107
BEAIRD, Joseph, 142
BEAL, Colo._____, 239
BECK, Jeremiah, 215-16
BEELER, Jacob, 172-73
    "   Lucy Jane, 173
BELL, Jno., 187
BENNETT, Richard,
BENSON, Wm. D. S., 35
BENTON, Daniel, 145
    "   Jessee, 145
    "   John, 145
    "   Sigh, 145
BERKELEY, Gov. William, 107
BLACKBURN, Andrew, 201
    "   Matthew, 200
BLACKMAN, Jeremy, 107, 126
BLAIN, Robert, 149
BLAND, Richard, 219
BLEDSOW, Carl E., 139
BLOCKER, Ocie, 221-222
BLUNT, Thomas, 187
BOGNALL, John, 127
BOSHARES, Elizabeth, 179
    "   Lindsay, 178-79
BOUGHMAN, Jacob, 145
BOWMAN, Robert, 145
BRADLEY, Wm., 68
    "   William, 56
BRANTLEY, Emily, 138
BRANTLEY, Thomas, 138
BREMARD, F., 36-37
BRIDENTOLL, Catherine L. L.,
       196
    "   David R., 196
BRIDGES, Emma, 162
    "   Isaac, 162
    "   Morris, 53, 153
    "   Newman, 162
    "   Ruth, 162
    "   William, 45
BRIM, Alice V., 235
    "   Betsy, 224, 229, 233
    "   Callie, 235
    "   Catherine, 224, 226, 229

BRIM, Charlotte, 224, 229
    "   Cynthia, 232
    "   Daniel, 224, 231, 242
    "   Daniel L., 232
    "   E. V., 234
    "   Elijah, 239
    "   Eliza, 242
    "   Elizabeth, 238, 240, 242
    "   Elizabeth C., 242-43
    "   Florence, 242
    "   George, 230, 234
    "   George W., 230-31, 233
    "   Henry, 224-27, 231
    "   Henry R., 232
    "   J. B., 234
    "   J. K. P., 234-35
    "   J. P., 242-43
    "   James, 224, 226, 231,
      240, 242
    "   James C., 242-43
    "   Jas. A., 231
    "   Jasper, N., 229
    "   John, 191-92, 224-25,
      230-32, 234-36, 238,
      240-43
    "   John A. R., 240, 242
    "   John C., 241
    "   John G., 232
    "   Jno., 238-39
    "   Joseph, 18, 224, 226,
      228-29, 231, 234, 239,
      241
    "   Julia, 242
    "   Katherine, 224
    "   Lavina, 2, 224, 227,
      231, 233, 243
    "   Lavina Rice, 225, 231
    "   Levina, 232
    "   Lewis, 1, 63, 191,
      224-28, 231, 233, 239,
      243
    "   Lima F., 242
    "   Linza R., 235-36
    "   Louis, 242
    "   Louisa, 232, 241
    "   Lucinda S., 232
    "   Lucy, 241

CALVATT, Frederick, 7, 9
CALVITT, Joseph, 6-7
CAMPBELL, Col. Arthur, 9
    "   John, 45
    "   Mathew, 160
CANTRELL, John, 66, 69
    "   Parntt, 69
CAPE, Wm., 56
CARDER, Robert, 210
CARMACK, John, 6
CARPER, Jacob, 23
CARTER, J., 105
CARTER, Col. John, 8
CASEY, John, 41
CASWELL, Gov., 186
CATTLETT, _____, 215
CATTON, Robt. H., 200
CAUSEY, Thomas, 128
CHAMBERLAIN, Jeremiah, 65
CHAMBERS, Elisha, 41
CHAMPION, Martha, 210
CHANDLER, Walter S., 124
CHAPPELL, Jo., 107, 126, 129
CHARLEMAGNE, 4
CHARLES I, King of England, 2
CHESHIRE, Edward, 59
CHILES, Major John, 25
CHIMM, Elijah, 59
CHISSLER, Edmund, 249
    "   James Pryor, 249
    "   John Baptist, 249
CHISSLERS, Edmond, 249
    "   Polly Ann, 249
CHRISMAN, Isaac, 45
CHRISTIAN, Capt., 9
    "   Colonel, 9, 244
    "   Lewis, 64
CHRISTOPHER, Mrs. Max A., 100
CLARK, Capt. Henry, 145
    "   Mildred, 109
CLAY, Mr., 214
    " William, 66
CLEVELAND, Martin, 68
COBB, William, 123
COCHRAN, John, 38
COCKS, Mr. Morris, 238
COKER, Ann, 249
COLE, William, 6
COLLVILLE, John, 118

COLVIN, Wm., 45
CONNER, Wm., 105
COONS, Elizabeth, 197, 218
    "   Michael, 197
COOP, Alfred, 195
    "   Caroline, 195
    "   Virginia C., 195
    "   Wm. R., 195
COPELAND, Thomas, 151
CORNISH, Thomas, 129
CORRETHERS, Ja., 80
COSHOW, America, 52, 54
COTSES, Richard, 66
COULTER, John, Gent., 7
COWAN, Wm., 6
COX, William, 13
COYLE, Robert, 6
CRAIG, Clara, 221
    "   David, 248
    "   Reuben, 53, 145
CRAVEN, Elijah, 45
CUMMING, Captain James, 25
CUNNINGHAM, David, 45
CURL, Elizabeth, 52, 54
CUTTER, Elizabeth Reeve, 219
DALE, Tho., 128
DAMERIN, Ledea, 194
DAVIES, Katherine, 129
DAVIS, Lucylle Rice, 60, 65,
       237, 249
DEALY, David, 77
    "   John, 77
    "   William, 77
DEAN, Matthew, 6
DELON, Capt. Henry, 186
DeLORME, Harold, Jr., 31
DEMPSEY, Bailey, 91, 94
    "   Frankline, 91, 94
DENNIS, Robert, 107, 126
DENT, William, 215
DENTON, Joseph, 122
DICK, William, 215
DICKSON, Michael, 13
DILLARD, Col. W. G., 170
DITTY, Edmond, 219
DOAK, Capt. Robert, 150
DOBSON, Nancy, 197
DODSON, Lazarus, 24
DONALDSON, Stockley, 120

288

JONES, Isaiah, 60
    "   James, 234
    "   Jessee, 201
    "   Captain Nehemiah, 186
    "   Sugar, 225
    "   T. F., 95
    "   Wm. Ellis, 238
JORDAN, Joseph, 187
JUSTICE, Wm., 107
KEENE, Tho., 127
KEER, Adam, 6
KEITH, Nancy, 179
KELLY, James, 6
KENNER, Mrs. John C., 217
    "   Rodham, 217
KEY, John, 145
KEYLE, Robert, 64
KILE, Capt. Robert, 145
KING, James, 41
    "   John, 6-7, 127
    "   Richard, 212, 214
KINKEAD, Joseph, 8
KNOTT, Wm., 127

LABRECHTS, _____, 118
LAINE, Joseph, 179
    "   Martha, 179
    "   Sarah, 179
LAKE, John H., 96
    "   Mary, 96
LAMBDIN, Jim, 162
LANEY, John, 200
LANGRAM, Rowland, 107
LAWSON, Isham, 105
LEA, Wm., 130
LEBO, Isaac, 6
LEE, Mr. Hugh, 214
    "   Needham, 102
LEMON, Sarah, 118
LEISSEN, George, 194
    "   Mary, 194
LETT, James, 45
    "   John, 45
LEWIS, Mr. John, 238
LIGHTFOOT, Marise, 222
    "   Marise, P., 222
    "   Mr. Phill, 238
LINDBERGH, Charles A., 218-19
LISBY, Moses, 197

LIPSCOMB, John, 20-21, 115
LITTLE, Gordon Rice, 117
    "   Melvin Weaver, 1, 154
    "   Ruby (Rema) Rice, 1,
           33, 49, 154
LOCK, John Sr., 119
LOCKART, Thomas, 18
LONG, Atn., 105
    "   John, 8
    "   Nicholas, 247
LONGMIRE, Elijah, 153-54, 247
    "   Mrs. Irwin, 139
    "   Myrtle, 135
    "   O. D., 140
    "   Obie D., 139
    "   Robert, 154
    "   Sarah Elizabeth, 154
LOXLEY, Robin of (Robin Hood),
        141
LOVE, J. A., 222
    "   John, 123
    "   Susie B., 221
    "   William T., 221
LOY, Elizabeth, 160-61
    "   Gibson, 162
    "   Haley, 162
    "   Hercules, 162
    "   Jacob, 118
    "   Job, 118
    "   John, 162
    "   Ola, 162
    "   Paris, 162
    "   Peter, 45
    "   Phebe Tillman, 118
    "   Will, 162
LUSTER, Franakey (Bailey),
        105
    "   S. D., 105
LYNCH, Elijah, 77
    "   Elizabeth, 77
    "   William, 77
LINCH, William, 77
LYTTE (Lyttle), Arch., 184

MACKEY, Sarah, 237
MADDISON, Mrs. Mary, 127
MALONE, Richard, 45
MARLOW, James, 45

MARROW, Cornelius C KATHER-
        INE, 219
"   Geo., 219
"   William, 219
MARROWE, Alen, 219
MARTIN, Jesse, 120
"   Jos., 105
"   Capt. Joseph, 145
"   Col. Joseph, 47
MASON, James, 128
"   John, 145
MASSENGILL, Michael, 149
MASSINGILL, Michael, 68
MATHEWS, Capt. Samuel, Esq.,
        130
MATLOCK, Martha Lucinda, 64
MATTOCK, Geo., 105
MAXWELL, George, 17, 116
"   Jessee, 17
MAY, Barbara, 140, 143, 152,
    164-65
MAYBERRY, Francis, 149
MEBANE, Isabella, 197
"   Nancy, 197
MEDLAM, Harvey, 118
MEDSTON, John, 107
MERONEY, Mary, 118
MERREDITH, Tho., 127
MEYERS, Eliza, 161-62
MICHAEL, W., 194
MILLER, Alfred, 48-49
"   Eve, 48
"   Eve Whitener, 47
"   Frederick, 118
"   George, 145
"   Isaac, 170
"   Jacob, 34
"   Captain John "Raccoon,"
            47-50
"   John, 48
"   Lewis, 145
"   Morris, 34
"   Nancy S., 56
"   Rebecca, 1, 20, 33,
            39, 47-48, 51, 237
"   Robt., 105
"   Thomas, Esq., 110
MILLIKAN, Capt. Elihu, 110
MINOR, Dodes, 238

MITCHELL, Aquilla, 68
"   Ephraim, 35
"   Genevieve, 162
"   Isaac, 65, 237
"   Isaac, Jr., 65, 237
"   Mary C., 65, 249
"   Mary Catherine, 65,
        237
"   Mary Williams, 65,
        237
"   Mordeci, 237
"   Morris, 237
"   Rhoda Emily, 237
"   Sarah, 65, 237
"   Ursula, 65, 237
MITTERBARGER, William, 225-26,
        231
MOONE, Abraham, 128
MOORE, John, 59
MORGAN, Capt. Rufus, 150, 152
MORROW, A., 205, 207
"   Adam, 200, 217
"   Adeline, 208
"   Alenda C., 210
"   Alex, 204-206
"   Alexander, 1, 183,
        197-98, 203-08, 212,
        214-18, 224
"   Alexr, 205-207
"   Alice R., 221-222
"   Allascander K., 207,
        209
"   Allaxander, 207
"   Alvin, 222
"   Amelia, 197, 202
"   Amelia J., 201
"   Anderson, 210
"   Andrew, 208
"   Andrew A., 220
"   Angeline, 201-03
"   Ann, 198, 200, 208,
        215-219
"   Ann S., 219
"   Anna, 209
"   Anna H., 201-02
"   Annie E., 221
"   Aretha, 209
"   Arthur, 211
"   Asbury, 209

MORROW, Benjamin, 203-04, 209
" C. F. R., 210
" Mrs. C. U., 222
" Caleb, 216
" Carnice H., 222
" Catherine, 209-10
" Charles, 183, 189-90,
198-99, 201-03, 217
" Charles Craig, 221
" Chls, 202
" Chris'r, 212
" Cintha C., 208
" Clyde A., 221
" Mrs. Clyde A., 220
" Connie U., 221
" Constance O., 219
" Daniel, 183, 189-90,
197-98, 209, 212,
214, 216, 218
" Daniel A., 209
" David, 197, 200, 211,
214-17
" Rev. David, 214-17
" David M., 210
" Dialtha, 200
" Dorothy, 214
" Dorothy May, 222
" Hon. Dwight Whitney,
218-19
" Dwight, Jr., 219
" E. J., 200
" Easther, 209
" Ebenazor, 200
" Edith Clementine, 221
" Edna A., 221
" Edwin Harlan, 221
" Eleanor Jane, 220
" Elijah, 220
" Elijah G., 210
" Eliza Ann, 209
" Elizth, 211
" Elizabeth, 198, 200-03,
205, 208-10, 215,
218-19
" Elizabeth Coons, 218
" Elizabeth R., 219
" Ellender U., 209
" Ellinor, 210
" Emily, 210

MORROW, Esther, 198-99, 201
" Esther E., 208
" Eva Gray, 222
" Ezekiel, 211
" Frances, 210
" Francis, 210
" Garfield, 220-21
" George, 198-99, 201,
204-07, 209, 211
" George D. L., 210
" George W., 209-10
" Hannah, 197, 200
" Hazle Paxton, 221
" Henry, 214
" Hester, 200
" Hezekiah, 200
" Hugh, 211, 219
" Ilione, 210
" Isaac D., 209
" Isabella, 198, 200-01,
203
" J. W., 221
" James, 183, 189-90,
198-200, 202-03, 207-
208, 210-11, 217
" James A., 209-10
" James Bemton, 222
" James Elmore, 218
" James K., 209
" James L., 208
" James M., 205-06, 210,
220-21
" Mrs. James M., 220
" James Murphy, 220
" James T., 221
" James William, 219
" Jas., 198
" Jas. F., 209
" Jas. M., 205-06, 220
" Jamima, 210
" Jane, 200, 208, 210
" Jay, 219
" Jeremiah, 216
" Jesse C., 210
" Jimmie H., 221
" John, 183, 189-90,
197-201, 203-210, 212,
214-17, 221-22
" John D., 209

MORROW, John E., 221
    "   John F., 209
    "   John J., 208
    "   John L., 209
    "   John M., 210
    "   John P., 220
    "   John Pinkney, 220
    "   John T., 209-10
    "   John W., 201-03, 222
    "   Jno., 211
    "   Jno. W., 205
    "   Jonathan, 214
    "   Joe Mack, 221
    "   Joseph, 201, 211, 218
    "   Joseph F., 220
    "   Joseph Franklin, 220-221
    "   Joseph Franklin, Jr., 221
    "   Joseph W., 208
    "   Josiah, 210
    "   Lavinia, 200
    "   Leffie B., 221
    "   Leonard, 203-06, 208
    "   Lettie A., 221
    "   Levi, 183, 189-90, 198
    "   Lewis, 219
    "   Louisa, 210
    "   Louisa E., 209
    "   Lumiza J., 210
    "   Lycurgus, 209
    "   Infant of Mr. & Mrs. M. W., 222
    "   Malinda, 201
    "   Malinda E., 202
    "   Malissa, 210
    "   Malissa P., 209
    "   Manerva, 209
    "   Manley W., 221
    "   Margt., 200
    "   Margaret, 200, 210
    "   Martha, 200, 209-10
    "   Martha A., 209
    "   Martha E., 209
    "   Martha J., 208
    "   Martha Jane, 209
    "   Martha Jean, 221
    "   Martha O., 209

MORROW, Mary, 200, 202-03, 207-211, 214-15, 222
    "   Mary A., 201, 208
    "   Mary C. C., 209
    "   Mary E., 200-03
    "   Mary F., 209
    "   Mary Jane, 208-09
    "   Mary Neomi, 209
    "   Mary R., 210
    "   Mary S., 209
    "   Mashie B., 209
    "   Masry, M., 209
    "   Mathew, 209, 212
    "   Matilda E., 221
    "   Melinda, 202
    "   Michael, 218
    "   Mildred N., 210
    "   Miles Leonard, 220
    "   Minerva J., 208
    "   Myra, 200
    "   Nancey C., 209
    "   Nancey D., 209
    "   Nancey L., 209
    "   Nancy, 209-10
    "   Nancy C., 208
    "   Nancy E., 201
    "   Nancy Roberta, 220
    "   Narcissa Jane, 209
    "   Narcissa Jane, 209
    "   Noah, 208
    "   Paul, 205
    "   Paul N., 221
    "   Polley, 203-05
    "   Priscilla, 198, 201
    "   Prudence, 201-03
    "   R., 202-03
    "   R. E., 209
    "   Rachel A., 208
    "   Richard, 197, 212
    "   Robt., 200
    "   Robert, 197, 199-203, 208, 210-12, 215, 222
    "   Robert A., 220
    "   Robert Andrew, 220
    "   Rosa Rice Spence, 190
    "   Rosanna, 198-99, 202, 205-06
    "   Rufus, 200
    "   Ruth Ann, 209

RICE, Neva Jane (Baker), 154
" Ora, 236-37
" Othniel, 34
" Patience, 56
" Polly (Mary), 34
" Rebecca, 34, 153-54, 157, 162
" Rhoadman Hickory, 70, 236
" Roaderman, 70
" Rosa, 1, 183
" Ruth Annette, 33
" Ruby Rema,
" Sally, 61-63
" Sarah, 25, 28, 61-62
" Sarah (Sally), 61
" Sarah Harper, 24
" Sousannah, 60
" Stephen, 34
" Susanna, 25, 42-44
" Susannah, 34, 40, 45, 56, 60
" Tabitha, 34, 39, 51, 53, 154
" Temperance, 56, 118
" Thomas, 3, 6, 25, 27, 56, 59-60, 82, 211
" Tillman, 118-19
" Virginai, 70
" Walter, 87, 89
" Westley S., 70
" Westley W., 70
" William, 1-2, 6, 9, 23-28, 61, 77, 244
" Wm. G., 93
" William G., 90
RICHARDSON, Lena, 220-21
RICHERSON, James, 149
RICHISON, James, 19, 67
RICOSTE, James, 126
RINEHART, Lydia, 118
ROADY, Josiah, 199
ROBERTSON, Capt. James, 9
" Dora Emily, 237
" Thomas Asbury, 237
ROBINSON, Absalom, 58
" Absolom, 56
" Elijah, 6
" Capt. James, 7

ROBSON, John R. (Chief Surgeon), 170
ROGERS, Jno. A., 105
" Pleasant M., 145-46
ROLLE, Capt., 147
ROSEBROUGH, William, 7
ROSS, Melanie, 86
" Melvina, 88
ROYSTON, Mr. Tho., 238

SAVAGE, Mrs. G. H., 117
" James, 98
SCARBURG, Littleton, 127
SCARBURGH, Edmund Jr., 127
SCHENK, Rev. W., 100
SCHLOTTERBECK, Seth S., 117
SCOTT, Harvey, 234
" Joseph, 234
" Rebecca, 234
" Samuel, 234
" Willie S. Morrow, 222
SEAL, John, 56
SEVERNE, Jo., 127
SEVIER, Burrell, 145
SHAMNESS, Asbery, 67
SHARP, A. B., 161
" Alfred, 145-46, 160-62
" Bratcher, 162
" Charles (Chuck), 33
" Clemmy, 162
" Colson, 52
" Conrad (Coonrod), 54, 248
" Coonrod, 40
" Daniel, 117
" Eli, 42-44
" Eliza, 52
" Elizabeth Black, 52
" Frank, 162
" George, 52
" Henry, 52, 226
" Henry (Sr.), 54
" Henry Sr., 117
" Isaac, 45, 52
" J. C., 53
" J. Crit, 51
" James, 161
" John, 45, 53
" Lewis M., 161

298

SHARP, Lorene Rogers, 33
  "   Mary, 52
  "   Nancy Heath, 52
  "   Nicholas, 45
  "   P. & J., 155
  "   Parley, 161
  "   Parlia, 161
  "   Parlia (Parley), 160,
        162
  "   Rachel, 161
  "   Rebecca, 53
  "   Robert, 162
  "   Sarah (Sally, Sallie),
        154
  "   Sarah Gibbs, 54
  "   Susan Leigh, 1
  "   Capt. Thomas, 150
  "   Wm., 155
  "   W. C. Jr., 140
  "   J. Wm. C., 140
  "   William, 52, 54,
        145-46
  "   William Foster, 33
SHARPE, Conrad, 120
  "   Conrad (Coonrod), 248
  "   Coonrod, 40, 119-120
  "   Elizabeth, 118
  "   Henry, 118
  "   Rebecca, 118
SHAW, Elizabeth, 215
SHELBY, General Evan, 47
  "   Evan, JUN., 6
  "   James, 6
  "   William, 45
SHELTON, Carolin, 99
SHIPE, Randall, 202-03
SHOSSHAN, Ph., J. P., 106
SHUTE, Mrs. Nan (Frances)
        Rice, 1, 3, 9, 20-21,
        24, 47-48, 51, 115-16,
        118
  "   Mrs. Nan Rice, 29
SIBSEY, John, 128
SIMMONS, Jane, 1, 39, 65
  "   John, 39, 248
SIMONTON, John, 118
SIMPSON, Betsy, 48
SKAGGS, J. D., 81
  "   Jno., 81

SKAGGS, Maggie, 81
  "   Mary, 81
SLACK, Jacob, 196
SMAYZE, H. D., 171
SMITH, Able, 250
  "   Ann, 250
  "   David, 1, 9, 18-20,
        38, 41, 154-55, 244-
        250
  "   David H., 248
  "   Edward, 247
  "   Elijah, 247
  "   Elizabeth, 2
  "   Betsy, 248
  "   Elizabeth Rice, 20,
        248
  "   Evan, 20, 247
  "   Jacob, 160
  "   Jane, 248
  "   John, 247
  "   Lt. Col. Jno., 238
  "   Joshua, 250
  "   Mary, 247
  "   Nancy, 52, 54
  "   Peter, 250
  "   Rachael, 20, 249
  "   Robert, 45, 247
  "   Samuel, 250
  "   Sarah, 52, 54, 200,
        202-203
  "   Thomas, 18, 247
SNODDERLY, A. H., 52
  "   Alvis, 52
  "   Anna, 52
  "   Daniel C., 52
  "   Earl, 140
  "   Elizabeth, 52-54
  "   Betsey, 54
  "   Gaines, 51
  "   George, 41-42,
        51-54, 150, 152, 154,
        247-48
  "   George III, 160
  "   George C., 52
  "   George W., 52
  "   Henry, 52-53
  "   (Henry) Rice, 244
  "   Henry Rice, 52-53,
        160, 244, 248

SNODDERLY, Huldah, 52-53, 153-54
"   Isaac, 45, 52
"   Jacob, 42, 52-53
"   James Hugh, 52
"   John, 51-53, 153
"   John W., 52
"   Lee Roy, 52
"   Lewis, 52
"   Lucy, 53
"   Mahala Nelson, 53
"   Malinda, 53
"   Margaret (Peggy) Burton Gibbs, 53
"   Mary, 52-53, 153
"   Nancy, 52
"   Nicholas, 53
"   Phoebe, 52-53
"   Rebecca, 52
"   Rice, 52, 153
"   Sarah, 51, 53, 154
"   Tabitha, 52-53
"   William, 52-53
SNODERLY, A. A., 153
"   Elizabeth, 54
"   George, 40, 42-45, 51, 54, 154, 160
"   Henry Rice, 53-54, 154
"   Jacob, 42-44
"   Jacob H., 54
"   John, 45
"   John Sr., 45
"   Lucy, 54
"   Rice, 54
"   Tabitha (Rice), 54
"   W. H., 153
SNOW, James, 77
"   John, 77
SORRELL, Edward, 208
SPENCE, A. E., 194
"   A. M. F., 194
"   A. R., 194
"   Abner, 196
"   Alex, 187
"   Alex Sen'r, 188
"   Alexander, 186-88
"   Alexr, 187, 211
"   Alsa, 196

SPENCE, Alson, 195
"   Ana, 196
"   Aramantha, 195
"   Bartholomew, 189-92
"   Bev. B., 196
"   Brent, 189-91, 194
"   Britton, 196
"   C. P., 194
"   Calvin, 193
"   Calvin T., 194
"   Cattern, 187
"   Charlotte B. C., 194
"   Chrlott, 196
"   Daniel, 196
"   Daved, 187
"   David, 186, 195
"   David H., 196
"   Delilah, 196
"   Dorety, 187
"   E. S., 194
"   Edward M., 194
"   Elisha, 196
"   Eliza, 195
"   Elizabeth, 189-92, 194, 196
"   Ellen, 195
"   Ellison, 193
"   Elaxander, 187
"   Emma, 196
"   Fanny, 196
"   Francis, 195
"   Franklin, 195
"   Geo. E., 194
"   Geo. W., 194
"   George M. D., 195
"   Geraldine, 195
"   GREVES, 186
"   H. E., 194
"   Henry, 194, 196
"   Hugh, 189-92
"   Incell, 185-86
"   Insell, 184
"   Ira, 196
"   Isabella, 193
"   J., 196
"   J. E., 194
"   J. M., 194
"   Jabez, 184-86
"   Jabiz, 186

SPENCE, Jas., 196
"   Jas. D., 196
"   Jam. Sen'r, 188
"   James, 1, 183-193,
        195-196
"   James Jn'r, 188
"   James C., 194
"   Jas. M., 194
"   Jane, 183, 189-92,
        195
"   Jerome, 195
"   Jinny, 183
"   John, 187, 189-92,
        195-96
"   John Senr, 188
"   John C., 189-91, 196
"   John D., 195
"   John E., 194
"   John F., 194
"   John L., 189-92, 195
"   John W., 194
"   Jno., 188, 194
"   Joseph, 186, 189-92,
        194, 196
"   Joseph A., 194
"   Josephine, 195
"   Kathleen, 195
"   Kinchen, 195
"   Levi, 196
"   Levy, 189-92
"   Louis C., 194
"   M. G., 189-92
"   M. J., 194
"   Madeline, 195
"   Mahala, 195
"   Mannaw, 189-90
"   Margaret, 194, 196
"   Margaret C., 194
"   Mark, 189-91, 194,
        196
"   Mark A, 195
"   Martha, 194-95
"   Martin V., 196
"   Mary, 194-96
"   Mary A., 195-96
"   Mary E., 194
"   Mary P., 194
"   Mary W. C., 196
"   Matilda, 196

SPENCE, Myea A., 195
"   Nancy, 195-96
"   Nancy C., 196
"   Nancy E., 195
"   Nancy T, 194
"   Nannie, 194
"   Parthena, 196
"   Pheoba, 195
"   Philip, 194
"   Polly, 183, 189
"   R. K., 194
"   Rachel, 189
"   Rebecca, 196
"   Renshaw, 196
"   Rhoda H., 194
"   Rhoda Tennessee, 194
"   Richard, 189-91, 196
"   Robt., 194
"   Robt. V., 193
"   Robert, 186-87
"   Rosa, 2, 183-84,
        196-98
"   Rosa Rice, 189, 214,
        217, 224
"   Rosana, 197
"   Rosanna, 183, 197-98,
        224
"   Rosanna Rice, 197
"   S., 196
"   Samuel, 183-85
"   Sarah, 193, 195-96
"   Sarah J., 195
"   Simon, 186
"   Stephen, 189-90, 195
"   Tanil, 195
"   Tennessee, 195-96
"   Thomas, 189-90
"   Thornton, 196
"   Thos., 196
"   Tiny, 195
"   Truman, 186
"   W., 189-91, 196
"   W. G., 195
"   W. W., 194
"   Wm., 191-92, 196
"   Wm. G., 195
"   Wm. P., 194
"   Will S., 193

SPENCE, William, 189-92,
   195-96
 " William G., 189-92
 " William H., 189-90
 " William J., 196
 " William M., 189-91
 " William W., 189-92,
   194
 " Wilson, 196
 " Wricker, 189-91
SPERRY, John N., 196
SPOTSWOOD, Honble Alexander,
   187
STAMPS, William, 23-24
STANFORD, Vincent, 107
STEELE, William, 13
 " William T., 30
STEPHENS, John, 34
STEVENSON, Mrs. Mattie, 100
STEWART, Capt. James, 153
 " Major, 62-63
STOAKES, Christopher, 127
STOCKTON, Mr., 127
STOOKSBURY, Hazy L., 161
STOREY, Elizabeth, 83, 88
 " Green, 83, 97
 " Matilda (Hensley), 97
STORY, Edy, 82
 " Green E., 82
 " James P., 79
 " Mary J., 78-79
 " Nancy B., 82
 " Sarah M., 82
STRASSBURGER, R. B., 3
STREATE, Jno., 238
STUBBLEFIELD, ____ 95
 " Hugh, 95
 " Wm., 64
STUKESBURY, Jacob, 145
 " Robert, 145
SYMMS, John, 3
TARPLEY, Linda Lee, 220
 " Minnie Lula, 220-21
TATUM, Jesse, 13
 " John, 38
 " Nath., 38
 " William, 38
TAYLOR, Elizabeth, 200
 " Frank, 100

TAYLOR, Irvin, 200
 " John, 200
 " Major T., 200
 " Mary, 200
 " Nancy, 200
 " Thomas, 195
 " Wm. H., 139
THIMPRIN, J., 64
THOMAS, Professor, 54, 139
 " W. H., 7, 48, 51
 " Professor W. H., 48
 " Wm. H., 140
 " Wm. Rice, 140
 " Professor William H.,
   139
 " William (Willie) Hen-
   derson, 53-54
 " Professor Willie H.,
   183
TILLMAN, Barbara, 117-18
 " Catherine (Sharp),
   117-18
 " Elizabeth, 120
 " ((Henry, 118
 " Jacob, 118
 " John Jr., 118
 " John Sr., 118
 " Many, 118
 " Margaret (Peggy),118
 " Nancy, 118
 " Nancy (Harless), 118
 " Rachael, 118
 " Sarah, 120
 " Tobias, 117-19
TILSEY, Tho., 128
TOWNSLAND, Mrs. Frances, 130
TOWNSLEND, Mrs. Francis, 130
TRUETT, George, 128
TUCKER, Branch, 106
 " John, 200
 " Wm., 68
TULLOS, Angie, 118
TUNNELL, James, 105
 " John, 200
Turnbow, Alva, 61
 " Alva Silas, 2, 33
 " Maude, 61
 " Maude Ina, 2, 33

TURNBOWS, The, 23, 44, 46,
        51, 53
TURNER, Geo., 238
    "   James W., 172-73
TUTTLE, Elizabeth J., 103
    "   George, 103
    "   James, 74, 103
    "   John, 103
    "   Joseph, 103
    "   Mary A., 103
    "   Rebecca C., 103
    "   Sarah A., 103
    "   Thomas, 103
    "   Wiley, 73-74, 103
    "   William, 103
USREY, William, 43, 45
USSARY, Elizabeth, 53
    "   Henderson, 53
    "   James, 53
    "   John, 53
    "   Louisa, 53
    "   Nancy Jane, 53
    "   Rebecca, 53
    "   William, 42-44, 53
    "   Zeba Annie, 53
VANCE, John, 6
VOSS, F. J., 222
    "   W. J., 222
WALDEN, Margery, 63-64
WALKER, Alexander, 217
    "   Edward, 126
    "   John, 159
    "   Netie A., 220
    "   Prudence, 197
WALLING, Jno., 64
    "   Wm., 64
WALTON, Worth, 162
WAMACK, Ann E., 201
WAREHAM, John, 127
WARY, Anne, 208
WATKINS, John, 130
WATSON, Abraham, 128
    "   Abram, 126
    "   Alexander, 127
    "   Alice, 127
    "   Alin, 128
    "   Andrew, 122, 125, 127
    "   Ann, 127
    "   Archibald, 122

WATSON, Art., 127
    "   Arthur, 128
    "   Asariah, 125
    "   Azariah, 125
    "   Betsey, 120
    "   Betsy, 115, 121, 128
    "   Catherine, 121, 125
    "   Christianna, 125
    "   Christopher, 126
    "   Cynthia, 115, 121
    "   David, 115, 120-22,
            124-25
    "   Eliazear, 125
    "   Elijah, 122
    "   Eliz., 127-28
    "   Elizor, 125
    "   Emeline, 121
    "   Francis, 126
    "   Geo., 127
    "   Godwin, 125
    "   Harden, 125
    "   Henry, 121, 128
    "   Isaac, 125, 127
    "   James, 122-23, 125,
            127
    "   Jeffery, 128
    "   Jo., 126
    "   Joane, 127
    "   John, 122, 125,
            127-28
    "   Josiah, 123-24
    "   Lydia, 115, 121
    "   Marg., 127
    "   Margaret, 121, 126
    "   Mary, 122, 127
    "   Molly, 2, 115, 123-24
    "   Molly Rice, 39, 121
    "   Nancy, 115, 120-21,
            128
    "   (Nathan), 117
    "   Nathan, 1, 16-18,
            21, 115-16, 120,
            123, 225
    "   Nicho., 127
    "   Nicholas, 126
    "   Peter, 121
    "   Pinkney, 121
    "   Pleasant, 125
    "   Richard, 127-28

WILSON, Louisie, 177
    "   Lucy, 180
    "   Luisey, 157
    "   Lydia, 140, 152,
            164, 166-67
    "   M. J., 178-79
    "   Maggie, 177
    "   Manervy J., 166, 176
    "   Margaret, 180
    "   Marry, 180
    "   Martha, 140, 180
    "   Martha A., 168, 171
    "   Martha Ida, 158-59
    "   Mary, 176, 178
    "   Mary B., 168
    "   Mary M., 176
    "   Matilda, 156, 167,
            177
    "   Maynard, 140
    "   Maynard O., 161
    "   D. Maynard, 139-41,
            157, 161-62, 165
    "   Merry E., 176
    "   Miller, 158-59, 161,
            163
    "   Milton, 179
    "   Myrtle, 161
    "   Myrtle B., 162-64
    "   McHenry, 156
    "   Nancy, 156, 175
    "   Nancy A., 177, 179
    "   Nancy J., 176
    "   Nellie B., 181
    "   Orvel, 158-59, 163
    "   Parlia, 158, 160-61
    "   Parley, 157, 159-60
    "   Pearley, 176
    "   Polly, 176
    "   Rex P., 166
    "   Rudolph, 162
    "   Rufus, 166
    "   Rufus P., 166
    "   S. E., 179
    "   Sampson, 140, 143-44
            151, 175-77
    "   Sampson D., 175-76
    "   Samuel, 147
    "   Sarah, 156, 178
    "   Sarah E., 176

WILSON, Scott, 162
    "   Smith, 147
    "   Square, 181
    "   Squire, 166
    "   Stella, 162
    "   Stella E., 176
    "   Susan, 147
    "   Thomas, 142
    "   Upias, 147
    "   V. M., 159-60
    "   Viola, 180
    "   Walhai?, 168
    "   Walter E., 176
    "   Washington W., 167,
            168
    "   William, 166, 214
    "   William S., 167
    "   Wm. E., 179
WINTON, _____, 237
WITT, _____. 153
WOREHAM, Thomas, 45
WORKFOLK, Major, 24
WOOD, Henry, 157
    "   James, 13
WRIGHT, George, 57

YANCY, Robert, 123
YORK, William, 45
YOUNG, John, 57
    "   John, Jr., 13
    "   Mary, 244
    "   Robert, 122
    "   William, 57

INDEX TO NAMES OF PLACES

307

INDEX TO NAMES OF PLACES (Continued)

Clarinda, IA, 53
Cleveland, OH, 219
Clinch Mountain (TN), 157
Clinch River (TN), 11, 15,
  48, 120, 124, 144
Clinton, TN, 11, 168, 171
Coffee County, TN, 210
Columbia, Maury County, TN
Copper Ridge (TN), 11
Corryton, TN, 140
Crook County, OR, 54
Cumberland Gap, 21, 49,
  169, 172
Cumberland Plateau (TN), 115
Curtiss Station (TN?), 145

Dallas County, MO,
Darke County, OH, 118
Davidson County, TN, 25,
  189, 190, 194
Decatur County, TN, 194
Doak's Creek (Knox County,
  TN), 197, 218
Dyer County, TN, 189, 190,
  194

East Dolan, MO, 87, 88
East Tennessee (first set-
  tled), 7
Edenton, NC, 187, 188
Edisto River ( ), 4
Elizabeth County, VA, 127
Elizabeth City County, VA,
  214
England, 4
Englewood, TN, 139
Essex County, VA, 218

Fayette County, AL, 205, 206
Fayette County (TN?) 194
Fayette County, TN, 189, 190
Forkvale, TN, 54
Fort Patrick Henry, 9
Fountain City, TN, 140, 180
Franklin (State of), 16
Franklin County, TN, 210
Fredericktown, MO, 111
Fredrickstown, SC, 4
Fresno, CA, 1

Germany, 2, 3
Gibson County, TN, 121, 128
Giles County, TN, 203-205,
  207, 209
Golden Creek (SC), 13
Goldings Creek (SC), 34
Grainger County, TN, 2, 13,
  14, 16, 18, 19, 30, 38, 59,
  65, 67, 68, 73, 74, 103,
  122-125, 129, 139, 148, 149,
  151, 198, 203, 224
Grassy Valley (TN), 142, 143
Gravelly Valley (TN), 24
Great Island (TN) (Long or
  Big Island), 10
Greene County, TN, 13, 15, 59,
  74, 75, 104, 122, 125, 141,
  148, 198-201, 203, 217
Greenville, Greenville County,
  SC, 211
Greenwood, MO, 98

Halls Cross Roads (TN), 11
Hamburg, SC, 4
Hancock County (VA-WV), 218
Hanover County, VA, 3
Hard Creek (Hord's Creek) (TN)
Hardin County, TN, 128

State Names are abbreviated
as follows:

AL	Alabama	MO	Missouri
AK	Alaska	MT	Montana
AZ	Arizona	NE	Nebraska
AR	Arkansas	NH	New Hampshire
CA	California	NJ	New Jersey
CO	Colorado	NM	New Mexico
CT	Connecticut	NY	New York
DE	Delaware	NC	North Carolina
DC	District of Columbia	ND	North Dakota
FL	Florida	OH	Ohio
GA	Georgia	OK	Oklahoma
HI	Hawaii	OR	Oregon
ID	Idaho	PA	Pennsylvania
IL	Illinois	RI	Rhode Island
IN	Indiana		
IA	Iowa	SC	South Carolina
KS	Kansas		
KY	Kentucky	SD	South Dakota
LA	Louisiana	TN	Tennessee
ME	Maine	TX	Texas
MD	Maryland	UT	Utah
MA	Massachusetts	VT	Vermont
		VA	Virginia
MI	Michigan	WA	Washington
MS	Mississippi	WV	West Virginia
		WI	Wisconsin
		WY	Wyoming

www.ingramcontent.com/pod-product-compliance
Lightning Source LLC
Chambersburg PA
CBHW080605270326
41928CB00016B/2931